Creativity in Direct Response Advertising

Creativity in Direct Response Advertising

By The Direct Marketing Creative Guild

Richard N. Harbert, Editor

PBC International, Inc. ▪ New York

DISTRIBUTOR TO THE BOOK TRADE IN THE UNITED STATES AND CANADA:
Rizzoli International Publications, Inc.
597 Fifth Avenue
New York, NY 10017

DISTRIBUTOR TO THE ART TRADE IN THE UNITED STATES:
Letraset USA
40 Eisenhower Drive
Paramus, NJ 07653

DISTRIBUTOR TO THE ART TRADE IN CANADA:
Letraset Canada Limited
555 Alden Road
Markham, Ontario L3R 3L5, Canada

DISTRIBUTED THROUGHOUT THE REST OF THE WORLD BY:
Hearst Books International
105 Madison Avenue
New York, NY 10016

PBC INTERNATIONAL, INC.
One School Street
Glen Cove, NY 11542.

Library of Congress Cataloging-in-Publication Data

Direct Marketing 2 : the graphics of direct mail and direct response marketing / by the Direct Marketing Creative Guild.
p. cm.

Includes Indexes.
ISBN 0-86636-061-1 : $55.00
1. Direct Marketing. 2. Mail-order business I. Direct Marketing Creative Guild.
II. Title. Direct marketing two.

HF5415. 122.D577 1988
658.8'4—dc19 88-17990
CIP

Color separation, printing and binding by
Toppan Printing Co. (H.K.) Ltd. Hong Kong
Typography by **RMP Publication Services**

PRINTED IN HONG KONG
10 9 8 7 6 5 4 3 2 1

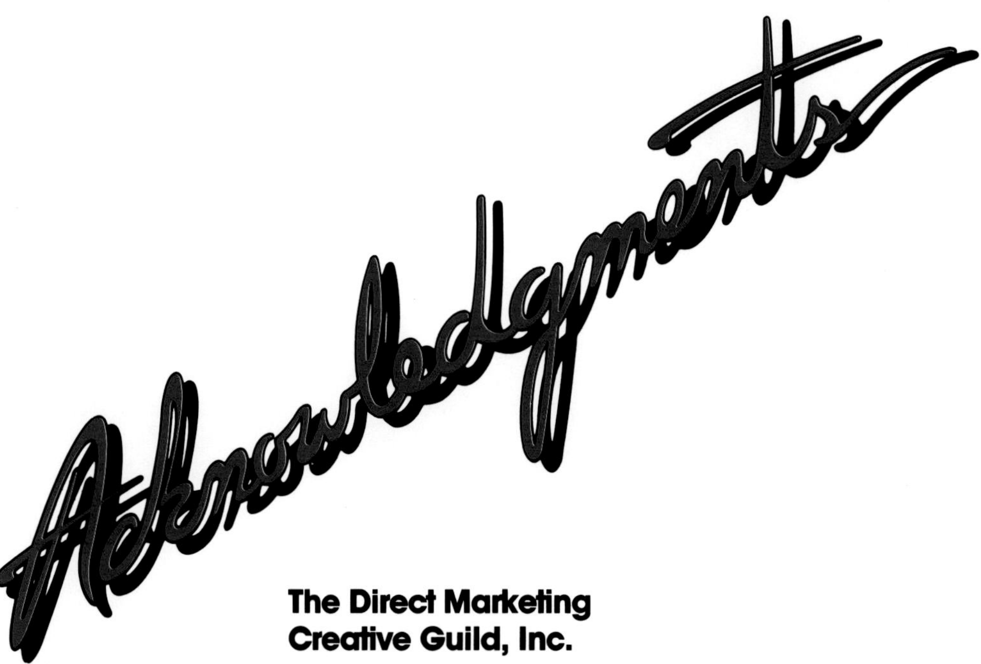

The Direct Marketing Creative Guild, Inc.

President
Shan Ellentuck

Executive Vice President
Stan Winston

Secretary
Dan Breau

Treasurer
Harriet Ballard

Vice President, Arrangements
Joan Greenfield

Vice President, Programs
Karen Hochman

Vice President,
Ralph J. Westerhoff

Vice President, Public Relations
Richard N. Harbert

Advisory Chairman
Richard Sachinis

Advisory Co-Chairman
Richard M. King

First Board Member-at-Large
Andi Emerson

Second Board Member-at-Large, Art
Jack Stern

Second Board Member-at-Large, Copy
Murray Rosenberg

For more information, write:
Direct Marketing Creative Guild
516 Fifth Avenue
New York, NY 10036

MANAGING DIRECTOR Penny Sibal-Samonte
CREATIVE DIRECTOR Richard Liu
FINANCIAL DIRECTOR Pamela McCormick
ASSOCIATE ART DIRECTOR Daniel Kouw
EDITORIAL MANAGER Kevin Clark
ARTISTS William Mack
Kim McCormick

POSTAGE
NECESSARY
IF MAILED
IN THE
UNITED STATES

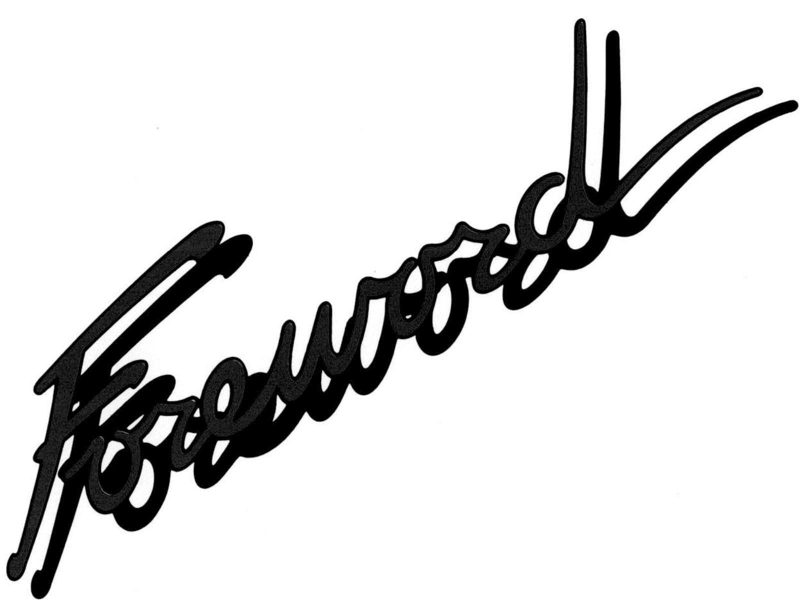

The book you hold in your hands is a treasury of direct marketing copy and design.

It is a celebration of the best creative work being done in our industry. It is a valuable historical record of current styles, trends, techniques and technology. And it is, above all, a sourcebook.

For a writer or designer, for a promotion manager of direct marketing manager, *Creativity in Direct Response Advertising* offers a vast amount of information and inspiration.

There are thousands of ideas to be found in these pages, ideas that can be translated into exciting new ways of meeting your own direct marketing challenges.

You may see things that have been done that you never knew *could* be done, technically. You may find inspiration in a new medium, a new technology, or a new way of using an established technology.

There is always the possibility of direct adaptation. The format that was effective for a business magazine may be exactly what is needed for a financial marketer.

Beyond that, there is the stimulation of seeing ingenious concepts developed; of looking at fresh, lively design; of reading crisp, clear and compelling copy.

Use this book. Browse through it now and then. Turn to it when you are stalled; for most of us the superb work of others is an effective starter for our creative motors, whether it functions as a goad or a carrot.

What makes a winner?

The one thing you must beware of, however, is thinking that this book has The Answers. You cannot simply duplicate what someone else has done, no matter how successful it has been, and assume that it will be successful for you.

Furthermore, a Caples Award-winning direct mail package, print ad, collateral piece, catalog or commercial may be an example of excellent creative work—but that does not necessarily mean that it was a winner in the marketplace.

Writers and designers sometimes do splendid work that fails for reasons entirely beyond their control.

Direct marketing campaigns are almost never the work of individuals. Copywriters don't normally choose products or make the list selections; designers don't devise offers, schedule mail drops or handle fulfillment.

In putting together a campaign a dozen or more people may have a hand in making it a winner—or a failure. Good creative is vital to success but even the most brilliant direct mail package can't sell the wrong product at the wrong price to the wrong people.

One can look at the creative work, however—even that of a failed effort, and say, "I think that was a brilliant idea...an ingenious way of dealing with that situation...an innovative way of meeting that challenge."

Caples Awards—for individual excellence

There are many awards in our industry that are given to organizations—to teams of creative, marketing and production people—for outstanding direct marketing efforts. These awards are based in large part on proven superior results.

The John Caples Award, from the Direct Marketing Creative Guild, is the only accolade given to *individuals* who, in the opinion of the judges, have found successful creative solutions to direct marketing problems.

For direct marketing creative professionals inclusion in this book is a distinct honor, reflecting the admiration of their peers.

There is much to admire in *Creativity in Direct Response Advertising*, much to learn from, and much to enjoy. Enjoy it!

Shan Ellentuck *President*
Direct Marketing Creative Guild

The John Caples Awards program celebrated its tenth anniversary in 1987 with far and away the largest number of entries it had ever received and record-breaking attendance at its gala awards luncheon in New York.

Given in recognition of individual creative excellence in direct response advertising, a Caples Award is the highest honor a copywriter or art director can achieve for direct marketing creativity. Named for a true pioneer in the field of direct marketing, each year's Caples Award winners are responsible for the best direct response creative work to be found anywhere.

This book presents a collection of selected finalists and winners from the 8th, 9th, and 10th Annual John Caples Awards, and we hope you enjoy it. But first, take note of the winners from those three programs, recognized on the roster below. It is their determined pursuit of the targeted brilliance exemplified by the work of John Caples himself that is the foundation of the entire Caples Awards program.

The Maxwell Sackheim Award

Initiated in 1983 to honor the memory of Maxwell Sackheim, another legendary direct marketing pioneer and innovator, each recipient of this award is specially selected by the board of directors of both The Direct Marketing Creative Guild and The John Caples Awards. The Maxwell Sackheim Award recognizes genuine marketplace innovation in the direct response industry, and is not presented every year. Only three times have winners of The Maxwell Sackheim Award been chosen.

THE 10th ANNUAL JOHN CAPLES AWARDS' MAXWELL SACKHEIM AWARD

Leo Yochim

THE 9th ANNUAL JOHN CAPLES AWARDS' MAXWELL SACKHEIM AWARD

Richard Armstrong

THE 6th ANNUAL JOHN CAPLES AWARDS' MAXWELL SACKHEIM AWARD

Rod Kilpatrick
Julie Vanatta

The Irving Wunderman Award

Established in 1987 and endowed by celebrated direct marketers Irving and Lester Wunderman, this award honors a single individual who, for a decade or more, has combined the highest levels of talent, imagination, curiosity and human insight into a unique body of creative work. The winner of the first Irving Wunderman Award was Tom Collins, a renowned copywriter and creative director responsible for many creative breakthroughs during his illustrious career.

THE 10th ANNUAL JOHN CAPLES AWARDS' IRVING WUNDERMAN AWARD

Tom Collins

Consumer Direct Mail
10th ANNUAL JOHN CAPLES AWARDS

1st Prize
Copy: Sue Levytsky, Norma Friedman, Suzanne Prince
Art Direction: Carol Dronsfield
Agency: Wunderman 'Worldwide
Client: American Express

2nd Prize
Copy: Fred Vallejo
Art Direction: Robin Bray
Agency: Time-Life Books In-House
Client: Time-Life Books

3rd Prize
Copy: Jim Punkre
Art Direction: Mike Sincavage
Agency: Brainstorms, Inc.
Client: Rodale Press, Inc.

Honorable Mention
Copy: Charles F. Herrmann
Art Direction: Pamela F. Miller
Agency: National Geographic In-House
Client: National Geographic Society

Business Direct Mail
10th ANNUAL JOHN CAPLES AWARDS

1st Prize
Copy: Rick Peterson
Art Direction: John Engerman
Agency: Sharp Hartwig
Client: Airborne Express

2nd Prize
Copy: Virg Viner
Art Direction: Cyndee Lamb
Agency: Children's Magazine Guide In-House
Client: Children's Magazine Guide

3rd Prize
Copy: Samuel Kirshenbaum
Art Direction: Timothy Claffey
Agency: Bozell, Jacobs, Kenyon & Eckhardt Direct/Chicago
Client: Wolverine Boots & Shoes

Honorable Mention
Copy: Suzie Becker
Art Direction: Jory Mason
Agency: HMBM/Creamer Direct
Client: Reebok

Consumer Direct Mail
9th ANNUAL JOHN CAPLES AWARDS

1st Prize
Copy: Richard Armstrong
Art Direction: Barbara Green, Adrianna Barbieri
Agency: The Oram Group
Client: The Center for Environmental Education

2nd Prize
Copy: Katie Hartley-Urquhart
Art Direction: Roy Sexton
Agency: Tracey-Locke Direct
Client: Princess Cruises

3rd Prize
Copy: Dianne Edlemann
Art Direction: Judy McCabe Smith
Agency: Ogilvy & Mather Direct
Client: The Atlanta Ballet

Honorable Mention
Copy: Sam Kirshenbaum
Art Direction: Tim Claffey
Agency: Bozell, Jacobs, Kenyon & Eckhardt Direct
Client: Mundelein College

Business Direct Mail
9th ANNUAL JOHN CAPLES AWARDS

1st Prize
Copy: Martha Westerman, Tom McNear
Art Direction: Bill Sowder
Agency: Kaiser Kuhn Bennett Inc.
Client: Health & Tennis Corp. of America

2nd Prize
Copy: Ellen Labb, Michael Fortuna
Art Direction: Jim Clattenburg, Keith Lane
Agency: Emerson Lane Fortuna
Client: Nantucket Inn at Nobadeer

3rd Prize
Copy: Raymond P. Clark
Art Direction: Rick Strode, Peter Simon
Agency: BDM Group, Inc.
Client: Digital Equipment Corp.

Honorable Mention
Copy: Betsy Sloan Thomas, Larrilee Frazier
Art Direction: Judi Kolstad, Bob Cesiro
Agency: Ogilvy & Mather Direct
Client: AT&T Public Communications

Consumer Direct Mail
8th ANNUAL JOHN CAPLES AWARDS

1st Prize
Copy: Peter Blau
Art Direction: Richard Koranda
Agency: Barry Blau & Partners, Inc.
Client: Citicorp Diners Club

2nd Prize
Copy: Sheila Stogol
Art Direction: Randy Howell
Agency: Kobs & Brady Adv.
Client: Western Publishing Co.

3rd Prize
Copy: George Mercer, Ruth Harris
Art Direction: Emelyn Albert
Agency: The DR Group Inc. Needham Harper Worldwide
Client: The Bank of Boston

3rd Prize
Copy: Nancy Cressler
Art Direction: Gerry Ulrich, Barry Underhill
Agency: Keller Crescent
Client: Evansville Dance Theatre

Honorable Mention
Copy: Emily Soell
Art Direction: Jim Pastena
Agency: Rapp & Collins, Inc.
Client: Conde Nast Publications

Honorable Mention
Copy: Martin Tarratt
Art Direction: Kathleen Tresnak
Agency: Time-Life Books In-House
Client: Time-Life Books

Honorable Mention

Copy: George T. Mercer
Art Direction: Russ Cevoli
Agency: The DR Group Inc. Needham Harper Worldwide
Client: The Bank of Boston

Business Direct Mail
8th ANNUAL JOHN CAPLES AWARDS

1st Prize

Copy: John Moon
Art Direction: Betsy Kitslaar
Agency: Campbell-Mithun Advertising
Client: 3M

1st Prize

Copy: Arthur Mitchell
Art Direction: Peter Barnes
Agency: W. B. Doner & Co., Advertising
Client: The Lee Company/V-F Jeans

2nd Prize

Copy: Laurie Shainwald
Art Direction: Robert Armstrong
Agency: Flair Communications
Client: North American Philips

3rd Prize

Copy: Edwin Roche
Art Direction: Angelo Sannasardo
Agency: Marquardt & Roche Inc.
Client: IBM Instruments Inc.

Honorable Mention

Copy: Randall Lorimor
Art Direction: Gail Dobbins
Agency: Robert Nichols & Associates
Client: A.E. Staley Mfg. Co.

Consumer Print
10th ANNUAL JOHN CAPLES AWARDS

1st Prize

Copy: Joyce Lapin
Art Direction: Carol Dronsfield
Agency: Wunderman Worldwide
Client: CBS Video Libraries

2nd Prize

Copy: Jeff Ostroth, Ralph Westerhoff
Art Direction: Derek Karsanidi
Agency: Kobs & Brady Adv.
Client: Foster Parents Plan

2nd Prize

Copy: Randy Haunfelder
Art Direction: Andy Greenaway
Agency: Ogilvy & Mather Direct
Client: Magnet

3rd Prize

Copy: Don Rudnick
Art Direction: Holly Pavlika
Agency: McCann Direct
Client: American Express Gold Card

Honorable Mention

Copy: Don Rudnick
Art Direction: Holly Pavlika
Agency: McCann Direct
Client: American Express Gold Card

Business Print
10th ANNUAL JOHN CAPLES AWARDS

1st Prize

Copy: Patricia Gannon
Art Direction: Lorraine Shaw
Agency: Bozell Jacobs Kenyon & Eckhardt Direct/Dallas
Client: American Airlines Freight

2nd Prize

Copy: Fred Wood
Art Direction: Sheldon Shacket
Agency: Cohen & Greenbaum
Client: Kemper Financial Services

Honorable Mention

Copy: Maureen Moore
Art Direction: Bob Meagher
Agency: Cramer-Krasselt/Chicago
Client: Citicorp Services Inc.

Honorable Mention

Copy: Alan Rosenspan
Art Direction: Lysle Wickersham
Agency: Ingalls, Quinn & Johnson
Client: Sigma Design, Inc.

Consumer Print
9th ANNUAL JOHN CAPLES AWARDS

1st Prize

Copy: George Watts, Bill Hemp
Art Direction: Tricia Bradley, Ellen Furguson
Agency: Young & Rubicam/Burson-Marsteller
Client: Metropolitan Life

2nd Prize

Copy: Jim Jenkins
Art Direction: Walter Halucha
Agency: Wunderman, Ricotta & Kline
Client: Johnson & Johnson Child Development Toys

3rd Prize

Copy: Joan Helfman
Art Direction: Tom Miano
Agency: Ogilvy & Mather Direct
Client: Direct Marketing Association

Business Print
9th ANNUAL JOHN CAPLES AWARDS

3rd Prize

Copy: Brown Hagood, Paul Levett
Art Direction: Vincent Picardi, Mal Karlin
Agency: Lowe Marschalk, Inc.
Client: Xerox Corp.

Honorable Mention

Copy: Paul Levett
Art Direction: Mal Karlin
Agency: Lowe Marschalk, Inc.
Client: Xerox Direct Marketing Div. of Xerox Corp.

Honorable Mention

Copy: Chuck Culver
Art Direction: Pam Levinson
Agency: Solem, Loeb & Associates
Client: Asian Yellow Pages

The complete listing of the John Caples Award Winners continues on page 246.

Chapter
1
PBC INTERNATIONAL
ONE SCHOOL STREET
GLEN COVE, NY 11542

DIRECT MAIL

Billions of marketing communications are mailed each year to thousands of different audiences around the world. A successful direct mail effort—whether it is aimed at only a small group of business executives or a huge segment of the general population—must meet at least one ultimate challenge. It must get a response from its recipient.

Along the road to a response, of course, there is much more that can be accomplished and an infinite number of ways to do it. Creative people in direct marketing, along with their teammates in strategic planning, media analysis and selection, database management, research and the printing and print production fields, are constantly seeking new ways to build *relationships* with people...endless networks of people whose business or consumer needs bind them together.

There is so much brilliant creativity in today's direct mail, as you will see in this chapter, that countless relationships must have been formed and many surely continue. In the process, a certain depth of image is invariably conveyed to the recipient by the mailer, who in turn learns more about his customer or prospect as their one-on-one connection expands.

Sending a manager $660 of real money, shredded into bits and pieces and packed in a plastic bag, is the way Airborne Express went about getting attention and opening a dialogue on shipping matters, especially shipping costs. In the imaginative direct mail effort on page 16, such tangible evidence reinforces the impact of the cost-saving opportunities discovered in the rest of the package, and the way is cleared for further contact.

Music has its own way of establishing contact, and the 45 RPM rock 'n' roll record sent by the Special Products division of Warner Communications may well have played a significant role in the proliferation of the licensing of rock and pop music for commercials in recent years. Advertising creative directors and television and radio commercial producers who receive and play the record hear samples of tunes to which the rights are available.

All sorts of attention-getting devices—ranging from the chrome-plated 3-pound exercise dumbbell offered in the Xerox Corporation's "Flex" effort on page 27 to V-F Jeans' balls of raw cotton and patches of blue denim in their five-part mailing on page 20—can be sent in cartons, crates and containers of myriad shapes and sizes. Most often used in business marketing, such mailings are usually low in quantity and relatively expensive on a per-piece basis. But compared to the average cost of one in-person sales call, more than $250, "three-dimensional" business mail can be targeted quite cost-effectively to reach a reasonable number of prospects.

Mass mailings, on the other hand, are routinely made to large groups of people, with quantities frequently reaching well into the multi-millions. Most experts agree that, almost without exception, among all elements of a direct mail package it is the mighty letter that provides most of the "pull" needed to generate responses. But the power of a direct mail letter—whether it's a short, long, extra-long, personalized or generic one—can often be dramatically enhanced by the other elements

And, as the role of direct response advertising within the marketing universe continues to expand, an ever-increasing amount of "clutter" threatens to dilute the impact of an advertiser's message. Never before has there been such great demand for spirited art direction and new, innovative production techniques in direct mail. Creative talents the world over are breaking through, year after year, to new levels of originality. Many copy-and-art teams cannot even envision the days, less than a generation ago, when many of the graphic decisions now made solely by the art director, or by mutual agreement, were then almost the exclusive domain of the copywriter. In today's award-winning direct mail, the concept, design, copy and execution all work together to create an integrated, well-constructed communication.

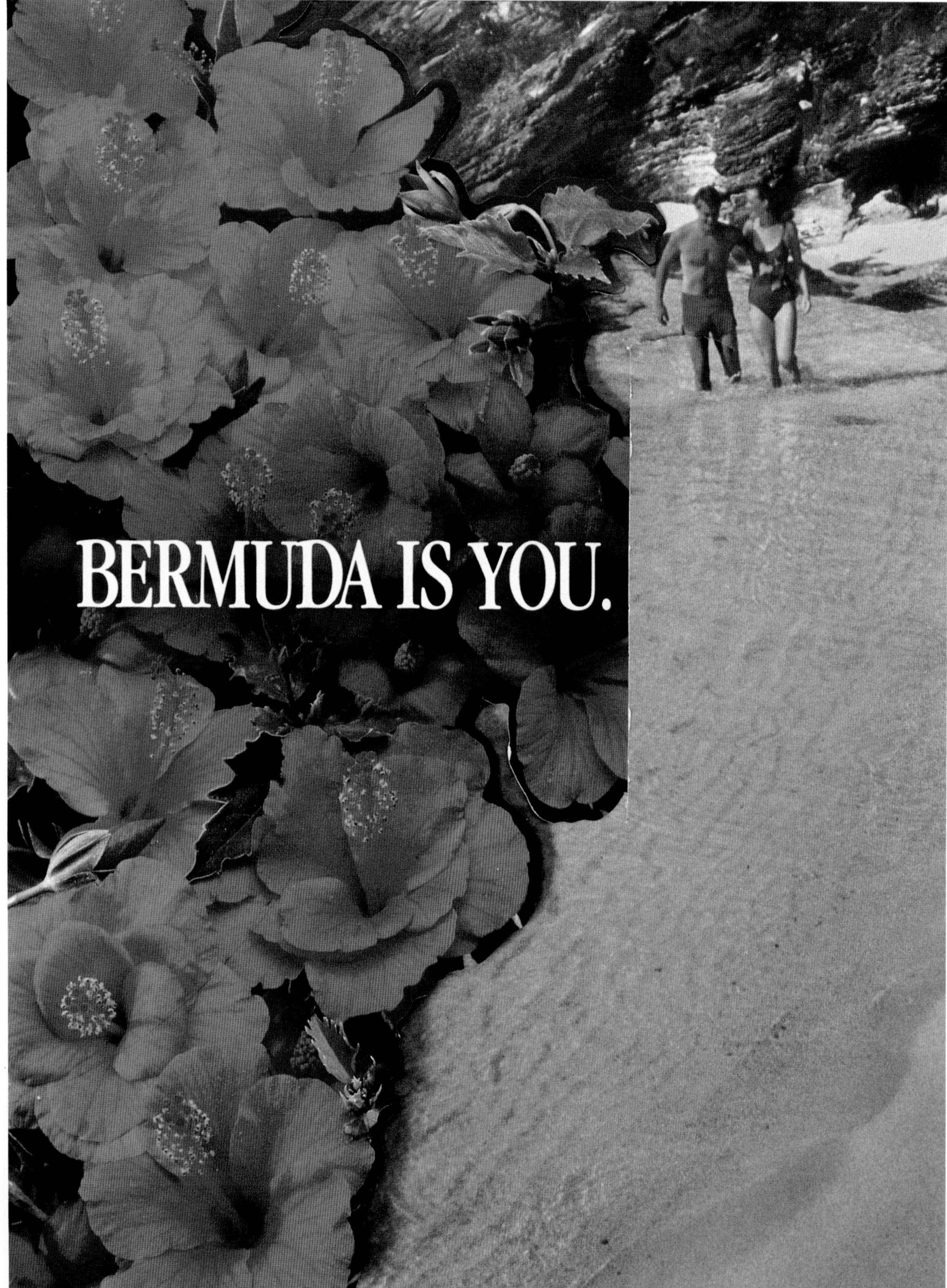
BERMUDA IS YOU.

Title: "Bermuda Is You"
Copywriters: Steve Snapp, Melanie Price
Art Director: Mitch Lunsford
Agency: Foote, Cone, Belding Direct
Client: Bermuda Tourism Bureau

If such a thing as dynamic simplicity exists, it is reflected in this evocative, double-die-cut mailer that speaks to one's instinctive desire for warmth, relaxation and fun.

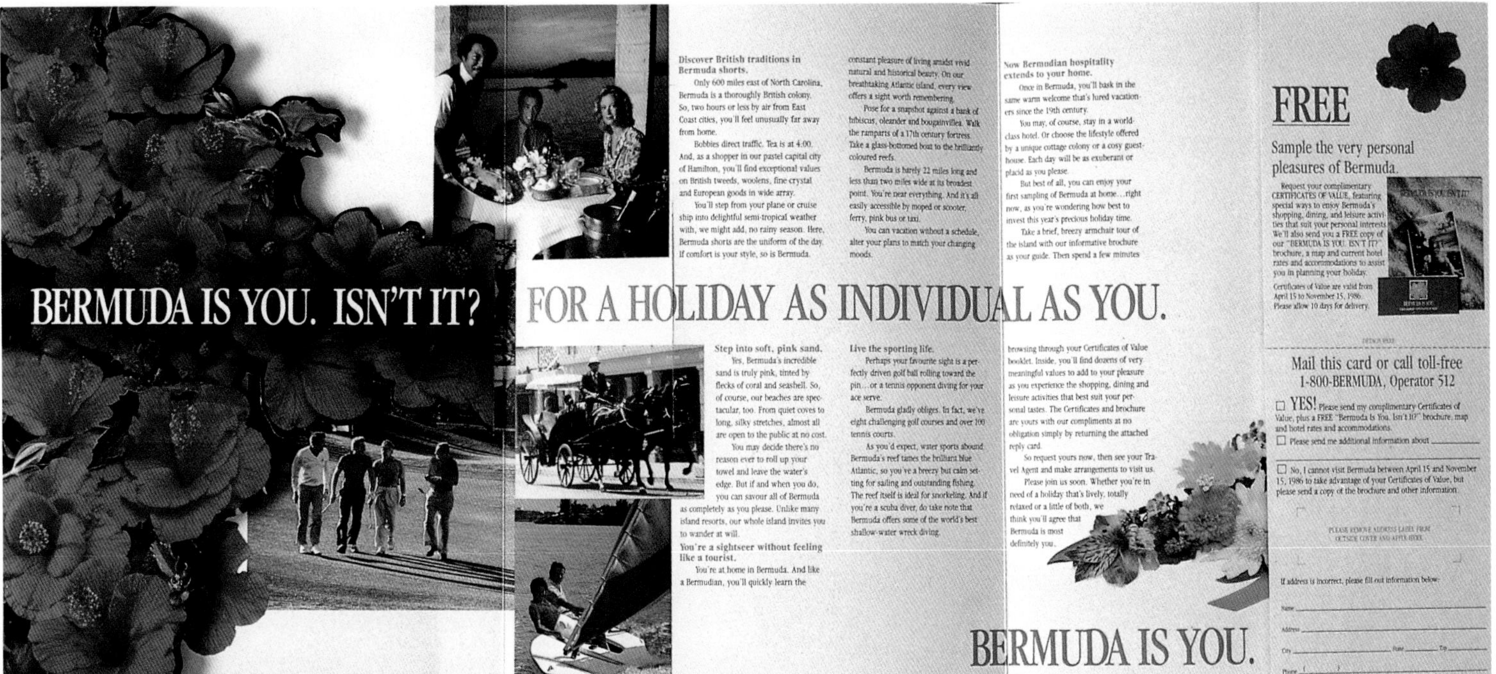

Dear Traveler,

As someone who plans thoughtfully how to spend your holiday time, you recently expressed interest in the island we proudly call home.

Now, please accept my invitation on behalf of all Bermudians to experience the satisfying sort of vacation you've been seeking—surrounded by all your favourite warm-weather leisure activities.

Everything about Bermuda is as diverse, exciting and friendly as you've heard...

...the traditions, shopping values and dining, all so reminiscent of Europe... the colourful and lush semi-tropical beauty...the fascinating history of Britain's oldest colony...the sports, both abundant and challenging...and, of course, our incomparable pink beaches.

And now through mid-November, we're presenting you with an even more convincing reason to pay us a visit during the island's loveliest, most active season.

Request your complimentary Certificates of Value, and enjoy a generous, extra measure of Bermudian hospitality.

Certificates in hand, you'll discover more of the qualities of Bermuda that best suit your interests. With them, you'll receive special considerations from many of the finest merchants, restaurateurs, and leisure facilities throughout the island.

Your Certificates of Value are free of cost or obligation. Certificates requested now are valid whenever you vacation with us, prior to November 15, 1986.

So request yours by mail or phone. Then see your Travel Agent to arrange your holiday in warm, peaceful, cordial Bermuda.

Take this chance to share in all of Bermuda. Whether you're in need of a vacation that's lively, totally relaxing, or a little of both, we think you'll agree that Bermuda is most definitely you.

Sincerely,

Stephen J. Flett
Director of Tourism

P.S. For your complimentary Certificates of Value, return the attached postage-paid card or call toll-free 1-800-BERMUDA and ask for Operator 512.

Global House, 43 Church Street, Hamilton 5-24 Bermuda

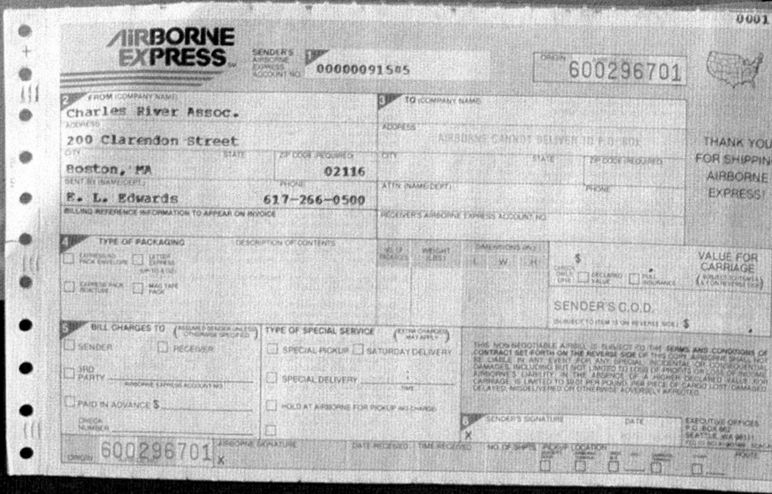

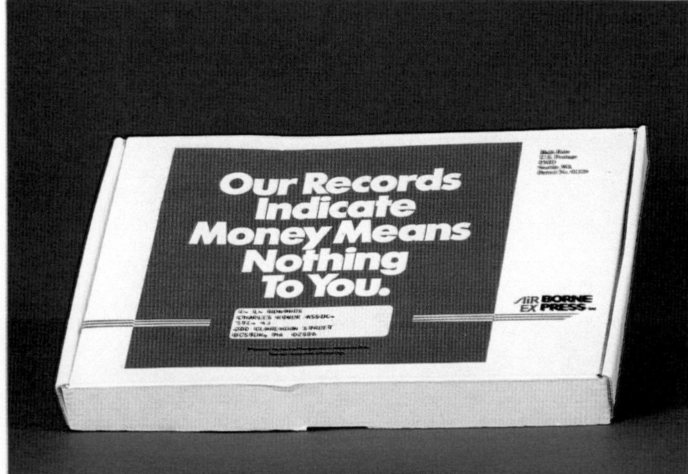

Title: "Our Record Indicate..."
Copywriter: Rick Peterson
Art Director: John Engerman
Agency: Sharp Hartwig
Client: Airborne Express

This dramatic business-to-business solicitation featured $660 of real U.S. currency, shredded, as a "gentle reminder that air express shipping with someone else is like tearing up money."

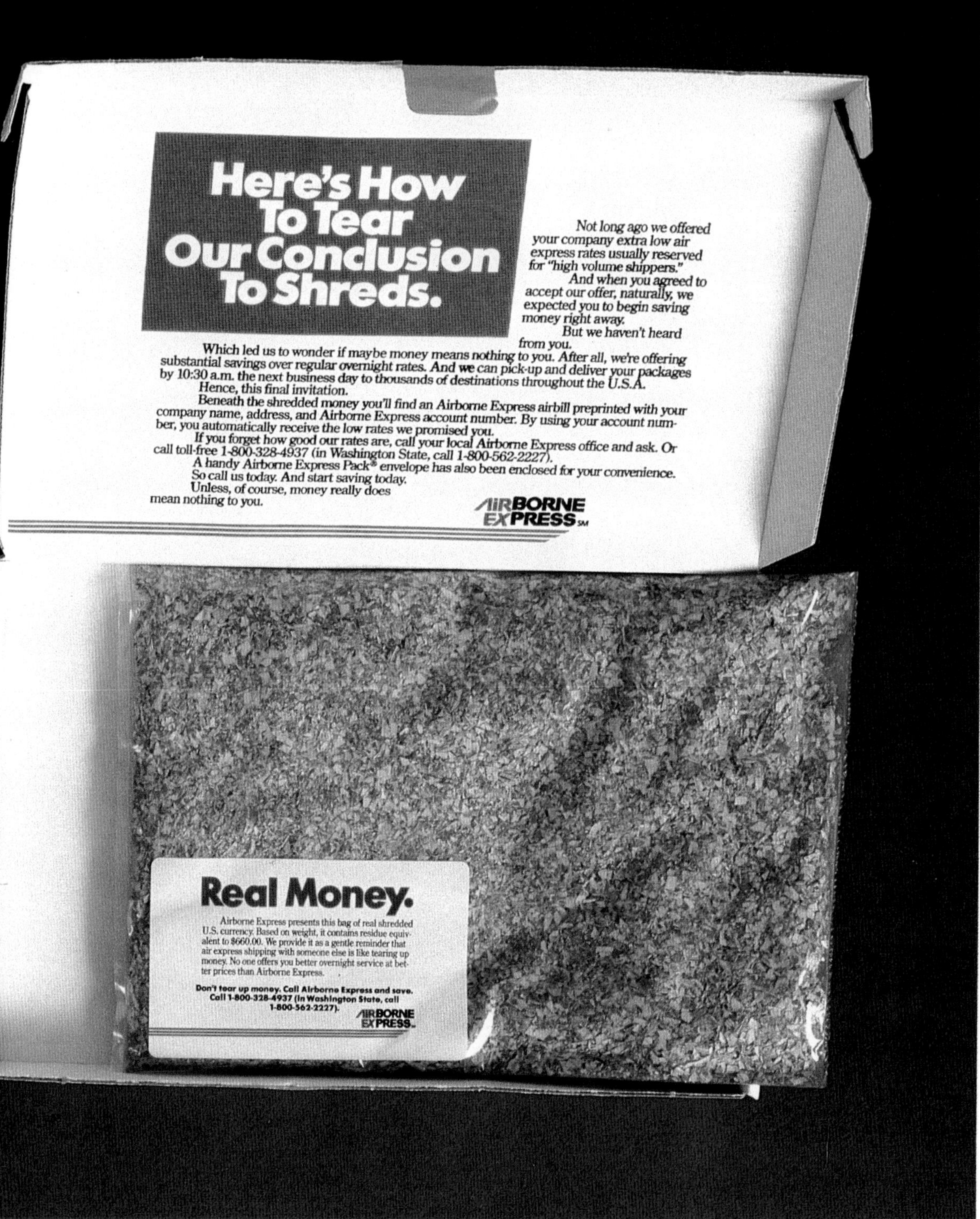
Here's How To Tear Our Conclusion To Shreds.
Not long ago we offered your company extra low air express rates usually reserved for "high volume shippers."
And when you agreed to accept our offer, naturally, we expected you to begin saving money right away.
But we haven't heard from you.
Which led us to wonder if maybe money means nothing to you. After all, we're offering substantial savings over regular overnight rates. And we can pick-up and deliver your packages by 10:30 a.m. the next business day to thousands of destinations throughout the U.S.A.
Hence, this final invitation.
Beneath the shredded money you'll find an Airborne Express airbill preprinted with your company name, address, and Airborne Express account number. By using your account number, you automatically receive the low rates we promised you.
If you forget how good our rates are, call your local Airborne Express office and ask. Or call toll-free 1-800-328-4937 (in Washington State, call 1-800-562-2227).
A handy Airborne Express Pack® envelope has also been enclosed for your convenience.
So call us today. And start saving today.
Unless, of course, money really does mean nothing to you.
AIRBORNE EXPRESS SM
Real Money.
Airborne Express presents this bag of real shredded U.S. currency. Based on weight, it contains residue equivalent to $660.00. We provide it as a gentle reminder that air express shipping with someone else is like tearing up money. No one offers you better overnight service at better prices than Airborne Express.
Don't tear up money. Call Airborne Express and save. Call 1-800-328-4937 (In Washington State, call 1-800-562-2227).
AIRBORNE EXPRESS

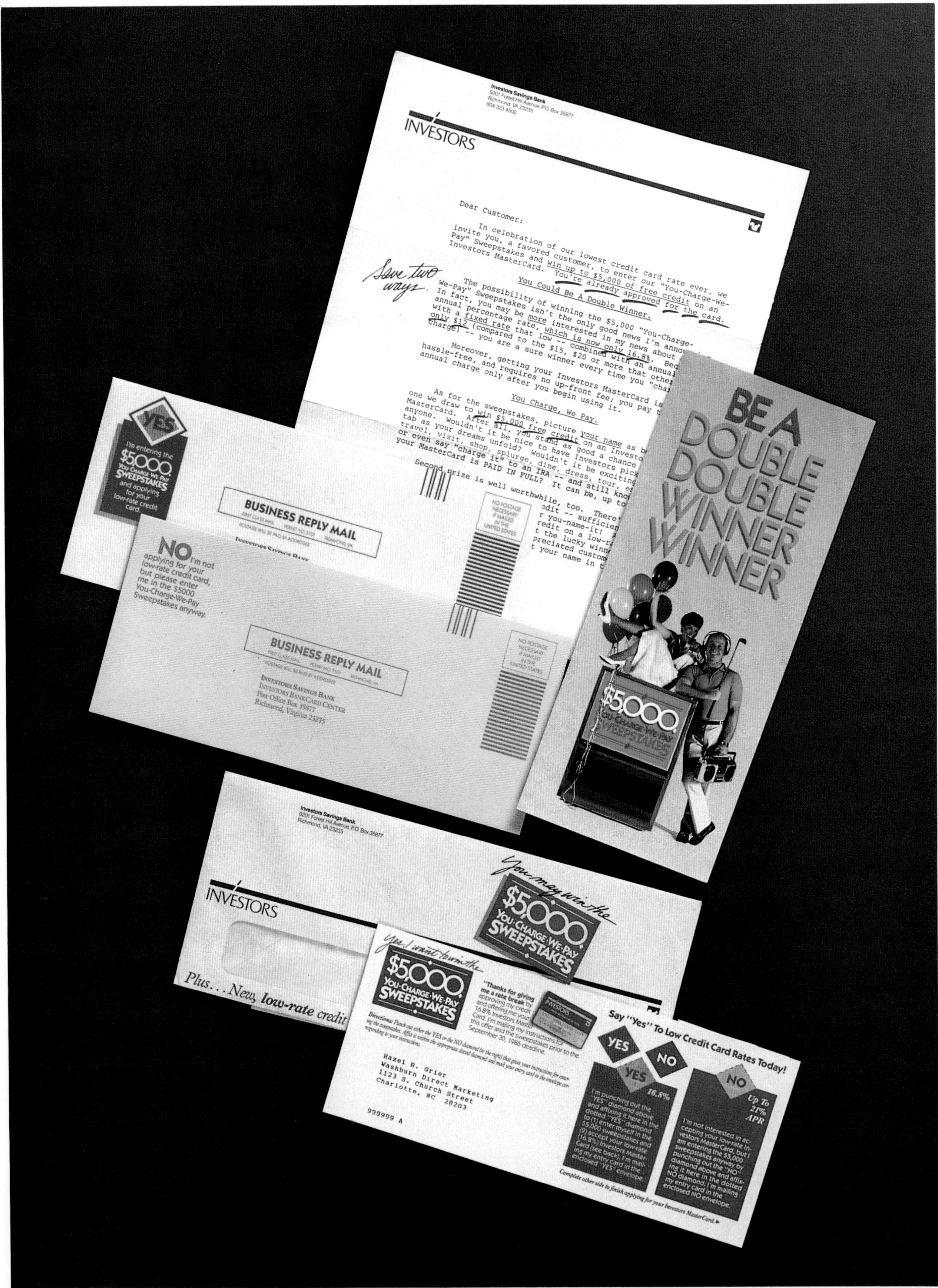

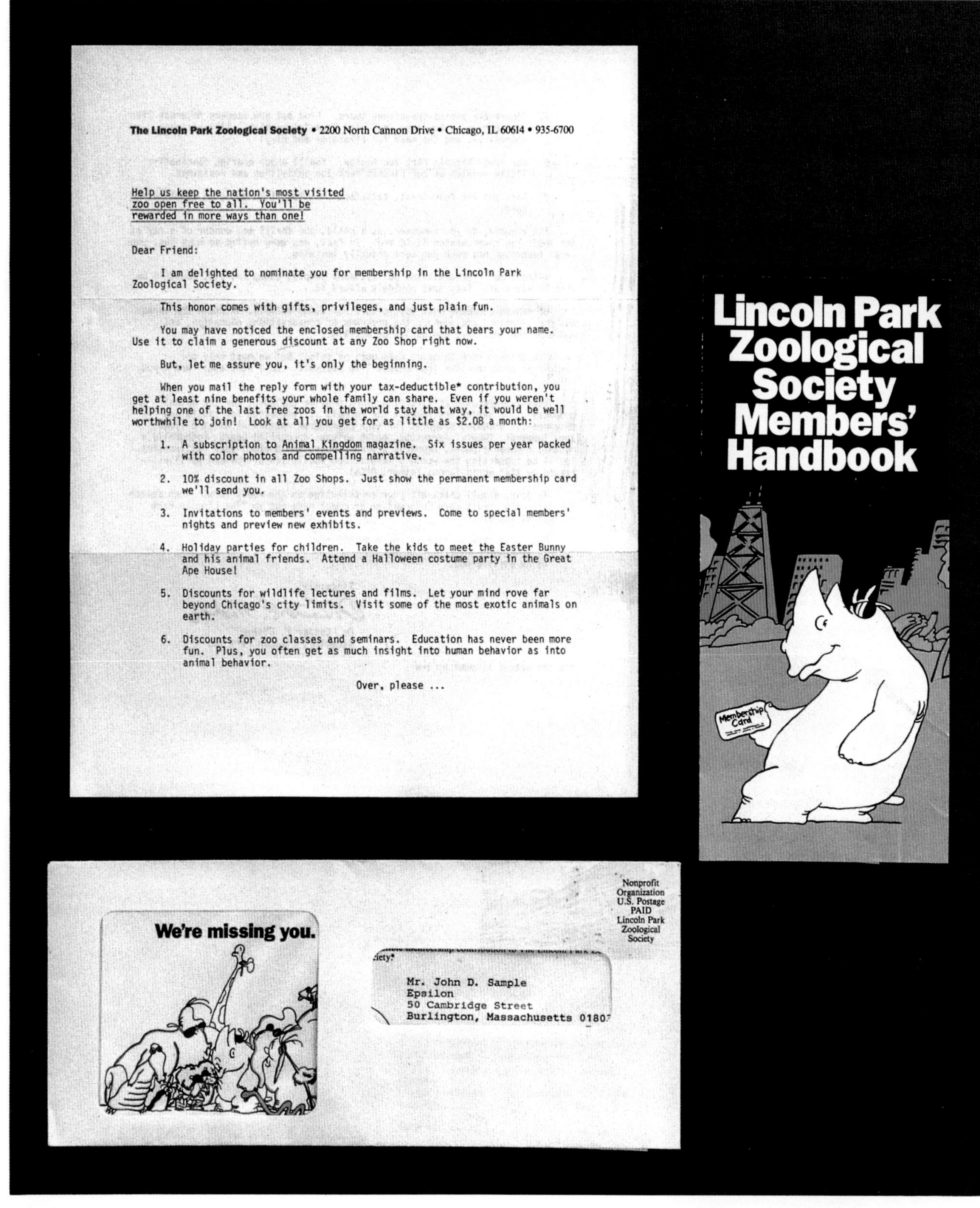

The Lincoln Park Zoological Society • 2200 North Cannon Drive • Chicago, IL 60614 • 935-6700

Help us keep the nation's most visited zoo open free to all. You'll be rewarded in more ways than one!

Dear Friend:

I am delighted to nominate you for membership in the Lincoln Park Zoological Society.

This honor comes with gifts, privileges, and just plain fun.

You may have noticed the enclosed membership card that bears your name. Use it to claim a generous discount at any Zoo Shop right now.

But, let me assure you, it's only the beginning.

When you mail the reply form with your tax-deductible* contribution, you get at least nine benefits your whole family can share. Even if you weren't helping one of the last free zoos in the world stay that way, it would be well worthwhile to join! Look at all you get for as little as $2.08 a month:

1. A subscription to Animal Kingdom magazine. Six issues per year packed with color photos and compelling narrative.
2. 10% discount in all Zoo Shops. Just show the permanent membership card we'll send you.
3. Invitations to members' events and previews. Come to special members' nights and preview new exhibits.
4. Holiday parties for children. Take the kids to meet the Easter Bunny and his animal friends. Attend a Halloween costume party in the Great Ape House!
5. Discounts for wildlife lectures and films. Let your mind rove far beyond Chicago's city limits. Visit some of the most exotic animals on earth.
6. Discounts for zoo classes and seminars. Education has never been more fun. Plus, you often get as much insight into human behavior as into animal behavior.

Over, please ...

Lincoln Park Zoological Society Members' Handbook
Membership Card
We're missing you.
Nonprofit Organization U.S. Postage PAID Lincoln Park Zoological Society
Mr. John D. Sample
Epsilon
50 Cambridge Street
Burlington, Massachusetts 0180

Title: "Investors Savings Sweepstakes"
Copywriter: John Gunderson
Art Director: Todd Baxter
Agency: Washburn Direct Marketing
Client: Investors Savings Bank

In a departure from predictability, this sweepstakes approach employs smart copy and complementary design to entice the consumer into mutually beneficial participation with an obviously trustworthy banking institution.

Title: "My Kind of Zoo"
Copywriter: Alan Fonorow
Art Director: Bob Meagher
Agency: Cramer- Krasselt/ Chicago
Client: Lincoln Park Zoo

Supported by broadcast efforts, this direct mail segment of a consumer multi- media campaign draws easy comparisons, through accessible illustrations and undistracted copy, between human prospective zoo members and their hosts, the animals.

Introducing V.F. Jeans.
The best made jeans in the world.

V.F. Jeans, a VF Company

The Fabric

Tight weave. Ring/Ring construction.
Unparalleled durability.

It's the best denim ever made. And the only one of its kind. Heavy, durable, yet incredibly soft.

How did we achieve it? Beefier yarns, tighter packing, and a few secrets our competitors would love to get their hands on.

Once you feel it, you'll know exactly why.

100% pure indigo. Dipped eight times.
Unprecedented depth and saturation.

Sure, we could have substituted cheaper dye. And we could have dipped the fabric fewer times.

But that wouldn't have given us the color we wanted. What we wanted was perfection.

And the color was just the start.

The Color

The Jeans

They're the best made in the world. Not the ones with the most unpronounceable name. Not the most authentic reproductions of the original Won-the-West jeans. Not the lower-than-low or high-as-the-sky priced ones either.

We left those lofty goals to others. And concentrated, instead, on making the best five-pocket jean ever.

It's why we used premium long staple cotton, pure indigo dye, and copper rivets and buttons.

It's why we specially sew the pockets and hems to keep them from curling after they're washed.

It's why we inspect them twice as often as the industry standard.

And it's why we'd rather throw out a pair than have your customers try on a size that's even *one-quarter of an inch* smaller than what the tag states.

But fanatical attention to detail isn't enough to make a pair of jeans as good as ours.

Nor is a simple passion for perfection.

It's the way the elements come together. That's the art that makes an original. New V.F. Jeans. If you could only sell one brand of jeans, this would be the brand.

Title: "V-F Jeans Introductory Mailing"
Copywriter: Arthur Mitchell
Art Director: Peter Barnes
Agency: W.B. Doner and Company
Client: The Lee Company/V-F Jeans

Five separate, well-crafted white boxes are utilized in this compelling use of business-to-business direct mail to introduce a new line of blue jeans to distributors. Samples of the actual raw materials used in making the jeans—and a moneybag indicating high profit potential—bring the promotional message home.

High. And we'll keep it that
53¢ on the dollar. It's better than anything you've seen in a very long time.
So is our product. That's one reason the margin's so good.
Another is exclusivity. A few select stores are all that will ever carry it.
The Margin

The Metal
Specially treated pure copper.
No rusting. Ever.
Some manufacturers get away with plated steel. It's an easy, inexpensive way to make buttons and rivets. Buttons and rivets that invariably rust.
We wanted perfection.
And using only pure copper was another way to get us there.

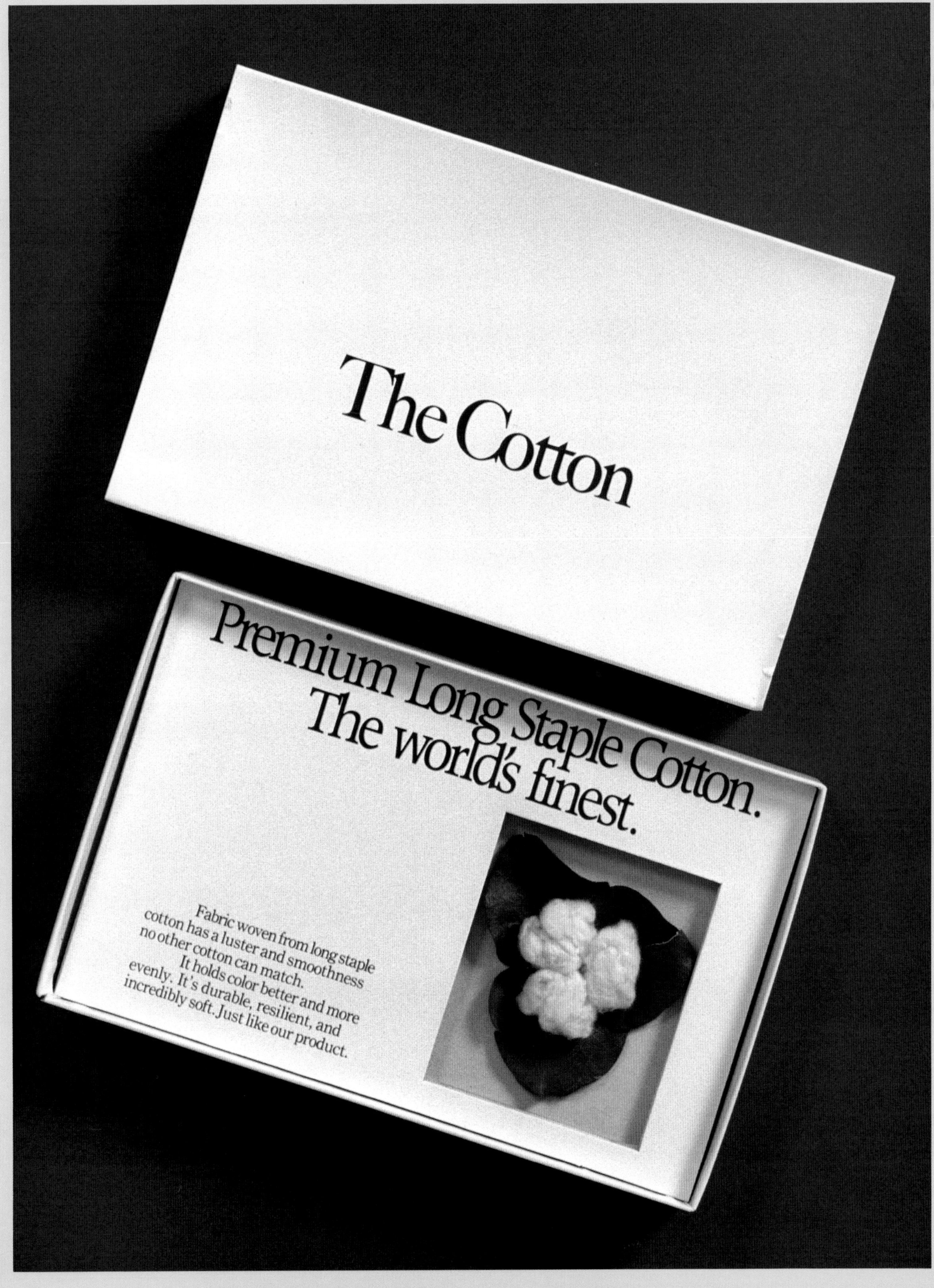

The Cotton

Premium Long Staple Cotton.
The world's finest.

Fabric woven from long staple cotton has a luster and smoothness no other cotton can match.
It holds color better and more evenly. It's durable, resilient, and incredibly soft. Just like our product.

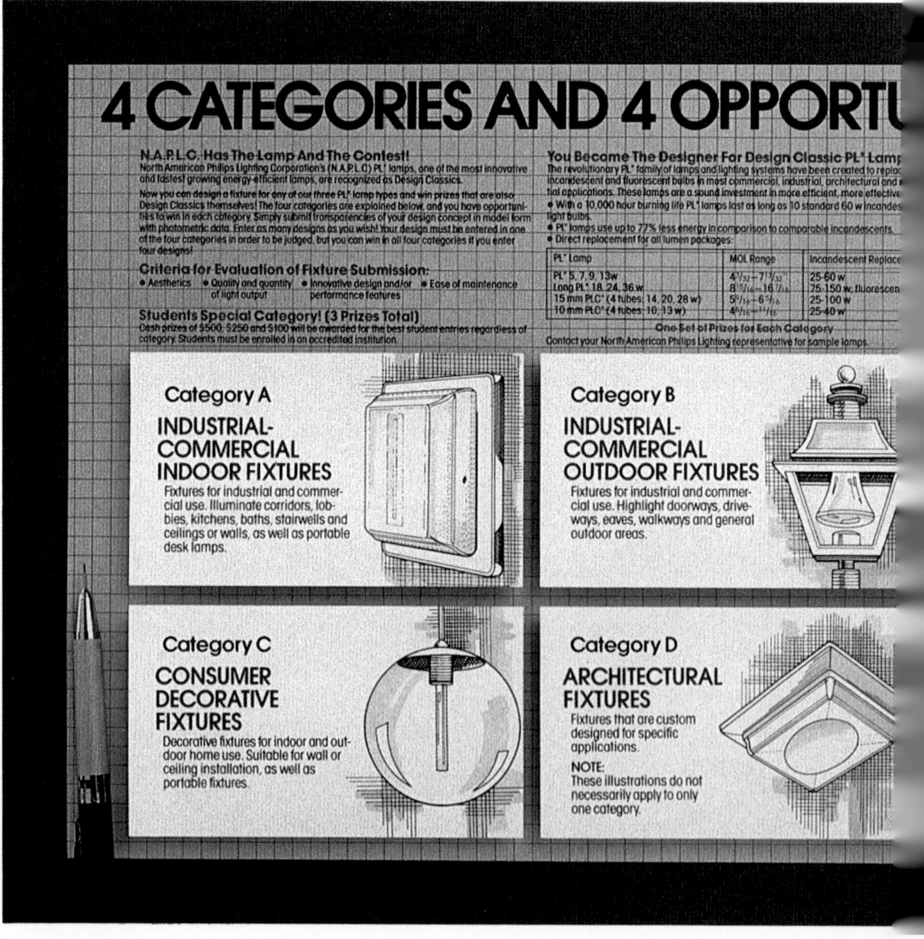

Title: "Design a Classic"
Copywriter: Laurie Shainwald
Art Director: Robert Armstrong
Agency: Flair Communications
Client: North American Philips Lighting

Already loaded with free belongings (a set of Pentels, a circle template, an engineer's ruler, a mechanical pencil), this business promotion to lighting suppliers and designers offers even more valuable awards by return shipment for excellence in lighting design.

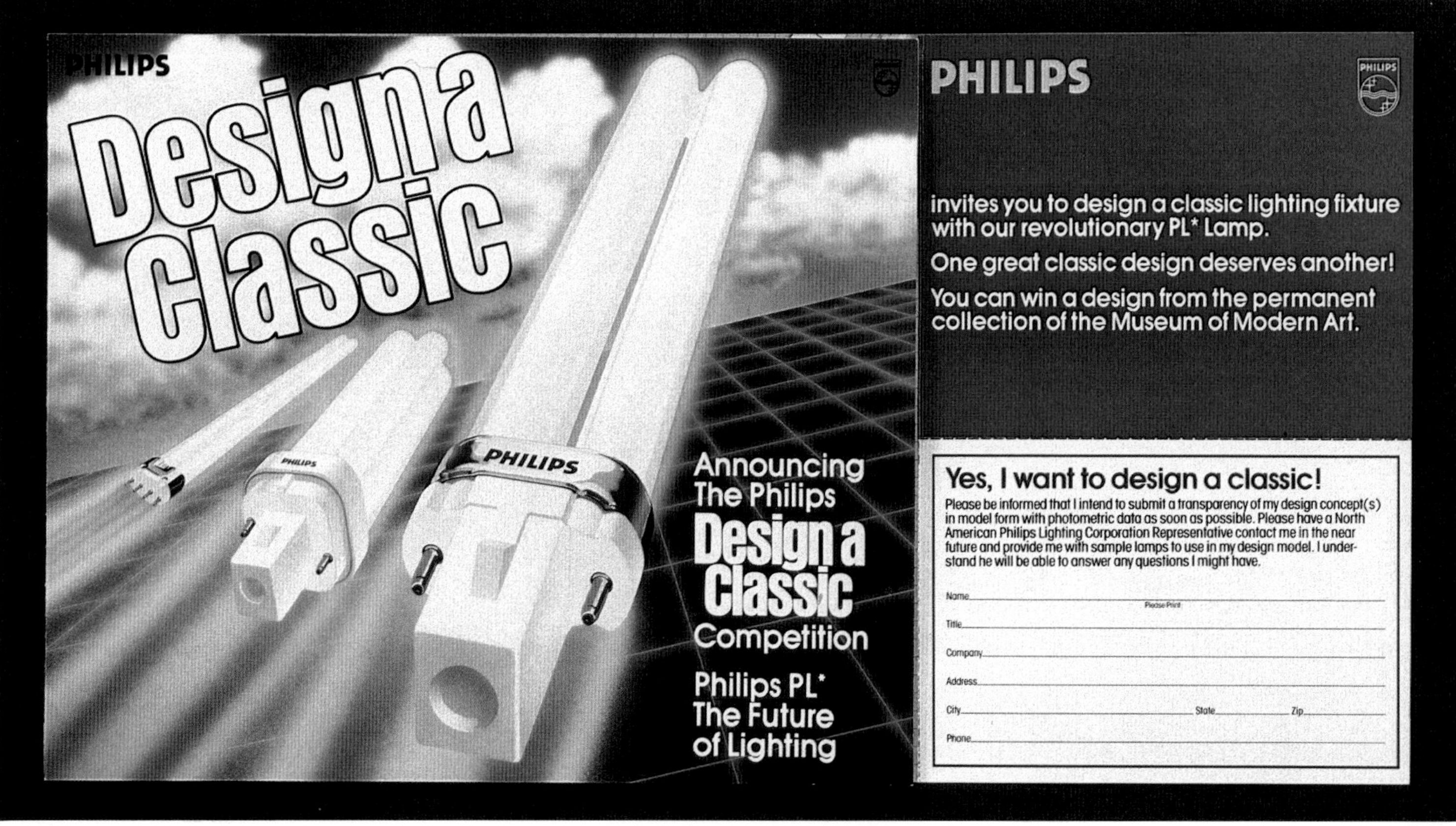
PHILIPS
Design a Classic
Announcing The Philips
Design a Classic
Competition
Philips PL*
The Future of Lighting
PHILIPS
invites you to design a classic lighting fixture with our revolutionary PL* Lamp.
One great classic design deserves another!
You can win a design from the permanent collection of the Museum of Modern Art.
Yes, I want to design a classic!
Please be informed that I intend to submit a transparency of my design concept(s) in model form with photometric data as soon as possible. Please have a North American Philips Lighting Corporation Representative contact me in the near future and provide me with sample lamps to use in my design model. I understand he will be able to answer any questions I might have.
Name
Please Print
Title
Company
Address
City
State
Zip
Phone

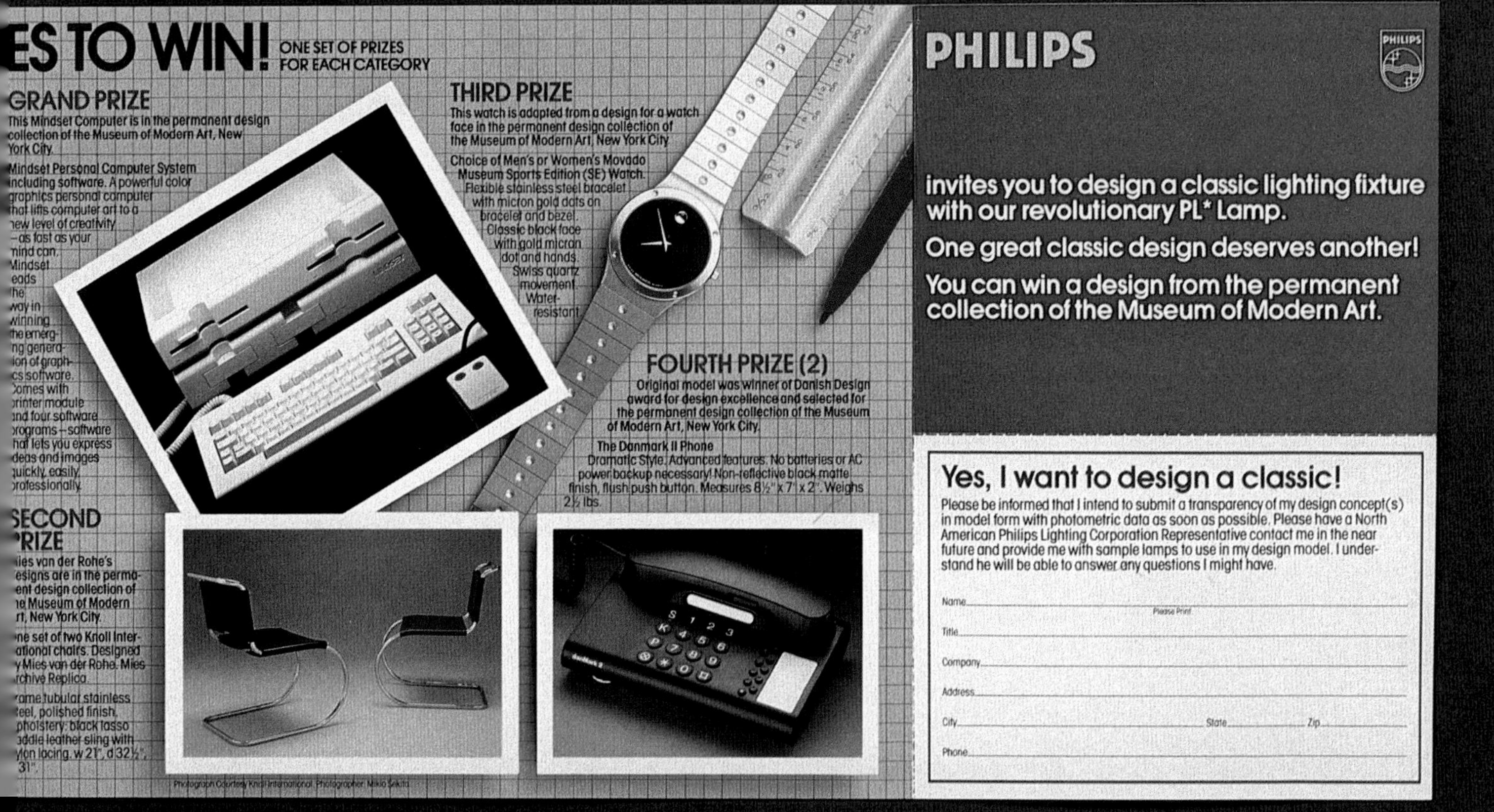
ES TO WIN!
ONE SET OF PRIZES FOR EACH CATEGORY
GRAND PRIZE
This Mindset Computer is in the permanent design collection of the Museum of Modern Art, New York City.
THIRD PRIZE
This watch is adapted from a design for a watch face in the permanent design collection of the Museum of Modern Art, New York City
Choice of Men's or Women's Movado Museum Sports Edition (SE) Watch. Flexible stainless steel bracelet with micron gold dots on bracelet and bezel. Classic black face with gold micron dot and hands. Swiss quartz movement. Water-resistant
FOURTH PRIZE (2)
Original model was winner of Danish Design award for design excellence and selected for the permanent design collection of the Museum of Modern Art, New York City.
The Danmark II Phone
Dramatic Style. Advanced features. No batteries or AC power backup necessary! Non-reflective black matte finish, flush push button. Measures 8½" x 7" x 2". Weighs 2½ lbs.
PHILIPS
invites you to design a classic lighting fixture with our revolutionary PL* Lamp.
One great classic design deserves another!
You can win a design from the permanent collection of the Museum of Modern Art.
Yes, I want to design a classic!
Please be informed that I intend to submit a transparency of my design concept(s) in model form with photometric data as soon as possible. Please have a North American Philips Lighting Corporation Representative contact me in the near future and provide me with sample lamps to use in my design model. I understand he will be able to answer any questions I might have.
Name
Please Print
Title
Company
Address
City
State
Zip
Phone

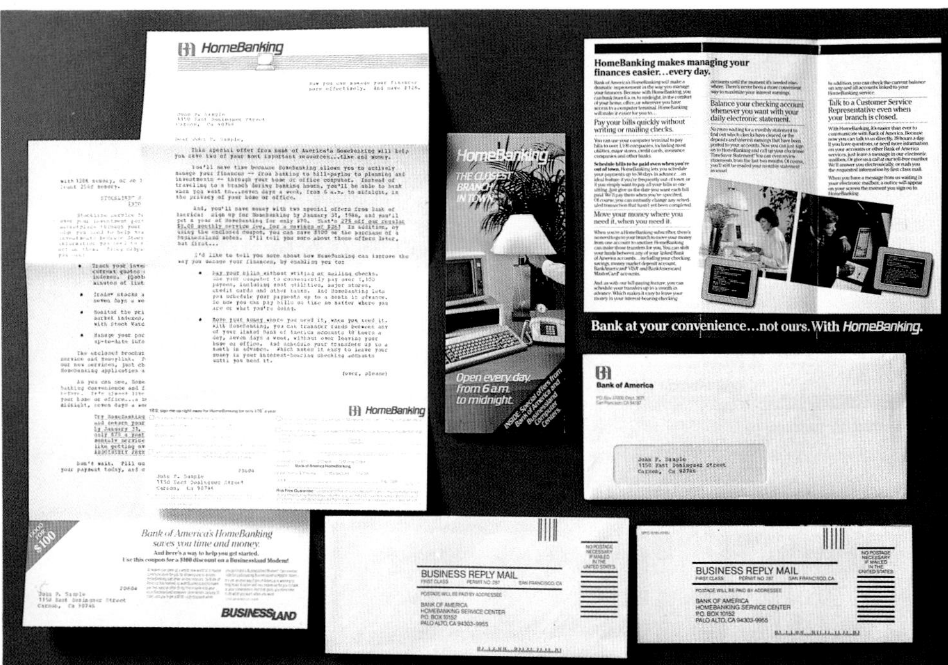

Title: "Easy Banking"
Copywriter: Martin Cohn
Art Director: Tom Joyce
Agency: Cohn & Wells
Client: Bank of America

This classic multi-element, four-color direct mail package appeals to the potential customer's desire for convenience and straightforward, uncomplicated banking services.

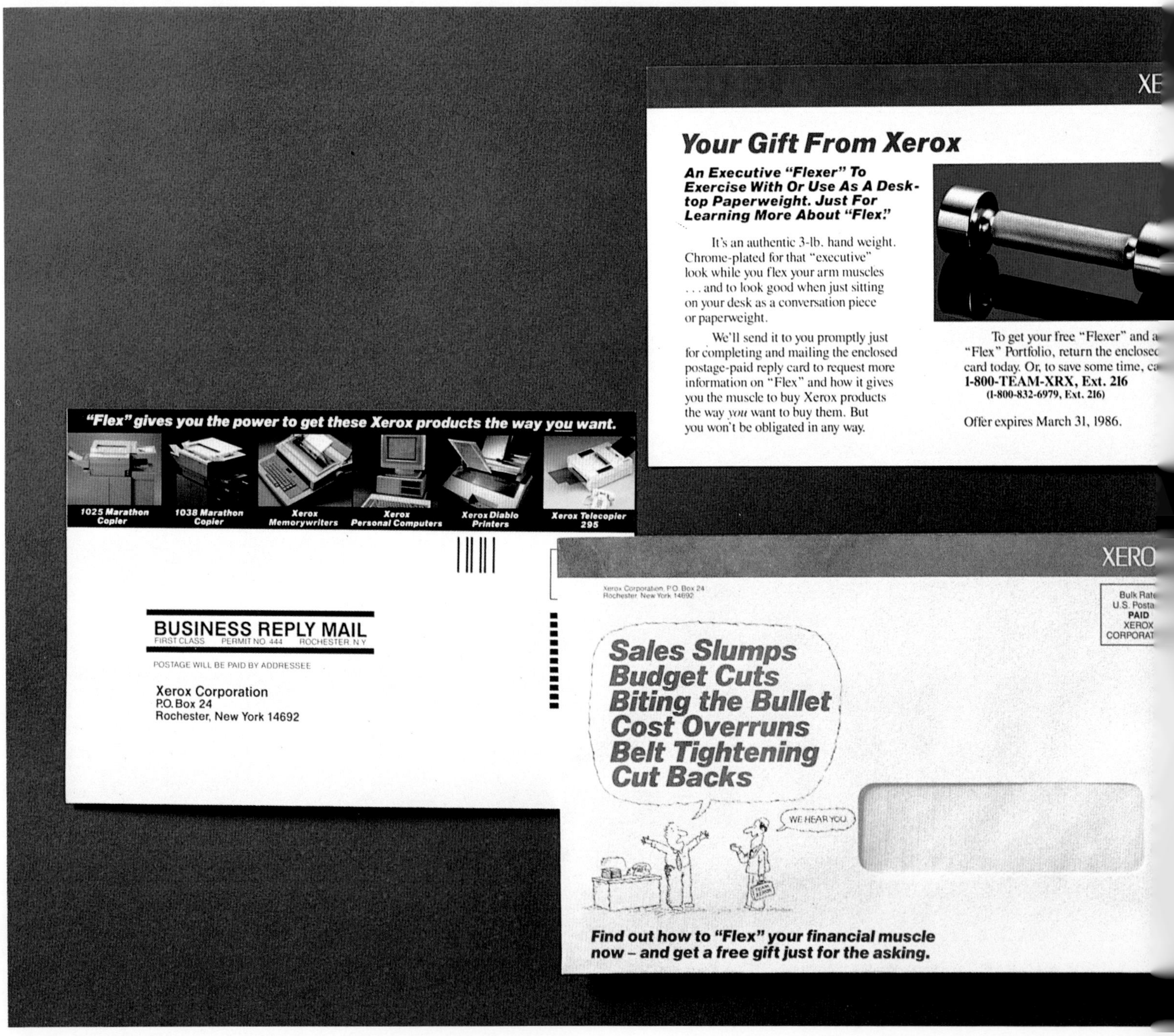

XE

Your Gift From Xerox

An Executive "Flexer" To Exercise With Or Use As A Desk-top Paperweight. Just For Learning More About "Flex."

It's an authentic 3-lb. hand weight. Chrome-plated for that "executive" look while you flex your arm muscles . . . and to look good when just sitting on your desk as a conversation piece or paperweight.

We'll send it to you promptly just for completing and mailing the enclosed postage-paid reply card to request more information on "Flex" and how it gives you the muscle to buy Xerox products the way *you* want to buy them. But you won't be obligated in any way.

To get your free "Flexer" and a "Flex" Portfolio, return the enclosed card today. Or, to save some time, ca

1-800-TEAM-XRX, Ext. 216
(1-800-832-6979, Ext. 216)

Offer expires March 31, 1986.

"Flex" gives you the power to get these Xerox products the way you want.

1025 Marathon Copier | 1038 Marathon Copier | Xerox Memorywriters | Xerox Personal Computers | Xerox Diablo Printers | Xerox Telecopier 295

BUSINESS REPLY MAIL
FIRST CLASS PERMIT NO. 444 ROCHESTER N.Y.
POSTAGE WILL BE PAID BY ADDRESSEE
Xerox Corporation
P.O. Box 24
Rochester, New York 14692

XERO
Xerox Corporation P.O. Box 24
Rochester New York 14692
Bulk Rate
U.S. Posta
PAID
XEROX
CORPORAT

Sales Slumps
Budget Cuts
Biting the Bullet
Cost Overruns
Belt Tightening
Cut Backs

WE HEAR YOU

Find out how to "Flex" your financial muscle now – and get a free gift just for the asking.

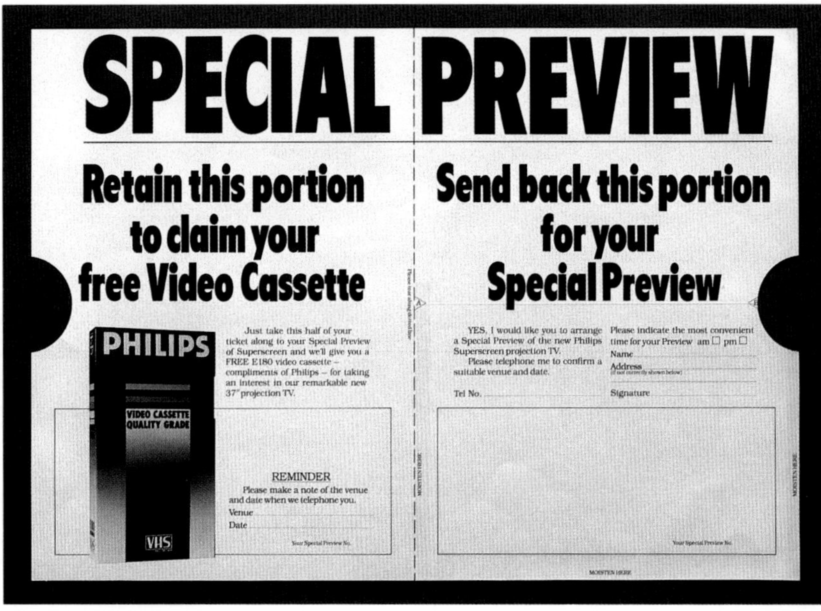
SPECIAL PREVIEW
Retain this portion to claim your free Video Cassette
Send back this portion for your Special Preview
PHILIPS
VIDEO CASSETTE QUALITY GRADE
VHS
Just take this half of your ticket along to your Special Preview of Superscreen and we'll give you a FREE E180 video cassette – compliments of Philips – for taking an interest in our remarkable new 37" projection TV.
REMINDER
Please make a note of the venue and date when we telephone you.
Venue
Date
Your Special Preview No.
YES, I would like you to arrange a Special Preview of the new Philips Superscreen projection TV.
Please telephone me to confirm a suitable venue and date.
Tel No.
Please indicate the most convenient time for your Preview am ☐ pm ☐
Name
Address
Signature
Your Special Preview No.
MOISTEN HERE

XEROX

Xerox Corporation
Xerox Square
Rochester, New York 14644

ANNOUNCING "FLEX" ...

our flexible new program that can increase your purchasing power now.

Dear Executive:

We've been listening to people who would prefer Xerox office products but think they have to settle for something "cheaper." And we've done something about it!

Now you can make your own deal on Xerox products. If you're expanding your facilities, opening a new office, or replacing the equipment you already have, you can get what you want from Xerox -- with "Flex."

Find out about it now and get a free gift!

We've put together a portfolio to tell you more about "Flex" ... and how its flexible options let you get the Xerox products that perfectly fit your business on terms that perfectly fit your business, too.

And if you ask for the "Flex" Portfolio now, we'll send you a free gift. But before I tell you more about the gift, let me tell you a little more about "Flex."

Flexible deals.

First of all, "Flex" gives you the muscle to acquire Xerox copiers, Memorywriters, printers and other products at one time. Because it offers you special terms and liberal trade-ins. So you can make the deal that best fits your needs.

If you've been shopping copiers, for example -- but you'd like to get other equipment, too -- you can get it without giving your budget a workout.

Flexible prices.

"Flex" also lets you wheel and deal on Xerox prices. That gives you the power to get quality, reliable Xerox products at the same prices you might pay for other brands you're not sure of.

Flexible financing.

And if cash flow is tight, or you need to conserve capital, "Flex" gives you financing options made to match your fiscal fitness needs. So you won't have to run lean to get what you really want.

Flexible product choices.

With "Flex," you also get options on these Xerox products ... to

(Over, please ...)

Title: "Flex"
Copywriter: Paul Levett
Art Director: Mal Karlin
Agency: Lowe Marschalk
Client: Xerox Corporation

This direct mail leg of a multi-media business-to-business lead generation campaign offers a chrome-plated, 3-pound exercise dumbbell along with the opportunity to "flex your financial muscle" through the use of cost-effective Xerox products.

The Watch, the Bear & the Hat

At first glance, I didn't see the relationship.

A pin-watch of the finest gold, delicately designed to reflect the gentility of its keeper. Old. An heirloom. Who would have left it in the store?

And the teddy bear. One ear torn off. An eye popped out—torn out, actually. It belonged, I imagined, to a rather free-spirited child. Stumbling along in tow behind his rather free-spirited mother.

But the hat. A subtle statement of a business man looking to escape the boardroom? Or an essential component of an adventurous wardrobe?

Three obviously different people had visited us that day. And behind they had left three obviously different impressions of themselves.

Articles left behind at Neiman-Marcus are my responsibility. I care for them until they're claimed—an interesting event that I enjoy. I like to imagine the kinds of people who leave these items behind. But I have to admit that my images rarely reflect the reality.

We found a shoe once that had been left by a dancer. This shoe was a rather well-worn Oxford. Not delicate or fragile at all. But its owner was. And I hadn't expected that.

So many different people shop Neiman-Marcus. And when I came to work here, I hadn't expected that either. Like the constantly changing collection of umbrellas that are turned in, people come in all sizes and shapes, fancy and plain, young and old, some bright and friendly, others quiet and reserved.

Many of the people who come to me looking for lost articles are very apologetic. They feel they must explain to me why they let a valuable object stray.

I tell them that there is no need to apologize. People become so involved with our merchandise that it's easy to overlook their personal belongings. I'm just glad that I can help them find their errant items.

[illegible] of misplaced items, I must return to the watch, the bear and the hat. [illegible] ve been more wrong in my assessment of the owners. All three articles [illegible] e same person—a woman who had bought the hat that day as a gift [illegible] llege student.

[illegible] to her grandson, whom she had also lost, but reclaimed the same [illegible] service department.

[illegible] ought, an heir- [illegible] s of this item [illegible] k to the [illegible] that, [illegible]

I [illegible] preciate Nei [illegible] ou haven't shop [illegible] ore, I hope you'll visit us s [illegible] nd if by chance the gremlins run off with any of your belongings, I'll find them for you. And keep them safe.

--A Longtime Employee of Neiman-Marcus

Dear Friend:

It's nice to find something that's been lost.

But it's especially nice to find something new. Something different. Something special.

That's how we want you to feel when you find Neiman-Marcus. And there's no easier way to find special things than with a Neiman-Marcus charge card.

All the wonders of Neiman-Marcus await you. And because we've already approved your account, you need only fill out the enclosed Acceptance Certificate and bring it to the Customer Service department of your Neiman-Marcus store.

And don't forget to bring in your Lost and Found claim tag. We've found something quite special we think will please you. Just bring in the tag we've enclosed and present it along with your Acceptance Certificate.

When you come, you'll discover that shopping is a pleasure at Neiman-Marcus. We've made it that way for you. Please find us soon.

Sincerely,

William H. Williams
Senior Vice President

P.S. Your Neiman-Marcus Charge entitles you to invitations to fashion shows and special events, our catalogs including the famous Christmas Book, advance notice of sales--and more. Bring in your Acceptance Certificate today, or fold, seal and mail it. Postage will be paid.

Neiman-Marcus
LOST AND FOUND

Please bring in this tag to claim the item we've found for you!

Title: "The Watch, the Bear and the Hat"
Copywriter: Charlie Piersol
Art Directors: Elizabeth Addison, Alan Blair
Agency: Ogilvy & Mather Direct/Chicago
Client: Neiman-Marcus

Not only is opening this package and unrolling a long scroll of a poster/story/letter a rather involving and, as it turns out, enjoyable process—but a "lift tag" and curled-up ordering vehicle make their presence known with just the right amount of impact to invite response.

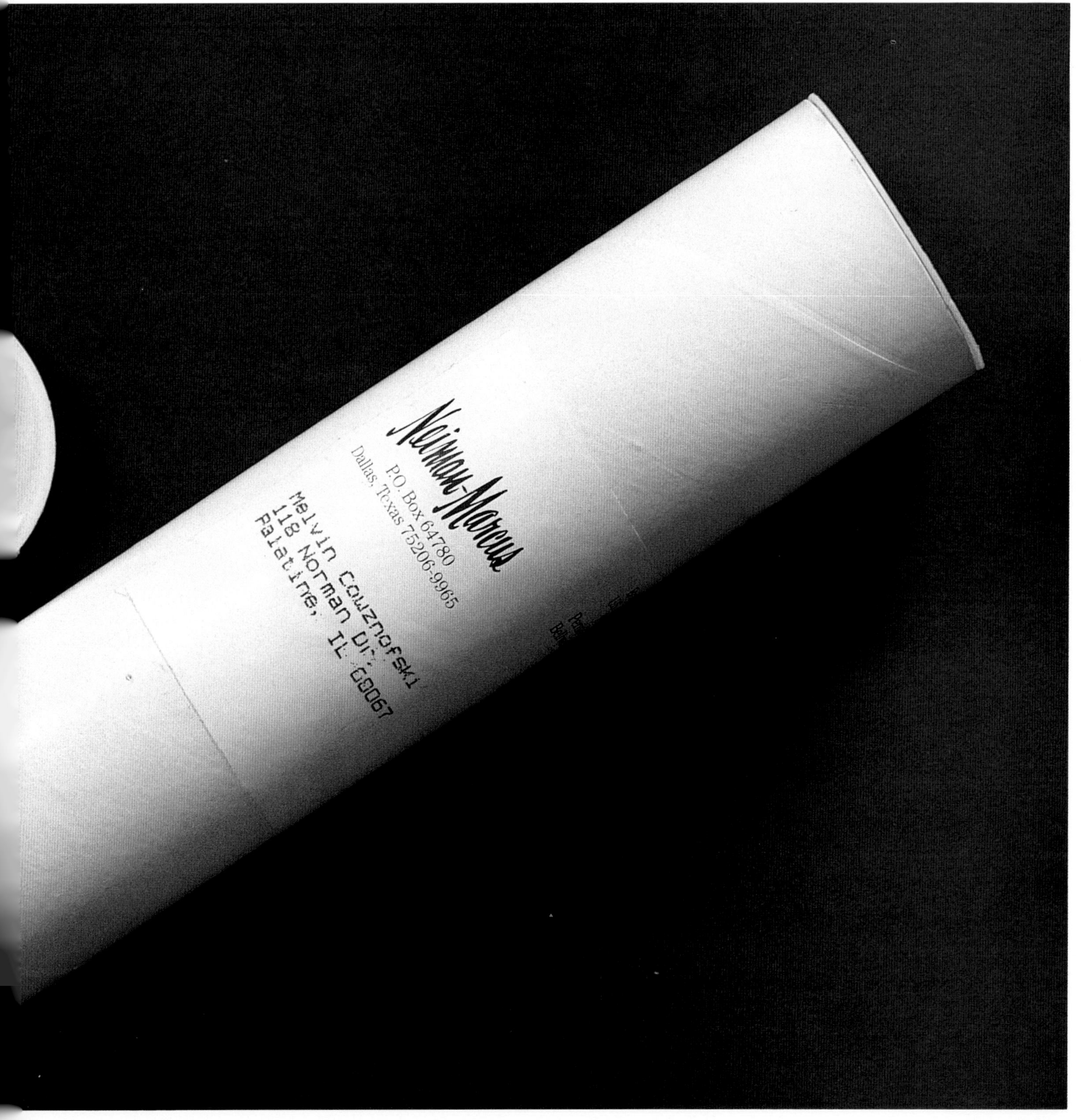

Title: 37 Reasons Chase Visa is Perfect For Any College Student

Copywriters: Johanna Thompson, Gary Bucca

Art Directors: Ken Messinger, Joe Schick

Agency: McCaffrey & McCall Direct Marketing

Client: Chase Manhattan Bank

Self-mailers can hold their own as message-bearing storytellers, as evidenced by this thoughtful yet upbeat consumer piece targeted with admirable accuracy to an up-and-coming student audience.

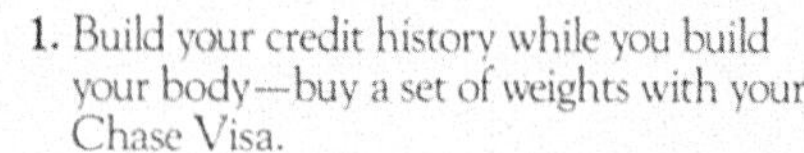

1. Build your credit history while you build your body—buy a set of weights with your Chase Visa.
2. Accounting 101: Spend less on credit with the card that has the lowest Visa interest rate of the top ten banks.†
3. Flying home for Christmas? Book your airfare on your Chase Visa card through the Travel Center and you get back a 5% cash travel bonus.
4. Head home for the weekend by train, and get a 5% cash travel bonus. (And don't forget to take your laundry.)
5. Make a car loan payment with a Chase Visa check.
6. You set up a last-minute date with your biology lab partner. Chase Visa gets you emergency cash at the nearby cash machine.
7. Start your good credit rating with Chase Manhattan, one of the largest financial institutions.
8. Congratulations! You passed with flying colors—treat your tutor to dinner at the local hangout with your Chase Visa.
9. Don't arrive home for the holidays empty-handed. Christmas shop with Chase Visa.
10. Earn CHASE BONUS DOLLAR$ for using your card. Use them to save up to 50% on a camera for your Intro. to Photography course.
11. No more cold shoulder at car rental counters now that you have Chase Visa. Plus, you'll get a 5% cash travel bonus.
12. Renting a car? Rent with Chase Visa and get up to $3,000 supplemental collision reimbursement when you charge to your card.
13. Need a canvas-bagful of art supplies? Pull out your Chase Visa and pay them off over the semester.
14. Avoid paying interest. Chase gives you a 25-day interest-free grace period on new purchases when you pay your bill in full each month.*
15. Add to your compact disc collection without adding to your out-of-pocket expenses. Use Chase Visa and pay in convenient monthly payments.
16. Spruce up the bare walls of your dormitory room. The decorating possibilities are virtually endless with a Chase Visa card—accepted at stores of *many* kinds.

17. If you're loaded down with textbook expenses, use Chase Visa and pay for them in smaller doses.
18. Now that you've bought all your books, use your Chase Visa to buy that last item on your list—a backpack.
19. Your favorite restaurant doesn't accept American Express. But Chase Visa is accepted at over 5 million places—don't be caught without one.

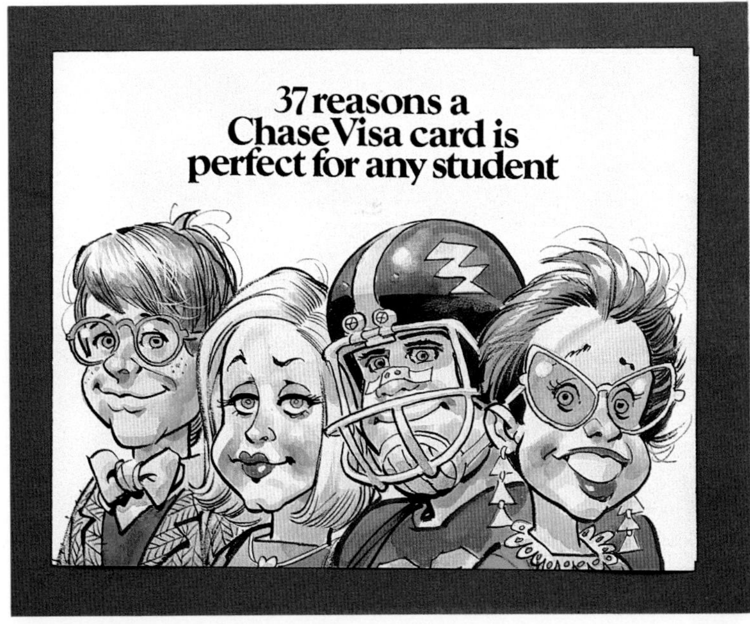
37 reasons a
Chase Visa card is
perfect for any student

re going out of town for a job
nake hotel reservations through
Center and you can get a 10%

lat and your wallet's empty.
can inflate your clout with the
an.

i-fridge for your dorm room
Visa.

– streak your hair magenta.
ns accept Chase Visa.

a semester abroad? Chase
gnized worldwide.

hase Visa can get you
cash at more than
iking locations

: "survival kit"
nplete without
orn popper.
to the

GMAT
course
VISA—

ost

el

and
ce at

29. Ready to start job hunting? Chase Visa helps you invest in an interview suit.

30. If you can't wait for the next paycheck to buy those new jeans, charge them with your Chase Visa and pay next month.

31. Go someplace exotic for spring break—when you reserve through the Travel Center, you can get 5% cash bonuses on special cruise and vacation packages.

32. Get personal attention with Chase Customer Service. We don't let you get lost in the shuffle.

33. The car has broken down. Good thing you've taken advantage of optional Road & Tow Service.

A13

34. It's time to start shopping for those back-to-school clothes. Put together your fall wardrobe with Chase Visa.

35. Taking off? Chase Visa can help—with a Travel Center that can guide you to the lowest available fares.

36. Sit back and relax when you travel—you're covered with $100,000 Common Carrier Travel Accident Insurance.**

37. Be daring this summer—try parasailing or white-water rafting. You can charge it to your Chase Visa.

Seal flap here.

*CHASE VISA CREDIT DISCLOSURE

**TRAVEL ACCIDENT DISCLOSURE

NOTICE

▼ FOLD HERE ▼

NO POSTAGE
NECESSARY
IF MAILED
IN THE
UNITED STATES

BUSINESS REPLY MAIL
FIRST CLASS PERMIT NO. 333 WILMINGTON, DELAWARE

POSTAGE WILL BE PAID BY ADDRESSEE

The Chase Manhattan Bank (USA), N.A.
802 Delaware Avenue
P.O. Box 35204
Wilmington, Delaware 19885-9955

AND TAKE YOUR CHANCE ON THE ORIENT EXPRESS IN THE AMERICAN EXPRESS® CARD SPECIAL AGENT SWEEPSTAKES.

Travel agents have always been special agents for arranging and coordinating your travel plans. But now, travel agents are information agents as well. Because now, travel agents can provide you with information on the American Express Card Special Agent Sweepstakes. With your chance to win the grand prize for two: first-class airfare to Europe on Pan Am, luxurious travel through Europe on the Venice Simplon-Orient-Express,® and two thousand dollars in American Express® Travelers Cheques.

To enter, simply contact your travel agent between April 1 and June 30, purchase an airline ticket with the American Express Card, and send in a copy of your ticket.* The Card not only gains you entry into the sweepstakes, but into fine restaurants, hotels and stores wherever you travel.

Don't leave home without it.®

*No purchase necessary for entering. Complete entry details available at participating travel agents in the Atlanta, Seattle, and Chicago areas.

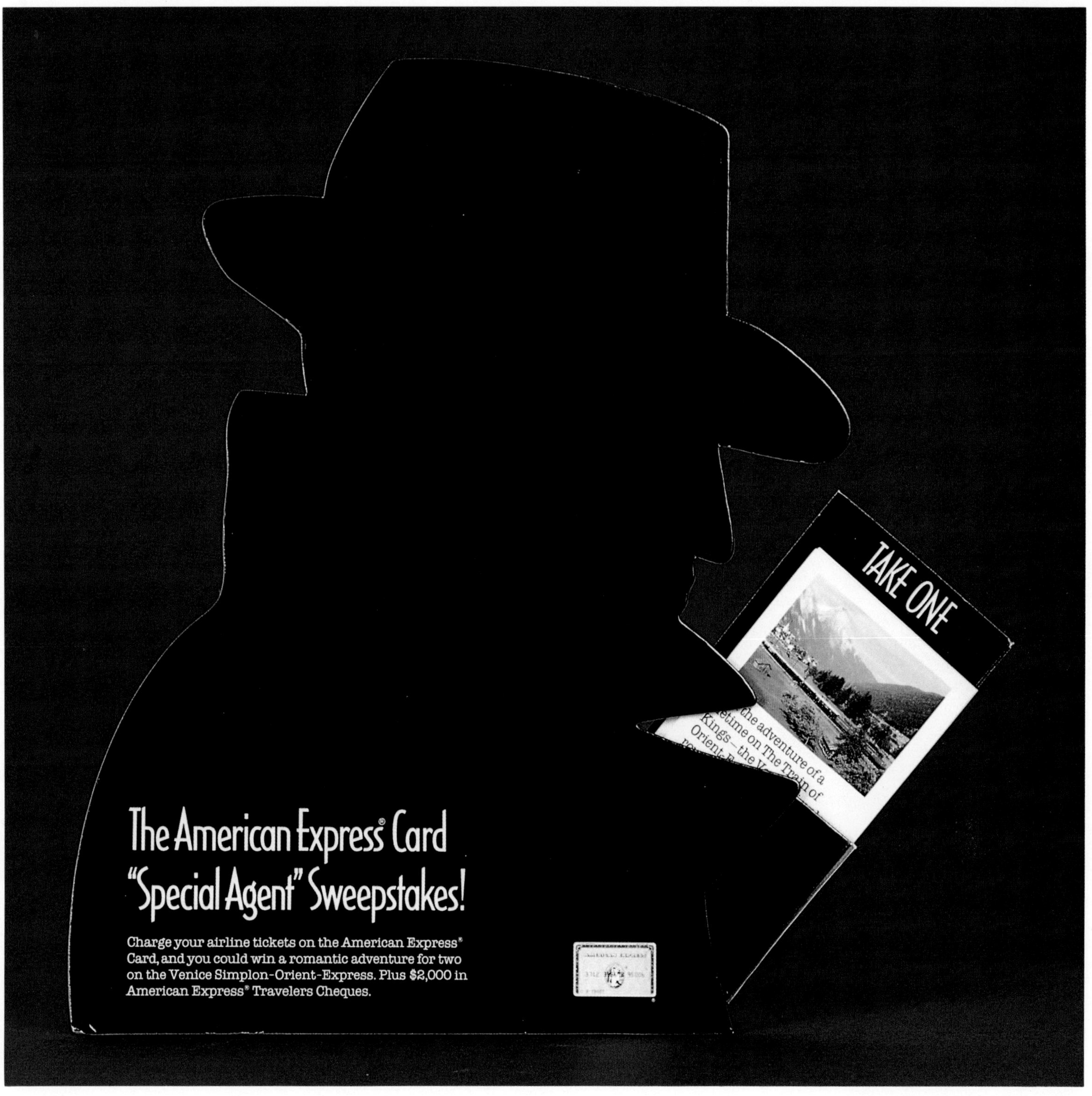
TAKE ONE
The American Express® Card
"Special Agent" Sweepstakes!
Charge your airline tickets on the American Express® Card, and you could win a romantic adventure for two on the Venice Simplon-Orient-Express. Plus $2,000 in American Express® Travelers Cheques.

Title: "Special Agent Program"
Copywriter: Rich Person
Art Director: Marjorie Millyard
Agency: Eastern Exclusives, Inc.
Client: American Express Travel Related Services

A strong theme with a tongue-in-cheek graphic treatment highlights this multi-element mailing to travel agents, encouraging them to book travel for their customers on the American Express Card. Also shown here are a print ad and an in-store "take one" display created to support the mailing effort.

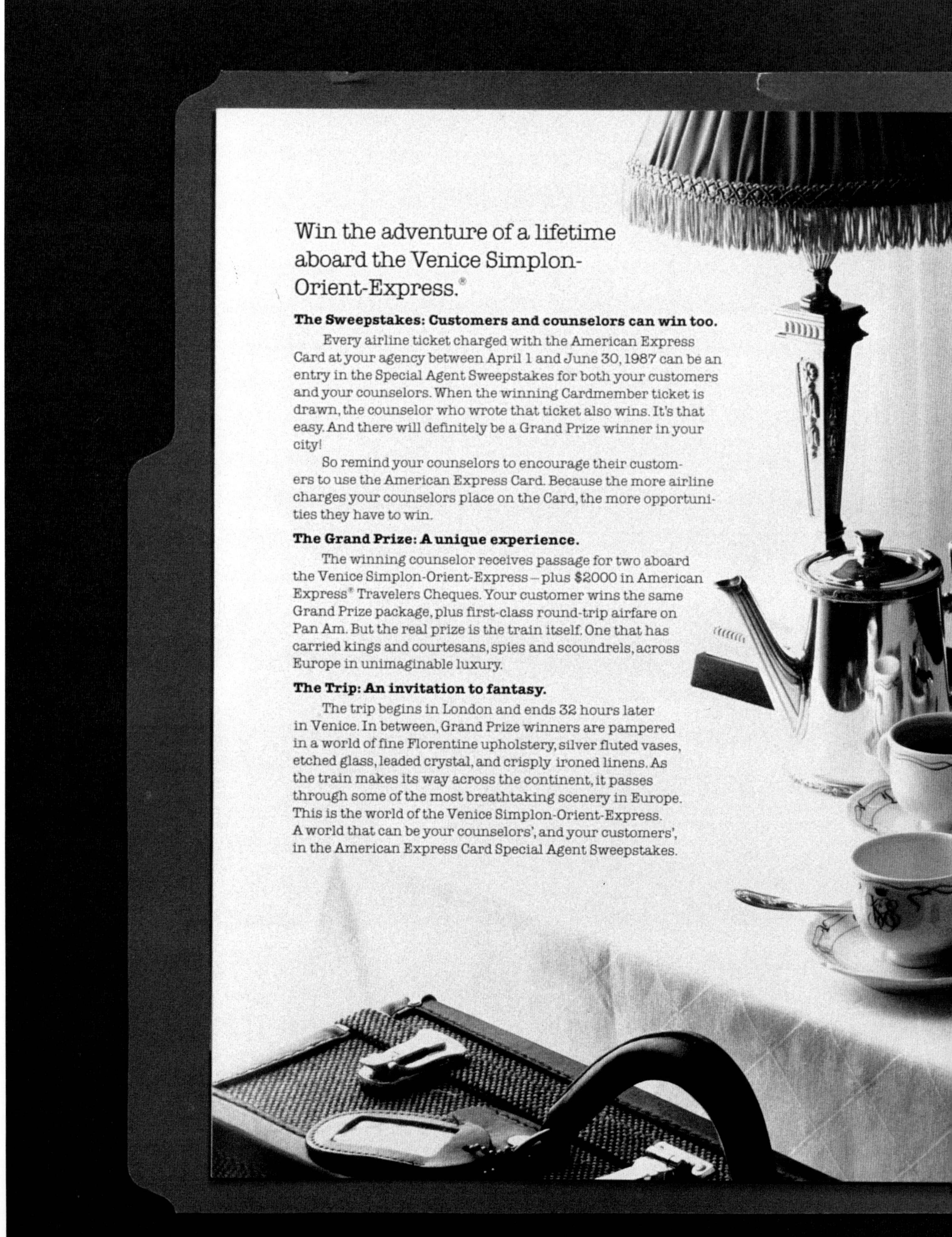
Win the adventure of a lifetime aboard the Venice Simplon-Orient-Express.®

The Sweepstakes: Customers and counselors can win too.
Every airline ticket charged with the American Express Card at your agency between April 1 and June 30, 1987 can be an entry in the Special Agent Sweepstakes for both your customers and your counselors. When the winning Cardmember ticket is drawn, the counselor who wrote that ticket also wins. It's that easy. And there will definitely be a Grand Prize winner in your city!
So remind your counselors to encourage their customers to use the American Express Card. Because the more airline charges your counselors place on the Card, the more opportunities they have to win.

The Grand Prize: A unique experience.
The winning counselor receives passage for two aboard the Venice Simplon-Orient-Express – plus $2000 in American Express® Travelers Cheques. Your customer wins the same Grand Prize package, plus first-class round-trip airfare on Pan Am. But the real prize is the train itself. One that has carried kings and courtesans, spies and scoundrels, across Europe in unimaginable luxury.

The Trip: An invitation to fantasy.
The trip begins in London and ends 32 hours later in Venice. In between, Grand Prize winners are pampered in a world of fine Florentine upholstery, silver fluted vases, etched glass, leaded crystal, and crisply ironed linens. As the train makes its way across the continent, it passes through some of the most breathtaking scenery in Europe. This is the world of the Venice Simplon-Orient-Express. A world that can be your counselors', and your customers', in the American Express Card Special Agent Sweepstakes.

Special Agent
ORIENT-EXPRESS
PASSENGER TICKET

Mr. Samuel Sample
President
XYZ Company
35 Morrissey Blvd.
Boston, MA 02125
American Express® Card Special Agent Program
P.O. Box 8009, Smithtown, NY 11787

Special Agent

EYES ONLY
USA 22
Richard Russell
USA 10c
Mr. Samuel Sample
President
XYZ Company
35 Morrissey Blvd.
Boston,MA 02125

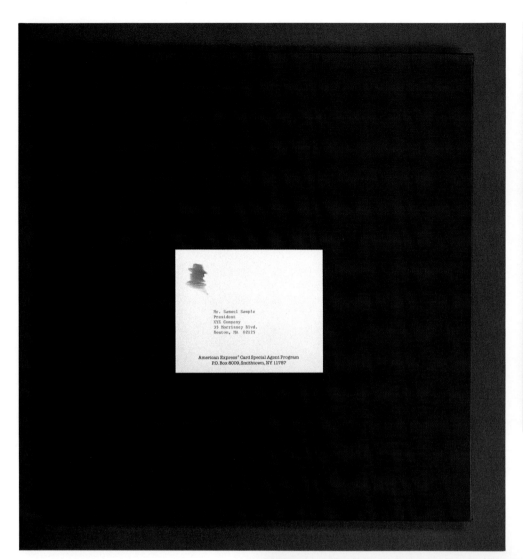

Title: "Special Agent Program"
Copywriter: Rich Person
Art Director: Marjorie Millyard
Agency: Eastern Exclusives, Inc.
Client: American Express Travel Related Services

A strong theme with a tongue-in-cheek graphic treatment highlights this multi-element mailing to travel agents, encouraging them to book travel for their customers on the American Express Card. Also shown here are a print ad and an in-store "take one" display created to support the mailing effort.

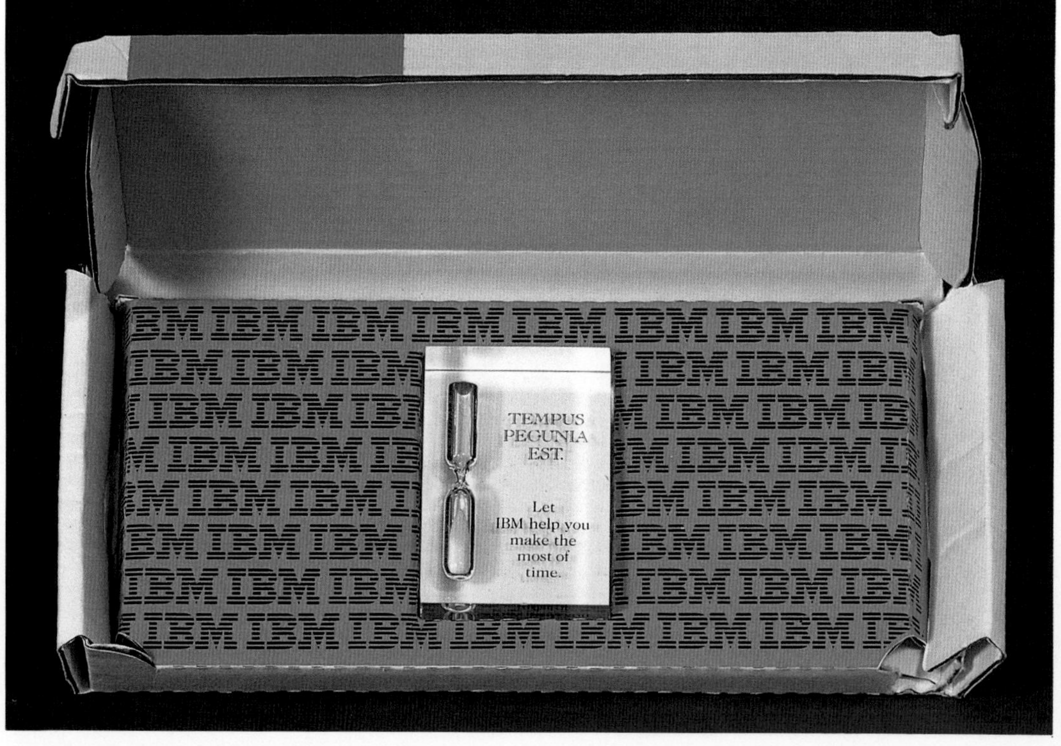

Title: "Legal Lead Generation"
Copywriter: Susan Hughes
Art Director: Mayme Allen
Agency: Tracy-Locke Direct
Client: IBM-IIS Software Mass Marketing

Simplicity of concept and execution sends this business direct mail piece's message home to attorneys who must agree to accept further information, as qualified leads, from the IBM software sales force.

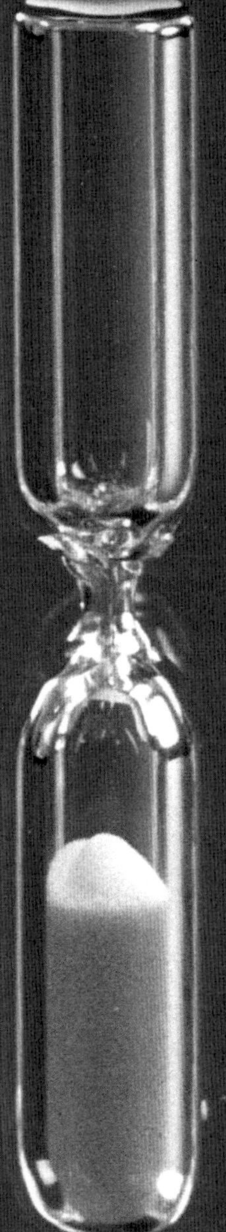

TEMPUS
PECUNIA
EST.
Let
IBM help you
make the
most of
time.

RYDER TRUCK RENTAL INC.
A Ryder System Company

RYDER

October xx, 1987

Mr. John Q. Sample
President
ABC Company
123 Main Street
Anytown, USA 00000

Dear Mr. Sample:

Before you buy a used truck, you deserve to know more about it than how it looks on the outside, and how many miles are on the odometer.

When you buy a Ryder used truck or tractor you'll know it's been well maintained, because by the time we're ready to sell it to you, a Ryder used truck will have been checked an average of 9,112 times.

- A new Ryder truck is thoroughly in-serviced by highly trained Ryder-certified technicians before it goes on the road -- that's 52 checks.
- Every time it stops for fuel at a Ryder service location, a 10-point service island inspection is carried out. And it stops for fuel at these locations an average of 347 times, so that's 3,470 more checks.
- An inspection of major components is made every 4,000 to 8,000 miles, depending on vehicle type. In addition, every 24,000 and 48,000 miles, various components are automatically replaced. On average, a total of 5,590 more checks.
- Finally, a thorough "Road Ready" inspection is required before we give one of our used trucks the Ryder "Road Ready" seal.

Our customers depend on us to keep them moving. And we take this responsibility so seriously that we've earned the reputation as one of the safest, most reliable fleets on the road. And that can only be good news for Ryder used truck buyers too.

Secondhand doesn't have to be second-best. Not if it's Ryder, that is. Contact us today to find out about the used vehicles we currently have available. You'll find them second to none.

Sincerely,

J.L. Langford
Director, Vehicle ...

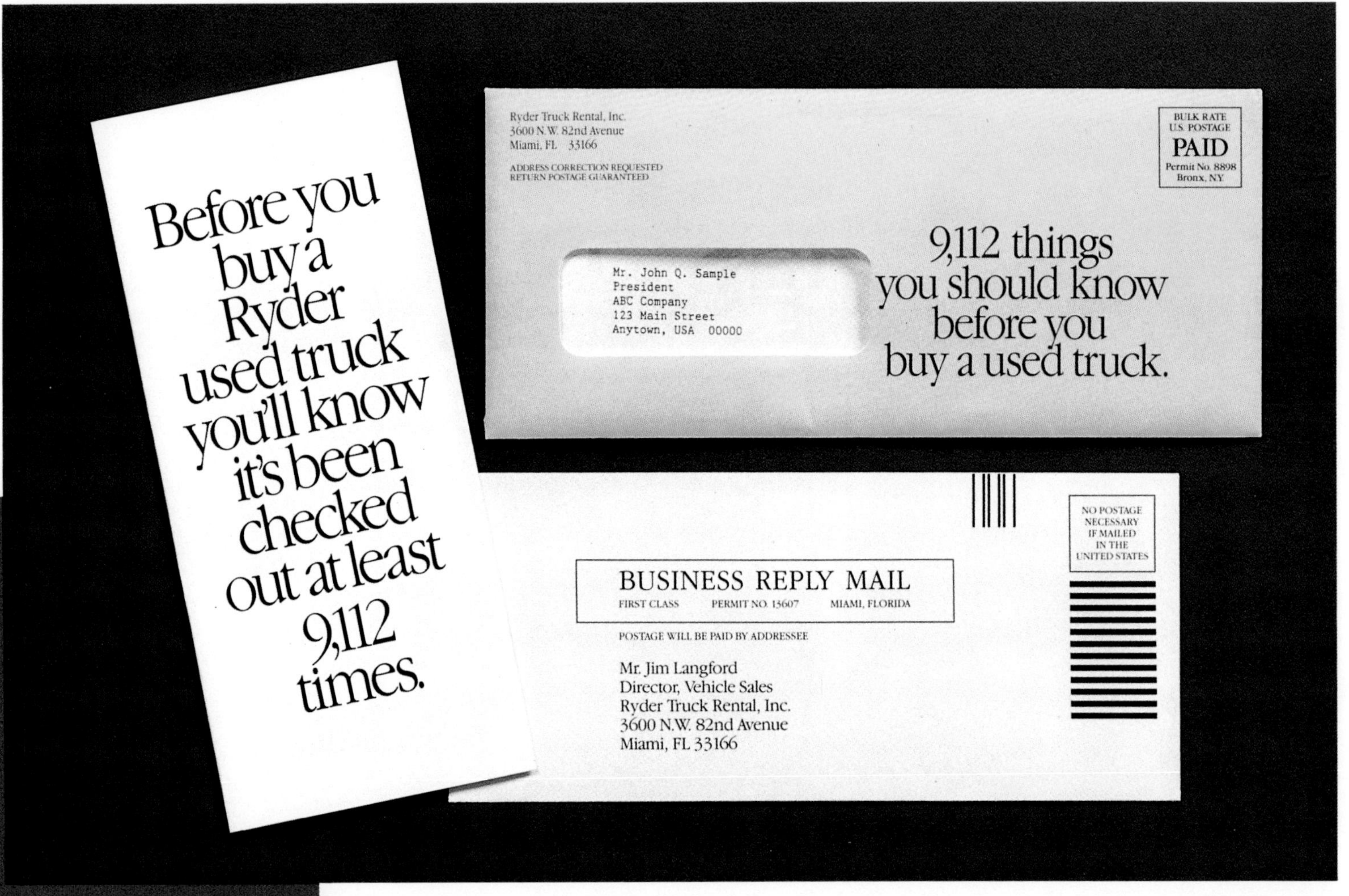

Title: "9,112 things you should know..."
Copywriter: Leila Vuorenmaa
Art Directors: Michael Cancellieri, Stan Smith
Agency: Ogilvy & Mather Direct
Client: Ryder Truck Rental

There's nothing like a strong creative concept, flawlessly executed, to drive home an attractive business-to-business proposition from a trustworthy name with a good, fair offer. This package exemplifies the art of effective direct mail.

Oriental Noodle and Chicken Salad with Creamy Peanut Sauce

NOW FROM Gourmet.

Zuppa di Pesce—(An Italian Fish Soup) and Arni Soupa Avgolemono—(A Greek Meat and Lemon Soup)

RECIPES ALIVE WITH CHARACTER

A SUMMER WEEKEND MENU

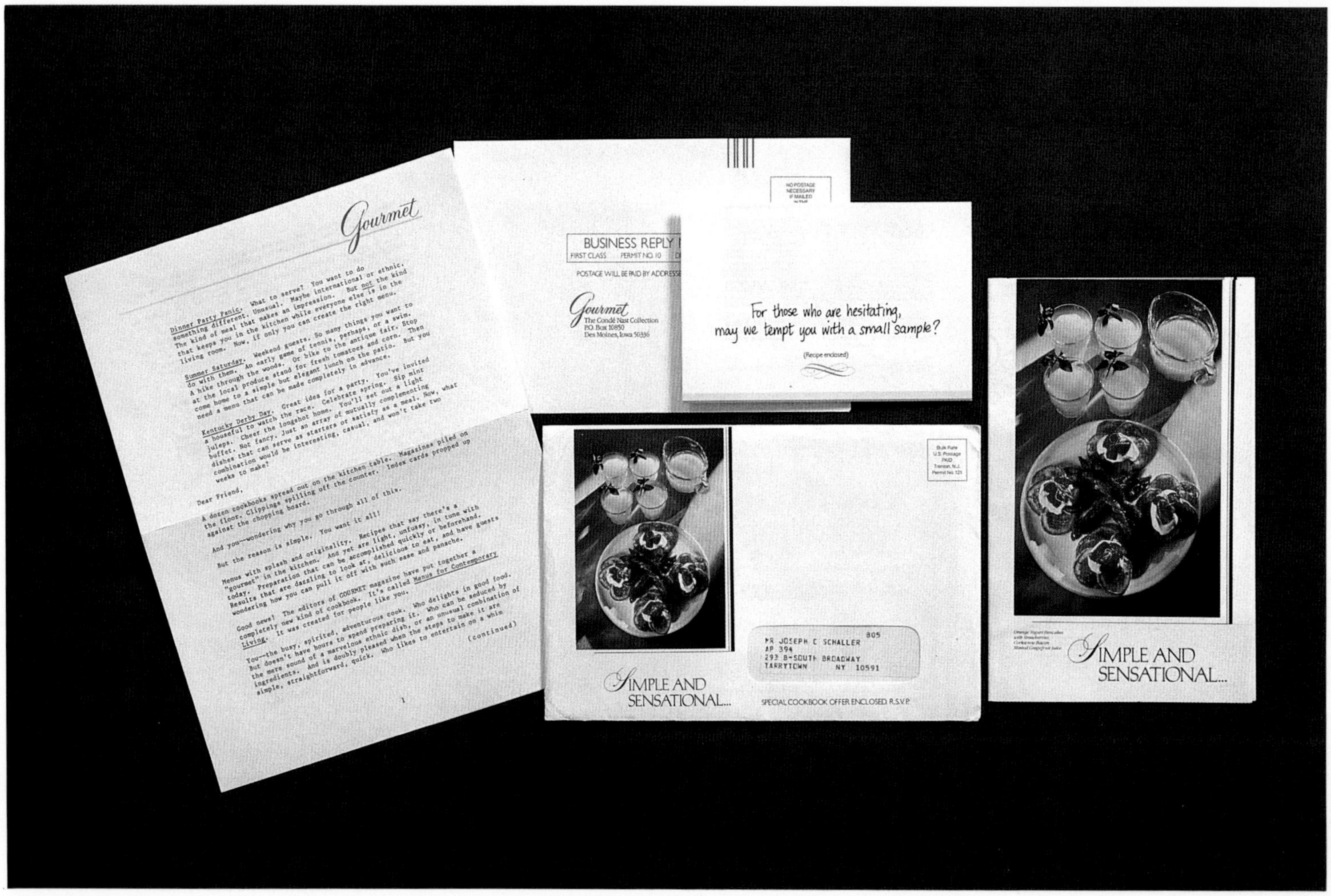

Rock Cornish Game Hens with Rosemary
Herb-Roasted Corn on the Cob
Tomato and Hearts of Palm Salad with Basil Vinaigrette
Nectarine Fool

Gourmet

Dinner Party Panic. What to serve? You want to do something different. Unusual. Maybe international or ethnic. The kind of meal that makes an impression. But not the kind that keeps you in the kitchen while everyone else is in the living room. Now, if only you can create the right menu.

Summer Saturday. Weekend guests. So many things you want to do with them. An early game of tennis, perhaps, or a swim. A hike through the woods. Or bike to the antique fair. Stop at the local produce stand for fresh tomatoes and corn. Then come home to a simple but elegant lunch on the patio. But you need a menu that can be made completely in advance.

Kentucky Derby Day. Great idea for a party. You've invited a houseful to watch the race. Celebrate spring. Sip mint juleps. Cheer the longshot home. You'll set out a light buffet. Not fancy. Just an array of mutually complementing dishes that can serve as starters or satisfy as a meal. Now, what combination would be interesting, casual, and won't take two weeks to make?

Dear Friend,

A dozen cookbooks spread out on the kitchen table. Magazines piled on the floor. Clippings spilling off the counter. Index cards propped up against the chopping board.

And you--wondering why you go through all of this.

But the reason is simple. You want it all!

Menus with splash and originality. Recipes that say there's a "gourmet" in the kitchen. And yet are light, unfussy, in tune with today. Preparation that can be accomplished quickly or beforehand. Results that are dazzling to look at, delicious to eat, and have guests wondering how you can pull it off with such ease and panache.

Good news! The editors of GOURMET magazine have put together a completely new kind of cookbook. It's called Menus for Contemporary Living. It was created for people like you.

You--the busy, spirited, adventurous cook. Who delights in good food. But doesn't have hours to spend preparing it. Who can be seduced by the mere sound of a marvelous ethnic dish, or an unusual combination of ingredients. And is doubly pleased when the steps to make it are simple, straightforward, quick. Who likes to entertain on a whim

(continued)

1

BUSINESS REPLY

FIRST CLASS PERMIT NO. 10

POSTAGE WILL BE PAID BY ADDRESSEE

Gourmet
The Condé Nast Collection
P.O. Box 10850
Des Moines, Iowa 50336

For those who are hesitating, may we tempt you with a small sample?

(Recipe enclosed)

MR JOSEPH C SCHALLER
AP 394
293 B-SOUTH BROADWAY
TARRYTOWN NY 10591

SIMPLE AND SENSATIONAL...

SPECIAL COOKBOOK OFFER ENCLOSED. R.S.V.P.

SIMPLE AND SENSATIONAL...

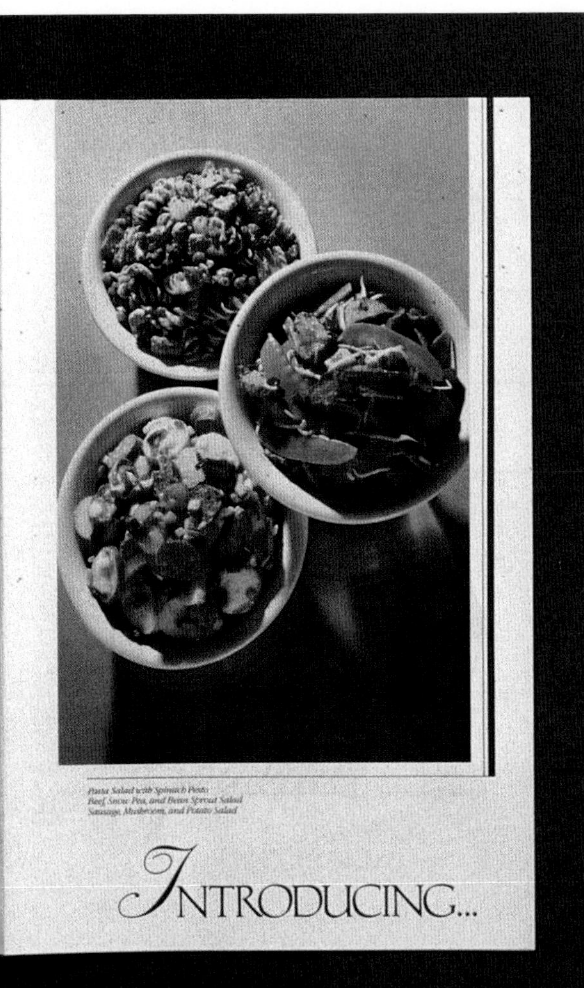

Title: "Gourmet's Menus for Contemporary Living"
Copywriter: Emily Soell
Art Director: Jim Pastena
Agency: Rapp & Collins
Client: The Conde Nast Publications, Inc.

This sophisticated direct mail package spares no effort to convey to prospective customers the desirability of the world-class cuisine that can be achieved with ownership of a book of menus from the publishers of Gourmet magazine, one of the leading upscale publications in the world.

Fast Food.

Now *you* can serve mouthwatering meals like this—in one hour or less!

Sincerely,

William J. Henry
President

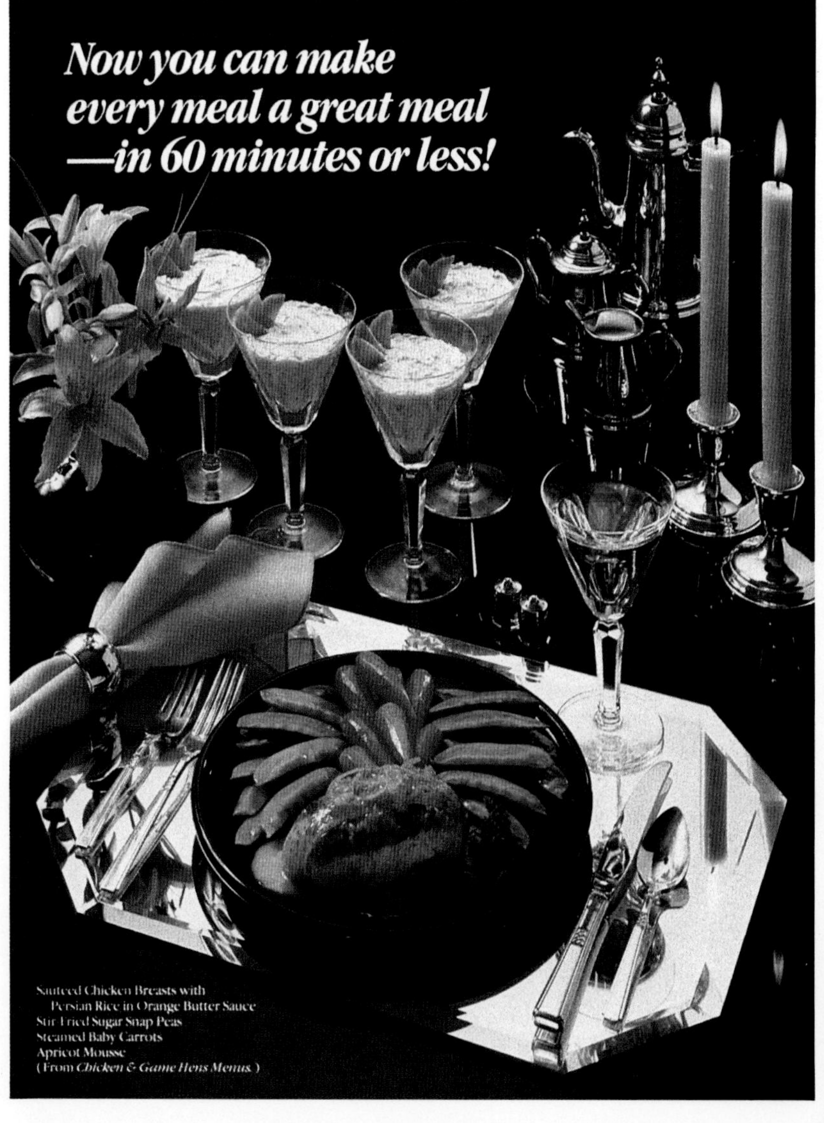

Title: "Fast Food"
Copywriter: Martin Barratt
Art Director: Kathleen Tresnak
Agency: In-House
Client: Time-Life Books

The full treatment is given in this 9″ x 12″ jumbo package for a continuity series of cookbooks, targeted to consumers who love excellent food but rarely have time to prepare it.

Beautiful Food.

Chili Shrimp
Smoked Bean Sprouts
Diced Chicken with
Fermented Black Beans
(From *Chinese Menus*)

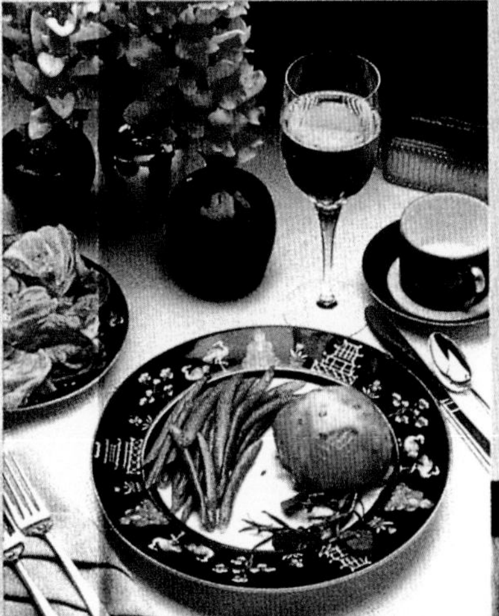

Fresh Food.

Spaghettini with Sausage
and Zucchini
String Bean Salad with
Nuts and Cream
(From *Pasta Menus*)

Healthy Food.

Baked Chicken Breasts
with Brandy Sauce
Green Beans
Boston Lettuce Salad
(From *Chicken & Game Hen Menus*)

Fast Food.

Champagne à l'Orange
Provençal Salad Platter
Cheese Pudding
Sliced Mangoes with Lime Wedges
(From *Brunch Menus*)

Scores of complete menus, fully illustrated and organized step by step.
And hundreds of foolproof recipes you'll find nowhere else!
GREAT MEALS IN MINUTES
Now TIME-LIFE BOOKS introduces a series of complete-menu cookbooks in which each meal is designed to go from your kitchen to your table in one hour or less!
With GREAT MEALS IN MINUTES, you'll be amazed at how easy it is to prepare meals that look good, taste good and are good for you—every day and for every occasion, even when you're on the busiest schedule.
You'll choose from an astonishing variety of menus (up to 30 in each volume). From meals built around chicken and fish, beef and pork, pasta, vegetables, eggs and cheese. From meals that include soups, salads and desserts. From authentic Italian, Chinese and Mexican meals.
You'll find each menu meticulously organized from start to finish. Ready-made shopping lists itemize ingredients and their exact amounts. Clear instructions guide you through each stage of preparation. Triple-tested recipes are sure to appeal to both your family and friends. And a full-color photograph shows you how each finished dish should look. In other words, the book does the worrying and you get everything onto the table at the same time—and all within 60 minutes!
Begin by examining Chicken & Game Hen Menus for 10 days FREE!
Great Meals IN MINUTES
PASTA ME
VEGETABLE M
CHICKEN & GAME HEN MENUS
GREAT MEALS IN MINUTES FISH & SHELLFISH MENU
GREAT MEALS IN MINUTES SALAD MENUS
GREAT MEALS IN MINUTES ITALIAN MENUS
GREAT MEALS IN MINUTES BRUNCH MENUS
TIME LIFE BOOKS
Each volume: Measures a large 8⅜" x 11" • Contains more than 100 pages
• Comes with durable, hardbound wipe-clean covers

From lunches, brunches and picnics to dinners for every day and every occasion, GREAT MEALS IN MINUTES does everything but the cooking for you!
Weekday meals your children will eat with gusto. No-fuss lunches. Brunches to stir the latest riser. Picnics you can prepare well ahead. Barbecues that would please even J.R. And special-occasion dinners so beautiful you eat them first with your eyes.
With GREAT MEALS IN MINUTES, you can now prepare truly extraordinary meals for your family and friends. All through the week and all year round, you can rely on a complete, 60-minute meal plan for every occasion.
Build a complete library of 60-minute menus!
From Salad Menus and Italian Menus to Vegetable Menus, Chicken & Game Hen Menus, and your introductory volume, Fish & Shellfish Menus, you'll enjoy far more than a unique collection of mouthwatering new recipes.
You'll find Pennsylvania Dutch dinners as traditional as a barn-raising in American Regional Menus. Inexpensive and infinitely varied meals in Pasta Menus (including a grandmother's recipe for Gnocchi and a Fettuccine alla Carbonara no godfather could refuse). Easy-to-prepare versions of famous dishes from Alsace, Burgundy and Provence in French Regional Menus. (Included are a superb 40-minute Boeuf Bourguignon...a simple Bouillabaisse...a quick Shrimp Provençal.)
Other volumes show you how to prepare authentic Mexican meals—as simple as tamales, as festive as Mole Poblano. Beef and veal menus with both cosmopolitan and country touches (everything from a 30-minute London Broil to 50-minute Stuffed Cabbage Leaves). And unhurried brunches that are as enjoyable for the cook as for the guests.
Begin by examining Chicken & Game Hen Menus for 10 days FREE!
Your first volume features no fewer than 27 new ways of serving chicken and game hens that you'll find nowhere else.
You can dazzle both family and friends with dishes that only look complicated. (The Basque Chicken Sauté shown on the envelope, for example. Or a dramatic brandy-flamed chicken.) Try crispy chicken with a specially invented Puebla-style mole sauce. Bake, poach, sauté, steam and stuff chicken breasts. Or combine game hens with green peppercorns for a novel eating adventure—all in one hour or less!
In all, more than 100 recipes are presented step by step and include soups, salads and desserts. Each has been triple-tested. At least once by the cook who created it for this volume. And twice by others following the same foolproof instructions you would use.
To put Chicken & Game Hen Menus to the test for 10 full days without cost or obligation, simply mail the accompanying postage-paid order card today!
TIME LIFE BOOKS
Great Meals IN MINUTES
CHICKEN & GAME HEN MENUS
Helpful hints
WHAT TO DRINK
SHOPPING LIST AND STAPLES
RECIPES
Handy shopping lists
save you time by itemizing everything you'll need and even pre-measure exact amounts for each menu.

If you were planning to cook tonight, which one of these menus would you choose?

Oven Barbecued Chicken
Southern-Style Black-Eyed Peas
Corn-Cake Crisps
Romaine Salad Vinaigrette

Poached Salmon Steaks with Green Sauce
Rice Pilaf with Scallions and Celery
Fresh Asparagus with Lemon-Mustard Glaze

Chilled Avocado Soup
Oriental-Style Marinated Beef Salad
Strawberries Dipped in White and Dark Chocolate

Dear Reader:

If you can believe it, you could put the first of these complete meals on the table in less than one hour.

Menu #2 would take you 30-40 minutes to prepare. And Menu #3 could be made in roughly 45 minutes.

When we say you can prepare each of these three meals in 60 minutes or less--soup, salad and dessert included--we mean it. We've cooked every one of them ourselves--using the same techniques and equipment, and following the same step-by-step instructions you would use--at least twice!

And because we always sample what we cook, we know the results are delicious. But, you don't have to go to a cooking school to achieve these results. Nor spend a fortune in a restaurant to enjoy such magnificent meals.

With GREAT MEALS IN MINUTES--an all-new concept in cookbooks from TIME-LIFE--you can now discover how easy it is to prepare meals that look and taste good every day, and for every occasion--even when you're on the busiest schedule.

Let me send you the first volume, Chicken & Game Hen Menus, to look at--and cook from--for 10 days FREE. It will provide you with 27 complete menus (and more than 100 foolproof recipes) that you will find nowhere else--no matter how many cookbooks you own!

Put Chicken & Game Hen Menus to the test in your own kitchen for 10 full days without cost or obligation. Try some of its exciting complete-menu ideas on your family and see who doesn't ask for more! Impress your friends with

TIME LIFE BOOKS

TIME LIFE BOOKS

FREE GIFT!

Handy Take Along Kitchen Timer

As a special welcome to GREAT MEALS IN MINUTES, you'll receive this ingenious Take Along Kitchen Timer—absolutely FREE—when you decide to purchase your introductory volume, *Chicken & Game Hen Menus.*

Made of durable plastic, this reliable 60-minute timer measures 2½-inches across. It has a black face with bold white numbers that are clear and easy to read. No batteries are needed. And the 30-inch nylon hanging cord is detachable in case you want to tuck the timer into a pocket.

To be sure of getting your FREE Take Along Kitchen Timer, send for *Chicken & Game Hen Menus* today!

Detach before mailing.

Great Meals in Minutes
Chicken & Game Hen Menus

Now...27 delicious chicken and game hen dinners you can make in one hour or less!

Order Card

YES! I would like to examine *Chicken & Game Hen Menus* as my introduction to GREAT MEALS IN MINUTES. Please send it to me for 10 days' free examination, along with future volumes, under the terms described in the accompanying letter.

If I choose not to keep *Chicken & Game Hen Menus*, I will return the complete package within 10 days.

DON'T FORGET! A handy, Take Along Kitchen Timer is yours to keep FREE with purchase of *Chicken & Game Hen Menus!*

SEND NO MONEY NOW.
Just mail this postage-paid Order Card today!

Please initial here ________
MLT

DÉTROIT DE DAVIS STRAIT
1587 - 1987
CANADA DOLLAR

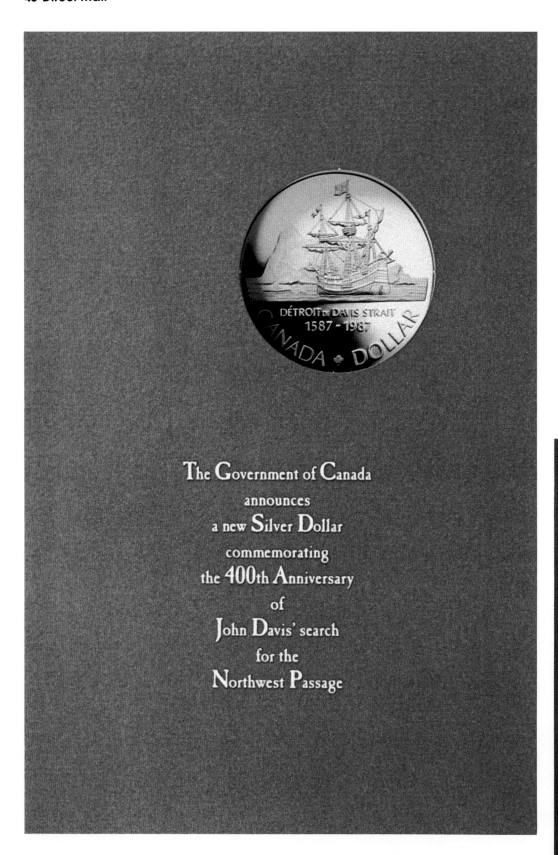

The Government of Canada
announces
a new Silver Dollar
commemorating
the 400th Anniversary
of
John Davis' search
for the
Northwest Passage

Title: "1987 Commemorative Proof Silver Coin"
Copywriter: Michael Beecher
Art Director: Cecilia Stevens
Agency: Barry Blau & Partners
Client: The Royal Canadian Mint

The "spirit of heroism and adventure" is evoked in this straightforward, effective mailing offering coin collectors the first chance to purchase a limited new issue.

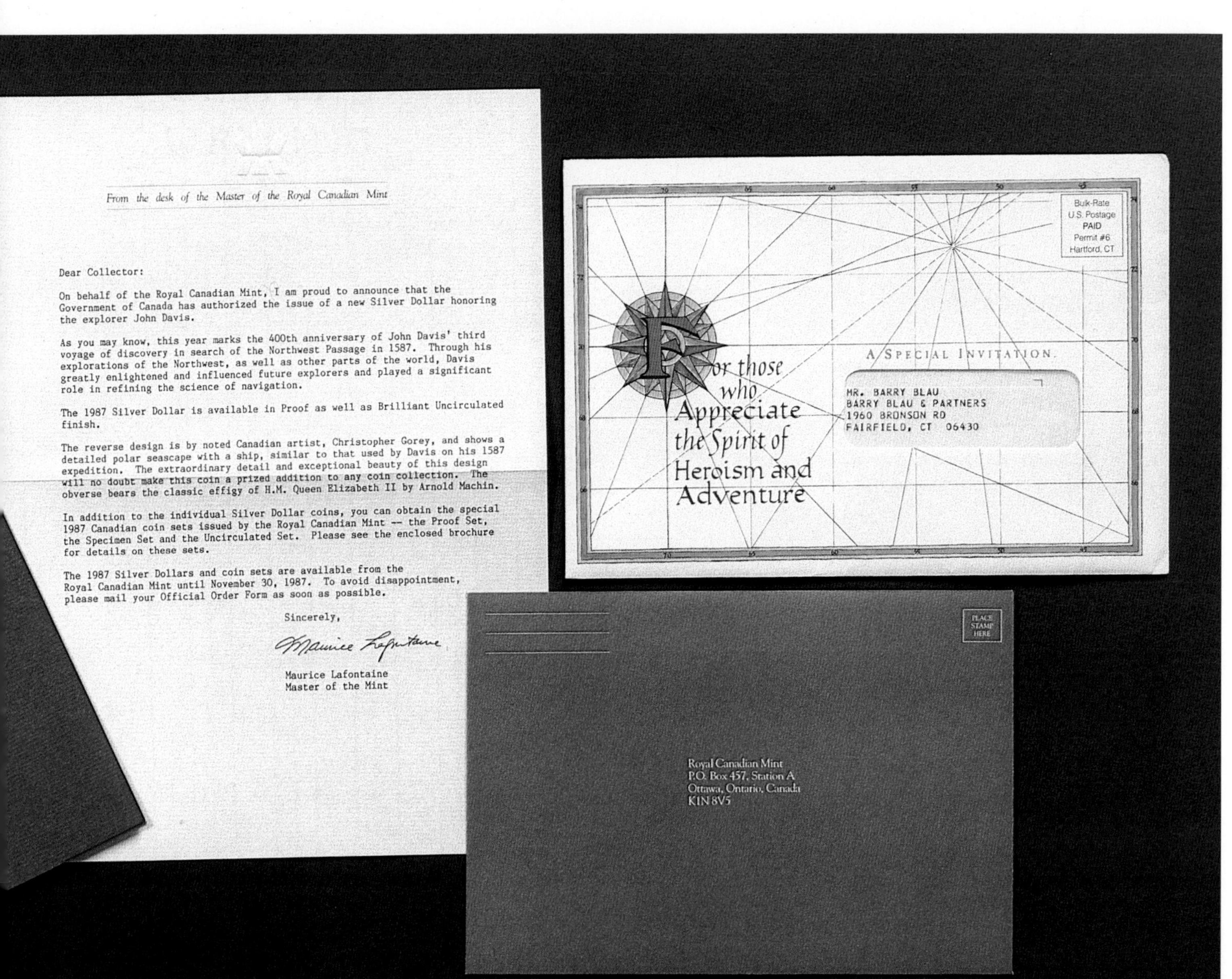

From the desk of the Master of the Royal Canadian Mint

Dear Collector:

On behalf of the Royal Canadian Mint, I am proud to announce that the Government of Canada has authorized the issue of a new Silver Dollar honoring the explorer John Davis.

As you may know, this year marks the 400th anniversary of John Davis' third voyage of discovery in search of the Northwest Passage in 1587. Through his explorations of the Northwest, as well as other parts of the world, Davis greatly enlightened and influenced future explorers and played a significant role in refining the science of navigation.

The 1987 Silver Dollar is available in Proof as well as Brilliant Uncirculated finish.

The reverse design is by noted Canadian artist, Christopher Gorey, and shows a detailed polar seascape with a ship, similar to that used by Davis on his 1587 expedition. The extraordinary detail and exceptional beauty of this design will no doubt make this coin a prized addition to any coin collection. The obverse bears the classic effigy of H.M. Queen Elizabeth II by Arnold Machin.

In addition to the individual Silver Dollar coins, you can obtain the special 1987 Canadian coin sets issued by the Royal Canadian Mint -- the Proof Set, the Specimen Set and the Uncirculated Set. Please see the enclosed brochure for details on these sets.

The 1987 Silver Dollars and coin sets are available from the Royal Canadian Mint until November 30, 1987. To avoid disappointment, please mail your Official Order Form as soon as possible.

Sincerely,

Maurice Lafontaine
Master of the Mint

Bulk-Rate
U.S. Postage
PAID
Permit #6
Hartford, CT
For those who Appreciate the Spirit of Heroism and Adventure
A Special Invitation.
MR. BARRY BLAU
BARRY BLAU & PARTNERS
1960 BRONSON RD
FAIRFIELD, CT 06430
PLACE STAMP HERE
Royal Canadian Mint
P.O. Box 457, Station A
Ottawa, Ontario, Canada
K1N 8V5

It's the premiere 1984-85 dance season

Number of subscriptions:

☐ Adult ☐ Student 16 & under

Subscription prices include entire season.

Section A	Section B
Adults: $36.00	Adults: $27.00
Student: $18.00 (16 & under)	Student: $13.00 (16 & under)

Performance dates:

- Nutcracker
  - ☐ Sat. Dec. 22 2 pm
  - ☐ Sat. Dec. 22 7 pm
  - ☐ Sun. Dec. 23 2 pm
- Sleeping Beauty
  - ☐ Sat. May 11 2 pm
  - ☐ Sat. May 11 7 pm
- Swan Lake, Requieum, Jazz 'n Break
  - ☐ Sat. Mar. 2 2 pm
  - ☐ Sat. Mar. 2 7 pm
- Peter & the Wolf, Clowns, Thriller
  - ☐ Sat. June 29 2 pm
  - ☐ Sat. June 29 7 pm

Payment: ☐ Visa ☐ MasterCard ☐ Check

NAME ____________________

ADDRESS ____________________

CITY ____________________ ZIP ____________

CHARGE CARD # ____________________

Evansville Dance Theatre
Old Court House
Evansville, IN 47708
812-423-9888.

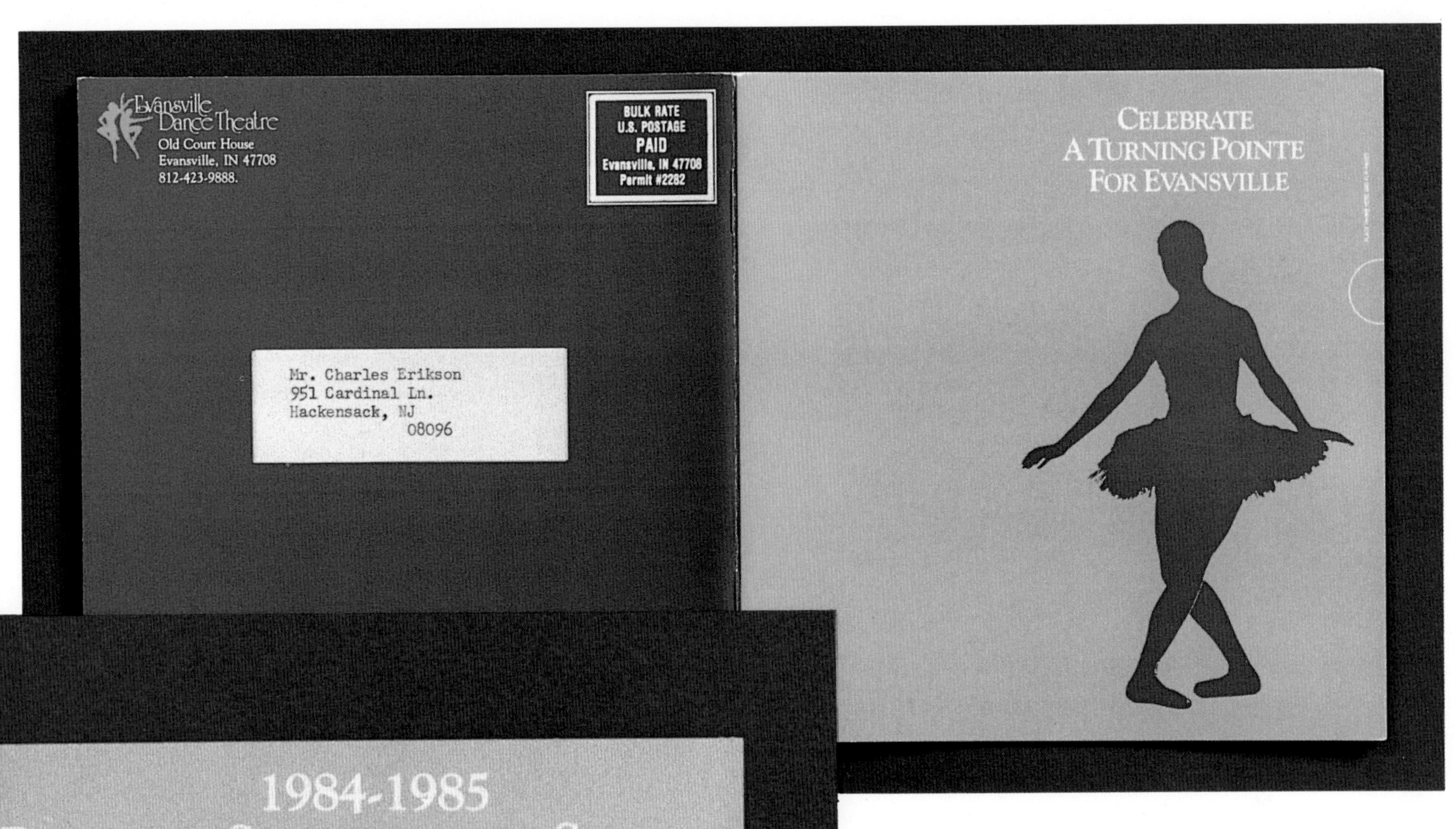

Title:	"Celebrate a Turning Pointe"
Copywriter:	Nancy Cressler
Art Directors:	Gerry Ulrich, Barry Underhill
Agency:	Keller Crescent
Client:	Evansville Dance Theatre

The simple principle of manual, "thumb-flip" animation turns this two-color self-mailer into an involving and eminently pleasing solicitation for support of a community's fine arts program, with the dancer doing a full turn in, of course, perfect form.

CELEBRATE
A TURNING POINTE
FOR EVANSVILLE

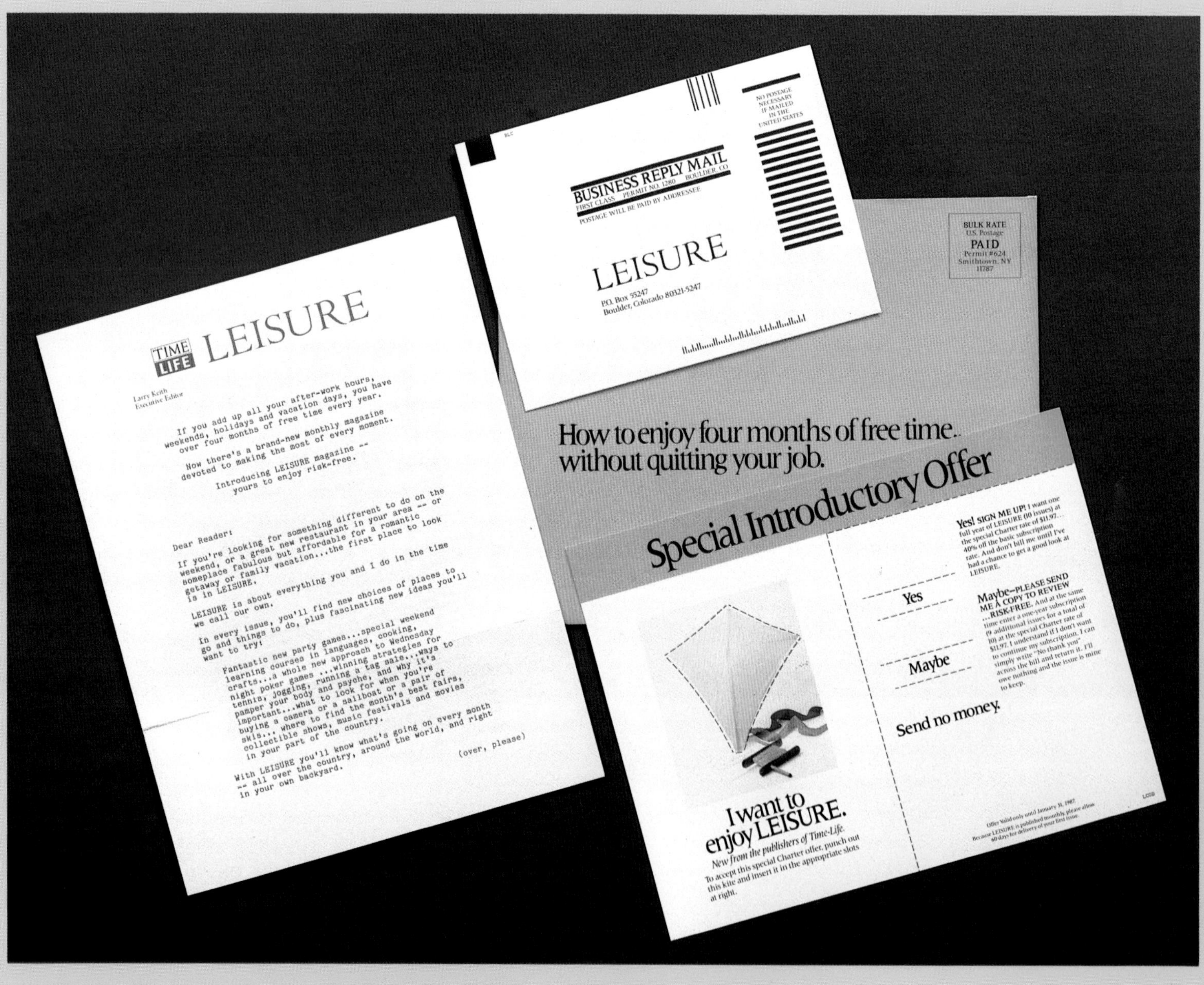
TIME LIFE LEISURE
Larry Keith
Executive Editor
If you add up all your after-work hours, weekends, holidays and vacation days, you have over four months of free time every year.
Now there's a brand-new monthly magazine devoted to making the most of every moment.
Introducing LEISURE magazine -- yours to enjoy risk-free.
Dear Reader:
If you're looking for something different to do on the weekend, or a great new restaurant in your area -- or someplace fabulous but affordable for a romantic getaway or family vacation...the first place to look is in LEISURE.
LEISURE is about everything you and I do in the time we call our own.
In every issue, you'll find new choices of places to go and things to do, plus fascinating new ideas you'll want to try:
Fantastic new party games...special weekend learning courses in languages, cooking, crafts...a whole new approach to Wednesday night poker games ...winning strategies for tennis, jogging, running a tag sale...ways to pamper your body and psyche, and why it's important...what to look for when you're buying a camera or a sailboat or a pair of skis... where to find the month's best fairs, collectible shows, music festivals and movies in your part of the country.
With LEISURE you'll know what's going on every month -- all over the country, around the world, and right in your own backyard.
(over, please)
BUSINESS REPLY MAIL
FIRST CLASS PERMIT NO. 1280 BOULDER, CO
POSTAGE WILL BE PAID BY ADDRESSEE
NO POSTAGE NECESSARY IF MAILED IN THE UNITED STATES
LEISURE
P.O. Box 55247
Boulder, Colorado 80321-5247
BULK RATE
U.S. Postage
PAID
Permit #624
Smithtown, NY
11787
How to enjoy four months of free time..
without quitting your job.
Special Introductory Offer
Yes! SIGN ME UP! I want one full year of LEISURE (10 issues) at the special Charter rate of $11.97... 40% off the basic subscription rate. And don't bill me until I've had a chance to get a good look at LEISURE.
Yes
Maybe
Maybe—PLEASE SEND ME A COPY TO REVIEW ...RISK-FREE. And at the same time enter a one-year subscription (9 additional issues for a total of 10) at the special Charter rate of $11.97. I understand if I don't want to continue my subscription, I can simply write "No thank you" across the bill and return it. I'll owe nothing and the issue is mine to keep.
Send no money.
I want to enjoy LEISURE.
New from the publishers of Time-Life.
To accept this special Charter offer, punch out this kite and insert it in the appropriate slots at right.
Offer Valid only until January 31, 1987
Because LEISURE is published monthly, please allow 60 days for delivery of your first issue.
LC0D

LEISURE
HAWAII
Join the new Leisure class for $11.97

Title: "How to enjoy..."
Copywriter: Claire O'Brien
Art Director: John Palisay
Agency: Ogilvy & Mather Direct
Client: Time- Life

An appealing idea—plenty of leisure time—is at the heart of this launch effort for a new magazine from one of the world's most important publishers.

You don't have to spend a million dollars or go a million miles to get away from it all.

Introducing LEISURE—a new magazine for America's active new leisure class.

What's for dinner? How about three appetizers and dessert?

It's a fresh, relaxed new way of eating that's attuned to the overdrive schedules of the 1980s. And it's become increasingly popular in top restaurants from Boston to L.A. It's called grazing—an invitation to wander around the menu, ordering anything you want. Like three soups and cherries jubilee.

It's more fun, and can often be much less expensive than a conventional soup-to-nuts kind of a meal. And it's a great idea for dining-in when you're entertaining at home some worknight and haven't time to pull off a complete dinner. We have recipes from some of the young chefs we talked to when we were grazing—and we'll be happy to share them with you, along with lots of other food ideas.

Magic places that can turn a week into the vacation of a lifetime.

Romantic hideaways, just hours away, where the breezes are soft and the sun is bright and the moon comes out at night for dancing... lovely old inns and hotels that tempt you to stay on and on and come back year after year... family cruises with built-in camps that let you take a vacation from the kids, and take the kids along. We'll give you all the details: how to cut costs (on car rentals, for example); when a splurge (on a 3-star meal perhaps) is worth it; where a special discount makes a luxury hotel suddenly affordable. In short, how to live it up at a cost that's down to earth.

A cross-country roundup of weekend events from cattle drives to antique shows.

Would you like to try your hand at being a cowhand some weekend? Or how about riding off Saturday morning with your family or a group of friends on a back-packing weekend bike trip? We've got 10 of the best, most scenic U.S. itineraries all mapped out for you. Plus over 10 pages of the best of everything that's going on this month in every part of the country. Film festivals, jazz festivals, collectors' shows, art exhibits, country fairs, concerts, triathlons, craft workshops, whale-watching expeditions, dogsled trips, windjammer cruises—and much, much more!

Relaxing ways to smooth away the rough edges of your day.

Whether you're creating something with your hands or swinging at a racquetball—or giving the family dog an evening run instead of a walk, nothing eases mental tensions faster than concentration on hard physical activity. At LEISURE, we're always searching out creative new ways to help you relax: things to do, new types of exercises (like aqua aerobics), interesting new craft workshops.

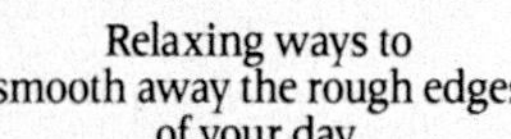

When there aren't enough hours in the day, for everything you want to do, learn to play for time...

The pleasures of learning to master a musical instrument—or learning to paint or make home movies, whatever attracts you—are immediate, and lasting. You find yourself *making* space in your day to fit in time for studying... time for yourself, away from the demands of work, friends, even family. It's an important part of leisure, yours and ours.

Great books at 55 M.P.H.

If reading's a favorite pastime, books-on-tape can turn the time you spend driving to work into hours of added "reading" time every week. We'll tell you about new tapes, and give you reviews of new videos and movies too—that let *you* decide if they're for you.

Enjoy a year of LEISURE.

In every issue, you'll find articles, features and columns on travel, food, sports, movies, videos, special events, hobbies... All for $11.97. Send for your introductory copy today.

You don't have to spend a million dollars or go a million miles to get away from it all.

Introducing LEISURE—a new magazine for America's active new leisure class.

Magic places that can turn a week into the vacation of a lifetime.

Romantic hideaways, just hours away, where the breezes are soft and the sun is bright and the moon comes out at night for dancing... lovely old inns and hotels that tempt you to stay on and on and come back year after year... family cruises with built-in camps that let you take a vacation from the kids, and take the kids along. We'll give you all the details: how to cut costs (on car rentals, for example); when a splurge (on a 3-star meal perhaps) is worth it; where a special discount makes a luxury hotel suddenly affordable. In short, how to live it up at a cost that's down to earth.

What's for dinner? How about three appetizers and dessert?

It's a fresh, relaxed new way of eating that's attuned to the overdrive schedules of the 1980s. And it's become increasingly popular in top restaurants from Boston to L.A. It's called grazing—an invitation to wander around the menu, ordering anything you want. Like three soups and cherries jubilee.

It's more fun, and can often be much less expensive than a conventional soup-to-nuts kind of a meal. And it's a great idea for dining-in when you're entertaining at home some worknight and haven't time to pull off a complete dinner. We have recipes from some of the young chefs we talked to when we were grazing—and we'll be happy to share them with you, along with lots of other food ideas.

Special Introductory Offer.

Join the new Leisure class for $11^97

EXTRA! SAVE $30
Connection Charge Waiver
(if you act now)
It costs $30 to have Custom Calling Service hooked up to your line. But if you return the enclosed card or call our toll-free number before June 30 we will provide your Custom Calling connection at no charge.
GTS CCR W3
TAKE A LOOK
at what could be one of the smartest residential telephones in existence today
Mr. John Q. Sample
123 Main Street
Anytown, USA 00000
PULL UP TAB
SURPRISED?

GTS CCR L5

General Telephone

GTE introduces Custom Calling,
a service to make your phone smarter.
Now you can try it free for one month!

Dear GTE Customer:

Imagine a phone that eliminates the frustration of a busy signal. That enables friends or business associates to get through to you even when you're talking. That connects you with your home, even if someone else is tying up the line.

Imagine a phone that could memorize frequently called or important numbers and dial them for you at the touch of a button. A phone that could automatically forward important calls to you when you're away from home. A phone that could instantly arrange a three-way conversation by bringing two outside people on your line at one time.

That might sound like the phone of the future. But it's your phone. Yes! The very same rotary or Touch Call phone that's been in your kitchen, bedroom or living room for years.

You see, GTE has found a way to plug these time-saving, problem-solving, stress-eliminating features into your home telephone. Not by giving you new equipment, or doing complicated installation work. But by wiring these services to you electronically. We call our service Custom Calling. And we would like you to try it free for a full month.

How? Simply call 1-800-525-3344, Ext.130 or mail the enclosed card before June 30, 1985, and ask for a free trial of our four Custom Calling features. It won't cost you anything. It won't involve a second of work or inconvenience on your part. It won't in any way obligate you to keep Custom Calling after the trial.

What it will do is show you just how smart your phone can be. And how ideal this service is for a busy person such as yourself.

YOUR PHONE WILL NEVER BE BUSY -- EVEN WHEN IT IS BUSY -- WITH CALL WAITING

How many times has this happened to you? You're desperately trying to call home and all you get is an annoying busy signal. Or you are home, awaiting an important phone call. But the call that comes in isn't the one you'd expected. And the person keeps talking and talking and you can't get off the line. Call Waiting reduces these aggravations. Because it enables you to answer an incoming call even while you're on the phone. With Call Waiting you can talk as long as you need to without the worry of missing other calls.

(cont'd)

SPEED CALLING

Now your phone can dial a number automatically (You just touch one or two buttons)

How does the phone dial automatically? Simple. You program any eight numbers you'd like into Speed Calling memory (including long distance numbers) by dialing a special code. Then you just press "2," "3," or "4" to make calls. Now, can you think of a better way to call close friends, remember phone numbers, or call for help in an emergency?

Now your phone can get two different people in two different places on the line with you at the same time

Now you can add a friend to your calls, and hold a three-way conversation without operator assistance. With Three-Way Calling you just:

1. Press the receiver button to put the original call on hold,
2. Dial the third party, and
3. Press the receiver button again for the three-way conversation to begin.

You can coordinate plans for the three of you without costly, confusing back-and-forth calling. Or have a happy get-together with family or old friends when you're miles apart!

SPEED CALLING

THREE-WAY CALLING

How to teach your telephone to solve five ticklish problems

1. Problem
What can you do with teenagers when they get on the phone? Those talkative kids won't let anyone's calls get through.

Solved
GTE Custom Calling Call Waiting lets incoming calls get through even while the phone is in use. Speak with the second caller while the original call is on hold, or acknowledge the calls for a call-back.

2. Problem
You've had an unexpected invitation to visit a friend. But you're expecting some important calls at home.

Solved
GTE Custom Calling Call Forwarding will transfer calls from your home phone directly to wherever you intend to be.

3. Problem
You're trying to make plans for the three of you to go out to dinner this week. But in trying to arrange things around everyone's busy schedules, you've already made three separate call-backs—and things still aren't set.

Solved
GTE Custom Calling Three-Way Calling eliminates the need for call-backs by letting you add a third party to your phone conversations.

4. Problem
You need to call a doctor and you can't remember the phone number or find your phone book. You don't want to waste time looking it up in the directory.

Solved
GTE Custom Calling Speed Calling remembers emergency numbers for you, and dials them, too! You just press one or two digits. Speed calling also remembers any other phone numbers you call frequently—up to 8 numbers.

5. Problem
You're sold on GTE Custom Calling, but your days are so busy, it's almost impossible to stay home to have it installed.

Solved
GTE Custom Calling needs no new equipment installation We can set up your service from our office in a matter of days. Just call 1-800-545-5400, Ext. 100 to start your free trial!

GTM CCR BR8

With GTE Custom Calling
YOU CAN TEACH YOUR OLD PHONE NEW TRICKS

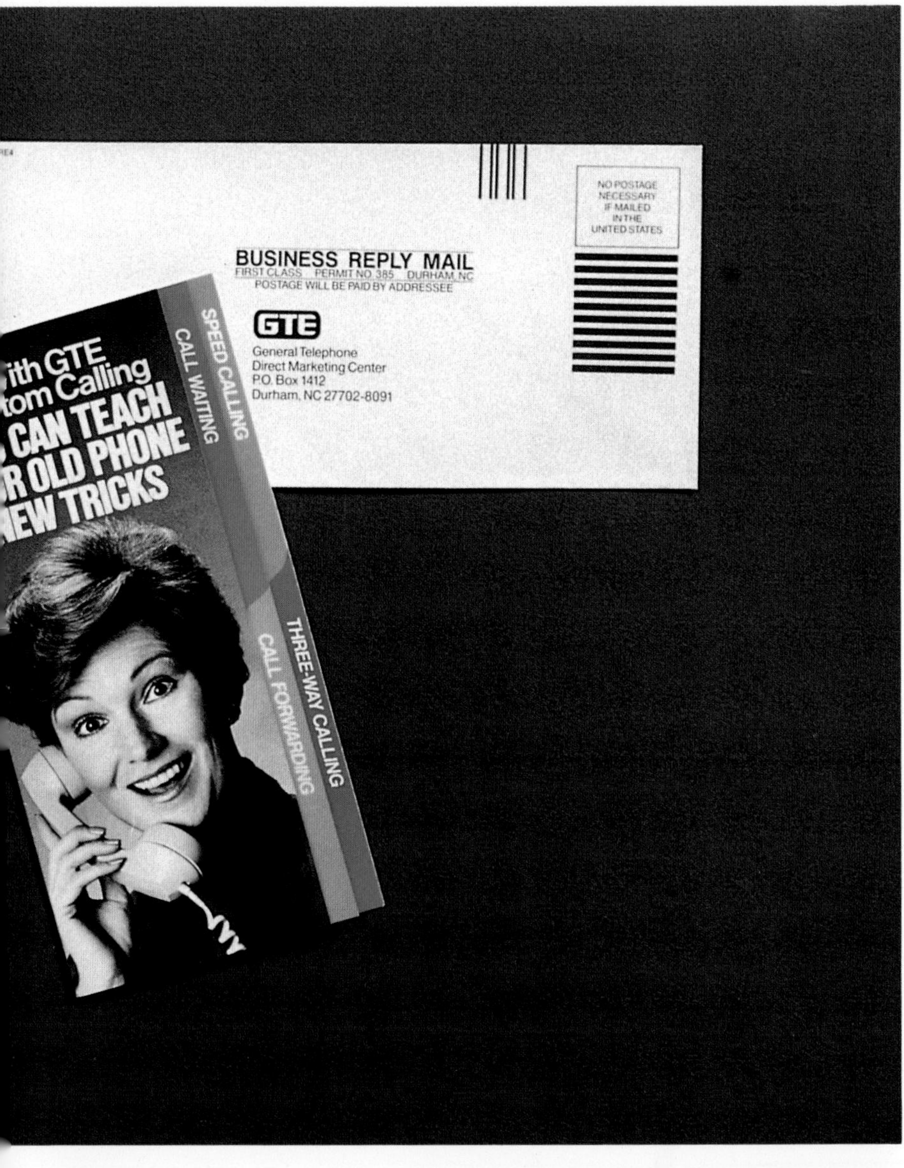

Title: "GTE Custom Calling"
Copywriter: Emily Soell
Art Director: Fernando Rola
Agency: Rapp & Collins
Client: GTE Service Corporation

In a state-of-the-art marriage of database capabilities and imaginative creativity, the direct mail recipient's actual telephone number was shown underneath a lift- up flap on the outer envelope of this package promoting new telephone services available with changing equipment.

CALL FORWARDING

Now your phone can find you for an important call when you're away from your home.

Have things to do, places to go? Don't waste time waiting around for your important calls. With Call Forwarding, your phone can transfer your calls to your new locale—or to a "phone sitter." Either way, you'll get added security and your important messages whenever you leave home.

Custom Calling brings the latest conveniences to your home phone with no installation–no new equipment

Possibly you're thinking, "I ought to try Custom Calling, but I'm working, or running a household or chauffeuring kids all day and can't wait around for installation." Or, "I just can't be bothered with new phone equipment. It's bound to be complicated. And buying new equipment always costs a lot."

That's part of the beauty of Custom Calling.

There's no new gadgetry of any kind. You can get Custom Calling Service through your present equipment, whether you have a rotary or Touch-Call phone.

And Custom Calling involves no equipment installation. We hook up the service electronically from our office, through the telephone lines.

So, you see, trying GTE Custom Calling couldn't be simpler or involve less work or headaches for you.

GTE

CALL WAITING

Now your phone can tell you that someone else is trying to get through to you.

With a faint "beep," your phone will alert you when a second caller is trying to reach you, when you have Call Waiting on the line. You then: press the receiver button to put the original call on hold, and answer the second call. Switch back and forth between calls...or acknowledge the second caller for a call-back.

CALL FORWARDING

digital™
Digital Equipment Corporation
Channels Marketing Group
4 Mt. Royal Avenue (1-P02-3)
Marlboro, MA 01752

BULK RATE
U.S. POSTAGE
PAID
BOSTON, MA
PERMIT NO. 1

HOW FUNNY LITTLE MAN (A) CAN HELP OVERWORKED OEM (B) DELIVER SOFTWARE SOLUTIONS FASTER AND FOR LESS. SEE INSIDE (C).

Reprinted with special permission of King Features Syndicate, Inc.

A simple method of inventing

(In the spirit of the great Rube Goldberg)

NO POSTAGE
NECESSARY
IF MAILED
IN THE
UNITED STATES

BUSINESS REPLY MAIL
FIRST CLASS PERMIT NO. 33 MAYNARD, MA

Postage will be paid by addressee

digital™
Digital Equipment Corporation
Channels Marketing (NR02-1/H3)
444 Whitney Street
Northboro, MA 01532-2599

digital™

When it comes to software,
the question is, to make or to buy?
The answer is as easy as (A), (B), (C).

Many years ago, a famous cartoonist named Rube Goldberg invented hilariously complicated machinery in order to accomplish simple tasks. His solutions were ingenious, and they always worked -- but they often took the long road.

We bring Rube Goldberg to your attention simply to dramatize a point: today, no OEM can afford to take the long road to providing software solutions. It's no laughing matter any more.

As an OEM, you face infinitely more complex tasks -- but the solutions are often simpler than you might suspect.

Your ability to offer added value in the form of higher performance, lower cost, greater efficiency, is the key to your success. And that ability often hinges on software.

The first question you must answer is, should you invent new software from the ground up, or buy existing solutions?

To do that, you have to balance benefits and costs. When you make software -- either as an in-house solution or a marketable product -- you have total control of the features you build in. But sometimes you can't control development costs, maintenance costs or the expenditure of your resources on base tools. When you buy, you may have slightly (and I emphasize the word "slightly") less control over features. But you have much greater control of costs. You can concentrate your resources on the value you add to the software. You get to market faster. Your vendor develops and maintains the product.

Certainly, there are times when developing software is worth your effort. But I'd like to suggest that you check with Digital before you commit to that long and often laborious process.

You see, Digital is better prepared than ever to help you deliver the added value that sets you apart from your competition. Our vast number of hardware and software products is increasing almost every day. They give you the modular products and tools you need to build imaginative and above all cost-effective solutions for your customers.

(continued)

Easy way to get full information that could save a lot of work.

Software
HANDBOOK

Fill out simple coupon (A), making sure name (B) is correct. Then send to (C) Digital Equipment Corporation today.

Detach here, complete and mail in enclosed postpaid envelope

(A)

YES, I'd like my copies of Digital's two books, *Software Handbook* and *VAX/VMS Software Language and Tools Handbook*. And enclose my free "Rube Goldberg" poster.

Please have a Digital representative call me immediately.
Phone (______)________________
Best time to call ________________

I'm particularly interested in
- ☐ Artificial Intelligence
- ☐ Languages and Productivity Tools
- ☐ Database/Information Management
- ☐ A-to-Z Integrated System

(B)

digital™
Digital Equipment Corporation
Channels Marketing Group
4 Mt. Royal Avenue (UP02-3)
Marlboro, MA 01752

(Are there others who should know about Digital's software products? Please list them on the reverse of this card.) CMG 003

You can choose from three software environments: the VAX/VMS virtual memory operating system that runs on all VAX processors from the MicroVAX II to today's most powerful VAX 8800 system; the VAXELN runtime executive, when you need real-time, runtime applications; and the ULTRIX system, Digital's enhanced UNIX™ operating system. With such a variety of operating systems, you can select the one that's best for your specific product. And Digital's networking allows you to tie environments together to create distributed applications.

And when it comes to individual software tools, the list fills a book -- two books, in fact. One is called the Software Handbook, and the other is VAX/VMS Software Language and Tools Handbook. These books give brief descriptions and price ranges of most Digital software products (new ones keep coming out!); they're indispensable for your working library. And I'd like to send them both to you free.

The brochure I've enclosed gives you a sampling of Digital's leadership software tools. When you read the brochure, please keep in mind that these are only a few of literally hundreds of available products.

I urge you to send for the two free books right away. And to check them before you commit major time and money to developing software on your own. You may find that your solution is as easy as (A) consult books; (B) find solution; (C) call Digital.

Sincerely,

Daniel P. Riordan
Systems Group Manager
Channels Marketing Group

P.S. Just for fun, I'll enclose a poster-sized reprint of our brochure cover with your books. It isn't exactly Rube Goldberg -- but it might just make the point.

digital™ Digital Equipment Corporation, Channels Marketing Group, 4 Mt. Royal Avenue (UP02-3), Marlboro, MA 01752

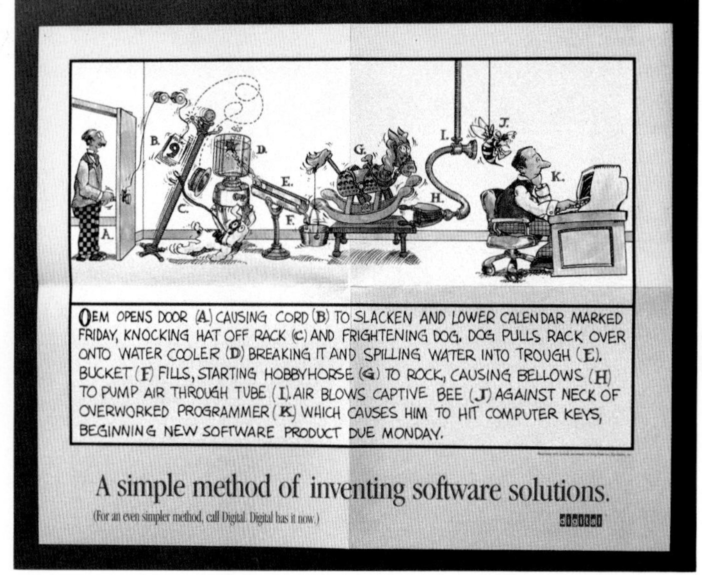

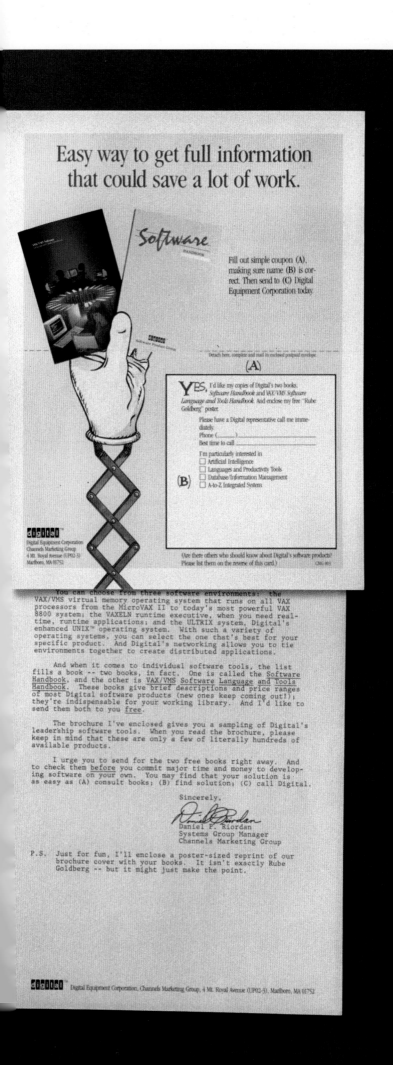

Title: "Rube Goldberg Mailing"
Copywriter: Raymond P. Clark
Art Directors: Rick Strode, Peter Simon
Agency: BDM Group, Inc.
Client: Digital Equipment Corporation

Computer software business customers are treated to the fun of what is perhaps the ultimate gadget of the moment in this fresh approach to a sometimes-intimidating subject.

Title: "Learn About Living"
Copywriter: Sheila Stogol
Art Director: Randy Howell
Agency: Kobs & Brady Advertising
Client: Western Publishing Company

A testimonial from television celebrity Michael Landon and a large, classic four-color brochure highlight this package promoting a series of books that can help parents explain serious, sensitive issues to their children.

The Golden Learn About Living™ Series

can help bring out all those questions your children wanted to ask, but didn't know how.

Developed and reviewed by experts and brought to you by Golden Press . . . to ease the pains of growing up in ways children understand.

Produced in cooperation with experts. Every book and newsletter is reliable and authoritative—without anything scary or upsetting. And because these books are created by some of the country's leading children's authors and illustrators, you can count on books every child will appreciate.

Each book even includes a special note to parents suggesting ways in which they can most effectively use the book and help ease their children's fears and anxieties.

And The Golden Learn About Living Series is reviewed by Dr. Bernice Berk, who will also contribute to the newsletter. She is Director of Psychological Services, Bank Street School for Children—Bank Street College of Education in New York City. Dr. Berk is also a Clinical Professor at the New York University, School of Psychology Program. She has had a private practice since 1968, providing help for children, adolescents and adults.

GOLDEN PRESS has been bringing families like yours fine children's books for over 40 years. Our Little Golden Books® have entertained and educated countless youngsters throughout the world. And our Golden Step Ahead® workbooks are used by grade schoolers to sharpen their skills on a variety of school subjects.

Now, with the Golden Learn About Living Series, Golden Press takes a new approach to childhood education . . . addressing some of the most serious and most sensitive issues facing our families in a way children can understand.

Today, we see more and more TV programs and stories in the news about children who are hurt or molested. We read about the problems of children trying to cope with changes in family lifestyle. And we worry about the many physical dangers that can befall our children.

That's why Golden Press decided to face the problems head-on. We turned to experts to develop a series of books that could help children understand the issues and help get them to talk about them. And we even added Parents' Newsletters to make it easier for parents to deal with the new questions.

In fact, Golden Press is the first major publisher producing such a comprehensive series for parents and children. But we felt, as we always have, that when there is a need that we can help fill . . . we will do our best to help out.

Provides 5 to 9 year olds with helpful, gentle advice on such sensitive issues as:

- Getting along with brothers and sisters.
- Dealing with strangers and protecting themselves from sexual abuse or molestation.
- Understanding the differences between family lifestyles.
- Dealing with a death in constructive ways.
- Learning that they are not "the boss."
- Getting to know people—and discovering how much alike we all are, not how different.
- Understanding Mommy's priorities when she goes to work.
- Overcoming the anger, fear and guilt associated with divorce . . . and bringing out the real concerns about remarriage and stepfamilies.
- Interacting with handicapped children.
- Remembering important safety rules—like buckling seat belts, knowing to call the police in an emergency, street safety, and the like.

You'll find important information and stories on these subjects and much more in the Golden Learn About Living Series.

Your child will get remarkable storybooks and you'll get newsletters that make parent-child discussions easier and more productive than ever.

Along with each book shipment, you get a Parents' Newsletter. You and your child can read the books together—to help get your child to talk about the issues. And, you can use the newsletters to help you answer your child's questions and address those concerns.

The idea behind the series is very simple: To get your child to talk about it—and for you to help make it better.

That's why every 32-page book is loaded with lovely, full-color illustrations to hold your child's interest. And why every book is written in easy-to-read style without anything threatening, scary or confusing. All to help you open the lines of communication with your child.

Plus, each 16-page illustrated newsletter is written specifically to help prepare you to best prepare your child. And each newsletter helps minimize your own self-consciousness and helps you get your child to open up and talk with you.

The Golden Learn About Living Series is truly unique. It offers the kind of two-way support you need to help raise a more secure, confident, and prepared child.

Try the Golden Learn About Living Series with your child today and GET ALL THIS!

FREE TRIAL

FREE BINDER

FREE GIFT STORYBOOK

- **Free Gift—*You Can Say "NO"* Storybook**
- **Free Gift—Newsletter Binder**
- **14-Day Free Trial—Storybook and Parents' Newsletter**
- **Plus, more helpful book-and-newsletter shipments.**

As soon as you say "YES" we'll ship you the introductory shipment to read and discuss with your child for 14 days absolutely free before you decide to buy. If you decide to keep the book and newsletter, you'll pay only $5.49 plus shipping, handling and applicable sales tax, or you can return the *Why Did Grandpa Die* Storybook and newsletter and owe nothing.

But whatever you decide, remember you get the free gift book—*You Can Say "No"*—and the Free Newsletter Binder to keep. They are our free gifts to you and your child.

Approximately a month after the first shipment, you'll get another book and newsletter—entirely on approval. Use this shipment free for a full 14 days. Again, you'll pay only $5.49, plus shipping, handling and applicable sales tax.

Then, to help you complete the entire series sooner, all the remaining books plus a newsletter will be mailed to you, on approval, approximately a month after you receive the second shipment. But you won't have to pay for them all at once. You will be billed for just two books and a newsletter a month at the low price of $5.49 each, plus applicable sales tax, with shipping and handling charges for the remainder of the series included in the first of these bills. The remaining newsletters will be mailed to you one per month along with your monthly billing.

There are no interest charges nor any other charges. And as always, you may return any books you don't want

Your Golden Press Assurance of Satisfaction

Use each shipment with your child for 14 days without obligation. You may return any shipments you do not wish to keep—and you won't owe any money. In fact, you are not obligated to buy a single thing—since there is no minimum purchase requirement. And the FREE GIFTS are yours to keep no matter what.

Each shipment features colorful storybooks and Parents' Newsletters to help you discuss things calmly and thoughtfully.

- Features stories that provide the springboard for discussion of sensitive subjects in a positive, non-threatening way.
- Sturdy, hardcover volumes designed to stand up to reading and re-reading.
- Each is a big 7½" x 9" with 32-pages and lots of appealing full-color illustrations.
- Filled with the tried-and-true hints from other parents and authoritative articles from the experts . . . to help you answer your child's questions—without fear or confusion.
- Provides the information *you* need, including "what if" games to help you monitor your child's progress.
- Each is a convenient 7" x 8¼" with 16 pages of thought-provoking information, plus helpful illustrations and photographs . . . ready to use or store in the free Newsletter Binder you get with the first shipment.

Don't delay! Help bring a childhood filled with happy endings into your home! Mail the Free Trial Certificate card today. And get valuable FREE GIFTS TO KEEP.

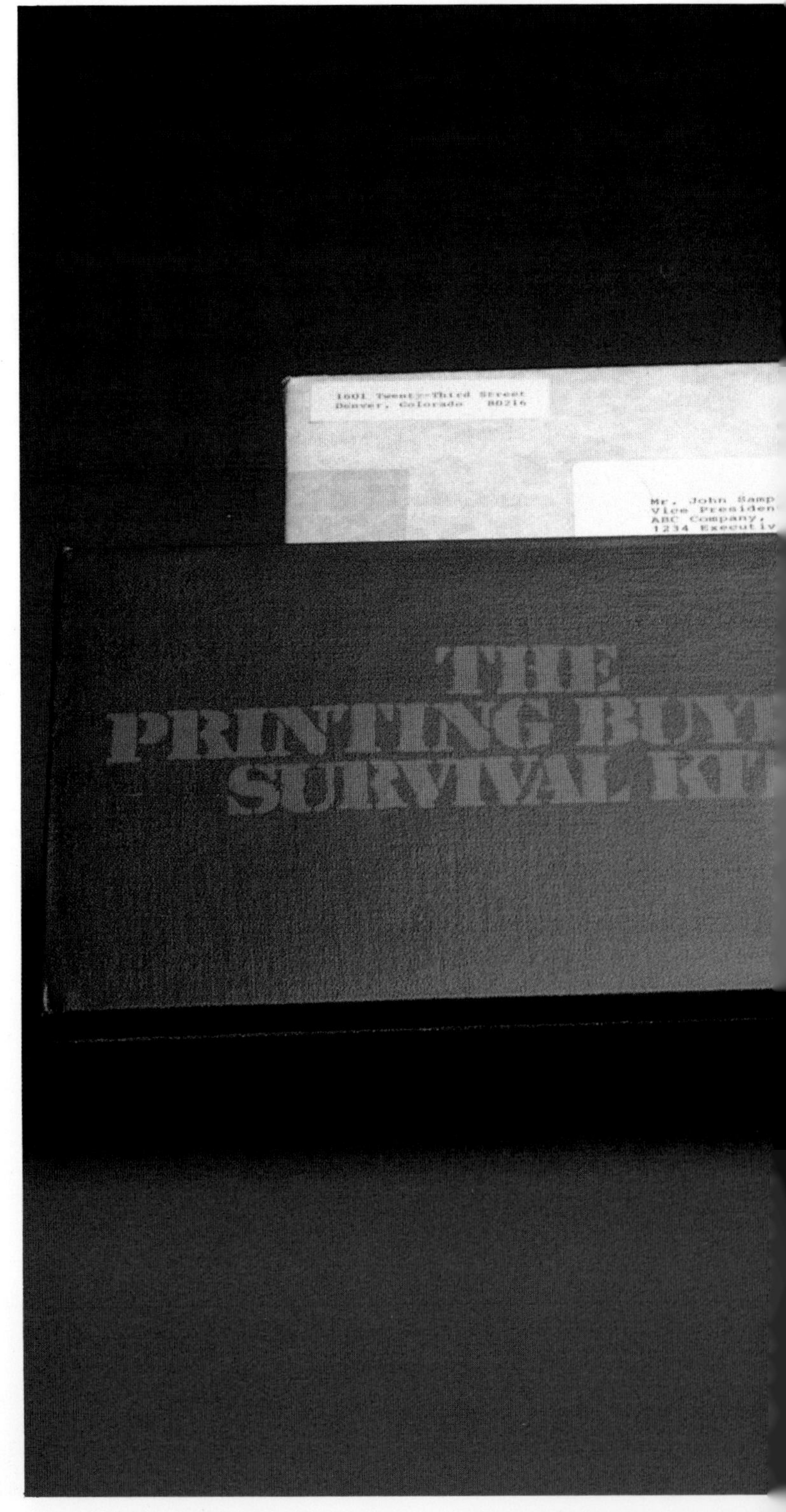
1601 Twenty-Third Street
Denver, Colorado 80216
Mr. John Samp
Vice Presiden
ABC Company,
1234 Executiv
THE
PRINTING BUY
SURVIVAL KI

Title:	"The Printing Buyer's Survival Kit"
Copywriter:	Chris Lawson
Art Director:	Dennis Machlica
Agency:	Karsh & Hagan Advertising
Client:	Hibbert West

Trail mix, a compass, Alka- Seltzer and a pocket-size booklet all aim to help printing buyers "find the right path around each potentially threatening situation" in this unique business mailing piece. The "kit" is contained in a sturdy box and shipped in a cardboard outer sleeve.

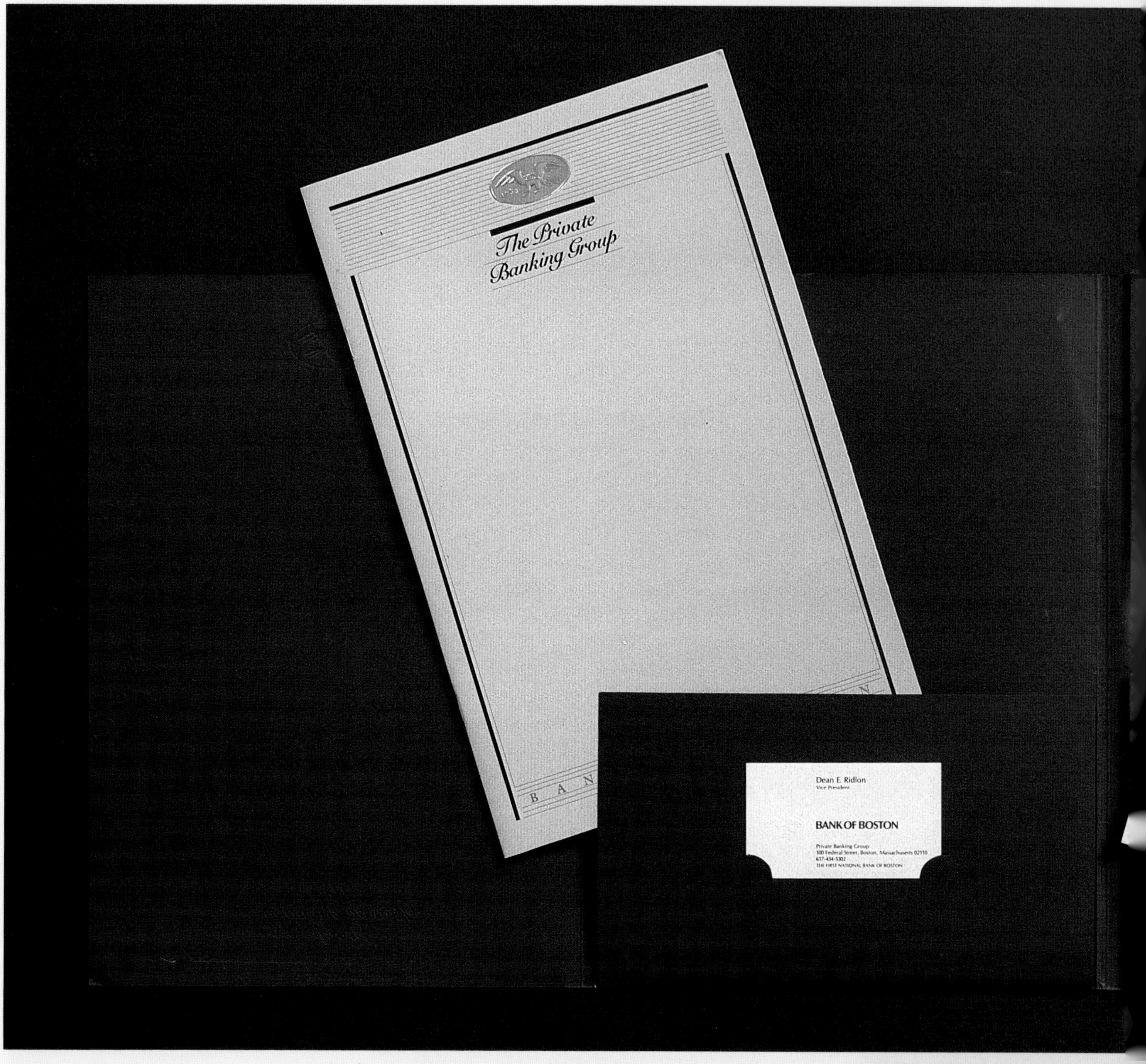

The Private Banking Group
Dean E. Ridlon
Vice President
BANK OF BOSTON
Private Banking Group
100 Federal Street, Boston, Massachusetts 02110
617-434-5302
THE FIRST NATIONAL BANK OF BOSTON

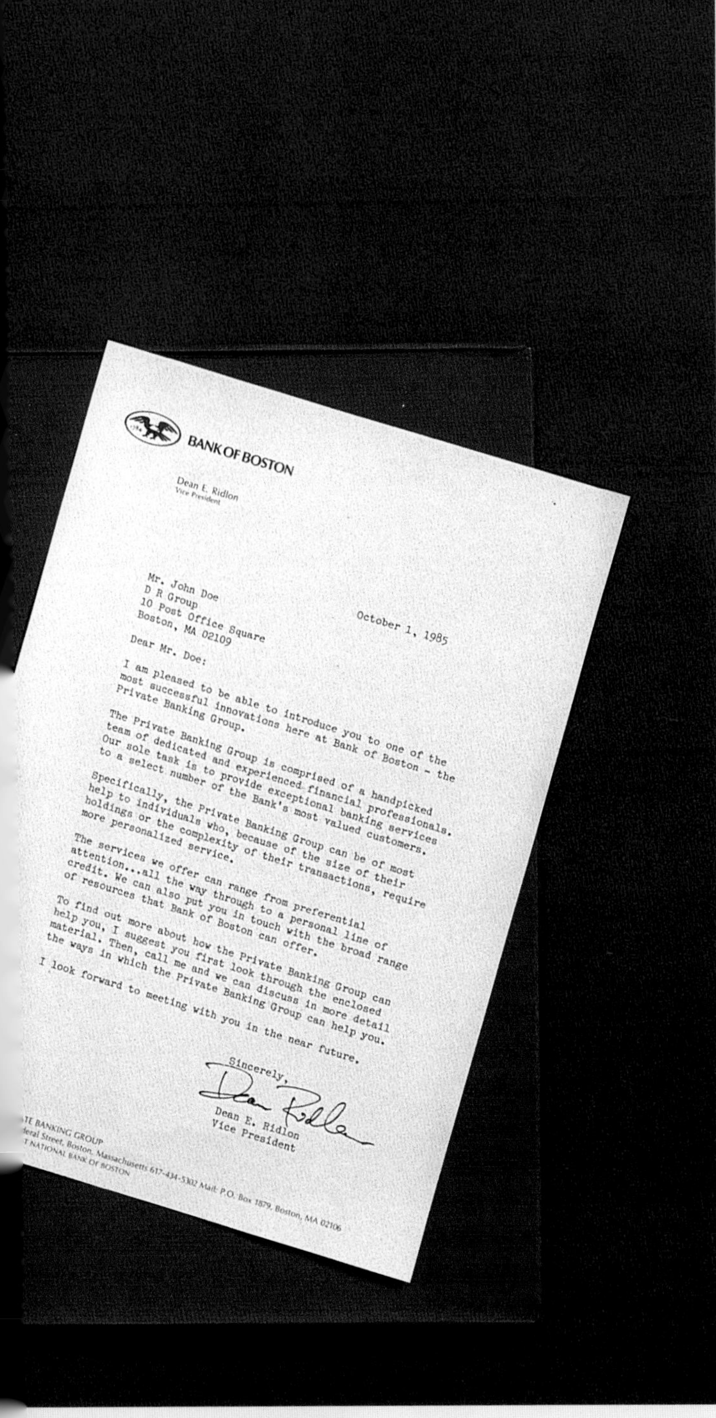

BANK OF BOSTON

Dean E. Ridlon
Vice President

October 1, 1985

Mr. John Doe
D R Group
10 Post Office Square
Boston, MA 02109

Dear Mr. Doe:

I am pleased to be able to introduce you to one of the most successful innovations here at Bank of Boston - the Private Banking Group.

The Private Banking Group is comprised of a handpicked team of dedicated and experienced financial professionals. Our sole task is to provide exceptional banking services to a select number of the Bank's most valued customers.

Specifically, the Private Banking Group can be of most help to individuals who, because of the size of their holdings or the complexity of their transactions, require more personalized service.

The services we offer can range from preferential attention...all the way through to a personal line of credit. We can also put you in touch with the broad range of resources that Bank of Boston can offer.

To find out more about how the Private Banking Group can help you, I suggest you first look through the enclosed material. Then, call me and we can discuss in more detail the ways in which the Private Banking Group can help you.

I look forward to meeting with you in the near future.

Sincerely,

Dean E. Ridlon
Vice President

…TE BANKING GROUP
…deral Street, Boston, Massachusetts 617-434-5302 Mail: P.O. Box 1879, Boston, MA 02106
…T NATIONAL BANK OF BOSTON

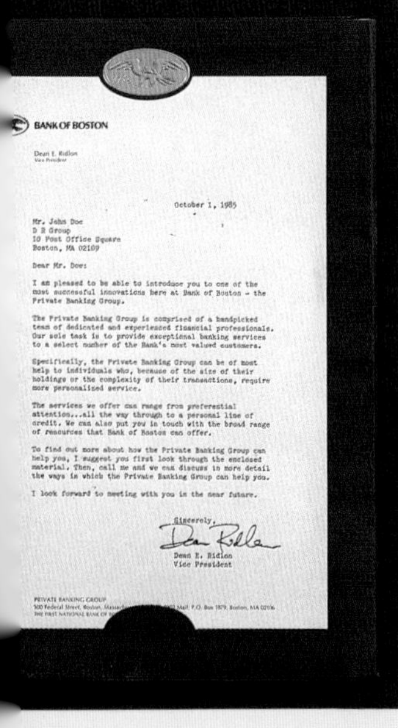

Title:	"The Private Banking Group"
Copywriter:	George T. Mercer
Art Director:	Russ Cevoli
Agency:	The DR Group
Client:	Bank of Boston

The most valued customers at a most prestigious banking institution are invited to receive exclusive personal financial services in this elegant, lavishly produced direct mail package—rendered even more valuable by the limited number of pieces produced.

A SINGLE SOURCE FOR A MULTITUDE OF FINANCIAL SERVICES.

Since no one knows the Bank's extensive resources better than your Private Banking Group officer, he or she is uniquely qualified to help you use all the resources of the Bank to build and manage your personal assets.

Your Private Banking Group officer is trained to be your liaison with the entire bank—both here and abroad—and you may very well find that he or she, once aware of your needs, can put you in touch with bank resources you were not aware existed.

Here are just a few of the areas you may wish to explore with your Private Banking Group officer:

Asset management advice. Your Private Banking Group officer can help you orchestrate your tax and investment plans. What's more, your Private Banking Group officer is always ready to work with your own outside specialists—stockbrokers, lawyers, and accountants—in developing a unified financial plan that will protect and increase your assets. Our own professionals also stand ready to be of help to you.

Investment Programs. Bank of Boston offers Keoghs, IRAs, IRA rollovers, and other tools for managing your assets more profitably including a unique Professional Retirement Account. Also, we can refer you to the Bank's new and extremely successful Special Investment Advisory Service.

Brokerage Services. Staffed by salaried professionals, this is a convenient and cost-conscious service you can depend on. Save up to 70% in fully-commissioned brokerage fees while you enjoy the convenience of dropping off securities at any one of the many Bank of Boston offices across the state—or, if you prefer, with your Private Banking Group officer.

Personal Trust & Financial Services Division. This department offers a wide range of personal trust and investment options from traditional trusts to growth-oriented investment programs. You can have your portfolio analyzed by our special computer system which utilizes charts and graphs to assess the status of your investments.

Precious metals, rare coins, fine art and other collectibles. The Group can help you handle the details involved in negotiating for and acquiring collectibles. We also work closely with such major firms as Sotheby's, should you need major works of art appraised or wish to purchase or sell fine artwork.

The Bank's Money Market Center trades in a wide range of commercial paper, treasuries, tax-exempt securities and certificates of deposit. As a member of the Group, you are entitled to two no-fee transactions per year.

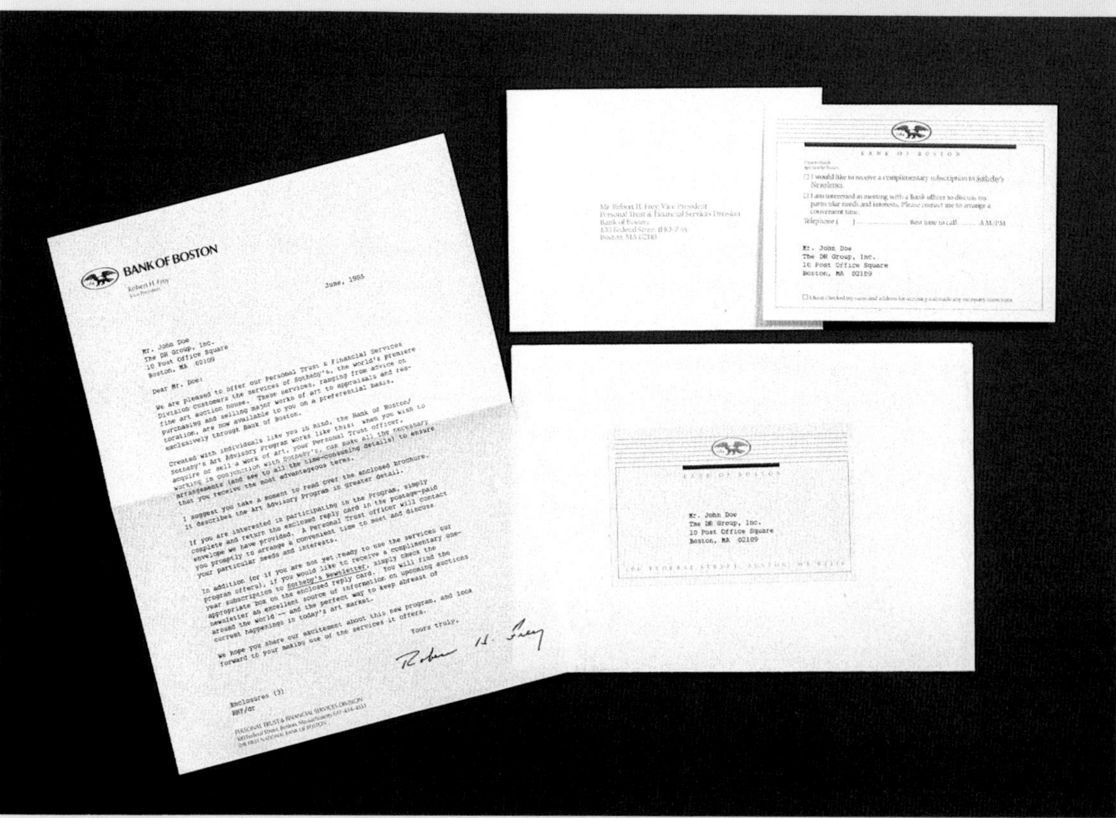

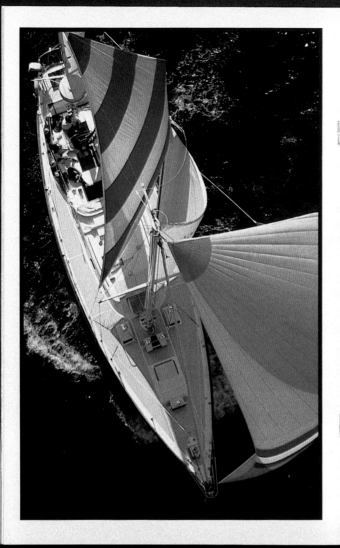

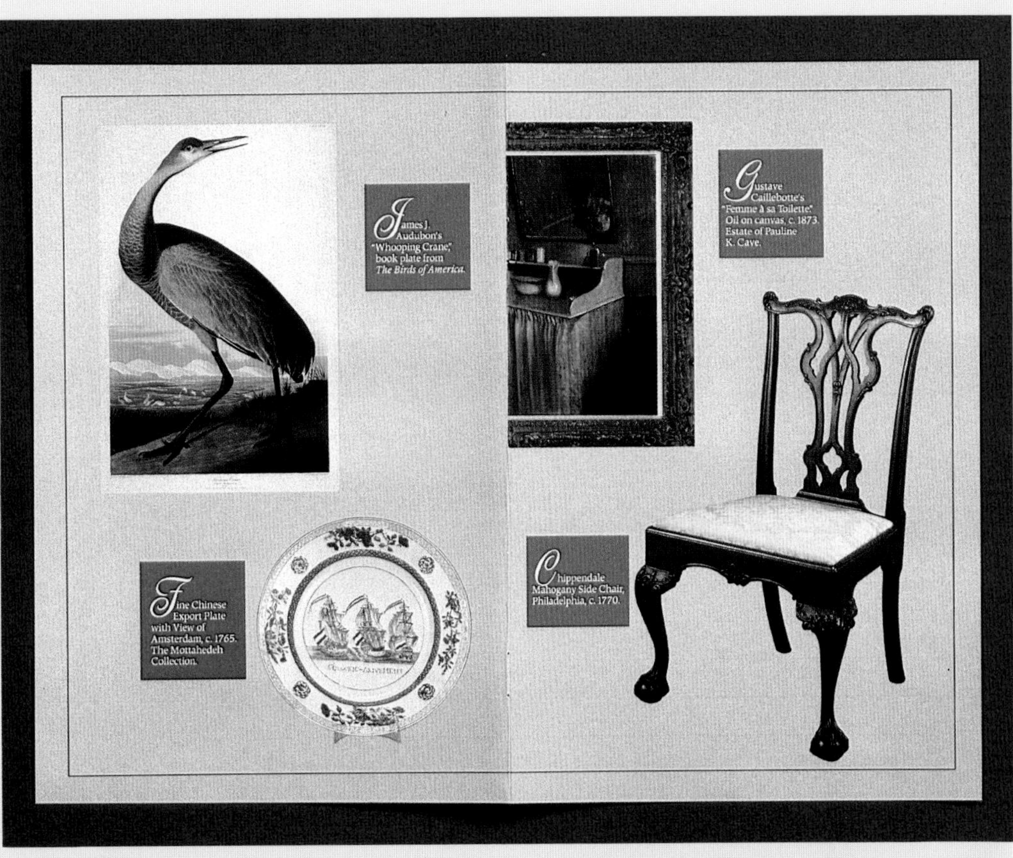

James J. Audubon's "Whooping Crane," book plate from The Birds of America.
Gustave Caillebotte's "Femme à sa Toilette." Oil on canvas, c. 1873. Estate of Pauline K. Cave.
Fine Chinese Export Plate with View of Amsterdam, c. 1765. The Mottahedeh Collection.
Chippendale Mahogany Side Chair, Philadelphia, c. 1770.

Advice and assistance on selling works of art.

If you would like to sell an item, Sotheby's is prepared to work with you to establish protective reserve prices and to devise a marketing plan tailored to your specific needs. Naturally, Sotheby's will strive to sell each item to your best advantage—at the best possible time, in the best possible location and at terms most preferential to you.

Once Sotheby's has inspected the item, you will be advised of its auction potential and the date and location of the next appropriate sale. If you decide to sell the property, Sotheby's can, in tandem with your Bank of Boston officer, make all the necessary arrangements, from shipping the property to the site of the sale to paying the net proceeds in accordance with your instructions. Sales by private treaty can also be arranged when appropriate and in keeping with your requirements.

Highly Important Emerald and Diamond Necklace. Mounted on platinum, set with 15 emeralds.

Additional services.

Appraisals.

Should you need an appraisal of an item, whether for inventory, charitable contributions, insurance or estate planning purposes, your Private Banking Group officer or Personal Trust officer will arrange for Sotheby's to review your existing collection, prepare a written inventory or appraisal and, if you so desire, make a color photograph or videotape record of each item. Because the appraisal is retained in Sotheby's computer, it can be easily updated whenever necessary.

Restoration and display services.

Through Bank of Boston, Sotheby's restoration craftsmen can advise you on costs for restoring antique furniture you own or are considering purchasing. Once you have made a decision to buy, Sotheby's can perform the restoration if you wish. In addition, you can receive advice on the display (including framing), storage, maintenance, care (including restoration and climate control), insurance, and security of your collections.

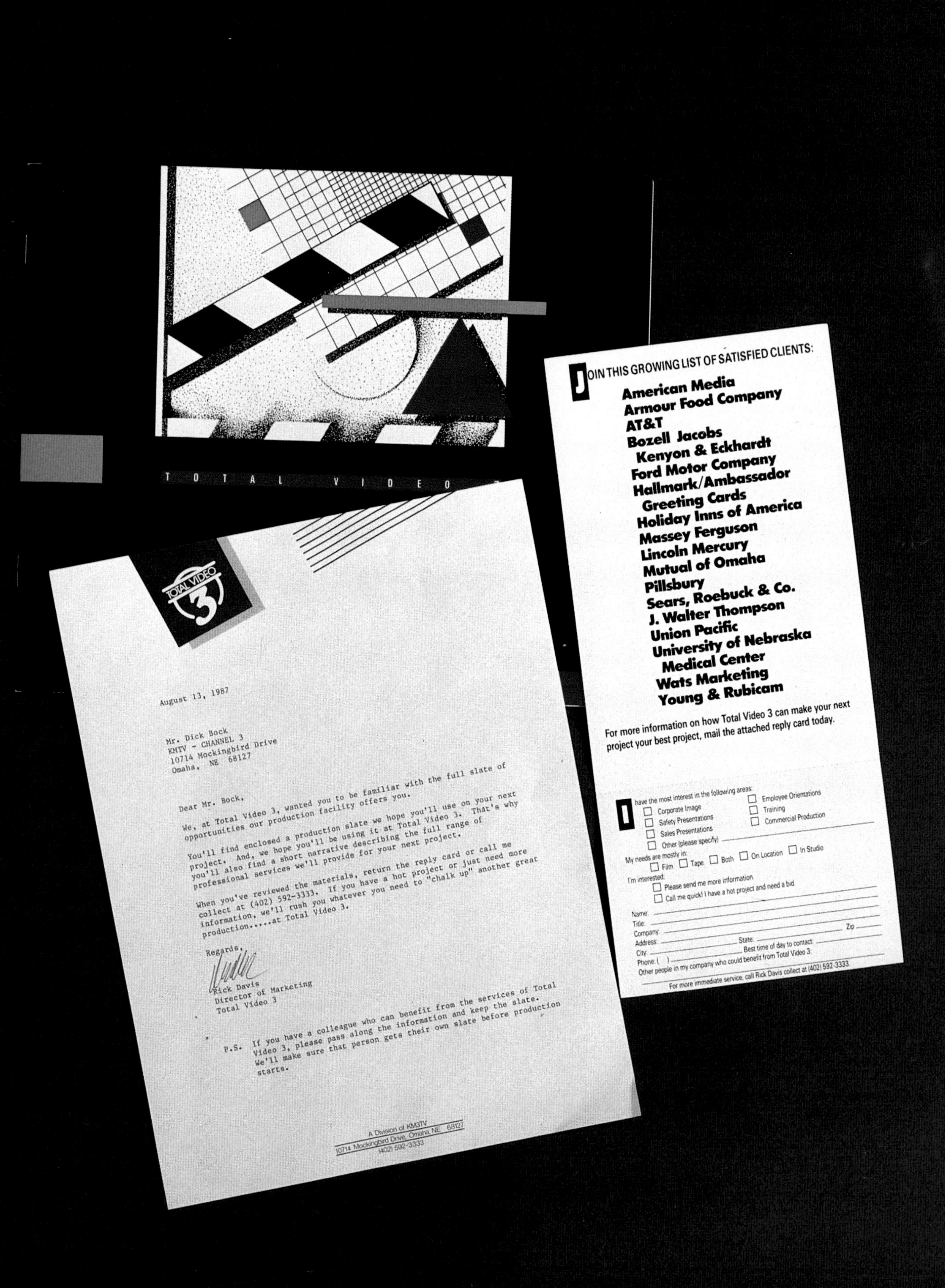

August 13, 1987

Mr. Dick Bock
KMTV - CHANNEL 3
10714 Mockingbird Drive
Omaha, NE 68127

Dear Mr. Bock,

We, at Total Video 3, wanted you to be familiar with the full slate of opportunities our production facility offers you.

You'll find enclosed a production slate we hope you'll use on your next project. And, we hope you'll be using it at Total Video 3. That's why you'll also find a short narrative describing the full range of professional services we'll provide for your next project.

When you've reviewed the materials, return the reply card or call me collect at (402) 592-3333. If you have a hot project or just need more information, we'll rush you whatever you need to "chalk up" another great production.....at Total Video 3.

Regards,

Rick Davis
Director of Marketing
Total Video 3

P.S. If you have a colleague who can benefit from the services of Total Video 3, please pass along the information and keep the slate. We'll make sure that person gets their own slate before production starts.

A Division of KM3TV
10714 Mockingbird Drive, Omaha, NE 68127
(402) 592-3333

JOIN THIS GROWING LIST OF SATISFIED CLIENTS:

American Media
Armour Food Company
AT&T
Bozell Jacobs
Kenyon & Eckhardt
Ford Motor Company
Hallmark/Ambassador
Greeting Cards
Holiday Inns of America
Massey Ferguson
Lincoln Mercury
Mutual of Omaha
Pillsbury
Sears, Roebuck & Co.
J. Walter Thompson
Union Pacific
University of Nebraska
Medical Center
Wats Marketing
Young & Rubicam

For more information on how Total Video 3 can make your next project your best project, mail the attached reply card today.

I have the most interest in the following areas:
☐ Corporate Image
☐ Safety Presentations
☐ Sales Presentations
☐ Other (please specify) ______
☐ Employee Orientations
☐ Training
☐ Commercial Production

My needs are mostly in:
☐ Film ☐ Tape ☐ Both ☐ On Location ☐ In Studio

I'm interested:
☐ Please send me more information.
☐ Call me quick! I have a hot project and need a bid.

Name: ______
Title: ______
Company: ______
Address: ______ Zip ______
City: ______ State: ______
Phone: ( ) ______ Best time of day to contact: ______
Other people in my company who could benefit from Total Video 3: ______

For more immediate service, call Rick Davis collect at (402) 592-3333.

Title:	"Total Video 3"
Copywriter:	Chris Carithers
Art Director:	Tim McDonald
Agency:	Culver & Associates
Client:	Total Video 3/KM3TV

Bringing a familiar sound-stage item—an authentic Hollywood "take" slate—into the prospective video client's office is accomplished with style in this effective three-dimensional business mailing.

L O C A T I O N

We can shoot anywhere. And we have. From the confined perspective inside a refrigerated box car to the scenic views shot by a camera man suspended from the Sears Tower, we've been there. We also have experience with the less extraordinary. We'll give you top quality work in any location. From manufacturing plants to the Board Room, we'll shoot it right. And we'll work around your schedule — day or night. That's how we've satisfied clients in Washington D.C., St. Louis, Dallas, Minneapolis, Kansas City, Denver, Chicago . . . and points in between.

STUDIO & SOUND STAGE

You're welcome at our place anytime. For any project. You can utilize our studio for everything from a dynamic table top of a ballbearing to dramatic studio scenes of a fleet of cars. You can take advantage of our 60′ x 75′ sound stage complete with 60′ CYC. Or if you need, you can take advantage of our kitchen. It's fully dressed for shooting or for just cooking that gourmet meal. You need a set? It will be ready. You need props? They'll be there. As with any of our projects, complete pre-production planning will have everything you need, ready when you need it. So you won't be waiting . . . you'll be shooting.

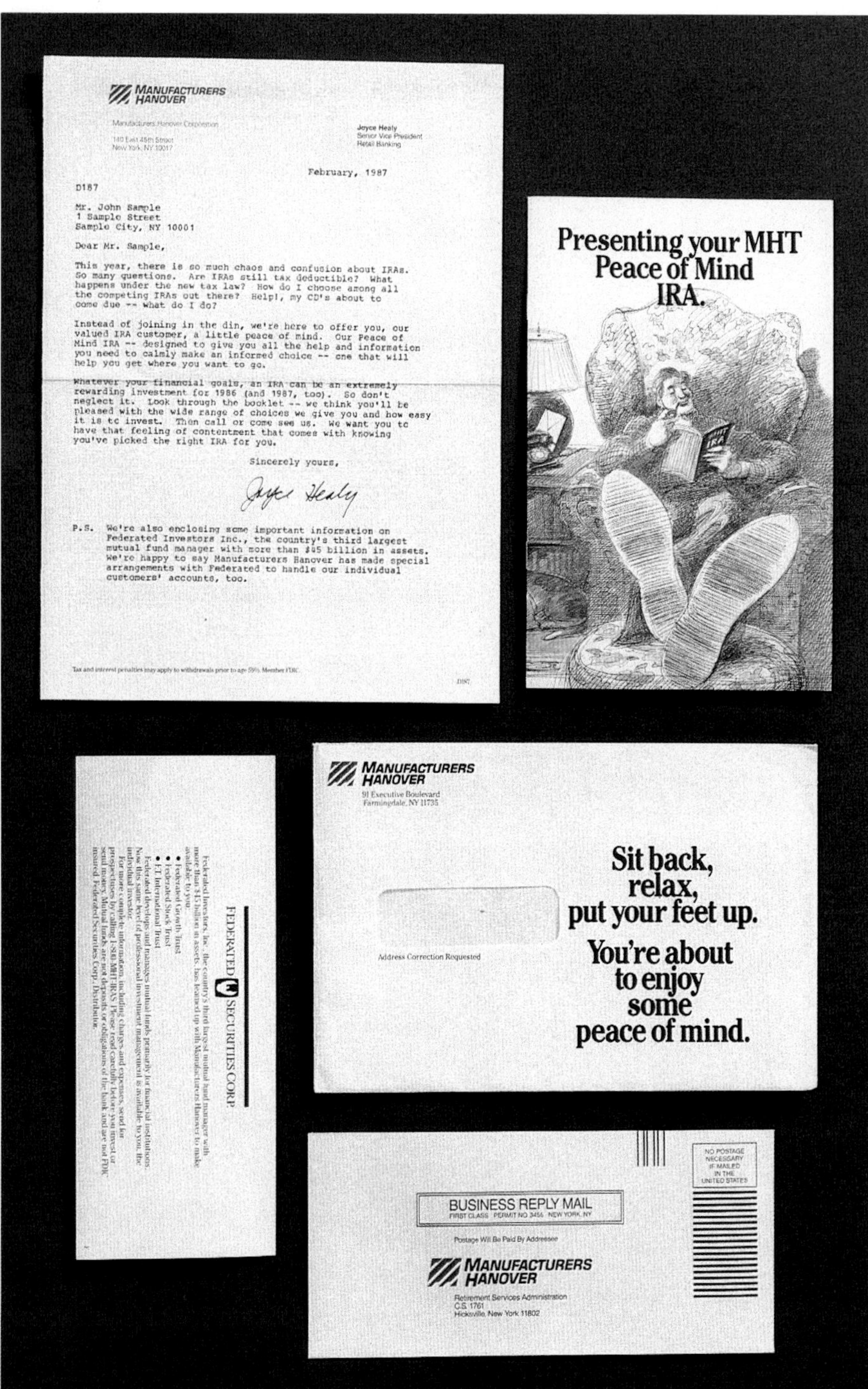

MANUFACTURERS HANOVER

Manufacturers Hanover Corporation
140 East 45th Street
New York, NY 10017

Joyce Healy
Senior Vice President
Retail Banking

February, 1987

D187

Mr. John Sample
1 Sample Street
Sample City, NY 10001

Dear Mr. Sample,

This year, there is so much chaos and confusion about IRAs. So many questions. Are IRAs still tax deductible? What happens under the new tax law? How do I choose among all the competing IRAs out there? Help!, my CD's about to come due -- what do I do?

Instead of joining in the din, we're here to offer you, our valued IRA customer, a little peace of mind. Our Peace of Mind IRA -- designed to give you all the help and information you need to calmly make an informed choice -- one that will help you get where you want to go.

Whatever your financial goals, an IRA can be an extremely rewarding investment for 1986 (and 1987, too). So don't neglect it. Look through the booklet -- we think you'll be pleased with the wide range of choices we give you and how easy it is to invest. Then call or come see us. We want you to have that feeling of contentment that comes with knowing you've picked the right IRA for you.

Sincerely yours,

Joyce Healy

P.S. We're also enclosing some important information on Federated Investors Inc., the country's third largest mutual fund manager with more than $45 billion in assets. We're happy to say Manufacturers Hanover has made special arrangements with Federated to handle our individual customers' accounts, too.

Tax and interest penalties may apply to withdrawals prior to age 59½. Member FDIC.

D187

Title: "Peace of Mind"
Copywriter: Mary Ann Donovan
Art Director: Jane Walsh
Agency: Wunderman Worldwide
Client: Manufacturers Hanover Trust

With concern rising over the effect of the new tax laws on Individual Retirement Accounts, Manufacturers Hanover launched a campaign to put current and prospective customers at ease and help clear up some of the confusion. Print advertising and radio commercials supported the direct mail pictured here.

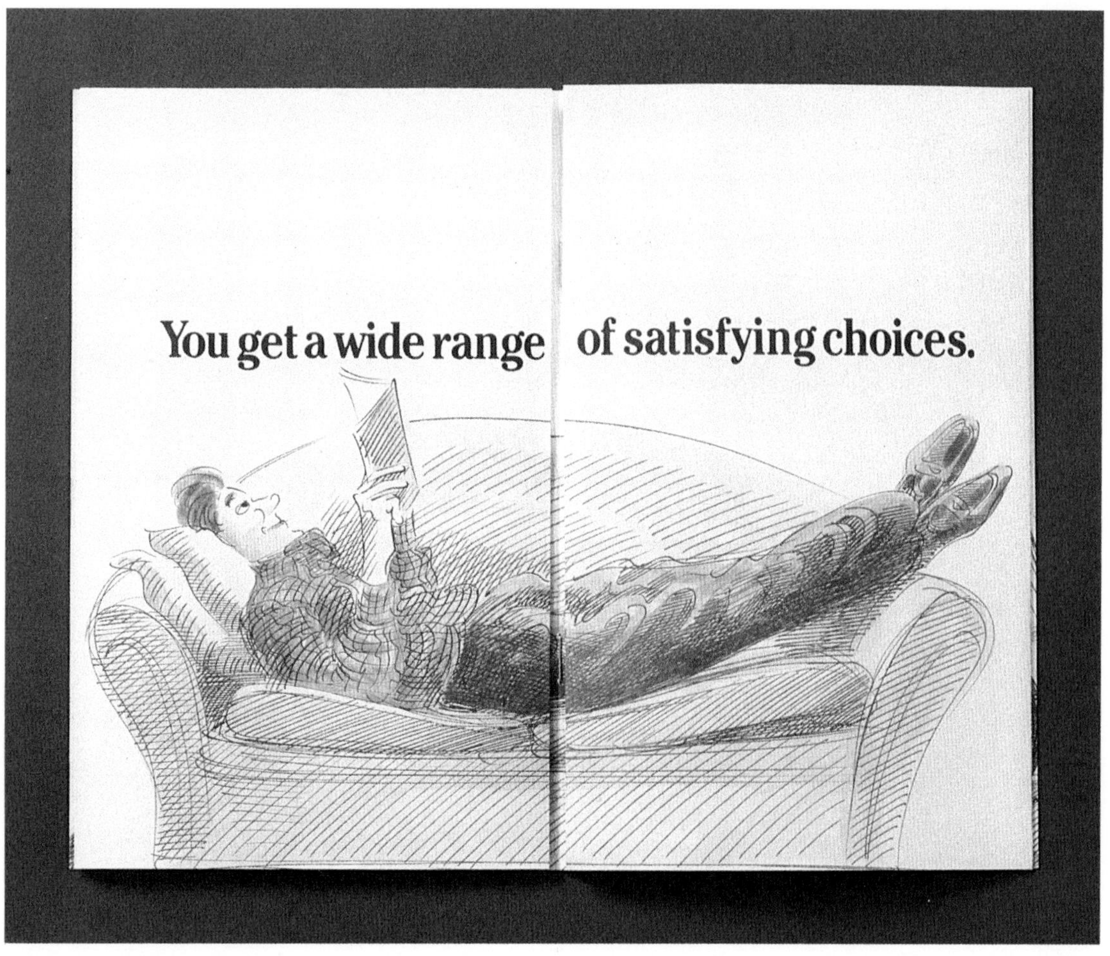
You get a wide range of satisfying choices.

s and Bonds
A is an easy way to buy ownership in companies you admire,
n most commissions, as compared to a full service broker.
pen an IRA Money Management Account. Then, you establish
rokerage account. We'll show you how. From then on, all
do is call in your order. Funds to cover it are automatically
rom your IRA Money Management Account. As you are
ly aware, investing in stocks and bonds involves some risk
ncipal can go up or down based on market conditions. But
lo give sophisticated investors a chance for a high return.
Deposit Accounts
Deposit Accounts offer you more guaranteed and worry-free
n ever before. For steady income at retirement, you can lock
te for 91 days, 5 years or just about any time in between.
ed*. For conservative investors, these accounts involve the
ou can start with as little as $500.
Zero Coupon Treasuries
Called STRIPS and CATS™**, these obligations are backed by the full faith of the government. Innovative securities, they can help you lock in a high yield for a long term if you hold them until maturity. You can even use CATS™ or STRIPS to build up a specific dollar amount for each year of your retirement. Our bond specialists will help you choose these investments.
Mutual Funds
MHT gives you direct access to a wide variety of diversified mutual funds through two of America's largest mutual fund companies: Dreyfus Corporation and Federated Investors, Inc. The funds that are available are no-load, which means there is no sales commission when you buy and sell. And you don't have to wrestle with picking securities. Professional money managers do the job for you. Your principal can go up or down in value, but mutual funds help you reduce stock market risk by spreading your money over a variety of securities.
Money Management Account
This FDIC insured* account provides you with money market interest at current rates. You automatically get a Money Management Account when you decide to invest in stocks, bonds, mutual funds or Zero Coupon Treasuries. So before you buy and after you sell securities, your money always works hard earning interest for you. All dividends and earnings are paid directly into this account.
Call toll free 1-800-MHT-IRAS.
*Your total IRA balances in Time Deposit Accounts, Money Management Accounts and Savings Accounts are separately insured up to $100,000 from other accounts you may have at MHT.
**CATS is a trademark of Salomon Brothers Inc.

Xxxxx
Mr. Sample A. Sample
1234 Anyplace
Anytown, U.S. 12345

Fly Free to London on British Airways—D

Title:	"British Airways/Member-Get- Members"
Copywriter:	Larilee Frazier
Art Director:	Michael Rosenbaum
Agency:	Ogilvy & Mather Direct
Client:	American Express Travel Related Services

What an offer! Find three people who can be approved as new American Express Cardmembers and get a free round-trip flight to London! This two-color package somehow makes such a goal quite within reach...but also warmly provides the promise of a "Be Our Guest" dinner certificate if only one or two new members are successfully referred.

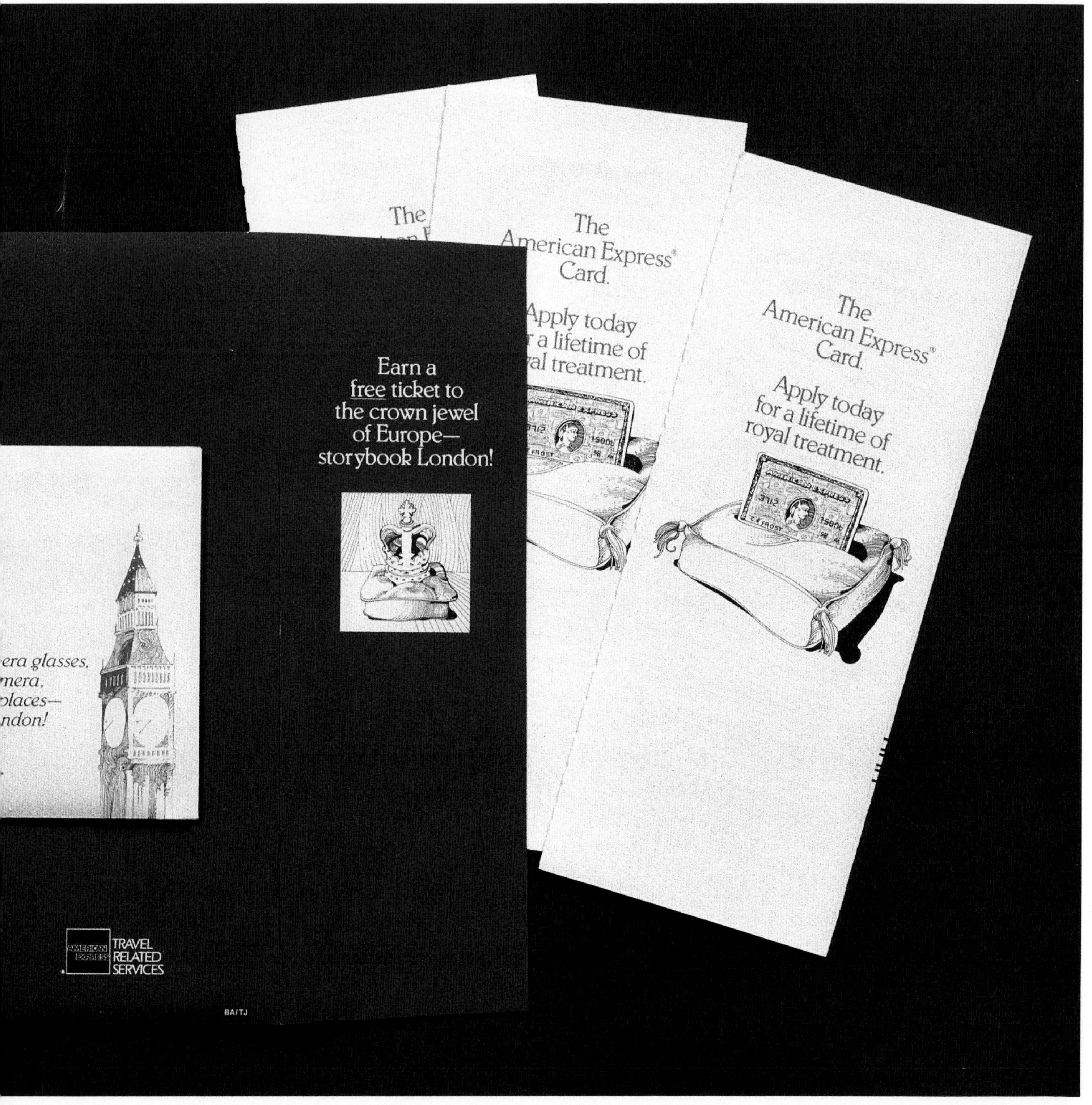

Something big is about to happen to the small screen...

POSTAGE PAID R PHQ 461

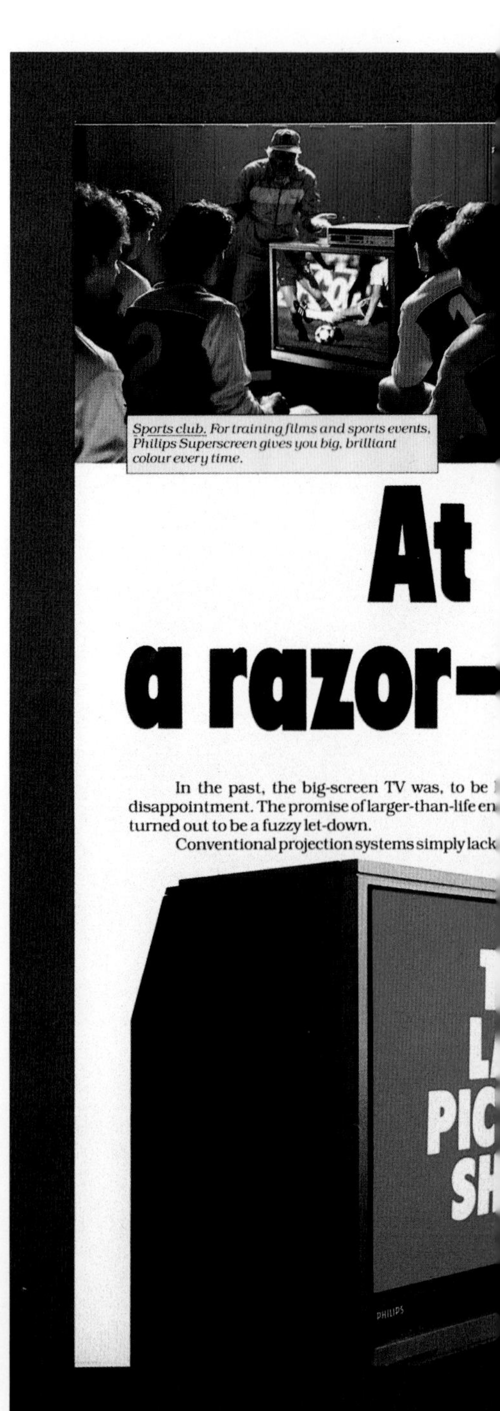

Sports club. For training films and sports events, Philips Superscreen gives you big, brilliant colour every time.
At
a razor-
In the past, the big-screen TV was, to be
disappointment. The promise of larger-than-life
turned out to be a fuzzy let-down.
Conventional projection systems simply
PHILIPS

Title: "Something Big"
Copywriter: Christian Digby-Firth
Art Director: Chris Jones
Agency: Ogilvy & Mather Direct
Client: Philips Electronics Limited

The dimensions of the huge outer envelope in this unusual consumer mailing are 19 7/8″ x 14 1/4″, and the four-color brochure inside unfolds to depict the actual size of a 37″ television screen. Everything else about the package is superjumbo, too, to create excitement about Philips' big new TV.

Hotel/Social clubs. Philips Superscreen gives you cinema-type viewing yet takes up no more space than a 26" stereo TV set.
Conference centres/educational institutions. Learning is a lot easier when the audience can clearly see what's being taught.
Trade fairs. When you're selling your product or service, Superscreen is an invaluable demonstration aid.

,a big screen that gives rp picture everyone can enjoy

to produce a large, clear, bright picture – mainly because ould not handle the high temperatures involved.

Now, Superscreen's e Liquid Optical Tube-Coupling uses liquid g to solve this problem.

The result is a uch sharper, higher-contrast picture than ou may have thought possible.

You'll certainly notice the difference nstantly. Indeed, the effect is astonishing. uperscreen gives you a brilliant, rich picture ith exceptional definition, covering the entire screen. dramatic improvement over its predecessors.

And Superscreen works just as well in daylight as a darkened room (again, unlike the old fashioned big-reen TV).

Here's another advantage. Our new "Black Stripe" screen produces an exceptionally wide horizontal viewing angle so you won't have to sit right in front of the screen to appreciate its quality.

And the vertical viewing angle is perfectly adjusted for armchair viewing.

If you have to entertain people...or nform them...or educate them...or just simply keep them amused...you'll realise the value of Superscreen. Imagine how much more interesting a sports event will be when it appears on the big screen. As a viewer, you'll feel a lot closer to the action.

Furthermore, the impact of big production movies won't be lost on a 37" TV either.

And if you have to show training films at conference centres or schools, everyone will have a clear view of what's being taught – when you show it on Philips Superscreen.

BIG PICTURE...SMALL SPACE

For a 37" TV, Superscreen takes up a remarkably small amount of space. Its 104cm x 52cm base area is no larger than a normal 26" stereo TV set. It's neat, too. The main tuning and adjustment controls are tucked away in a concealed drawer at the front of the set. And for normal operation (TV reception, teletext, sound, VCR), you can use your infra-red remote control unit.

To see the amazing new Philips Superscreen for yourself, send back the reply portion of your Special Preview ticket enclosed. We'll be glad to arrange a convenient time and place.

And be sure to take your Special Preview ticket with you, as you'll be entitled to a FREE Philips E180 Video Tape as a 'Thank you' for coming to see Philips Superscreen.

Remote control. You can control TV reception, teletext, sound and VCR functions from a convenient distance with this sleek remote keypad.

ontrols drawer. ain tuning and djustment contols are hidden a concealed awer at the ont of the uperscreen set.

Best seats in the house. Vertical viewing angle adjusts for perfect viewing, no matter where you sit.

PHILIPS

Now open up to see just how big it really is...

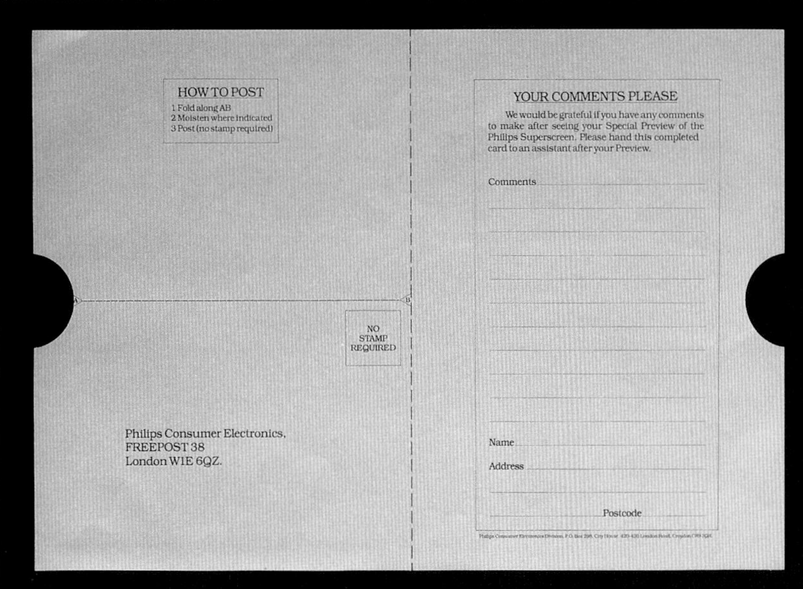

HOW TO POST

1 Fold along AB
2 Moisten where indicated
3 Post (no stamp required)

NO
STAMP
REQUIRED

Philips Consumer Electronics,
FREEPOST 38
London W1E 6QZ.

YOUR COMMENTS PLEASE

We would be grateful if you have any comments to make after seeing your Special Preview of the Philips Superscreen. Please hand this completed card to an assistant after your Preview.

Comments ....

Name ....

Address ....

Postcode ....

PHILIPS

VIDEO-SUPERSCREEN 37

Big, isn't it?

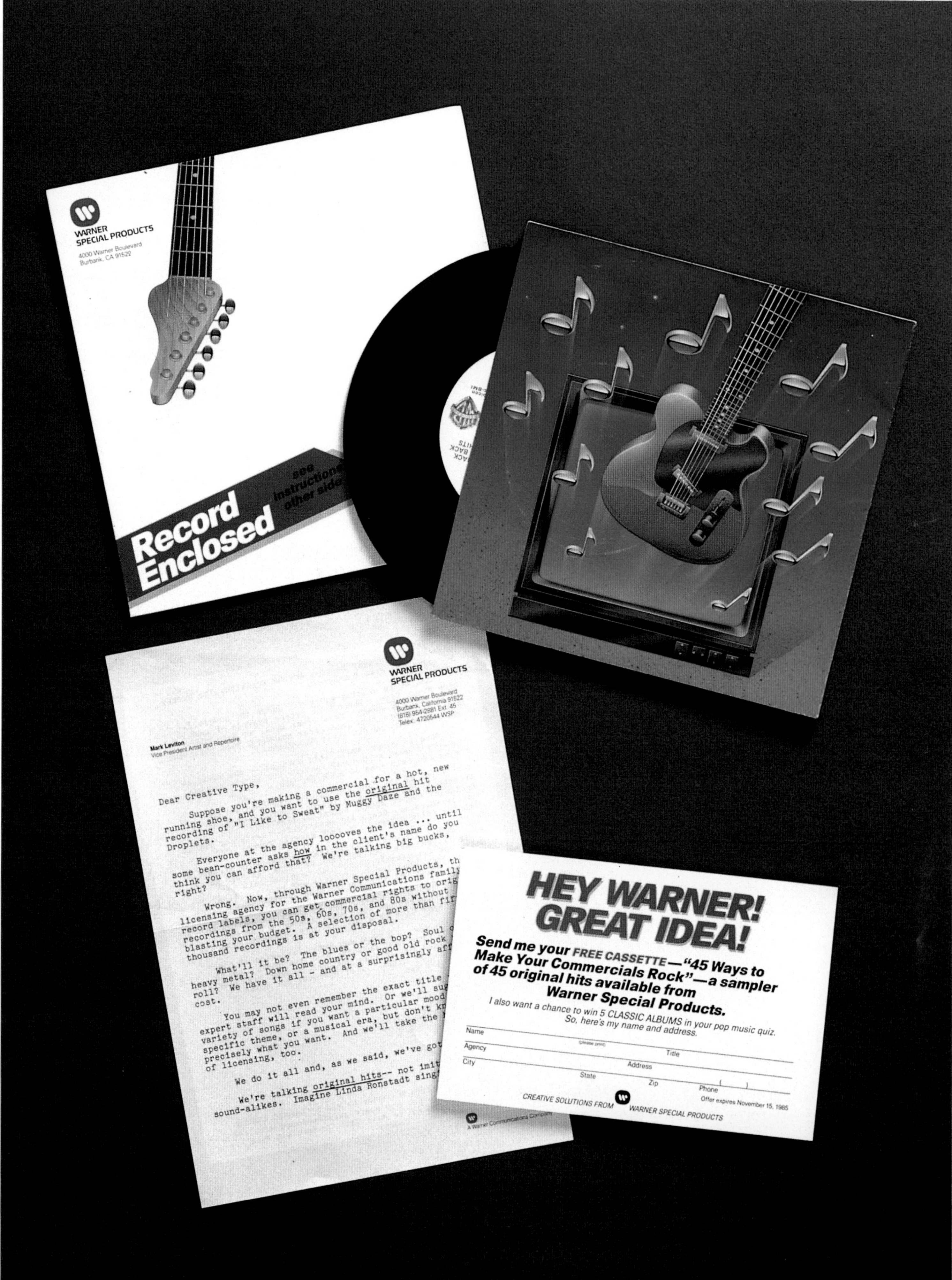
WARNER SPECIAL PRODUCTS
4000 Warner Boulevard
Burbank, CA 91522
Record Enclosed
see instructions other side
WARNER SPECIAL PRODUCTS
4000 Warner Boulevard
Burbank, California 91522
(818) 954-2881 Ext. 45
Telex: 4720544 WSP
Mark Leviton
Vice President Artist and Repertoire
Dear Creative Type,
Suppose you're making a commercial for a hot, new running shoe, and you want to use the original hit recording of "I Like to Sweat" by Muggy Daze and the Droplets.
Everyone at the agency looooves the idea ... until some bean-counter asks how in the client's name do you think you can afford that? We're talking big bucks, right?
Wrong. Now, through Warner Special Products, th licensing agency for the Warner Communications famil record labels, you can get commercial rights to orig recordings from the 50s, 60s, 70s, and 80s without blasting your budget. A selection of more than fi thousand recordings is at your disposal.
What'll it be? The blues or the bop? Soul heavy metal? Down home country or good old rock roll? We have it all - and at a surprisingly af cost.
You may not even remember the exact title expert staff will read your mind. Or we'll su variety of songs if you want a particular mood specific theme, or a musical era, but don't k precisely what you want. And we'll take the of licensing, too.
We do it all and, as we said, we've go
We're talking original hits-- not imit sound-alikes. Imagine Linda Ronstadt sing
A Warner Communications Company
HEY WARNER! GREAT IDEA!
Send me your FREE CASSETTE—"45 Ways to Make Your Commercials Rock"—a sampler of 45 original hits available from Warner Special Products.
I also want a chance to win 5 CLASSIC ALBUMS in your pop music quiz.
So, here's my name and address.
Name
Agency
Title
City
Address
State
Zip
Phone
CREATIVE SOLUTIONS FROM WARNER SPECIAL PRODUCTS
Offer expires November 15, 1985

Title: "How To Make A Commercial Rock"
Copywriters: Dan Von der Embse, Dolores Banerd
Art Director: D. Villefort-Sima
Agency: Rapp & Collins/West
Client: Warner Special Products, Inc.

A 45-RPM single record offers a sampling of rock 'n' roll music available for commercial licensing in this business-to-business effort that sets the tone, cuts the groove and paves the way for a response.

Title: "Traveler"
Copywriter: James V. Bullard
Art Director: Pamela F. Miller
Agency: In- House
Client: National Geographic Society

A single sheet of lightweight, coated card stock is the medium that carries this self-mailer's subscription offer for a new travel publication. A poly sleeve affixed to the front holds the personalized order card, which the respondent can simply pull out, sign, and drop into the mail.

A LITTLE GOSSIP

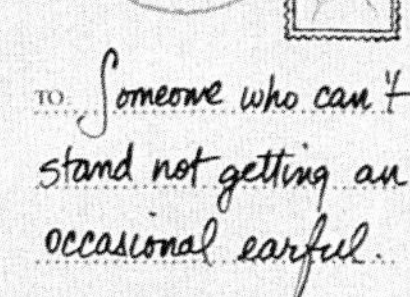

When I'm feeling deliciously wicked, I read Vanities. VF's monthly sampling of total irreverence, delivered with a dose of fun. For tidbits, potshots, and blows below pompous belts, all is Vanities, and nothing is fair.

Adieu.

October's Vanities. Illustration by Ken Maryanski.

TO: Someone who can't stand not getting an occasional earful.

A LITTLE SATIRE

Sometimes I think satire's the truest art form. And here's where I get my fill. Read a wonderful "interview" with Fidel Castro recently. And discovered five hilarious new possibilities for vice president.

Snicker, Snicker

Olympic Dames. Photograph by Bill King.

TO: An aficionado of the tongue-in-cheek.

A LITTLE ROMANCE

Did you hear the latest about Keith Richards and Patti Hansen? Jessica Lange and Sam Shepard? Dorothy Stratten and Peter Bogdanovich? Alfred and Betsy and Vicki?

I did.

Jessica Lange and Sam Shepard. Photograph by Bruce Weber.

TO: The hopeless romantic

A LITTLE STYLE

I thought nobody could show me anything new and exciting in fashion ... until I saw Vanity Fair. Only it could take sequined gowns and pair them with bathing caps! Put Raquel in swim suits and furs. (She looked fabulous, of course.) And did something I love... men's clothes on women.

Got to go... shopping.

Clothing by Emanuel Ungaro. Jewelry by Butler & Wilson. Photograph by Snowdon.

TO: The fashion fanatic

A LITTLE CULTURE

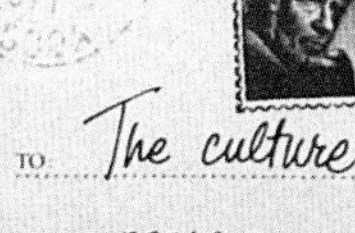

In one issue alone, I read Mailer, Cheever, and a scene from Wendy Wasserstein's hit play. Saw three marvelous works by outrageous artist Eric Fischl, too. And a portfolio of Barbara Norfleet's photos. If that isn't a good, healthy dose of culture, what is?

Sayonara.

Norman Mailer. Photograph by Irving Penn.

TO: The culture maven

A LITTLE FUN

Who is Whoopi Goldberg, and what is she doing in Vanity Fair? Well, if you read VF you'd know—she's only the new Lenny Bruce. And you could have discovered the likes of Pee Wee Herman, Ann Magnuson, Steven Wright, and Gilbert Gottfried, the newest New Wave of very, very funny people.

Still laughing

Lily Tomlin. Illustration by Robert Risko.

TO: The last of the real laugh lovers.

To get *Vanity Fair* for yourself, see the enclosed order card for details.

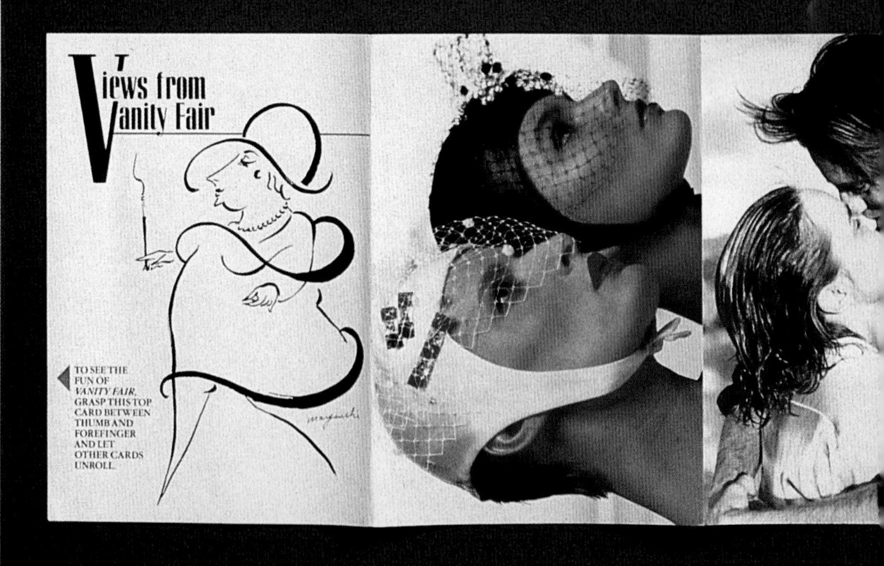

Views from Vanity Fair
TO SEE THE FUN OF VANITY FAIR, GRASP THIS TOP CARD BETWEEN THUMB AND FOREFINGER AND LET OTHER CARDS UNROLL.

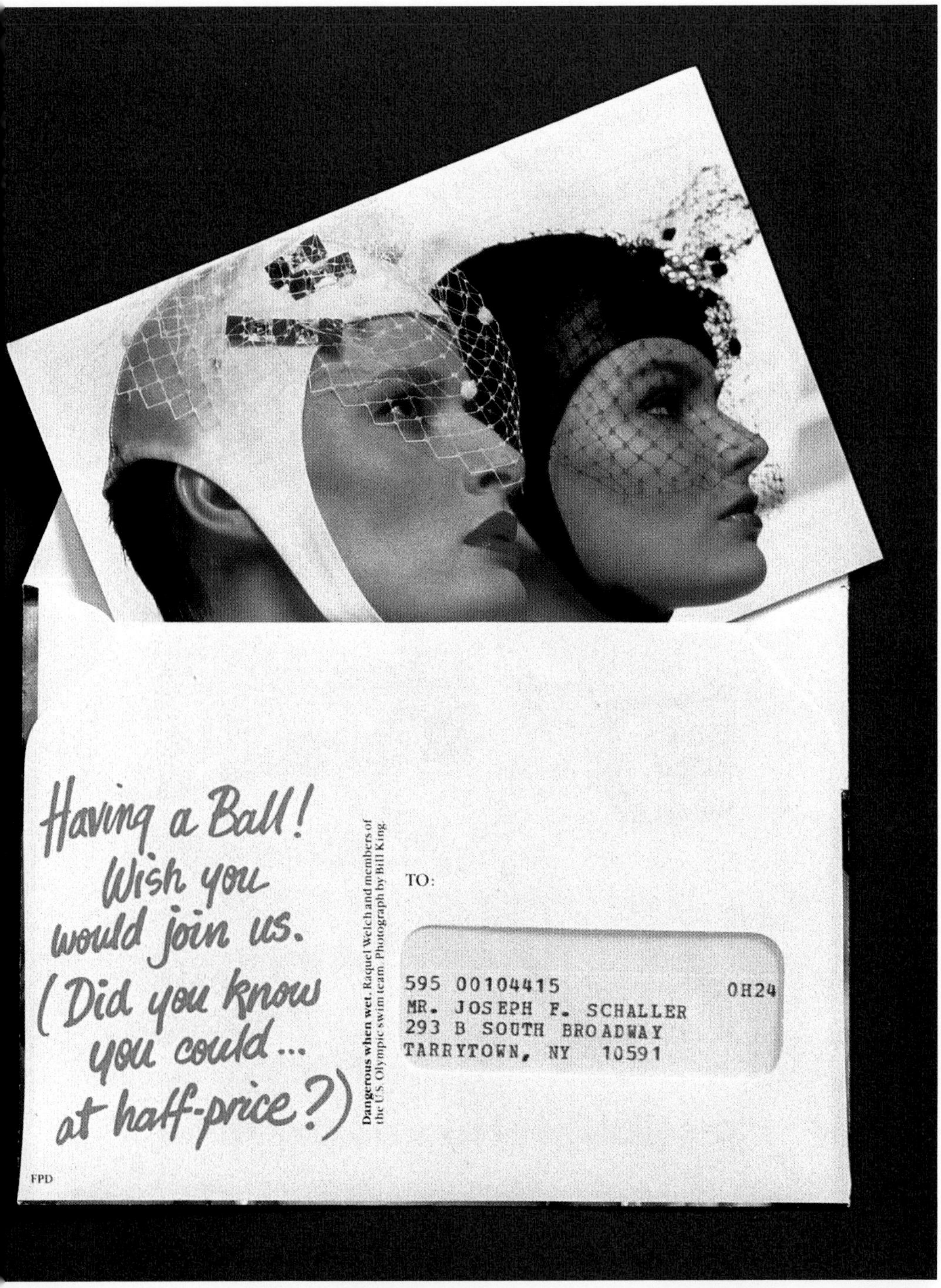

Title: "Having a Ball"
Copywriter: Gina Bruce
Art Director: Jim Pastena
Agency: Rapp & Collins
Client: The Conde Nast Publications, Inc.

This compact, four-color Vanity Fair subscription solicitation package features a six-panel foldout brochure that, in postcard form, highlights the contents of the magazine.

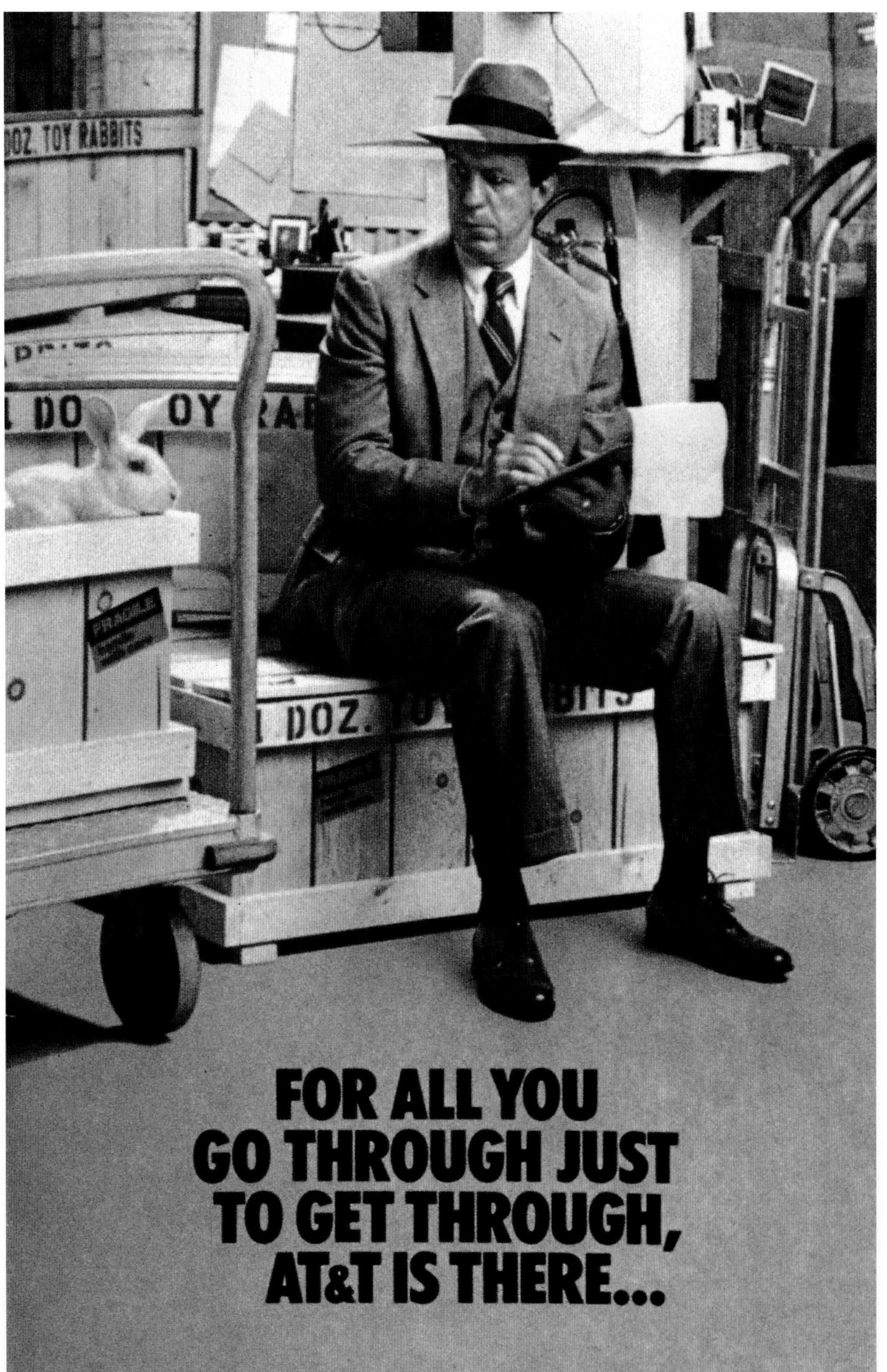
DOZ. TOY RABBITS
FOR ALL YOU
GO THROUGH JUST
TO GET THROUGH,
AT&T IS THERE...

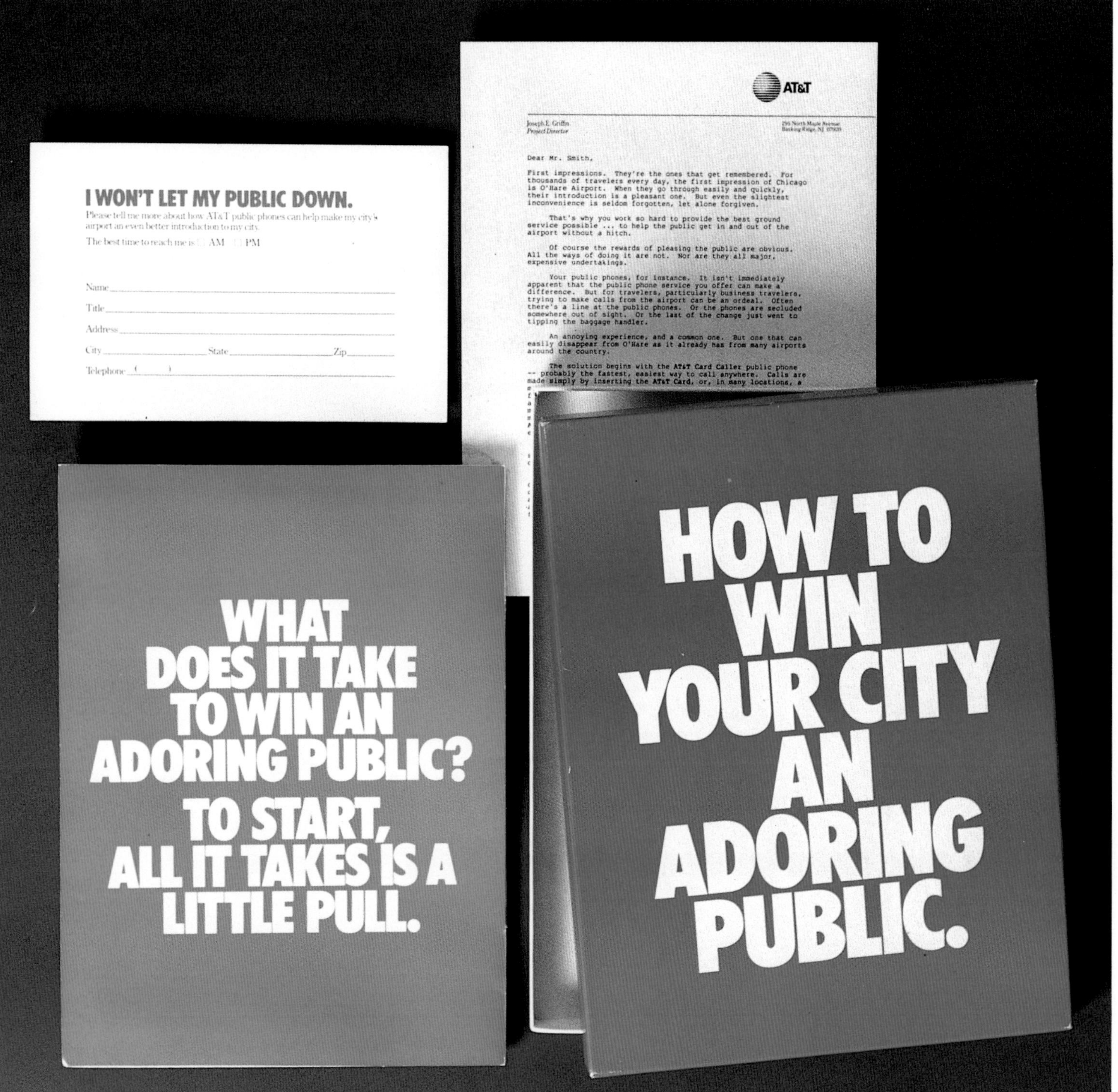

Title:	"Sales Professional Package"
Copywriters:	Betsy Sloan Thomas, Larri-lee Frazier
Art Directors:	Judi Kolstad, Bob Cesiro
Agency:	Ogilvy & Mather Direct
Client:	AT&T Public Communications

Millions of telephone calls per year are made from airports, and this elaborate business-to-business direct mail package speaks to airport managers of the advantages of installing AT&T public phones in their terminals. The involving booklet features eight die-cut windows and a pull-out tab that changes travelers' expressions from frustrated to satisfied.

THE AT&T LONG DISTANCE NETWORK OFFERS YOU SEVERAL WAYS TO BILL YOUR CALLS.

Need to call your boss in a hurry but haven't any coins? Don't worry. AT&T's network offers you a variety of billing options. So you can make all your long distance calls without having to carry a lot of change in your pocket.

For fast, convenient, coinless calling, use your **AT&T Card** or **AT&T Card** number. Simply punch in your billing number and your calls will be automatically charged to your account. Plus, they'll be grouped together on your bill so you can easily identify all your long distance business calls.

With the **AT&T Card**, calling long distance is not only easy. It's also less expensive than most AT&T coin calls, collect or other operator-assisted calls. And you can get an **AT&T Card** free. Just phone 1 800 CALL ATT, Ext. 17, or mail in the enclosed order form, and we'll send one out to you.

In addition, AT&T's network also gives you the option of placing your calls collect or billing them to a third number.

"Hi, boss? Yeah, I picked up the new merchandise. But listen, I think there's been a little misunderstanding here..."
1 DOZ. TOY RABBITS
1 DOZ. TOY RABBITS
1 DOZ. TO

PULL

MAKE TRAVELI
THROUGH YOUR AI
EASIER FOR TH
PUBLIC TO FAC
YOU CAN DO IT
WITH SOME PRACT
HELP FROM AT

PULL

Every day, millions of people fly to American cities like yours. They trudge through airports. Wait for baggage. Line up for taxis. And in doing so form their first impression of the cities they visit.

The smoother the trip through the airport, the better the impression. Which is why you devote so much time and energy to providing top-of-the-line ground service—a good first impression can bring lasting benefits to your city.

THERE'S SOMETHING IN THE AIR...ARE YOU ON TO IT? Now, public phones might not be the first thing you think of when you're looking to improve your airport. But executives at other airports *have* already thought about them. And they've seen the advantages of knowing their public phone service is as up-to-date as the rest of their facilities.

Of course, this is by no means the only way to attract more travelers to your city. But in this highly competitive arena, can you afford to overlook anything—particularly something this simple—that can make your airport's good reputation even better?

THE AT&T CARD CALLER. IT'S CHANGING THE FACE OF TELECOMMUNICATIONS. The public phone that's rapidly gaining popularity all across the country is the **AT&T Card Caller.**

Why? First, it's fast. To place a call, the user simply inserts the **AT&T Card** (or, in many locations, a major commercial credit card) into the space provided. And then calls anywhere. Instantly. A multitude of calls can be made, one after the other, at the touch of a button. And of course calls can also be made collect, billed to a third party, or by punching in your **AT&T Card** number or local phone company card number.

Second, it's so easy, you don't have to know how to use it, to use it! The **AT&T Card Caller's** unique video screen spells out, step by step, how to place calls. And does so in four languages...because your public isn't necessarily limited to English-speaking travelers.

Third, it's thoughtful. There's a three-stage volume control button, so conversations can be heard clearly, even over airport clatter and clamor. It's self-diagnostic, so it spots problems *before* they happen. The **AT&T Card Caller** even issues a warning tone—and the video screen tells you to take your card —should the card be left behind.

The result of this simple improvement? Faster calling, fewer lines at the phones, no need for travelers to fumble for the right change—a generally happier public.

80% OF AIR TRAVELERS CAN'T BE WRONG. A recent survey of travelers in a major international airport revealed an interesting statistic: 80% of those questioned who used the **AT&T Card Caller** phone said that, given the choice, they would use it again over a regular coin phone.

Through such surveys, and through a number of promotional efforts, travelers are becoming more and more aware of the **AT&T Card Caller.** Which means that if the public saw it in your airport, they'd recognize it. And use it. And appreciate it. And that's a good impression to make on your share of the traveling public.

And since this technologically advanced product is backed by AT&T, you can feel confident about its quality and reliability.

AT&T PUBLIC PHONES—THE RIGHT CHOICE. What's coming next in telecommunications? You can be sure it's going to come from AT&T. Innovative thinking isn't just our history...it's our stock in trade. We're constantly exploring new ways to make communication better and easier, whether it's developing new equipment or developing new ways to use it more efficiently.

We also offer innovative ways to help you. Our flexible cancellation policy makes it easy to work with us. And we offer a generous commission plan.

In every way, AT&T is the acknowledged telecommunications leader. And your adoring public—and you—deserve nothing less.

YOUR PUBLIC AWAITS YOU. First impressions mean a lot. Your airport can be welcoming, easy to get through, and a great introduction to your city. Or not. It can provide the fastest, most up-to-date communications service. Or something less.

It's up to you. You've got the pull to make it happen. Now exercise a little push. Call your AT&T account executive, or complete the enclosed reply card and send it back to us. You'll see how winning your city an adoring public can be a lot easier than you thought.

Every day, millions of people fly to American cities like yours. They trudge through airports. Wait for baggage. Line up for taxis. And in doing so form their first impression of the cities they visit.

The smoother the trip through the airport, the better the impression. Which is why you devote so much time and energy to providing top-of-the-line ground service—a good first impression can bring lasting benefits to your city.

THERE'S SOMETHING IN THE AIR...ARE YOU ON TO IT? Now, public phones might not be the first thing you think of when you're looking to improve your airport. But executives at other airports *have* already thought about them. And they've seen the advantages of knowing their public phone service is as up-to-date as the rest of their facilities.

Of course, this is by no means the only way to attract more travelers to your city. But in this highly competitive arena, can you afford to overlook anything—particularly something this simple—that can make your airport's good reputation even better?

THE AT&T CARD CALLER. IT'S CHANGING THE FACE OF TELECOMMUNICATIONS. The public phone that's rapidly gaining popularity all across the country is the **AT&T Card Caller.**

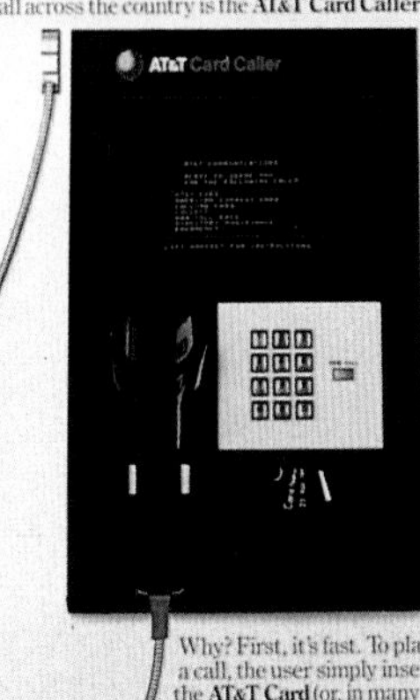

Why? First, it's fast. To place a call, the user simply inserts the **AT&T Card** (or, in many locations, a major commercial credit card) into the space provided. And then calls anywhere. Instantly. A multitude of calls can be made, one after the other, at the touch of a button. And of course calls can also be made collect, billed to a third party, or by punching in your **AT&T Card** number or local phone company card number.

Second, it's so easy, you don't have to know how to use it, to use it! The **AT&T Card Caller's** unique video screen spells out, step by step, how to place calls. And does so in four languages...because your public isn't necessarily limited to English-speaking travelers.

Third, it's thoughtful. There's a three-stage volume control button, so conversations can be heard clearly, even over airport clatter and clamor. It's self-diagnostic, so it spots problems *before* they happen. The **AT&T Card Caller** even issues a warning tone—and the video screen tells you to take your card —should the card be left behind.

The result of this simple improvement? Faster calling, fewer lines at the phones, no need for travelers to fumble for the right change—a generally happier public.

80% OF AIR TRAVELERS CAN'T BE WRONG. A recent survey of travelers in a major international airport revealed an interesting statistic: 80% of those questioned who used the **AT&T Card Caller** phone said that, given the choice, they would use it again over a regular coin phone.

Through such surveys, and through a number of promotional efforts, travelers are becoming more and more aware of the **AT&T Card Caller.** Which means that if the public saw it in your airport, they'd recognize it. And use it. And appreciate it. And that's a good impression to make on your share of the traveling public.

And since this technologically advanced product is backed by AT&T, you can feel confident about its quality and reliability.

AT&T PUBLIC PHONES—THE RIGHT CHOICE. What's coming next in telecommunications? You can be sure it's going to come from AT&T. Innovative thinking isn't just our history...it's our stock in trade. We're constantly exploring new ways to make communication better and easier, whether it's developing new equipment or developing new ways to use it more efficiently.

We also offer innovative ways to help you. Our flexible cancellation policy makes it easy to work with us. And we offer a generous commission plan.

In every way, AT&T is the acknowledged telecommunications leader. And your adoring public—and you—deserve nothing less.

YOUR PUBLIC AWAITS YOU. First impressions mean a lot. Your airport can be welcoming, easy to get through, and a great introduction to your city. Or not. It can provide the fastest, most up-to-date communications service. Or something less.

It's up to you. You've got the pull to make it happen. Now exercise a little push. Call your AT&T account executive, or complete the enclosed reply card and send it back to us. You'll see how winning your city an adoring public can be a lot easier than you thought.

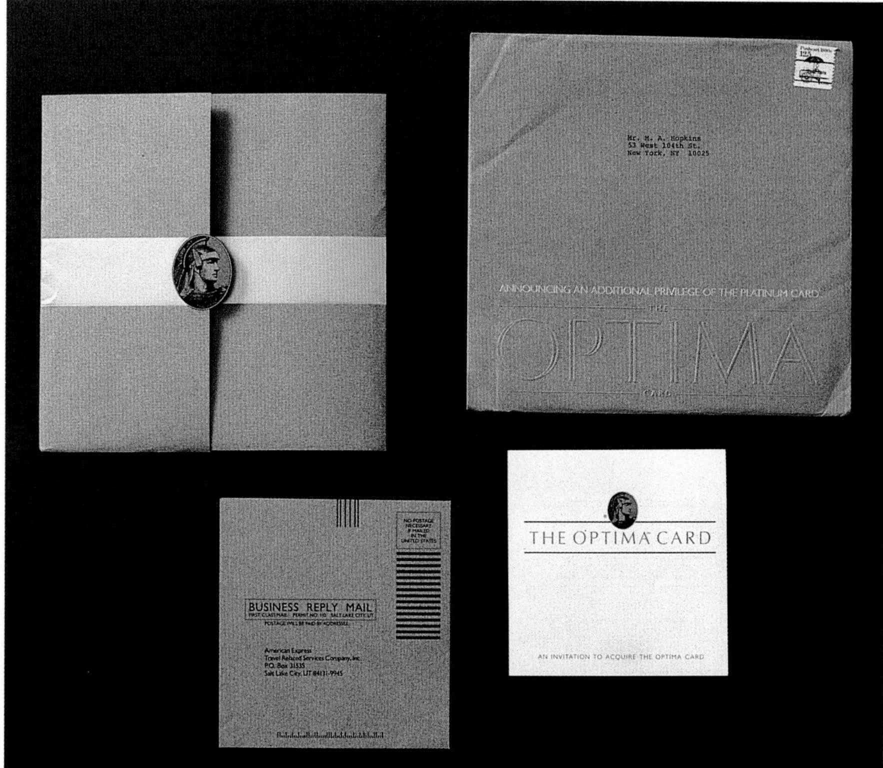

Title: "Platinum" Package
Copywriters: Sue Levytsky, Norma Friedman, Suzanne Prince
Art Director: Carol Dronsfield
Agency: Wunderman Worldwide
Client: American Express Travel Related Services, Optima Card Division

Elegance and sophistication characterizes this black, white and gray direct mail package sent to upscale American Express cardmembers.

CREATED FOR THE PERSONAL NEEDS OF THOSE WITH A DEMANDING LIFESTYLE.

Commanding, personal, convenient. The world's finest markets stand ready to recognize your Platinum Card status.

You already know the immediate recognition and respect that is accorded to you when you present the Platinum Card.

Now, the Optima Card gives you an additional financial resource you can use almost anywhere in the world. With the full knowledge that

THE DEFINITION OF OPTIMA

WHY DO I NEED THE OPTIMA CARD IN ADDITION TO THE PLATINUM CARD?

Many Cardmembers have asked us to make extended payment available; many indicated that they preferred to access it via a second card. Hence, the Optima Card. It is an additional financial resource that carries with it the level of recognition and service you enjoy with the Platinum Card.

DO I NEED TO MAINTAIN MY PLATINUM CARD ACCOUNT?

Yes. The Optima Card is a privilege of Cardmembership. You will continue to enjoy the benefits of the Optima Card, so long as you are a Platinum Card member.

HOW DO I SELECT MY CREDIT LINE FOR THE OPTIMA CARD?

It's easy. We have established a personal credit line range for you based upon your past spending, payment patterns and financial resources. You can select your credit limit within this range according to your requirements.

WHAT IS THE INTEREST RATE?

The privileged Annual Percentage Rate, currently 13.50%, will be adjusted semiannually in relation to the Prime Rate, as listed in the Wall Street Journal.

DOES HAVING THE OPTIMA CARD AFFECT MY ABILITY TO SPEND WITH THE PLATINUM CARD?

No. Your personalized credit line on the Optima Card in no way affe… your spending power with the Platinum Card.

WILL I RECEIVE A SEPARATE STATEMENT FOR CHARGES O… THE OPTIMA CARD?

Yes, you will be billed separately … charges made on the Optima Card. This monthly, descriptive statement will contain, without receipts, the k… of useful information you expect fr… American Express. As a Platinum C… member, you will also receive a ye… end report summarizing all the Op… Card activity. This chronological account of transactions will be sim… to, yet separate from, the Platinum Card Year-End Summary of Char…

WHERE IS THE OPTIMA CARD ACCEPTED?

You will find a warm welcome … the Optima Card at fine shops, se… vices and other establishments ar… the world, just as you do with the Platinum Card.

WHAT IS THE FEE FOR THE OPTIMA CARD?

The Optima Card is offered only to selected Platinum Card members at no …

THE ADVANTAGES OF OPTIMA

The authority of the world's most respected Card delivers increased financial leverage, starting with a preferred interest rate.

One of the hallmarks of success is the ability to seize an opportunity while maintaining maximum flexibility and control. The Optima Card, presented to you with our compliments, is designed to enable you to do exactly this with unmatched authority and convenience.

The Optima Card offers you the luxury of extending payments. The interest rate for these deferred payments is the preferred Annual Percentage Rate, currently 13.50%, adjusted semiannually in relation to the Prime Rate as listed in the Wall Street Journal.

THE POWER OF OPTIMA

A personalized credit line brings maximum control. The luxury of time provides maximum flexibility.

THE CONTROL OF OPTIMA

Your fully descriptive monthly statement and year-end summary of purchases combine for more effective financial management.

The Optima Card gives you increased control over your money management. It is designed to conform to your needs, rather than asking you to adapt to its requirements.

For greater control, you will receive a separate billing statement for charges made on the Optima Card. This monthly, descriptive statement will contain, without receipts, the kind of useful information you expect from American Express.

As a Platinum Card member, you'll also have the convenience of a separate year-end summary of all purchases billed to the Optima Card, further facilitating your personal financial management.

These features, combined with your personalized credit line, make the Optima Card the most individualized financial resource available. And the combination of the Platinum Card with the Optima Card gives you even better financial control.

Here, at last, is a combination of financial resources that fully recognizes the position you have achieved. And the privileges you have earned.

Edwin M. Cooperman
President
Consumer Card Group, USA

May 20, 1987

Dear Mr. Hopkins:

The manner in which you use the Platinum Card® distinguishes you as one who appreciates the better things in life -- and new opportunities to enjoy them.

It is for people such as you that American Express® has created an important new service: the Optima Card℠, the new companion to the Platinum Card. You may use the Optima Card on those occasions when it is to your advantage to extend payment over time, rather than pay in full.

As a Cardmember, you will be entitled to an advantageous Annual Percentage Rate, currently 13.50%, tied to the Prime Rate as listed in the Wall Street Journal. You will also receive a choice of a personalized credit line to suit your financial picture.

And as you might expect, the Optima Card grants you the same exclusive array of Cardmember benefits and worldwide acceptance you are accustomed to.

I invite you to begin enjoying the Optima Card and all its privileges with our compliments.

You will not only be among the first to carry the Optima Card, but the first to appreciate the rewards of doing so.

Sincerely,

P.S. Simply sign the enclosed invitation and return it by the end of June, 1987. This invitation is open to you as long as you are a Cardmember in good standing. And it's your assurance that you receive one of the first Optima Cards ever issued.

American Express Travel Related Services Company, Inc., American Express Tower, World Financial Center, New York, New York 10285-3492

ALLANTÉ

Title: "Allante"
Copywriters: A. MacMillan Eichman, Kenneth Sidlow, James Stano, Richard Wolf
Art Directors: Connie Stone, Martha Schiebold, Jack Carmichael, Paul Zimmerman
Agency: Intergroup Marketing & Promotions
Client: Cadillac Motor Division

Trendsetters and luxury car owners with incomes of $150,000 per year and above qualify to receive this lavish test-drive offer that includes an oversize 40-page booklet with two gatefolds, an even larger 72- page book filled with lush four-color photography, a two-page letter, reprints from automotive magazines, and a specially- packaged VHS preview videocassette—all contained in a sturdy, laminated portfolio.

Cadillac

THE ALLANTÉ COLLECTION

"With the Allanté, Cadillac has produced a precise balance of luxury and performance. Allanté has a firm, positive feel that inspires confidence. Here is truly an automobile for the connoisseur, the aficionado, the driver who is very discriminating. A driver like you who can fully appreciate the extraordinary caliber of Allanté."

John O. Grettenberger
Vice President, General Motors Corporation
General Manager, Cadillac Motor Car Division

ALLANTÉ VIDEOTAPE

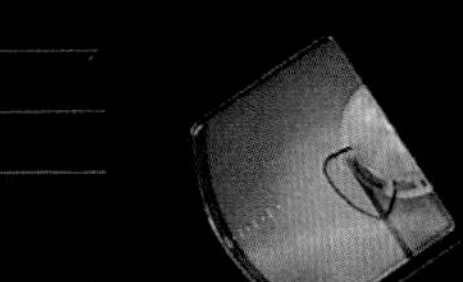

ALLANTÉ PROSPECTUS AND COMMENTS

Allanté road test offer

Please print.

☐ **Yes,** I would very much like to road test the new Cadillac Allanté. I understand that in the near future my Cadillac Dealer will be calling to schedule the road test.

Your Name

Your Street Address

Your City State ZIP Code

Your Phone Number

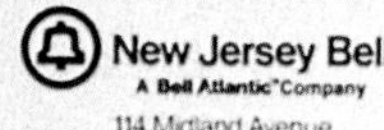

New Jersey Bell
A Bell Atlantic™ Company
114 Midland Avenue
Kearny, NJ 07032

6JRE6LTR5

Can your phone handle two calls at once, transfer calls, let you dial with a single digit, or make three-way calls?

You bet it can!

Dear Customer:

How well do you really know your phone?

Do you think of it as a faithful, but not terribly exciting household fixture? Well if you do, you could be in for a big surprise...

Because today your rotary dial or Touch Tone phone can bring you greater convenience, efficiency, and peace of mind than ever before—without a single piece of new equipment, or a visit from the installer.

How is all this possible?

With Custom Calling Services, four impressive telephone service enhancements that can turn your ordinary phone into a...SUPERPHONE!

What's more, if you order by May 30, 1986, you won't have to pay an installation charge. And that's a SUPERPHONE savings of $21.00!

Custom Calling Services include such SUPER features as:

- Call Waiting ...that lets you put your first call on "hold," then answer a second call. PLUS, it enables you to get through on a call home when your line is tied up—which can be a life saver in an emergency.
- Call Forwarding ...allowing you to forward your calls electronically, from your home phone to a phone where you can be reached. So your family and friends get you, not your answering machine.
- Three-Way Calling ...making it possible for you to talk to two different people, in two different locations, at the same time.
- Speed Calling ...which enables you to dial frequently-called and emergency numbers with just one or two digits. And that saves you time and helps prevent dialing errors.

With Custom Calling Services, you'll have a SUPERPHONE at your service 24 hours a day, 7 days a week. Which means you'll be able to:

- Get through to your spouse when your teenager is on the phone.

(Over, please)

Now, with a single call to New Jersey Bell, you can transform your ordinary phone into a

See inside to find out how you can save an extra $21.00!

Now you can turn your ordinary phone into...

WITH AMAZING CUSTOM CALLING SERVICES.

Order Form

To order your Custom Calling Services at a special discounted package price—**and SAVE the $21.00 Installation Charge**—simply sign and complete this form and return it in the enclosed envelope by May 30, 1986. Or call TOLL FREE 1 800 772-2184, between 9:00 AM and 5:00 PM, Monday through Friday. No installation visit or special equipment is necessary.

CHECK YOUR CHOICE:

- ☐ SUPER PACKAGE: Call Waiting, Call Forwarding, Three-Way Calling, Speed Calling (8-number memory)...$9.15/month*
- ☐ Call Waiting, Call Forwarding, Three-Way Calling, Speed Calling (30-number memory)...$10.29/month*
- ☐ Call Waiting, Call Forwarding, Speed Calling (8-number memory)...$8.01/month*
- ☐ Call Waiting, Call Forwarding, Three-Way Calling...$8.01/month*
- ☐ Call Waiting, Call Forwarding...$5.73/month*
- ☐ Call Waiting, Speed Calling (8-number memory)...$5.73/month*
- ☐ Call Waiting, Speed Calling (30-number memory)...$6.85/month*

220404

Mcmann
7 Swift Ct
Clifton, NJ 07014

(____) ________________ ________________
Telephone Number Signature

IMPORTANT! YOU SAVE THE INSTALLATION CHARGE OF $21.00 IF WE RECEIVE YOUR ORDER BY MAY 30, 1986. PLEASE ACT NOW! 6JRE6OC5

*Rates and charges are before taxes and subject to change.
The offer of free installation is made possible by an Order of the New Jersey Board of Public Utilities.

BULK RATE
U.S. Postage
PAID
New Jersey Bell

PULL HERE

Free Installation for a Limited Time Offer

Now serving mankind and especially:

Underneath your phone's mild-mannered exterior is a thrilling new identity...

6JRE/U6OEW

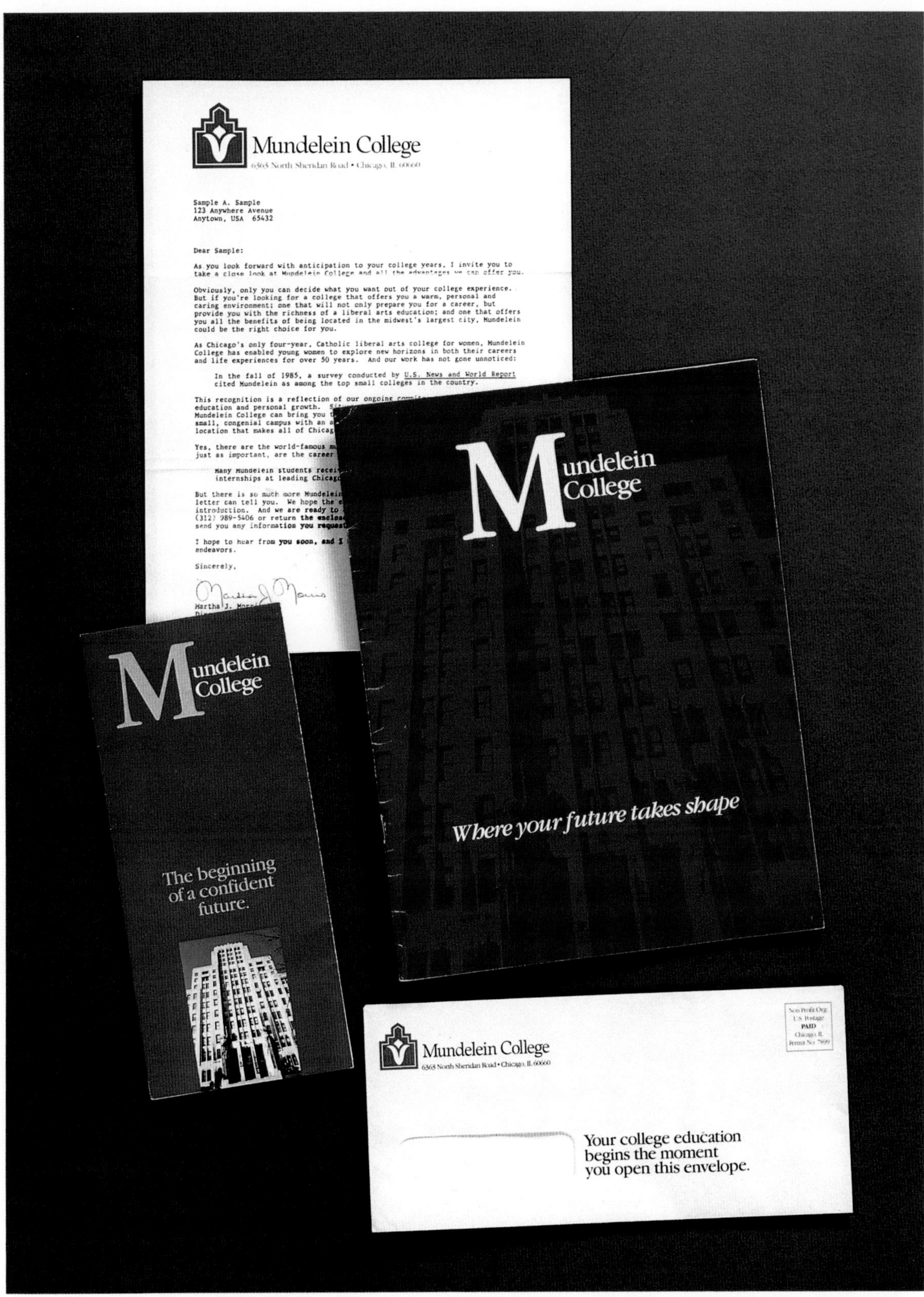

Title: "Superphone"
Copywriters: Martha Craig, Jerry Danzig
Art Directors: Laurie Scibetta, Joe Pavale
Agency: Ketchum Direct
Client: New Jersey Bell

Instantly recognizable logotype, repeated for impact, provides a foundation for this memorable upsell consumer direct mail effort promoting expanded telephone capabilities.

Title: "Mundelein College Direct Mail Campaign"
Copywriter: Sam Kirshenbaum
Art Director: Tim Claffey
Agency: Bozell, Jacobs, Kenyon & Eckhardt Direct
Client: Mundelein College

A relatively small Chicago institute of higher learning explains its benefits to prospective students in this balanced direct mail package, combining a no- nonsense copy approach with lively but sophisticated graphics.

Title: "Inside are your keys..."
Copywriter: Todd Moore
Art Director: Frank Luca
Agency: Della Femina, Travisano & Partners
Client: Isuzu

Technical data and equipment shown in this brochure are based upon the latest avai
time, without notice, in prices, colors, materials, equipment specifications, and to d

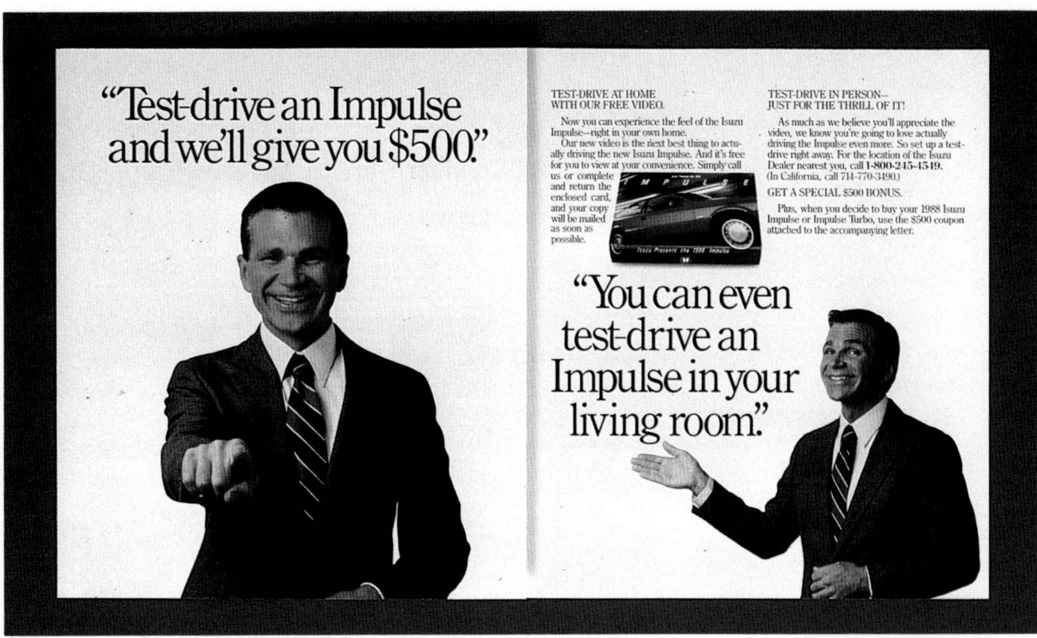

The famous national television campaign starring "honest" Joe Isuzu is brought to life through the mail with this good-natured consumer package encouraging test drives of the new Isuzu Impulse.

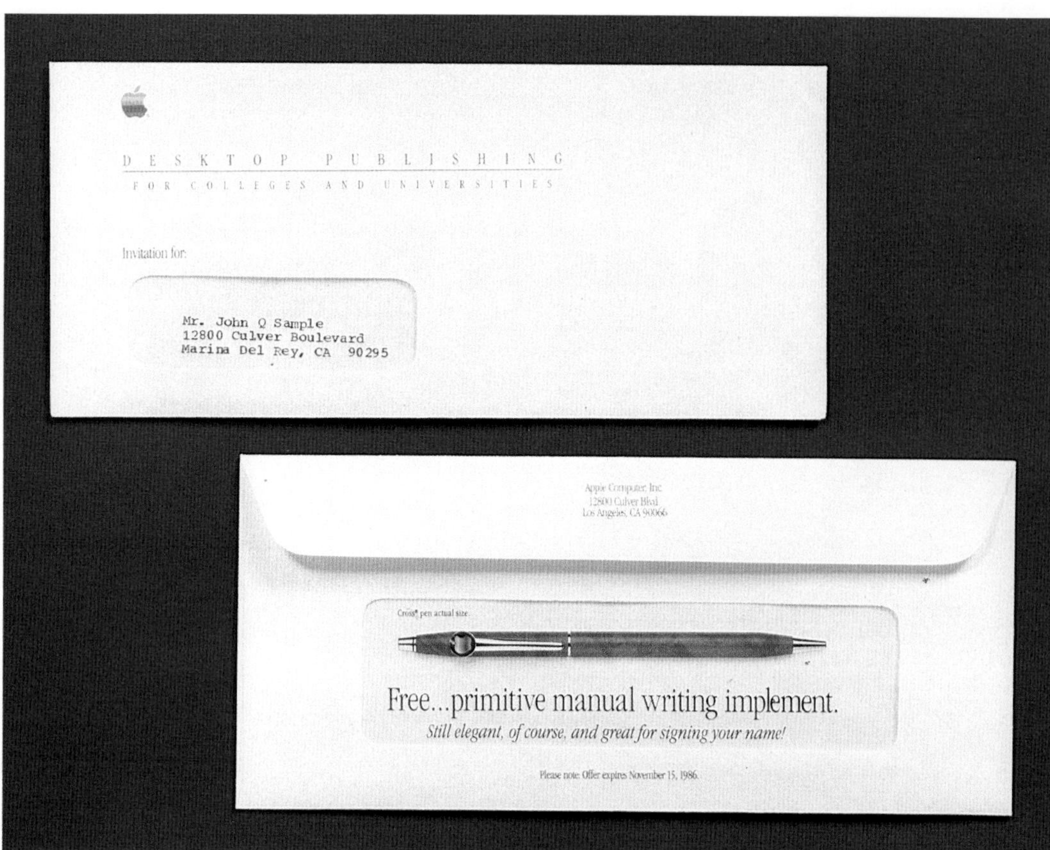

Title: "Apple Desk Top Publishing"
Copywriters: Gary Wexler, Lee Lefton
Art Directors: Neel Muller, David Ayriss
Agency: Krupp/Taylor
Client: Apple Computer

An enticing offer of a free Cross pen is made through a special window before the envelope of this business mailing is even opened. Targeted to college administrators and education professionals, this package makes good on its Cross promise once the respondent has registered for a demonstration seminar.

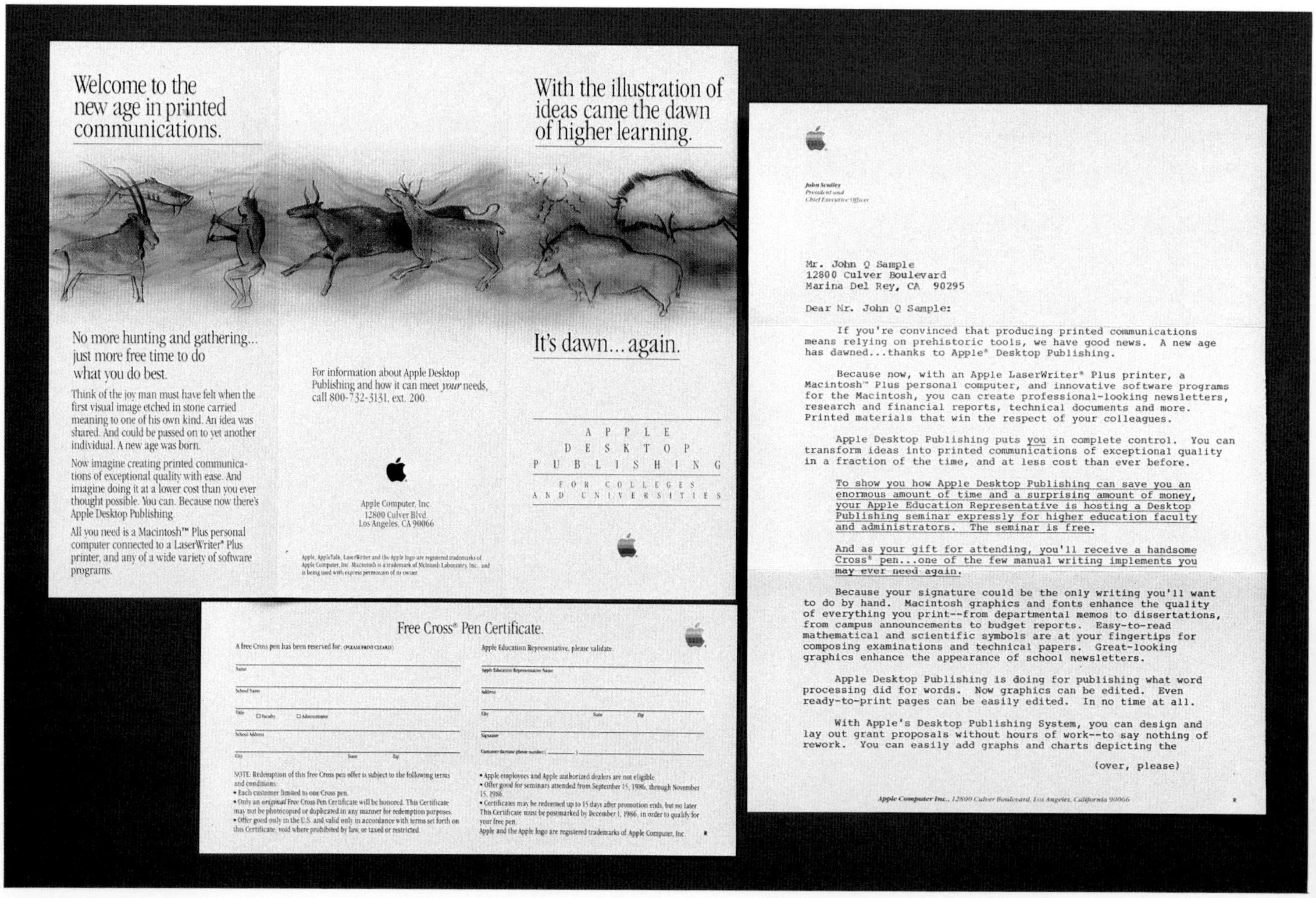

Welcome to the new age in printed communications.

With the illustration of ideas came the dawn of higher learning.

No more hunting and gathering... just more free time to do what you do best.

Think of the joy man must have felt when the first visual image etched in stone carried meaning to one of his own kind. An idea was shared. And could be passed on to yet another individual. A new age was born.

Now imagine creating printed communications of exceptional quality with ease. And imagine doing it at a lower cost than you ever thought possible. You can. Because now there's Apple Desktop Publishing.

All you need is a Macintosh™ Plus personal computer connected to a LaserWriter® Plus printer, and any of a wide variety of software programs.

For information about Apple Desktop Publishing and how it can meet *your* needs, call 800-732-3131, ext. 200.

Apple Computer, Inc.
12800 Culver Blvd.
Los Angeles, CA 90066

It's dawn... again.

A P P L E
D E S K T O P
P U B L I S H I N G
F O R C O L L E G E S
A N D U N I V E R S I T I E S

Free Cross® Pen Certificate.

John Sculley
President and
Chief Executive Officer

Mr. John Q Sample
12800 Culver Boulevard
Marina Del Rey, CA 90295

Dear Mr. John Q Sample:

If you're convinced that producing printed communications means relying on prehistoric tools, we have good news. A new age has dawned...thanks to Apple® Desktop Publishing.

Because now, with an Apple LaserWriter® Plus printer, a Macintosh™ Plus personal computer, and innovative software programs for the Macintosh, you can create professional-looking newsletters, research and financial reports, technical documents and more. Printed materials that win the respect of your colleagues.

Apple Desktop Publishing puts you in complete control. You can transform ideas into printed communications of exceptional quality in a fraction of the time, and at less cost than ever before.

To show you how Apple Desktop Publishing can save you an enormous amount of time and a surprising amount of money, your Apple Education Representative is hosting a Desktop Publishing seminar expressly for higher education faculty and administrators. The seminar is free.

And as your gift for attending, you'll receive a handsome Cross® pen...one of the few manual writing implements you may ever need again.

Because your signature could be the only writing you'll want to do by hand. Macintosh graphics and fonts enhance the quality of everything you print--from departmental memos to dissertations, from campus announcements to budget reports. Easy-to-read mathematical and scientific symbols are at your fingertips for composing examinations and technical papers. Great-looking graphics enhance the appearance of school newsletters.

Apple Desktop Publishing is doing for publishing what word processing did for words. Now graphics can be edited. Even ready-to-print pages can be easily edited. In no time at all.

With Apple's Desktop Publishing System, you can design and lay out grant proposals without hours of work--to say nothing of rework. You can easily add graphs and charts depicting the

(over, please)

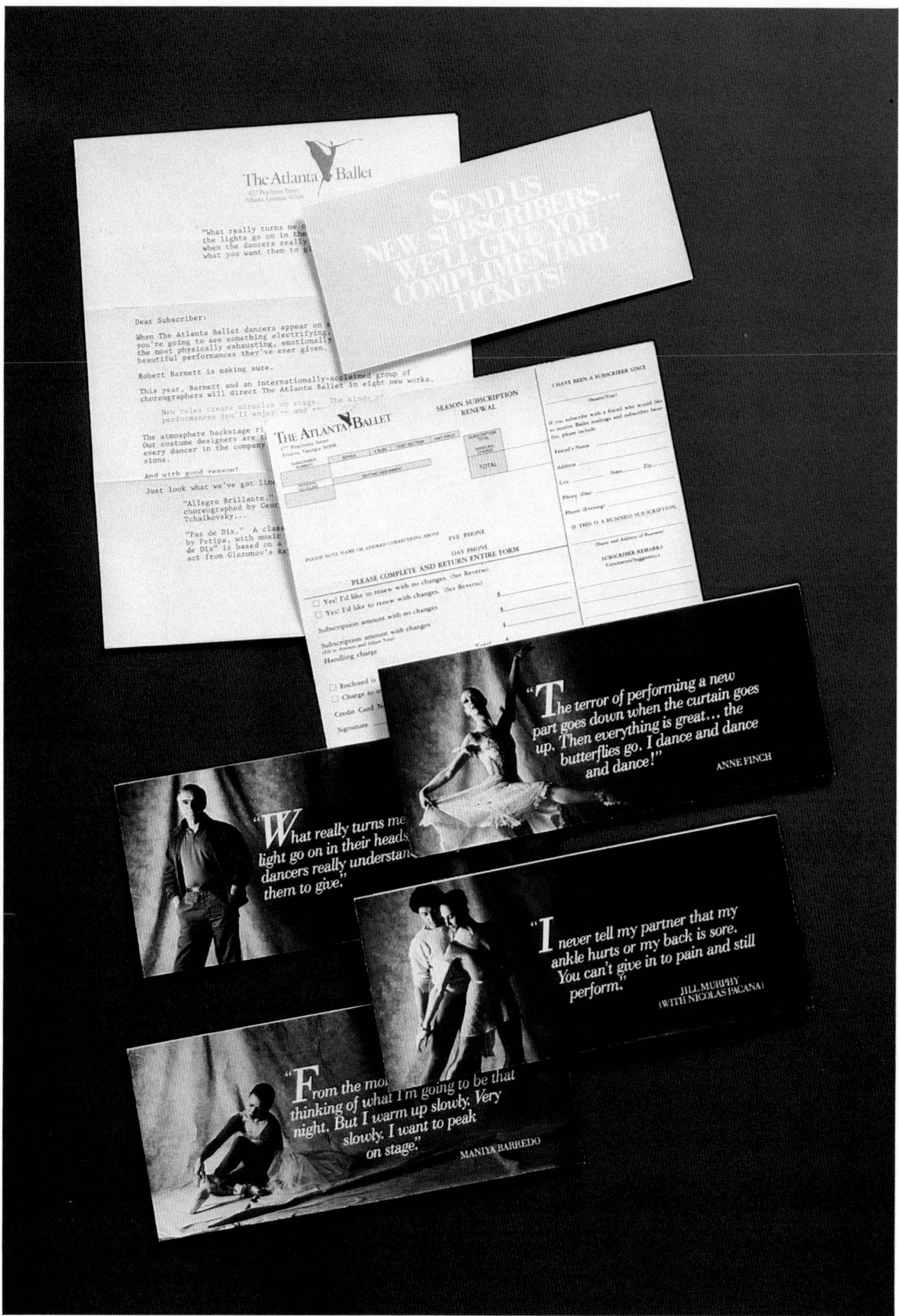

Title: "Get To Know The Dancers"
Copywriters: Dianne Edlemann, Carey Smith
Art Director: Judy McCabe Smith
Agency: Ogilvy & Mather Direct
Client: The Atlanta Ballet

Inner feelings of dancers are reflected so that the reader of these direct mail efforts can join in creative secrets not so often shared with the general public. The graphics and copy approach are in complete harmony, paralleling what is promised of the forthcoming performances.

Chapter
2
PBC INTERNATIONAL
ONE SCHOOL STREET
GLEN COVE, NY 11542

PRINT ADVERTISING

Direct response print advertising in newspapers and magazines is subject to greater limitations than the wide-open possibilities of direct mail. There is more advertising clutter to contend with, not to mention the distraction of the editorial environment that motivated the reader to pick up the publication in the first place.

And, compared with direct mail, there are severe restrictions on the amount of copy that can be included in print advertising (also called space advertising). Whatever you call it, there just isn't enough room to run paragraph after paragraph explaining the benefits and advantages of products, premiums and offers.

Heightening the creative challenge even further, there is a critical need for well-designed graphics that are not only attention-getting but practical and functional, too. Art direction in space ads must support the copy theme and be a catalyst, moving the reader to act. The most effective coupons are easy to understand and use, and in their absence, toll-free telephone numbers or other ways to respond must facilitate the call-to-action without a shadow of a doubt.

Furthermore, as if the degree of difficulty in creating great print advertising wasn't already harsh enough, there is *serious* competition among the many bright young professionals and seasoned veterans practicing the craft of direct marketing today. And, more people with talent and enthusiasm are joining the field all the time. In light of recent growth, trends in the amount of advertising space sold by magazines and newspapers—which simply means that a space ad is up against more and more clutter vying for attention and action from the reader—direct response space advertising in the late 1980s finds itself in a rather challenging situation.

But, as you can see in this chapter, the challenge is being met brilliantly. "Firewood," for instance, on page 123, a full page black-and-white ad for Foster Parents Plan, was not only Second Prize winner in the Consumer Print division at the 10th Annual John Caples Awards, but a 1987 ECHO Award winner as well, for superior marketplace results.

Before writing "Coffee Cup," another Second Prize winner from the 10th Annual Caples Awards, an enterprising copywriter from Ogilvy & Mather Direct in London called one of her client's field offices and—without revealing her ulterior motive—arranged and conducted an interview in her own home to plan the remodeling of her kitchen. The client was Magnet, one of Great Britain's largest home-improvement contractors. The advertisement created from her experience, on page 111, succeeds on all levels, with flawless art direction and a trustworthy ring of truth in the copy both working together in a solid, engaging concept.

Virtually all of the print ads here, in fact, are sparkling examples of copy-and-art teamwork, even when the product or service requires extremely long, traditional copy. As with direct mail, the art director's role in direct response print advertising has become crucial to its effective conceptual development and execution. And as the disciplines of direct marketing and image advertising grow closer together and more dependent upon each other, we can look forward to the state of the art reaching exciting new levels of excellence in the years ahead.

Xerox announces a printer promotion that isn't built on the same old principle.

At Xerox, we think the most profitable promotional programs are built on help. Not hype.

And our first printer promotion for 1986 is a perfect example.

It's designed the way dealers told us they wanted to see a printer rebate promotion designed. Without restrictions and long-term commitments.

It's simply strong dealer support with no strings attached.

NO MINIMUMS, NO MAXIMUMS.

You can purchase as many or as few Xerox printers as you want. Because there are no minimum or maximum purchase requirements.

And the promotion covers our full line of leading edge printers, including both our Diablo dot matrix and daisy-wheel models.

What's more, the promotion for your customers will run for a full three months, from May 1 through July 31, 1986. And that means you'll have the time it takes to really make the promotion work.

CONSUMER REBATES ON ALL NINE XEROX PRINTERS.

Your customers will get substantial rebates of $25 to $500 on our full line of Xerox Diablo printers purchased from May 1 through July 31, 1986.

Also, since these rebates come directly from Xerox, your profit margin will be fully protected.

It's simple. You do the selling, we do the paying.

DEALER REBATES ON ALL NINE XEROX PRINTERS.

You'll receive a 5% rebate off your distributor's price on every printer, sheet feeder or tractor you purchase between March 14, 1986 and June 30, 1986. Whether you purchase one or one thousand.

In addition, we'll supply you with free merchandising materials, including customer rebate certificates, posters, statement enclosures, counter cards, and ad slicks.

NATIONAL ADVERTISING AND DIRECT MAIL SUPPORT.

We'll be supporting you with an aggressive national advertising and direct mail campaign that will run throughout May, June and July in leading publications like Time, Inc., Venture, The Wall Street Journal, Byte, MIS Week, Computer Decisions, Business Computer, and Personal Computing.

Also in many of the most popular in-flight magazines like TWA Ambassador, Delta Sky, US Air, and East West Network.

Plus a heavy schedule in major market newspapers.

And, we'll be sending hundreds of thousands of targeted mailings to prospective printer customers throughout the nation. It's a media blitz that adds up to over 44 million reader impressions.

GET BONUS POINTS ON ALL NINE XEROX PRINTERS.

We're offering you and your sales people extra bonus points on all nine printers in the promotion.

So make sure you're enrolled in the Xerox Points Program before the promotion starts.

XEROX QUALITY AND RELIABILITY.

When you sell Xerox Diablo printers you'll be selling high quality, reliable products. Also, every printer in the promotion is compatible with Xerox, Apple and IBM personal computers.

What's more, every printer is backed by a one-year limited warranty on parts and service.

So if you'd like a printer promotion that has all of the carrots with none of the strings attached, be sure to enroll today.

It's easy to sign up: just call us toll free, at ***1-800-TEAM XRX ext. 157A.***

Or send in the coupon. And, we'll take care of the rest.

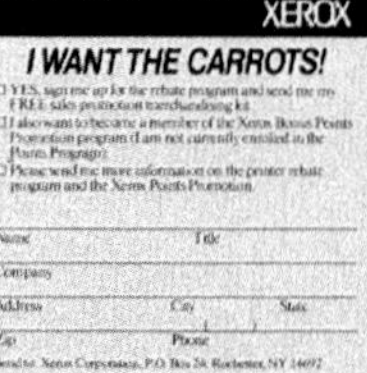

Title: "Carrots"
Copywriter: Paul Levett
Art Director: Mal Karlin
Agency: Lowe Marschalk, Inc.
Client: Xerox Corporation

The first line of copy in this business advertising spread sets up the premise and the promise of Team Xerox, and the rest of the ad carefully leads the reader to reach for more by using the coupon.

Title: "The Xerox 2510"
Copywriters: Brown Hagood, Paul Levett
Art Directors: Vincent Picardi, Mal Karlin
Agency: Lowe Marschalk, Inc.
Client: Xerox Corporation

More capability for less money, always a strong selling point, is instantly visualized here, and is reinforced by confident copy and two response options—a mail-in coupon or toll-free telephone number.

Title: "What most meetings do..."
Copywriter: Paul Levett
Art Director: Mal Karlin
Agency: Lowe Marschalk, Inc.
Client: Xerox Direct Marketing

A novel visual allegory provides the graphic foundation for this comprehensive, well-written message promoting one key practical business application of a technological innovation.

XEROX

What most meetings do is reduce smart thinkers to copiers.

It's an amazing business phenomenon.

Bright, productive, highly paid people sit down in a meeting and POOF! . . . they're reduced to copiers.

Now it's not their fault. After all, in today's fast-paced, one-meeting-after-another world of business, if you want to keep up you have to copy everything down.

So most people spend most of their time in meetings copying, not thinking.

XEROX INTRODUCES THE CONFERENCE COPIER

That's why what your meetings really need is a copier.

But not just any copier. The Xerox Conference Copier. It does the copying. So you can do the thinking.

You can work out a problem on the Conference Copier just as you would on an easel pad. But with one gigantic difference.

When you're finished, you just push a button and in 15 seconds you get a sharp, 8½" x 11" copy of everything you wrote.

PUTS A MEETING INTO MOTION

The Xerox Conference Copier can turn a work session into a session that really works. Because everyone can really be involved.

The Conference Copier's five big 3' x 4' screens give you 60 square feet of work space. So you have plenty of room to work out even the biggest problems.

You can use a variety of colored, felt-tip markers to add impact and interest.

Then when you're ready, you can make copies of one, two, or up to four screens, all on a single sheet of paper.

The Conference Copier can even make up to 99 copies at a time.

Its nonglare, white plastic surface makes it an ideal screen for slides or films, too.

And it's easy to operate. After all, it's just a copier.

TURNS IDEAS INTO ACTION

When you roll the Xerox Conference Copier into a meeting, everyone can roll out of the meeting and get the work rolling fast.

Because everyone can leave the meeting with an exact copy of exactly what needs to be done.

You won't have to wait for a secretary to type up all those loose pages of scribbles and cross-outs. Then edit the manuscript. Then make copies. Then get them distributed.

The Xerox Conference Copier could literally save you days, maybe even weeks.

15 DAY TRIAL. RISK-FREE.

Once you work with the Xerox Conference Copier, you won't want to work without it. That's why we'd like you to try it for 15 days, at absolutely no risk.* If for any reason you decide not to keep it, we'll come and take it away at no cost to you.

Team Xerox

And you'll be backed by Team Xerox. One of the largest service and support organizations in the business.

So call 1-800-828-9090 or send in the coupon today. We'll take care of the rest.

MARKETING PLAN

But be sure to act today. After all, the sooner you do, the sooner you'll turn your copiers back into thinkers.

XEROX

I THINK I WANT IT.

☐ Yes, I'd like to arrange a risk-free trial. Please call me.
☐ Yes, I'd like more information on the Xerox Conference Copier.

Send to: Xerox Corporation, P.O. Box 22855, Rochester, NY 14692

or call **1-800-828-9090**

XEROX

The Xerox 2510 Engineering Copier presents two major breakthroughs in paper.

36"

(plain paper copies)

$3,695

It's a little like having your cake and eating it, too.

For it lets you copy virtually everything you've always needed to copy—onto just about any material up to 36 inches wide. Right in your own office.

For only $3,695—a fraction of what it would have cost you up to now.

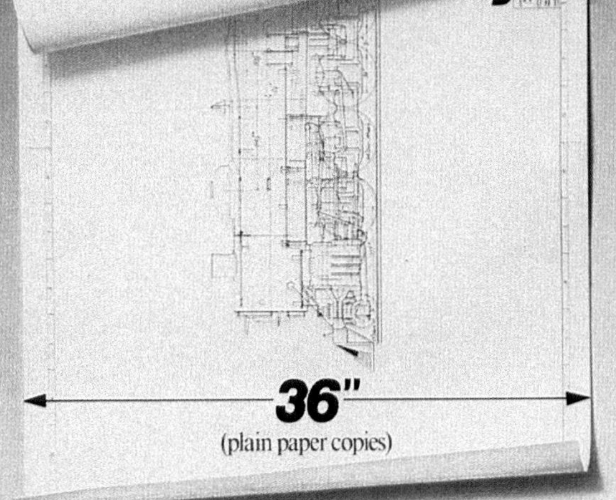

You can copy translucent *and opaque* originals. Vellums, bluelines, sepias. In fact, you can copy just about anything—even illustration boards up to ⅛ inch thick.

You can even copy cut-and-taped originals. (Think of all the hours and money *this* will save.)

Sound good? Look at what you can copy *onto*. Ordinary bond. Vellum. Polyester drafting film. In rolls or cut sheets.

And you'll get presentation-quality copies—plus all the other benefits of xerography.

For example, there's no separate room needed. No unpleasant chemicals. No shelf life to worry about. No test exposures to make. And no wasted copies.

All you need is plain paper (or vellum or film) and xerographic toner.

The Xerox 2510 is obviously more than just two major breakthroughs in paper.

Team Xerox

It's two major breakthroughs for you.

It's also an important addition to the complete line of Xerox engineering and graphic products.

Call ***1-800-TEAM-XRX ext. 282A.*** Or mail the coupon today.

You'll not only make your operation a lot more productive.

You'll have one of the largest service and support organizations in the business backing you up.

XEROX

It sounds good to me.

☐ Please send me more information on the Xerox 2510 Engineering Copier.
☐ Please have a sales representative call me.

Send to: Xerox Corporation, P.O. Box 24, Rochester, NY 14692

or call **1-800-TEAM-XRX ext. 282A**

How to make beans and francs.

Once there was a company that made jelly beans better than anybody. After success here, they expanded overseas.

Before long they were an international concern with international concerns.

A good deal of their money was involved in international payments. So they were always looking for better ways to manage their cash—and their costs—worldwide.

What they needed was WorldLink.[SM] This part paper, part electronic, international payment system lets you issue checks from your office in the world's major trading currencies.

Instead of wiring funds to the nice people in your Nice office, you could send a WorldLink check and do the same job for one-third of the cost.

Because you write the check in French francs at your end, you don't pay Foreign Exchange penalties at the other end.

And with the WorldLink system you can check status or stop payment on any item anywhere, most anytime you please!

Whether you want more control over your payments or just a way to save some francs, use your bean. Call Michael Gamburg at 1 (312) 380-5215 and find out what WorldLink can do for you.

A better way to move money around the world. CITICORP WORLDLINK

Title: "How to Make Beans and Francs"
Copywriter: Maureen Moore
Art Director: Bob Meagher
Agency: Cramer-Krasselt/Chicago
Client: Citicorp Services

Financial executives at international corporations see a great deal of tedious, fine-print advertising, so it's undoubtedly a welcome change of pace to find such a light-heated yet information-packed full page as this.

Title:	"The Reason We Use Red Stripes"	One might never realize how much in-depth research is required to design a proper baby rattle were it not for informative advertising such as this.
Copywriter:	Jim Jenkins	
Art Director:	Walter Halucha	
Agency:	Wunderman Worldwide	
Client:		

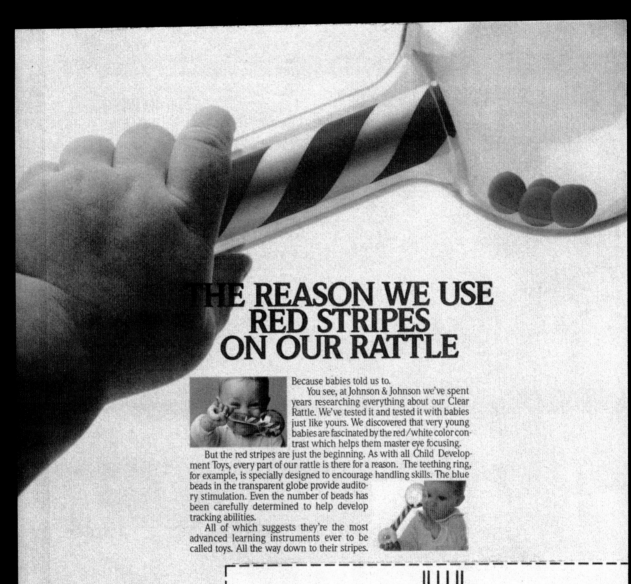

THE REASON WE USE RED STRIPES ON OUR RATTLE

Because babies told us to.

You see, at Johnson & Johnson we've spent years researching everything about our Clear Rattle. We've tested it and tested it with babies just like yours. We discovered that very young babies are fascinated by the red/white color contrast which helps them master eye focusing.

But the red stripes are just the beginning. As with all Child Development Toys, every part of our rattle is there for a reason. The teething ring, for example, is specially designed to encourage handling skills. The blue beads in the transparent globe provide auditory stimulation. Even the number of beads has been carefully determined to help develop tracking abilities.

All of which suggests they're the most advanced learning instruments ever to be called toys. All the way down to their stripes.

The Clear Rattle is yours FREE (Reg. price $6.50) **just for examining a second toy from Johnson & Johnson.**

(See other side for details.)

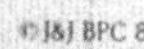

NO POSTAGE NECESSARY IF MAILED IN THE UNITED STATES

BUSINESS REPLY MAIL

FIRST CLASS PERMIT NO. 1999 HICKSVILLE, N.Y.

POSTAGE WILL BE PAID BY ADDRESSEE

Johnson & Johnson

CHILD DEVELOPMENT TOYS
6 Commercial Street
Hicksville, NY 11801-9955

HOW TO REDUCE CORPORATE WAIST.

Every American corporation could save money by running lean and mean. Not by trimming the size of its staff, but by making its staff trim.

The fact is, corporations are losing money because of out-of-shape employees.

Heart disease alone accounts for 52 million lost workdays every year. Simple back pain affects 75 million workers, accounting for more than $1 billion in lost output each year. And the cost of hypertension is more than $10 billion annually.

THE PROBLEM ISN'T JUST FATNESS. IT'S FITNESS.

The modern workplace doesn't satisfy the needs of anybody's body. The human anatomy simply isn't built for sitting behind a desk eight hours a day.

As a result, we're attacked by all sorts of degenerative diseases. Not to mention stress-induced psychological and physical ailments.

The result: Decreased efficiency. Decreased productivity. Increased turnover. Increased absenteeism. Increased probability of on-the-job accidents. Rising health care costs. And lowered employee morale.

But companies all over the country have found that corporate fitness plans can help reduce these problems and expand profitability.

A CORPORATE FITNESS PROGRAM CAN GIVE YOU A HEALTHIER BOTTOM LINE.

For instance, Mesa Petroleum found that employees who exercised had 38% less sick time than those who didn't. And reduced absenteeism means reduced expense.

The Health Research Institute, in a study of America's 1500 largest corporations, found that health care costs for companies with fitness programs averaged 27% less than those without.

And now, the Corporate Fitness Plans available from Chicago Health Clubs offer companies of every size a way to enjoy the benefits of employee fitness, without the substantial capital expense of building and maintaining in-house facilities.

YOU COULDN'T HAVE A BETTER PROGRAM IF YOU DID IT YOURSELF.

Chicago Health Clubs operates 23 of America's finest health and fitness centers. Our large facilities offer the most sophisticated equipment available. The best in aerobic exercise. As well as swimming and racquetball in many locations. And since we're part of Health & Tennis Corporation of America, the world's largest operator of quality fitness centers, your Chicago Health Clubs Corporate Membership can be good at all of our 300 affiliated clubs nationwide. That means your employees can stay in shape, even when they have to stay on the road.

Our Corporate Fitness Plans are flexible, offering different levels of financial participation. You tell us your needs, and we'll tailor a fitness plan to fit your company and budget.

THE HAPPY ENDING TO OUR SHORT STORY.

There's much more to tell you about how a Chicago Health Clubs Corporate Fitness Plan can benefit your company. So give us a call now, or send in the coupon below.

Our programs will not only cut down on corporate waist. They'll do good things for your whole corporate body.

(312) 390-1000

Call now for more information on Chicago Health Clubs Corporate Fitness Plans.

Your shorts made a big impression on me, and your figures were pretty good, too.

☐ Please call ___ me ___ my secretary for an appointment to further explain the Corporate Fitness Programs.

☐ Please send me more information on your programs.

NAME__________

TITLE__________

SECRETARY'S NAME__________

COMPANY__________

ADDRESS__________

CITY__________

STATE__________ ZIP__________

PHONE NUMBER (____)__________

T1

Chicago Health Clubs
Corporate Sales Office
1011 Touhy Ave., Suite 530
Des Plaines, IL 60018

© 1986 Chicago Health Clubs

Introducing the environment that sets the business mind free.
Las Colinas Inn and Conference Center
A new concept from Four Seasons Hotels

Title: "Four Seasons Hotels: Group Meetings"
Copywriter: James Overall
Art Director: Jerry Sukenick
Agency: Scali, McCabe, Sloves Direct
Client: Four Seasons Hotels

A calm, distraction-free business conference environment is reflected in this four-page, four-color insert designed to generate leads for the Las Colinas sales staff. A preview videocassette is available simply by filling out and returning the bind-in card.

Title: "How to Reduce Corporate Waist"
Copywriters: Martha Westerman, Tom McNeer
Art Director: Bill Sowder
Agency: Kaiser Kuhn Bennett
Client: Health & Tennis Corp. of America

The "can't-be-missed" visual in this two-page spread lends immediate impact to the vital, long-copy message concerning physical fitness programs for corporate executives—and how important they can be to overall good health and business productivity as well.

Title: "401(K) Watch"
Copywriter: Fred Wood
Art Director: Sheldon Shacket
Agency: Cohen & Greenbaum
Client: Kemper Financial Services

An eye-catching gold watch works nicely with the headline in this appealing offer for more information about mutual funds. Requests are fulfilled with a free videocassette as well as comprehensive printed materials.

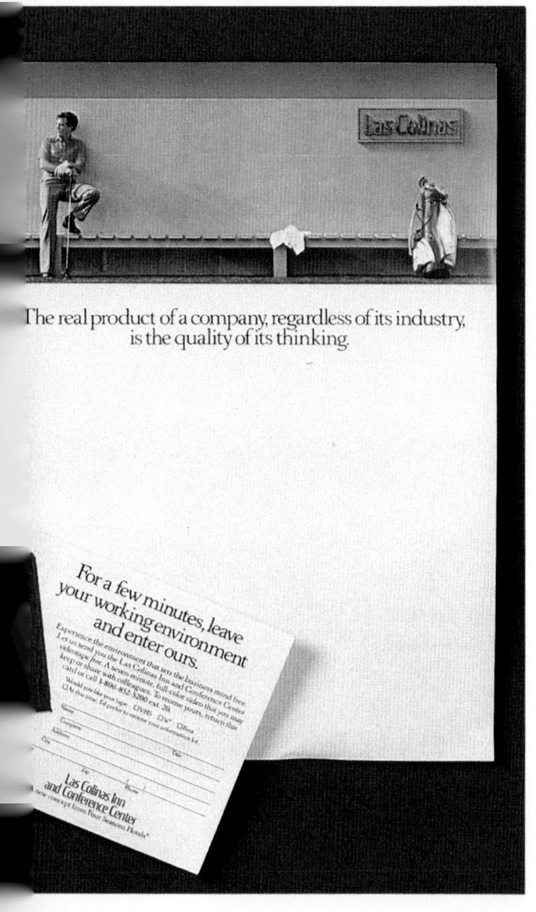

Las Colinas
The real product of a company, regardless of its industry, is the quality of its thinking.
For a few minutes, leave your working environment and enter ours.
Las Colinas Inn and Conference Center

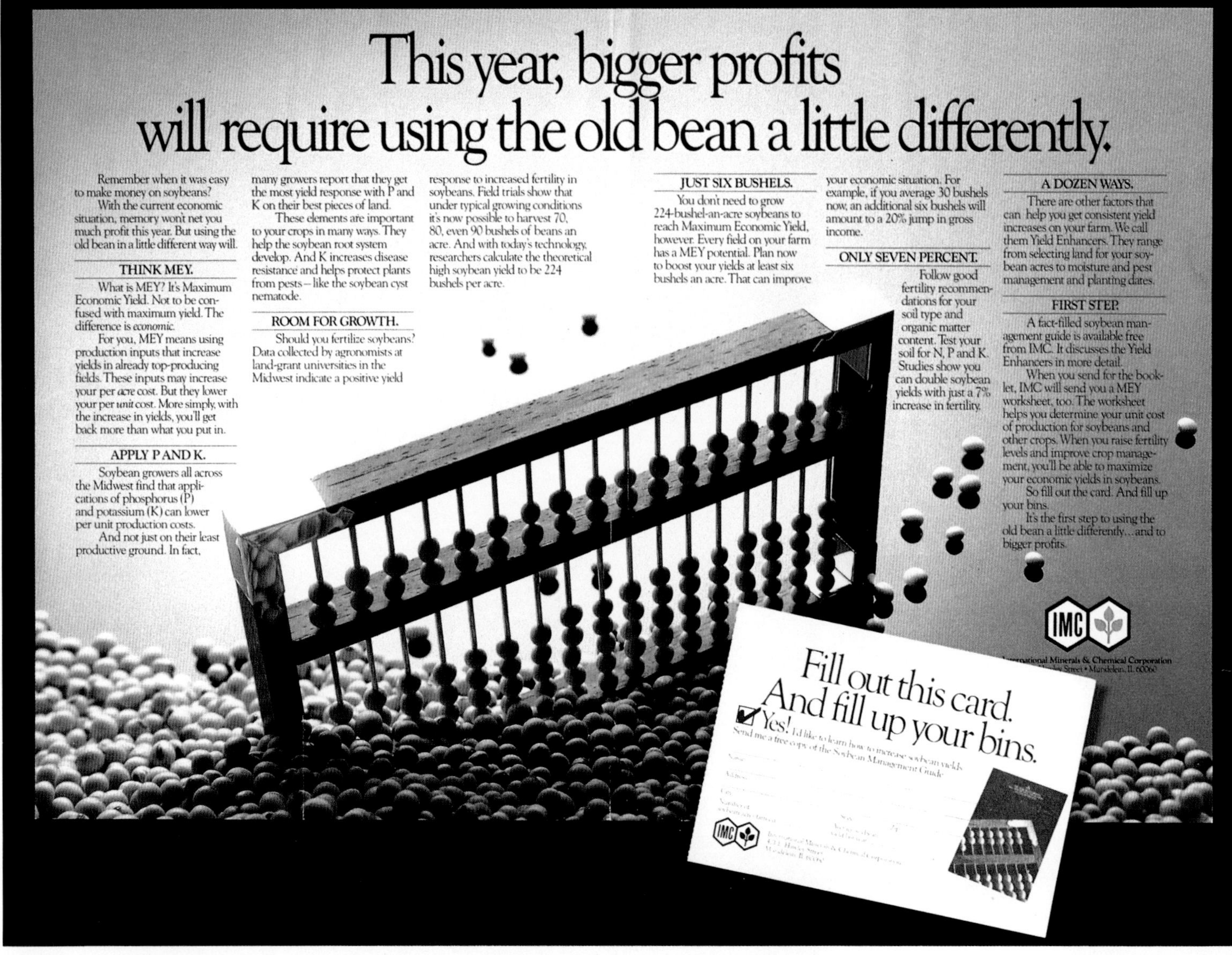

This year, bigger profits will require using the old bean a little differently.
Remember when it was easy to make money on soybeans?
With the current economic situation, memory won't net you much profit this year. But using the old bean in a little different way will.
THINK MEY.
What is MEY? It's Maximum Economic Yield. Not to be confused with maximum yield. The difference is *economic*.
For you, MEY means using production inputs that increase yields in already top-producing fields. These inputs may increase your per *acre* cost. But they lower your per *unit* cost. More simply, with the increase in yields, you'll get back more than what you put in.
APPLY P AND K.
Soybean growers all across the Midwest find that applications of phosphorus (P) and potassium (K) can lower per unit production costs.
And not just on their least productive ground. In fact, many growers report that they get the most yield response with P and K on their best pieces of land.
These elements are important to your crops in many ways. They help the soybean root system develop. And K increases disease resistance and helps protect plants from pests – like the soybean cyst nematode.
ROOM FOR GROWTH.
Should you fertilize soybeans? Data collected by agronomists at land-grant universities in the Midwest indicate a positive yield response to increased fertility in soybeans. Field trials show that under typical growing conditions it's now possible to harvest 70, 80, even 90 bushels of beans an acre. And with today's technology, researchers calculate the theoretical high soybean yield to be 224 bushels per acre.
JUST SIX BUSHELS.
You don't need to grow 224-bushel-an-acre soybeans to reach Maximum Economic Yield, however. Every field on your farm has a MEY potential. Plan now to boost your yields at least six bushels an acre. That can improve your economic situation. For example, if you average 30 bushels now, an additional six bushels will amount to a 20% jump in gross income.
ONLY SEVEN PERCENT.
Follow good fertility recommendations for your soil type and organic matter content. Test your soil for N, P and K. Studies show you can double soybean yields with just a 7% increase in fertility.
A DOZEN WAYS.
There are other factors that can help you get consistent yield increases on your farm. We call them Yield Enhancers. They range from selecting land for your soybean acres to moisture and pest management and planting dates.
FIRST STEP.
A fact-filled soybean management guide is available free from IMC. It discusses the Yield Enhancers in more detail.
When you send for the booklet, IMC will send you a MEY worksheet, too. The worksheet helps you determine your unit cost of production for soybeans and other crops. When you raise fertility levels and improve crop management, you'll be able to maximize your economic yields in soybeans.
So fill out the card. And fill up your bins.
It's the first step to using the old bean a little differently…and to bigger profits.
IMC
Fill out this card. And fill up your bins.
Yes!

Title: "Old Bean"
Copywriter: Matt Murphy
Art Directors: Bill Winchester, Ken Schmitt
Agency: Miller Meester Advertising
Client: International Minerals & Chemical Corp.

The solid marriage of copy and art in this business appeal has soybean farmers anxious for information, which they can easily obtain via the bind-in reply card.

Title: "Coffee Cup"
Copywriter: Randy Haunfelder
Art Director: Andy Greenaway
Agency: Ogilvy & Mather Direct
Client: Magnet

From Great Britain comes this anonymous testimonial, in conversational first-person style, explaining how easy and pleasant it can be to plan a major home remodeling project.

"How I got a professional designer to measure and plan my new kitchen.

This is all it cost me".

I was pretty fed up with my old kitchen. I barely had counter space to make a sandwich. And I had to yank my cutlery drawer open with both hands – it was sticking so badly.

The time had come to do something. But where to begin? And to be honest, I was a little worried about the cost.

Then I read an article about Magnet's Kitchen Planning Service.

They design a new kitchen for you by computer… free!

"This sounds too good to be true", I thought. "But what have I got to lose?"

Here's what I found

I called my nearest store to ask when a kitchen planner could visit my flat. (I called their Golders Green store but this service is available from any Magnet Superstore.)

It was so easy. I phoned on Tuesday and he came on Friday.

The planner, David Wells, arrived at 9:10 neatly dressed in a pin-striped suit and apologised for being 10 minutes late.

He was friendly and professional. He went straight to work.

First he planned where to put the new units

Did I need a tall cupboard like I have now?

He thought a row of low units would look better. Did I especially want a double sink? A 1½ bowl sink would give more counter space. Did I want new appliances?

"Yes please" (My old gas cooker had character but it was downright ugly.)

While he was measuring the place and drawing a floor plan, I fired questions at him.

I was surprised to learn Magnet has been going for over 100 years. Today, they're one of the UK's largest manufacturers of quality kitchens and bedrooms.

Then he explained how Magnet make their own kitchens

Magnet make their own kitchens, unlike a lot of places. That's why a Magnet kitchen is one of the best you can buy.

After all, with 100 years' experience working with wood, they should know how to build a cabinet better than anyone else.

When he had finished his floor plan, he showed it to me over coffee. It looked wonderful.

"This is great", I exclaimed. "There's enough counter space here for a whole sandwich bar!" (I was starting to get excited.)

"Just you wait", he laughed. "These measurements will go into our computer as soon as I get back to the store. You can pick up your three-dimensional computer drawing tomorrow or I can post it first thing next week". (That's what I call service.)

The big question: "What's this going to cost?"

"You'll receive a computer drawing together with a price", he said. "Then think it over…show it to your friends…even mail a copy to your mother."

"And if I decide against it?"

"If you don't want the kitchen, that's entirely up to you. We're not into hard sell at Magnet", he said proudly.

"Another coffee", I asked.

"No thanks", he smiled. "This is supposed to be a free service".

(For your free catalogue, write to Magnet, Ref THI0, FREEPOST, Royd Ings Avenue, Keighley, West Yorkshire BD21 1BR. Or ring 01-200 0200).

PERSPECTIVE VIEW 3.2

Here's the free computer plan of my new Magnet kitchen I got in the post just a few days after David Wells' visit.

Magnet can do the same for your kitchen–or bedroom–or bathroom. Ring 01-200 0200 for details. For your FREE catalogue write to Magnet, Ref THI0, FREEPOST, Royd Ings Avenue, Keighley, West Yorkshire BD21 1BR.

Name__________

Address__________

Postcode__________

magnet

ALL AROUND THE HOME

TEAM UP WITH THE HUSKERS AND HIKE UP YOUR INTEREST.

Now everytime the Huskers win, you win. Open an American Charter 12-month C.D. with our Big Red Bonus anytime between now and November 8th.

Each time the Huskers win, you'll earn bonus interest* on top of American Charter's already competitive rate. All it takes is $500 or more.

Visit your American Charter branch office today and ask about our Big Red Bonus. It can give you another reason to cheer. And put a little snap in your savings.

*The American Charter Big Red Bonus is bonus interest added to American Charter 12-month C.D.s opened between September 4 and November 8, 1986. Each Cornhusker win during the regular season will increase your rate by .05%. A win at a bowl game will increase your rate by .10%. Interest compounded annually from date of deposit. Bonus rates do not apply in the case of early withdrawal. Penalty for early withdrawal.

AMERICAN CHARTER
Federal Savings and Loan Association
Member FSLIC

Proud to be here. Ready to help.

FSLIC

Title: "Team Up With The Huskers..."
Copywriters: Joshua Mandel, Dave Ullman
Art Director: Ginni Selle
Agency: Cramer- Krasselt/ Chicago
Client: American Charter Savings & Loan

Every home-game Saturday during college football season, the population of Lincoln, Nebraska exceeds that of any other city in the state while better than 60,000 fans cheer their team on. This crisp, image-oriented message capitalizes on that fervor.

Title: "Nanny Care"
Copywriter: Claire O'Brien
Art Director: Stefanie Palermo
Agency: Ogilvy & Mather Direct
Client: Kinder-Care Learning Centers

Parents in Atlanta, Georgia are promised much more than mere daytime child supervision in this full-page black-and-white ad—they're promised complete, loving care by a real "nanny."

If you want someone to hold your child's hand through the wonderful, often puzzling world of childhood and to always be there when you're not... to respond quickly to every need but not give in to every whim... to awaken wonder and put dragons to sleep and build castles in the sand...

Call Nanny Care

Introducing a special kind of child care created for parents who believe children are best cared for at home: Nanny Care—Atlanta's first complete nanny service.

A Nanny Care nanny is given intensive classroom training plus practical experience working with infants and children. She's bright, responsible, warm... someone you can count on to keep your child or children safe and well cared for.

For more information dial
(404) 457-2229

To find out more about the kind of care children enjoy with a trained nanny from Nanny Care...

Dial (404) 457-2229. Or simply return this coupon.

Name ____
Address ____
City ____ State ____ Zip ____
Daytime Telephone ____

Nanny Care
4375 Chamblee-Dunwoody Road
Atlanta, Georgia 30341

THE SOLDIERS IN THESE FILMS TOOK HOME PURPLE HEARTS, NOT OSCARS.®

Photo Courtesy of U.S. Marine Corps

THE CBS VIDEO LIBRARY PRESENTS THE VIETNAM WAR WITH WALTER CRONKITE.

Narrated by Walter Cronkite

These soldiers aren't actors. And these films aren't movies.

This is actual war footage, shot in the heat of combat. Presenting *The Vietnam War with Walter Cronkite*.

In this landmark videocassette series, you'll see Vietnam the way it really was. Because every mortar blast, every sniper, every land mine is real. You'll see Medevac pilots saving lives against incredible odds. B-52 air strikes pounding the hills. From the streets of Hue to the suffocating jungle, through ambushes and booby traps, you'll witness it all as it really happened.

Start with "The Tet Offensive," considered by some to be the most important event of the war. Here the Vietcong violate a cease-fire on their most sacred holiday to launch a stunning and deadly attack. You'll see the siege at Khe Sahn, where 6,000 marines defend their mountain base surrounded by 40,000 North Vietnamese. And at Hue, you'll watch Marine "grunts" advance their position, inch by bloody inch. Much of the footage in this remarkable videocassette was filmed even as the enemy sniped at the cameramen. And it's yours for a ten-day, risk-free trial for just $4.95, if you join today.

As a subscriber, you'll receive a new videocassette every six weeks, always for the same risk-free trial. Each cassette is insightfully narrated by Walter Cronkite. Each features a different chapter of the war.

For each cassette you decide to keep, the price is just $39.95 plus shipping and handling. There's no minimum number to buy. And you can cancel your subscription at any time.

The Vietnam War with Walter Cronkite brings you Vietnam as it really happened. So start with "The Tet Offensive" by sending in the coupon below. For faster service, use your credit card, and call toll free: **1 800 CBS-4804**. (In Indiana, call 1 800 742-1200.)

"THE TET OFFENSIVE," JUST $4.95.

with subscription

CBS VIDEO LIBRARY, 1400 North Fruitridge, Ave., Terre Haute, IN 47811

CBS VIDEO LIBRARY

Dept. AT7, P.O. Box 1111, Terre Haute, In 47811

YES, enter my subscription to *The Vietnam War with Walter Cronkite* under the terms described in this ad. Send me "The Tet Offensive" for the introductory price of just $4.95 which I'm paying as indicated below (*fill in*). Also, send me future cassettes (at $39.95 plus $2.45 shipping and handling) on ten days' approval, with no obligation to buy.

Check one: ☐ **VHS** ☐ **BETA** Check how paying:

☐ **CHECK ENCLOSED** for $4.95* (future cassettes billed with shipment). V11

☐ **CREDIT CARD** Charge my series purchases, beginning with $4.95* for my first cassette, to:

☐ American Express ☐ VISA ☐ MasterCard ☐ Diners Club V12

Account # ______________________ Expiration date __________

Signature ______________________

Name ______________________

Address ______________________

City ____________ State ____________ Zip ____________

NOTE: All subscriptions subject to review. CBS Video Library reserves the right to reject or cancel any subscription. Offer limited to continental U.S. ***Applicable sales tax added to all orders.**

Oscar is a registered trademark of the Academy of Motion Picture Arts and Sciences

Title: "OSCAR"
Copywriter: Joyce Lapin
Art Director: Carol Dronsfield
Agency: Wunderman Worldwide
Client: CBS Video Libraries

In an unflattering reference to Hollywood's acute awareness of the current commercial value of the Vietnam War, this ad depicts combat Marines and discusses their very real wounds while making available a complete video history of the conflict.

Good Fortune Is On Your Doorstep

When You Know How To Sell To The Bay Area's No. 1 Market.

We come from Mainland China and Manila. Hong Kong and Taiwan. We're from Japan and Thailand. From Singapore and Viet Nam. Some of us arrived on these shores well established. Others have had to struggle for generations to be financially comfortable. But together we form a population of more than 500,000 called the Asian-Americans. And almost all of us rely on the Asian Yellow Pages to help us select goods and services.

Proud To Be No. 1!

We're proud of what we are. Hard-working. Thrifty. Family oriented. We cherish our traditions, but we're glad to be a vital part of this community. We're also proud to be important economic contributors:

- The most affluent group in the Bay Area ($27,435 average household income)
- The fastest growing (133% from 1970 to 1980)
- The best educated (33% of adults are college graduates)
- The best credit risks (even though studies show most of us prefer to pay cash)

In other words, we are an extremely important group for almost any business selling virtually any product or service. And, our near relatives, Asian tourists, spend more money per capita than any other foreign visitors to the Bay Area.

How Can Your Business Reach Us?

Well, it will take more than your traditional advertising...conventional yellow pages, newspapers, radio or television. In reaching our market, you will have to overcome two major problems:

Language: Most of us can speak functional or better English, *so your staff will be able to transact business with us easily.* However, most Asian-Americans read only the character language well or at least prefer to read in our native language.

Think of it this way: If you moved to Taiwan, you would start to speak some of the language within six months to a year. But your reading skills would still be well behind. *In fact, studies show, even 20 years from now, you would prefer to read in your mother tongue.*

Acceptance: We've come a long way, but many Asian-Americans are still keenly aware of racial prejudice. We patronize those businesses that welcome our trade. And, to us, an ad in the Asian Yellow Pages is like an engraved invitation.

How Do You Begin?

The Asian Yellow Pages, has published a free booklet, "How To Sell To The Asian Market," which is full of helpful information on how to trade with both Asian-Americans and Asian tourists. This book can show you what to say in ad copy and how to say it. How to position products and services for our market. Even how to make your business more accessible to Asian consumers. And all you have to do to receive your free copy is send in the coupon below.

Where Do You End?

As you begin to understand the Asian-American market, you'll see why the Asian Yellow Pages is so important. It's a complete, full-service directory with listings and display ads in Chinese, Japanese and English. It is distributed to all Asian households, Asian businesses and most hotel and motel rooms in the Bay Area. It is heavily used by Asian-American consumers and has more advertisers than any other ethnic yellow pages in the United States.

As they have for other smart business owners, the Asian Yellow Pages publishers would like to help you reach the Asian-American market. If you would like more information, just check the appropriate box on the coupon below. They'll be glad to send it to you.

To Your Good Fortune.

My family, my friends and all of us in the Asian-American community will be looking for you. And we'll find you... if your ad is in the Asian Yellow Pages. Then you'll find that good fortune truly is on your doorstep.

Asian Yellow Pages

The Source of Good Fortune*

HOW TO SELL TO THE ASIAN MARKET

FREE **"How To Sell To The Asian Market"**

This unique booklet shows you how to reach the Asian-American (or Asian tourist) customer. Learn the unique characteristics of the market. What your advertising should say (and not say). And more. For your copy, at no obligation, just send in this coupon.

YES! I'm ready to tap into the Bay Area's No. 1 market.

☐ Please send me my free copy of **"How To Sell To The Asian Market"**
☐ Also enclose information and rates on the Asian Yellow Pages.
☐ Also enclose copies of the Asian Yellow Pages for my review.

Name __________
Title __________
Company __________
Address __________
City __________ State ______ Zip ______

Asian Yellow Pages
346 9th Street, San Francisco, CA 94103
Call (415) 626-4111

A Division of Direct Language Publishing, Inc.

Title:	"Good Fortune Is On Your Doorstep"
Copywriter:	Chuck Culver
Art Director:	Pam Levinson
Agency:	Solem, Loeb & Associates
Client:	Asian Yellow Pages

The sizable and growing Asian population in the San Francisco area, as explained here, represents a customer base of strong potential for a wide variety of marketers, who can easily get more information by using the coupon.

Title: "ARRIS Leading Edge"
Copywriter: Alan Rosenspan
Art Director: Lysle Wickersham
Agency: Ingalls, Quinn & Johnson
Client: Sigma Design, Inc.

A catchy headline, sound art direction and a no-nonsense bind-in card make it easy and logical for architects and builders to ask for more information about the latest computer-assisted design software promoted here.

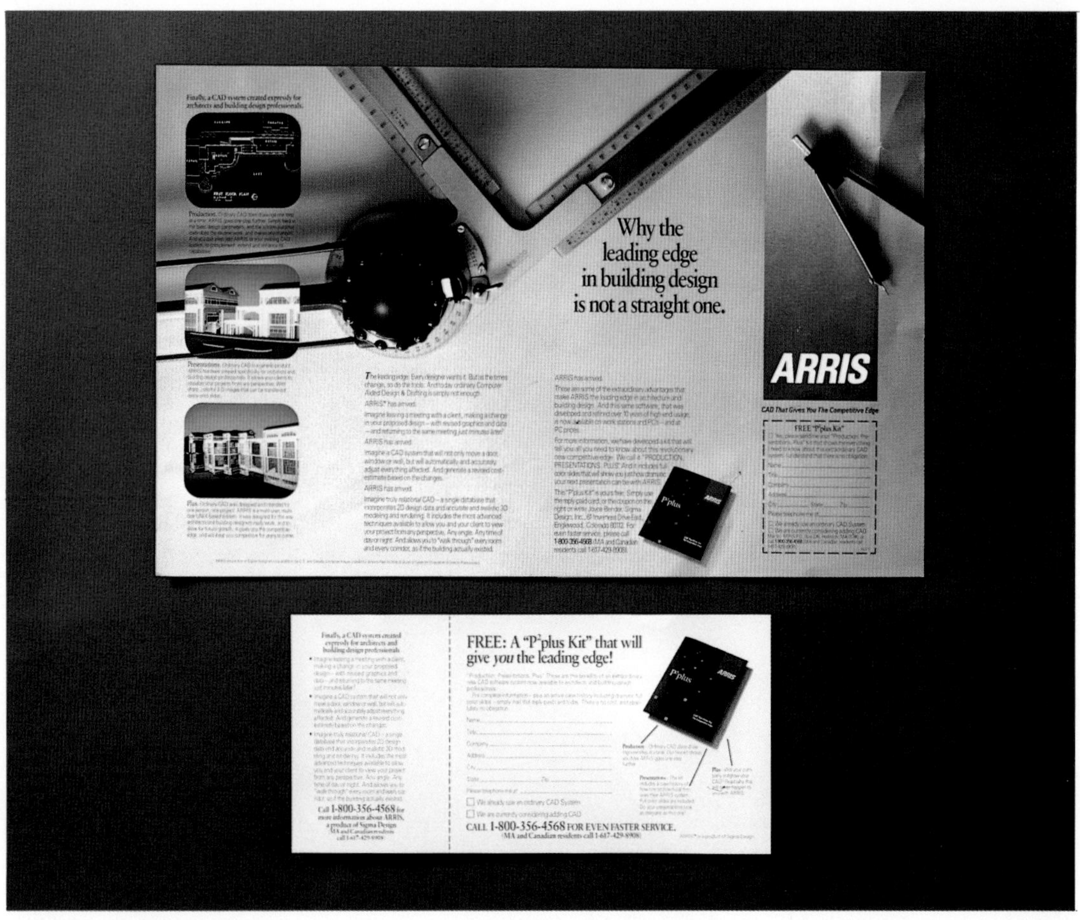

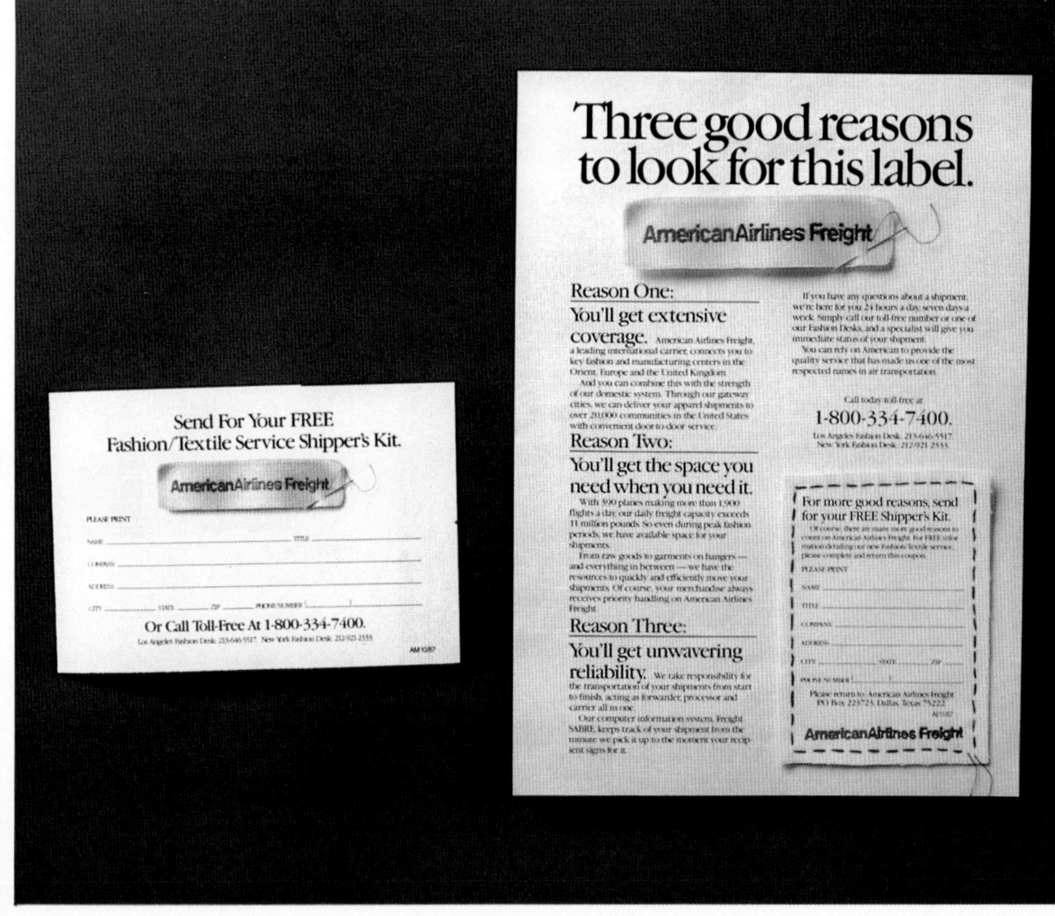

Title: "Look For This Label"
Copywriter: Patricia Gannon
Art Director: Lorraine Shaw
Agency: Bozell, Jacobs, Kenyon & Eckhardt Direct/Dallas
Client: American Airlines Freight

Fashion and textile business professionals are delighted to find an actual clothing label and coupon pinned to this ad, and the accompanying easy-to-use, no-obligation response card encourages additional replies.

Title: "Your Reports Are Also Judged..."
Copywriter: Alan Fonorow
Art Director: Judy Savage
Agency: Cramer-Krasselt/Direct
Client: General Binding Corporation

If business presentations are an extension of one's own personal image, as this ad suggests, nothing but the best will do.

Your reports are also judged by the way they're dressed.

There you stand. A representative of your company.

You're on a roll. Ideas well thought out. Clearly and persuasively expressed. Shouldn't matter how you're dressed.

But, as everybody knows, it matters terribly.

And it also matters how you dress your reports and proposals.

Ironically, many well-tailored professionals think nothing of binding their less-formal documents with staples and clips. Formal reports are often clothed in ordinary office supply covers. Those documents represent you, your department, your company. You deserve better.

GBC binders are far more handsome than standard office supply folders—yet they cost about the same!

Now you can dress up your best ideas in covers that suit your image, taste, and objectives. You can bind them professionally—in-house. Make them colored or clear, personalized or plain, textured or smooth. Possibilities are endless! We'll help you select the look that's right for you!

Most GBC binding systems are no bigger than electric typewriters and are as easy to operate as office copiers. And you'll be amazed that it costs so little to dress your reports so well!

Free "dress-up" booklet available now.

Just complete and mail the coupon or call our toll-free number: 1-800-DIAL-GBC. We'll see that you get a free fact-filled copy of *How To Dress Up Your Reports & Presentations*. No obligation at all.

You'll soon discover how easy it is to dress your presentations for impact, respect, success, and power!

GBC®
1-800-DIAL-GBC.

FREE "DRESS-UP" BOOKLET
Please send me *How To Dress Up Your Reports & Presentations*—with valuable facts and tips—at no cost or obligation.

Name (please print) ____ Title ____
Firm ____
Address ____
City ____ State ____ Zip ____
Phone ( ) ____

STAPLE BUSINESS CARD HERE AND MAIL.

Call toll-free: 1-800-DIAL-GBC. Or mail to GBC
One GBC Plaza, Northbrook, IL 60062

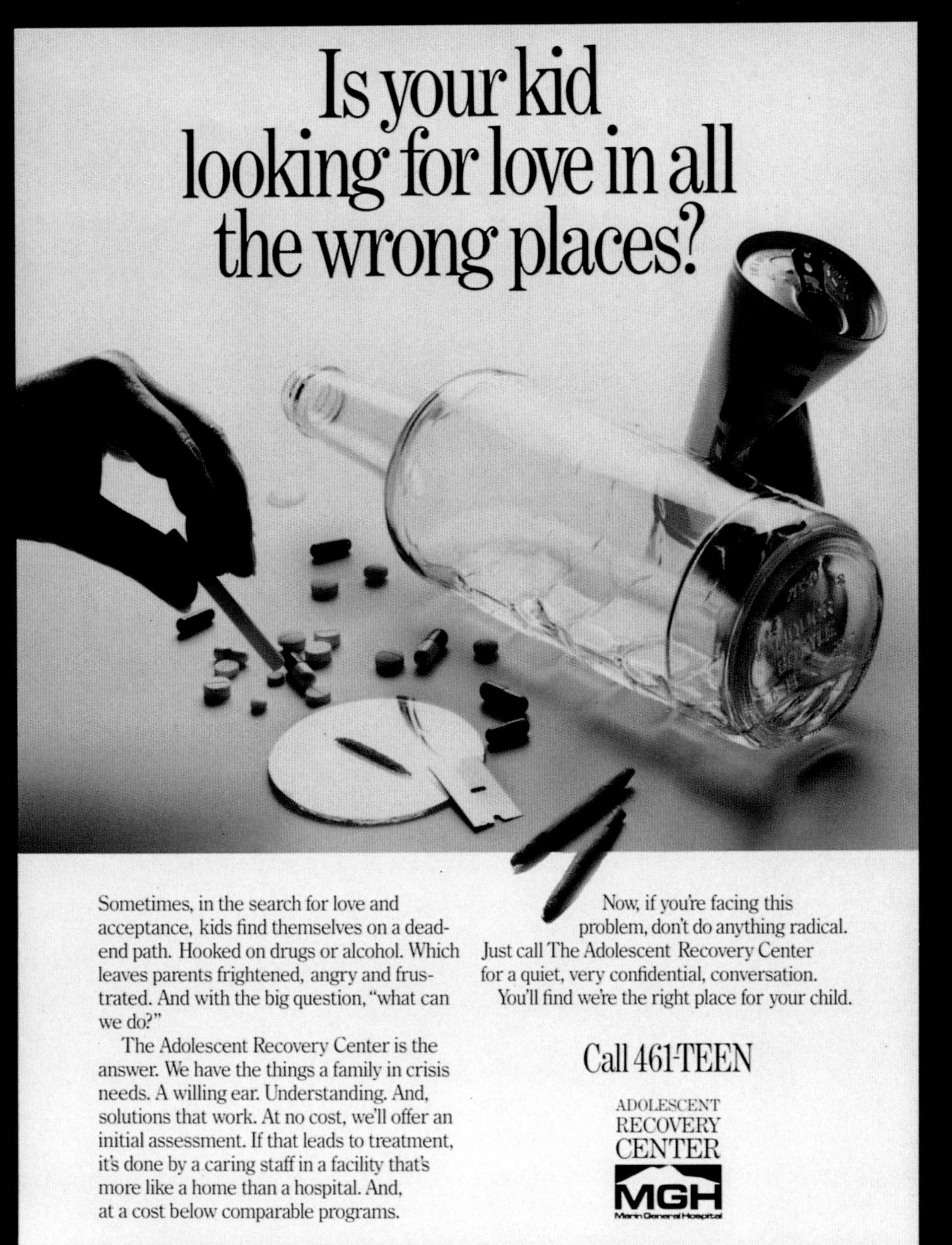

Is your kid looking for love in all the wrong places?
Sometimes, in the search for love and acceptance, kids find themselves on a dead-end path. Hooked on drugs or alcohol. Which leaves parents frightened, angry and frustrated. And with the big question, "what can we do?"
The Adolescent Recovery Center is the answer. We have the things a family in crisis needs. A willing ear. Understanding. And, solutions that work. At no cost, we'll offer an initial assessment. If that leads to treatment, it's done by a caring staff in a facility that's more like a home than a hospital. And, at a cost below comparable programs.
Now, if you're facing this problem, don't do anything radical. Just call The Adolescent Recovery Center for a quiet, very confidential, conversation.
You'll find we're the right place for your child.
Call 461-TEEN
ADOLESCENT RECOVERY CENTER
MGH
Marin General Hospital

Title: "Looking for Love"
Copywriters: Jeff Loeb, Chuck Culver
Art Director: Pam Levinson
Agency: Solem, Loeb & Associates
Client: Marin General Hospital

When teenage drug and alcohol abuse threaten to ruin a kid's life—or end it—help is nearby in the San Francisco/Marin County area, as publicized by this simple, emotional black-and-white message. A telephone "hot line" is the only means of direct response.

Earning it has never been easy.

Applying is.
Call 1-800-458-AMEX.

In a world that is becoming increasingly complex, it's reassuring to know that some things have never been simpler. Like applying for the Gold Card.®

Now, all you have to do to apply is call 1-800-458-AMEX.

With the Gold Card, you'll enjoy an extensive array of financial benefits, including worldwide charge privileges with no pre-set spending limit. In fact, your purchasing power with the Gold Card is limited only by your personal resources and the spending and payment patterns you establish.

And to help you keep track of that spending, Gold Card membership offers you the Year-End Summary of Charges—a comprehensive, chronological account of your Gold Card transactions, clearly broken down by expense category and location.

The Gold Card also gives you access to cash and American Express® Travelers Cheques 24 hours a day in the U.S. and around the world. And it may even include a personal line of credit to draw upon at your discretion.

There's also the convenience of American Express® ENVOY, a personalized 24-hour travel service. Plus a customer service network that is available to you any time of the day or night.

All of which makes the Gold Card a much sought-after credential. And one that has never been easier to apply for.

To acquire the Gold Card, simply call 1-800-458-AMEX.

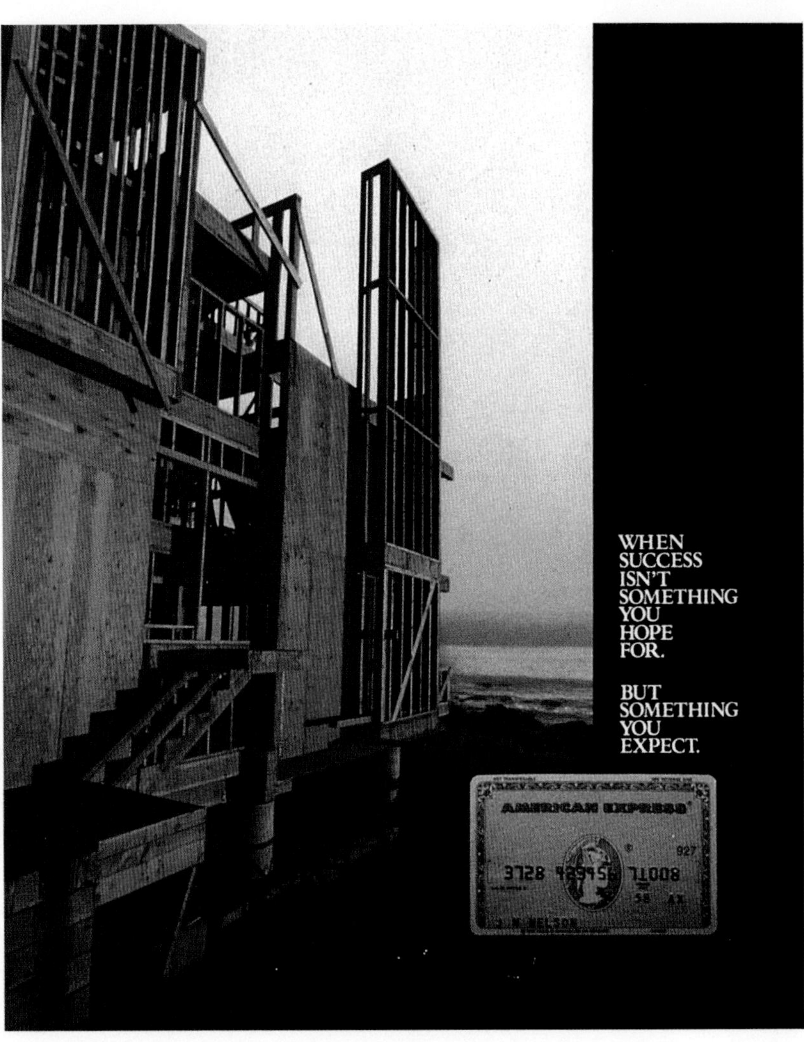
WHEN
SUCCESS
ISN'T
SOMETHING
YOU
HOPE
FOR.
BUT
SOMETHING
YOU
EXPECT.
AMERICAN EXPRESS

There are those who dream. And those who watch their dreams take shape each day.

For the latter, there is the Gold Card.® A card whose commitment to quality and service is evidenced by the select group who call themselves Gold Card members.

Join this group and you'll enjoy an extensive array of financial benefits, including worldwide charge privileges with no pre-set limit imposed upon your spending. In fact, your purchasing power with the Gold Card is limited only by your personal resources and the spending and payment patterns you establish.

And to help you keep track of that spending, Gold Card membership now offers you the Year-End Summary of Charges, a comprehensive, chronological account of your Gold Card transactions, clearly broken down by expense category and location.

The Gold Card also gives you access to cash and American Express® Travelers Cheques 24 hours a day in the U.S. and around the world. And it may even include a personal line of credit to draw upon at your discretion.

There's also the convenience of American Express® ENVOY, a personalized 24-hour travel service. Plus a customer service network that is available to you any time of the day or night.

All of which makes the Gold Card a much sought-after credential. But one that you, no doubt, have always expected to carry.

To acquire the Gold Card, simply fill out and return the accompanying application. Should it be missing, call 1-800-648-AMEX.

THE GOLD CARD®
APPLY TODAY

The Gold Card® Application

U.S. RESIDENTS ONLY

YOUR PERSONAL DATA
First, Middle, Last Name
Soc. Sec. Number | Date of Birth
Street Address | City | State | Zip Code
Home Phone ( ) | Own Home / Rent | Yrs./Mos. There | No. of Other Dependents
Previous Home Address | Years There
Nearest Relative or Friend Not Living With You
Their Address | City | State | Zip Code
Print in the boxes below how you would like your name to appear on the Gold Card. Spell last name completely. Full name must not exceed 20 spaces.

YOUR JOB
Employer | Nature of Business
Position | Yrs./Mos. There
Street Address
City | State | Zip Code
Business Phone ( ) | Self-Employed
If Employed By Above Less Than 3 Years Previous Employer, College or University | Yrs. with Firm or Graduation Date
Street Address
City | State | Zip Code

YOUR INCOME
Your Annual Salary | Amount and Source of Other Income†
Name for Verification of Other Income | Phone ( )
†List other Income and Source (Banker, Broker, Employer, etc.) whom we can call for confirmation. (Alimony, separate maintenance or child support need not be revealed if you do not wish to rely on it.)

CREDIT REFERENCES
Checking Acct. Number | Bank
Bank Address | City | State | Zip Code
Major Credit Card | Account Number
Major/Other Credit Card | Account Number

AMERICAN EXPRESS® CARDMEMBER EXPERIENCE
Present / Past / None | Account Number
Mail bill to office | Mail bill to home

An applicant, if married, may apply for a separate account.

I am asking American Express Travel Related Services Company, Inc. or its participating subsidiaries ("Amex") to open an account and issue me a Gold Card. If I currently have an American Express® Card account, I understand it will not be cancelled unless I so request. I agree to be liable for all charges to my Gold Card account. I agree to be bound by the agreement accompanying the Gold Card unless I cut the Card in half and return it to Amex. If either Amex or I cancel my account or Card, all Cards issued on my account will be cancelled automatically. I am asking to be considered for a Line of Credit from a participating financial institution selected by Amex; should my request for a Line of Credit be denied, my signature constitutes my application for a Gold Card without a Line of Credit. I agree if the financial institution approves this application and if I use the Line of Credit for any purpose, I will be bound by the agreement sent to me by the financial institution. Should my application be denied, my signature below constitutes my application for an American Express Card. I authorize American Express and the financial institution to verify the information supplied above and to receive and exchange credit information about me now and in the future.
Do not enclose the $65 annual Gold Card fee. We will bill you later.

X Signature of Applicant | Date

FOR FINANCIAL INSTITUTION USE ONLY IH
Financial Institution Name | Institution No. | Credit Line $
Routing Symbol | ABA No. | Line of Credit No.
Date Opened | Recommended by | Approved | Declined

PLEASE SEE REVERSE SIDE OF APPLICATION G-06-05-0022-0

PLEASE DETACH, FOLD IN HALF, MOISTEN, SEAL AND MAIL.

Title: "Earning It"
Copywriter: Don Rudnick
Art Director: Holly Pavlika
Agency: McCann Direct
Client: American Express Gold Card

Upwardly mobile magazine audiences are the targeted readers of this comprehensive appeal to acquire a Gold Card. Dominant photography, long copy and a complete application form comprise self-contained opportunities in various editorial environments.

Your Search Is Over—EM Is here!

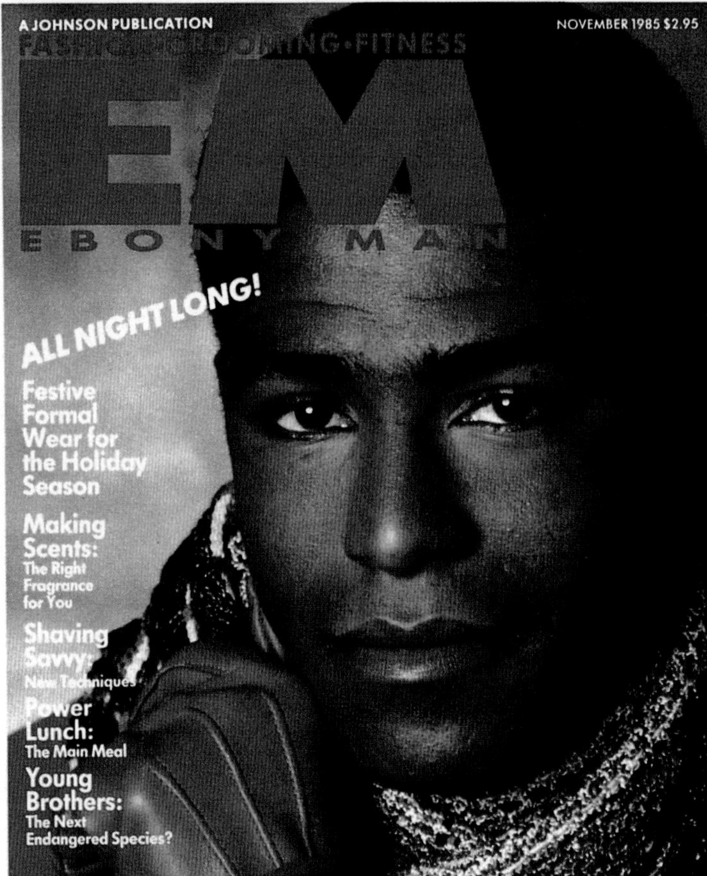

A JOHNSON PUBLICATION
NOVEMBER 1985 $2.95
FASHION·GROOMING·FITNESS
EM
EBONY MAN
ALL NIGHT LONG!
Festive Formal Wear for the Holiday Season
Making Scents: The Right Fragrance for You
Shaving Savvy: New Techniques
Power Lunch: The Main Meal
Young Brothers: The Next Endangered Species?

EM—EBONY MAN— is the definitive Black men's magazine. All these years you've been searching for a magazine that speaks to everything you are, and now there's EM—the magazine for the total Black man!

Each month **EM** will present photo-editorials prepared specifically for you on:

Fashion
Fitness
Grooming
Health
Careers
Finances
Male-female relationships
Home life
Electronic equipment
Entertainment guide

EM will debut in November 1985 with great articles like these: "Is There A New Black Masculinity?," "Tribal Carving: The New African Influence In Black American Hair," "How Never To Be Unemployed," and "How To Talk To The New Black Woman."

SPECIAL CHARTER SUBSCRIPTION RATE:

12 ISSUES ONLY $19.95!
A Savings Of 44% Off The Newsstand Cost!

Clip and Mail Today

EM 820 South Michigan Ave., Chicago, IL 60605
YES, I Want To Subscribe To EM
At The Special Charter Rate of 12 issues for just $19.95
☐ My payment Is Enclosed ☐ Bill Me

Name ____________
Address ____________
City ____________ State ____________ Zip ____________
Signature ____________
Offer Good in USA Only EMON85

Title:	"Your Search is Over..."	To introduce the new magazine Ebony Man, bold red logo repetition and straight-to-the-point copy surround a large four-color reproduction of the publication's debut cover.
Copywriter:	Lydia J. Davis	
Art Director:	Norman L. Hunter	
Agency:	In-House	
Client:	Johnson Publishing Company	

A twenty-dollar donation in the name of Liberty isn't much to ask, considering what some have given.
Since that day our forefathers first realized that a "Land of Liberty" could be more than a dream, men have risked their lives for it. First, to achieve it. And since, to preserve it.
To these men of principle, we, as a nation, award these strips of colored ribbon. Symbols. Symbols of lives willingly risked, and lives taken. Of friendships made, and friendships ended. Of love letters sent, but never answered. Of fathers. Of brothers. Of sons.
The very fundamental which these men left their homes and families to protect also has a symbol: The Statue of Liberty.
October 28, 1986 will mark 100 years she has been our proud representative. And as citizens of these free states, it is our obligation to see to it that her restoration is completed by then.
The opportunity to take a stand for liberty is now yours. Your generous donation will help ensure that Miss Liberty celebrates her birthday in a manner befitting a lady of her stature. And that the legacy left us by so many brave men and women shall never be forgotten.
Give today, others have already given so much.
Send your check to: Statue of Liberty-Ellis Island Foundation, P.O. Box 1992-Dept. M, N.Y., NY 10008.
An appeal to the American public by Ogilvy & Mather Direct.
Vietnam Cross of Gallantry Second Class
Air Medal
Armed Forces Expeditionary Campaign
Air Force Commendation
Medal of Honor
WW II–Victory
Joint Services Commendation
Asiatic–Pacific Campaign
Army Commendation
Marine Expeditionary Campaign
United Nations
WW II–Occupation of Germany Berlin Airlift
United States Coast Guard Commendation
Distinguished Service Cross Navy
Distinguished Service Cross Air Force
American Red Cross
Merchant Marine Combat Ribbon
American Campaign
Silver Star
Republic of Vietnam Campaign
National Defense
Soldier's Medal
Vietnam Service
WW I–Victory
Airman's Medal
Combat Action Ribbon
Women's Army Corps
Armed Forces Reserve
Merchant Marine Atlantic War Zone
Korean Service
Legion of Merit Legionnaire
Philippine Independence
Bronze Star
Distinguished Flying Cross
American Defense
China Service
Purple Heart
WW I–Occupation of Germany
European–African–Middle Eastern Campaign
Philippine Defense
Air Force Longevity
Secretary of Navy Commendation for Achievement
Navy–Marine Corps Medal
Naval Reserve

Title: "Twenty dollars isn't much..."
Copywriter: Vincent Chieco
Art Director: Jon Grondahl
Agency: Ogilvy & Mather Direct
Client: Time Magazine/Forum for Freedom

This appeal for donations to the Statue of Liberty centennial rebuilding fund utilizes the symbolism of war decorations to represent veterans who gave their lives protecting America's freedom. The copy makes a compelling case for all citizens to make a contribution.

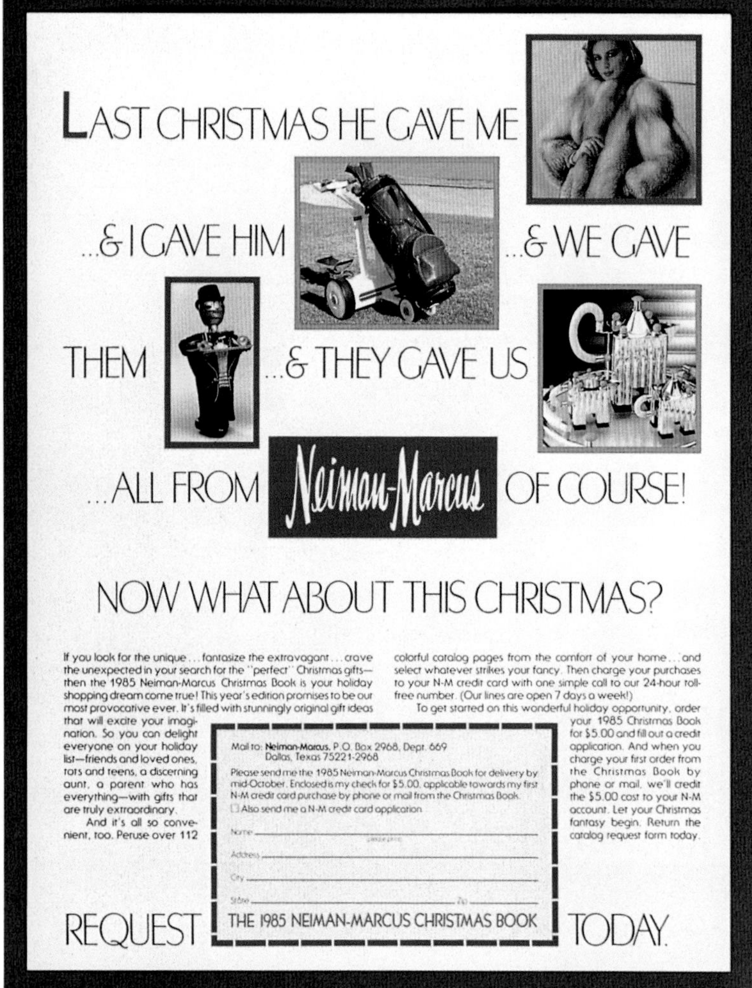

Title:	"The Rebus"
Copywriter:	Jerry Ricigliano
Art Director:	Jerry Genova
Agency:	Rapp & Collins
Client:	Neiman-Marcus

The reader has no choice but to take the time to understand the headline in this interesting, accessible one-page promotion for The Christmas Book, a catalog, from one of the world's best-known department stores.

Title: "Firewood"
Copywriters: Ralph Westerhoff, Jeff Ostroth
Art Director: Derek Karsanidi
Agency: Kobs & Brady Advertising
Client: Foster Parents Plan

This award-winning ad reaches the reader down deep, but offers hope and a way to help.

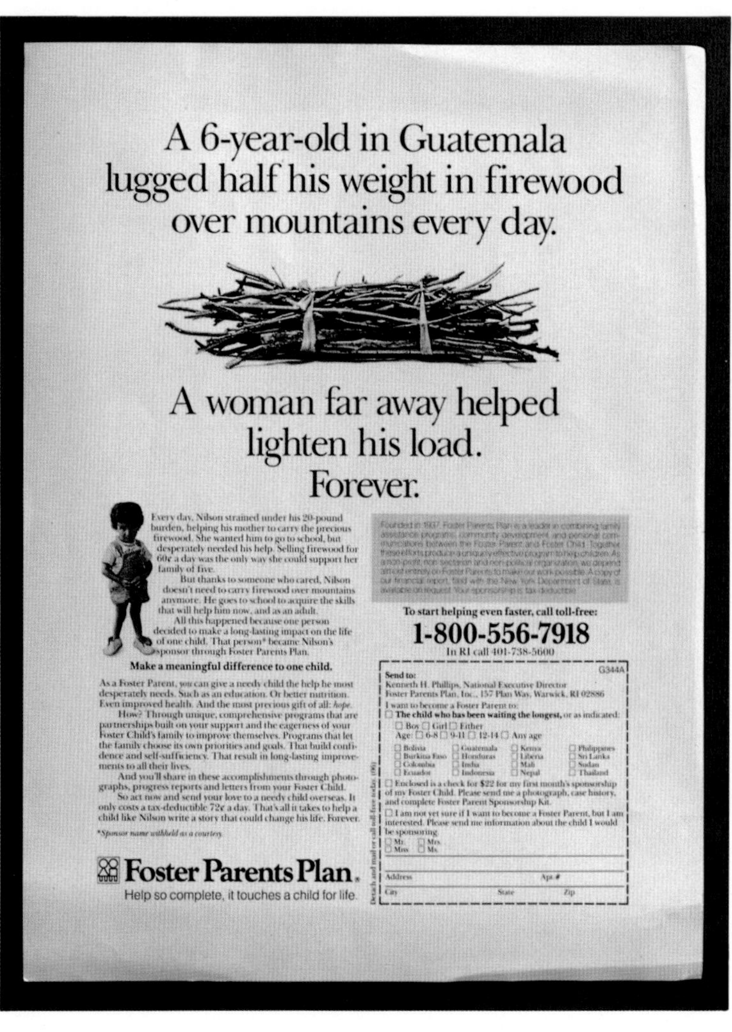

Title: "The 38-Minute Foolproof Chocolate Chip Souffle"
Copywriter: Jerry Ricigliano
Art Director: Lucia Barrientos
Agency: Rapp & Collins
Client: Margrace, Inc.

Previously marketed as a set of recipe cards, the 60-Minute Gourmet series is re-positioned in this one-page-plus-bind-in as a means of obtaining delicious food, not as a collection that comes in a handy plastic case.

Chapter
3
PBC INTERNATIONAL
ONE SCHOOL STREET
GLEN COVE, NY 11542

CATALOGS

There are no precise figures available on the number of different catalogs published each year, but what is certain is that the field has seen explosive growth since the late 1970s. Between consumer and business-to-business catalogs, some direct marketing experts estimate that as many as 7,500 distinct efforts are created annually, with mailing quantities running into the billions of pieces.

Coupled with the many remarkable advances being made (and those on the horizon) in computer technology and database manipulation, not to mention a steady stream of intelligent marketing strategy, the catalog has been busy breaking important new ground for itself. To millions of people, catalogs are "the other half" of an ongoing one-to-one relationship.

An immense measure of responsibility for the success or failure of a catalog rests with its creative identity, from concept and development to execution and production. One customer may respond to the "voice" of the copy while another gets more involved in the "presence" of the merchandise as he perceives it within the catalog's graphic environment. Either way, or when both influences are equal, the catalog as a complete entity must manage to keep the lines of communication wide open. It must maintain a certain continuity through dozens, hundreds, even thousands of different products. Winning catalogs, no matter what their specialty, are polished, finely-tuned, fully-developed creative presentations.

In the spring of 1988, the challenge to publish successful catalogs in the United States suddenly became more difficult. Heavy increases in postal rates for business mail went into effect, and, almost at the same time, bulk paper prices rose significantly. The cost of producing and distributing a catalog shot up by more than 40 percent in some cases, slashing profits and curtailing the ability to grow.

Two immediate priorities are faced by catalog marketers, who must defend their chances for prosperity or even protect their very survival. New economies must be imposed to lower the total cost of getting catalogs into the mail, and each of these catalogs must sell more than it did before. So, the burden becomes even heavier on copywriters and art directors to maximize the selling power of their creativity.

The catalogs in this chapter have already done that—and some, notably The Sharper Image and Banana Republic, have expanded into the retail marketplace, with stores that embody the themes first created for the two-dimensional, printed page.

Other catalogs, including the 10th Annual Caples Awards First Prize winner in the Consumer division, Armstrong Roses' "The Rosebook" on pages 140-141, are truly a sight to behold.

Observing the superior talent and craftsmanship of the people who created these efforts, and that of their many colleagues, it is fair to expect that adjustments to alleviate less-than-ideal conditions in the American catalog field can and will be made. Globally speaking, the opportunities seem virtually unlimited as their pursuit continues.

THE SHARPER IMAGE®

November 1986 $1.00

Order direct.
800 344-4444

Take home an American beauty.

Title: "The Sharper Image Catalog"
Copywriters: Deborah Bishop, Doug Payne, Tim Murray
Art Directors: Pat Margis, Noren Schmitt, Trisha Stricklan, Carole Czapla
Agency: In-House
Client: The Sharper Image, Inc.

Time after time, The Sharper Image finds a fresh approach to the presentation of its unusual merchandise and its must-have but hard-to-find mainstays—and the creative execution and production values remain consistently high.

Keep a golden tan all year round. On the improved home solarium.

Compared to last year's model, Portatan's newest home Solarium tans you more efficiently, saves energy, and weighs *over 20 lbs. less*. With all these improvements, it should sell for $1,000 or more. Yet it's yours through The Sharper Image for the same low price as last year's model—just $745.

Now you can get an even, golden tan at home—without the inconvenience of a heavy, bulky machine. Portatan is the first home solarium to eliminate cumbersome starter ballasts. Instead, a new electronic circuit instantly lights the bulbs—without flicker or delay. This patented printed circuit uses approximately half the energy for bulb start-up as conventional ballasts. Heat build-up is also reduced, eliminating noisy fans.

With its trimmer base and new slimline canopy, Portatan is easier to move and store. Weighs just 57 lbs. New gas-filled strut lets you adjust the canopy easily with one hand.

6' canopy adjusts to any angle and any height from 25½" to 32½".

New, one-piece molded plastic reflectors disperse light more evenly than old-style aluminum reflectors. And they strengthen the canopy, making it more rigid. Reflectors span at 45° angles to tan your *sides* as well as your front and back.

To store, simply lock the canopy into the upright position and roll into a closet on easy-gliding casters. Measures 78¾H × 32½W × 6½D" folded for storage.

Precision built in England of vinyl-coated steel. Ten minute assembly (attaching 2 bolts) requires an adjustable wrench. Plugs into regular AC outlet. Long-life Phillips tubes last for 2,000 ½-hour sessions. Comes with instructions, goggles, and audio cassette with tips on safe, fast tanning. One-year warranty. A Sharper Image exclusive.

Variable 1–30 minute timer makes sure you never burn.

Take 30 days to discover the glow of confidence that comes with a total tan—whatever the weather.

■ Portatan Electronic Solarium #JPT600 $745 (79.00)

Please include address and daytime phone number when ordering.

30 minutes to a tropical tan.

Stretch out on your couch, bed, or chaise lounge and bask in the restful glow. Phillips TL-09 bulbs produce even more mild UVA tanning rays than last year's bulbs. FDA-approved bulbs filter out 99.7% of harmful UVB rays—leaving just enough to activate your body's natural tanning process.

After 4–8 initial sessions, you're rewarded with a rich, golden tan. Then just two 30-minute sessions a week will keep your tan.

Indoor tanning vs. the sun. How safe?

Compared to the sun, indoor tanning systems emit just a fraction of the wavelengths of light that can cause burning of the skin. And this percentage has been greatly reduced as technology has improved.

Although no one should tan to excess, following the schedule recommended in your solarium's instructions will leave you looking great. And feeling confident about your appearance.

When purchasing a tanning system, look for a protective safety grid across the lamp array. If a lamp should become dislodged, the grid prevents costly breakage—while protecting you from the hazards of broken glass. Some cheaper versions on the market lack this essential safety requirement.

26

Penetrate the mysteries of perpetual motion.

Silently, the polished rotor rolls back and forth. Four times a minute. In a day, travelling more than a mile. What unseen force propels it? Is this the perpetual motion machine that eluded so many great minds throughout history?

Almost. Space Wheel™ is modern physics turned into fascinating kinetic art. Each time the rotor rolls past the center, an electronic coil concealed in the base gives a gentle boost to three magnets hidden inside the rotor arms. Patented design runs five months on one 9v battery (included). Made of polycarbonate and ABS. 3H × 2½W × 13D", 7 oz. 30-day warranty.

The rhythmic motion of Space Wheel casts a calming spell over any room. And inspires brisk speculation among your science-minded friends. While they proclaim, "Impossible!" Space Wheel rolls on—silently and inexorably.

■ Space Wheel #JWC910 $25 (3.00)

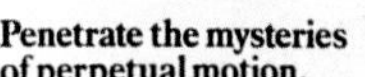

Technology opens new underwater worlds.

Molded of surgical-grade, allergy-tested silicone, Tekna's new diving mask and snorkel are virtually immune to the effects of sunlight, saltwater and age. The mask's anatomically curved, low-volume design insures easy clearing. Optical-grade lenses minimize distortion and reflection. Unique roller-locks on straps adjust with one hand.

New self-draining snorkel with large diameter one-way valve automatically purges 90% of trapped water. Patented tube-tab mouthpiece swivels 360°, has collapsible tooth lugs that conform to your individual bite, eliminating jaw fatigue. 13" long ⅞" diameter.

Flexible fins: new power for swimmers.

Force Fin® is engineered to generate the greatest kicking power with the least effort. Unlike a stiff, heavy rubber fin, Force Fin's molded polyurethane blade folds down on the upkick to reduce water resistance, and snaps open for full power on the downstroke. The water flows backward rather than up and down, so you don't have to work as hard. Force Fin is lighter than rubber (just 24 oz.) and your toes are free to bend naturally. Adjustable nylon straps with quick-release plastic buckles assure a perfect fit. 18" long. One-year warranty.

■ Tekna Scuba Mask #JTE132 $49 (3.50)
■ Snorkel #JTE145 $22 (3.50)
■ Force Fin® #JBT520 $49 (3.50)

Please indicate size (see chart).

SIZE CHART by shoe size		
Force Fin	Men	Women
Small	5–6½	7–8½
Med.	7–8½	9–10½
Med.–Lg.	9–10½	11–12½
Lg.	11–12½	

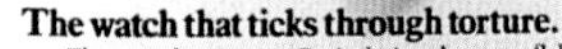

The watch that ticks through torture.

The crowd at a recent Paris design show was flabbergasted: after 10 hours strapped to the wheel of a motorcycle, turning continuously over solid brick, the Stunt's precision Swiss ETA movement was *still in perfect condition*. Shielded by a patented anti-shock system, this European marvel is built to withstand up to *two tons* of pressure—with no effect on its quartz-accurate performance.

Under the hardened mineral glass crystal, the luminescent hands are readable day or night, on land or under sea (watertight to 330 ft.). Case, stem, backing and bracelet are 100% tough stainless steel—yet the watch is just 8mm thin, comfortable enough to wear skiing, diving, or through a hard-fought rugby match. Accurate to ±15 seconds per month. Comes with three-year battery and year warranty. Order the rugged watch that sets new standards of shock resistance.

■ Stunt Watch #JKZ850 $89 (3.50)

Please indicate man's or woman's when ordering.

December 1986 | $1.00
OVER 20 MILLION READERS MONTHLY

THE SHARPER IMAGE

THE SHARPER IMAGE

Beverly Hills store
now open.
See back cover.

Order direct.
800 344-4444

THE SHARPER IMAGE®

October 1986 $1.00

OVER 20 MILLION READERS MONTHLY

Now open: New Orleans and Newport Beach. See back cover.

Find her before she finds you.

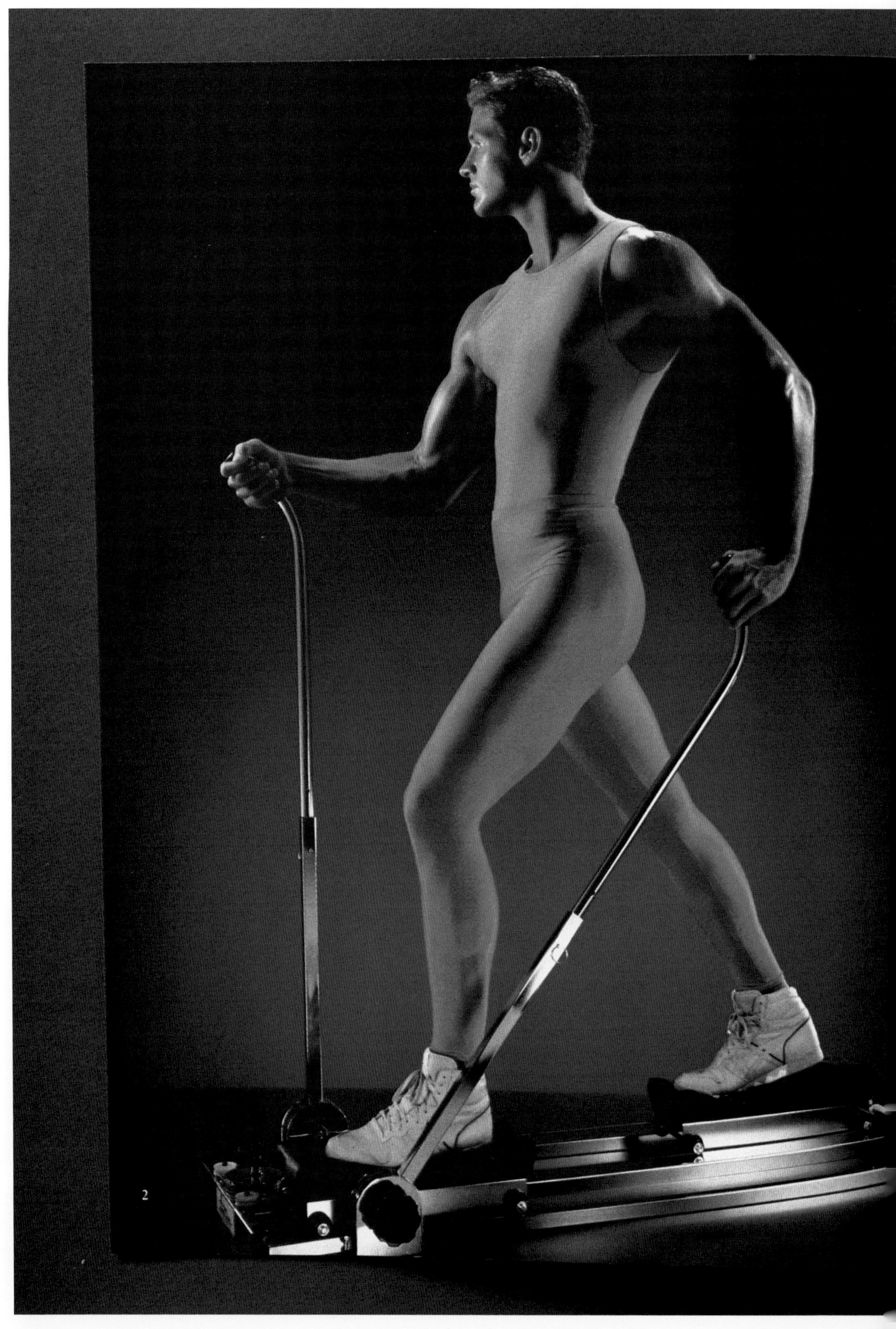
2

Move cross-country.

Treat your body to the *best* aerobic workout.

If you've ever spent an afternoon skiing cross-country, you know how invigorated you feel. Fitness experts say it's the best aerobic exercise you can do. In fact, a hardy group of endurance cross-country skiers in Scandinavia have the highest cardiovascular capacities ever measured.

The smooth, rhythmic movements tone every major muscle group in your body—legs, buttocks, torso, shoulders, and arms. Without the repetitive impact to your body of jogging or aerobic dancing.

Now you can get the fitness and muscle toning benefits of this popular sport at home. New Fitness Master™ is the most effective cross-country skiing simulator we've seen (see box).

Tension adjustment knobs on the poles and footpad pulley let you dial in the exact resistance that's right for you.

Aerobics made easy.

This is the surprise of a Fitness Master workout: *you don't feel like you're working.* You're not straining. Your muscles aren't crying out with pain. Yet within minutes, you can easily elevate your respiration and pulse to the aerobic target rate for your age.

Cross-country skiing is the best aerobic exercise because it rhythmically works so many muscles. And since so many muscles are in motion, *less effort is required from each muscle.* The best exercise is also the easiest to do.

To begin, just step into the cushioned footpads (with or without shoes) and grasp the handgrips. Now, push and pull on the arm poles as you slide your feet back and forth—as if you were gliding across a snow-covered hillside. Repeat this simple 20-minute workout three times a week: 3-minute warm-up, 12 minutes at your target pulse rate, 5-minute cool-down. That's all there is to it.

As your stamina grows, you can increase your workout by striding faster, lengthening your poling motion and stride, or increasing the resistance. Tension adjustment knobs on the poles and footpad pulley let you dial in the exact resistance that's right for you (up to 50 lbs. resistance on the armpoles and 280 lbs. on the footpads). Resistance is both positive and negative for fullest muscle development.

Burn 500–900 calories per hour.

There's a good reason you won't find an inch of fat on experienced cross-country skiiers. This sport burns calories prodigiously. Sustained aerobics can also raise your body's metabolic rate. So even *at rest,* you burn more calories. You can permanently lower your body's "set point"—the point at which your weight tends to stabilize. So you can control your weight without starvation diets.

Built in the U.S., Fitness Master's chrome-plated steel construction will stand up to many years of rugged use. Non-slip vinyl covers the padded footpads, linked by aircraft cable. Sturdy handlebars adjust to five heights. To store, just push the handles down flat and roll into a closet or under a bed. Folded, measures only 5H × 24½W × 52L", weighs 36 lbs. Minor assembly (attaching knobs) requires pliers. Comes with exercise guide and *two year* warranty.

Feel younger. Look better.

One hour every week working out on Fitness Master can bring profound changes. You'll feel your heart and lungs growing stronger, reducing your risk of cardiovascular disease. Also growing stronger are your joints, bones, and lower back. You'll fall asleep easier, sleep better, and wake with more energy. You'll find that you can work longer, with less fatigue. Your performance in sports will improve. And you'll feel a sense of pride in your trim, toned, and healthy body.

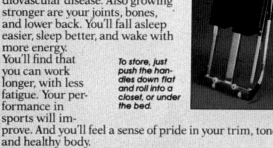

To store, just push the handles down flat and roll into a closet, or under the bed.

Call now to invest in a healthier life. Order Fitness Master for a 30-day trial.

■ **Fitness Master #LFT350 $399 (18.50)**

Fitness Master: The better choice.

Here's how Fitness Master stacks up against the other leading brand*:

Fitness Master	Nordic Track®
• Two-way adjustable resistance—backwards *and* forwards.	• One-way adjustable resistance—backwards only.
• Comfortable upright exercise position.	• Stressful forward-leaning exercise position.
• Footpads linked for coordinated movement.	• Footpads move independently. Awkward if both skis move backwards at same time.
• Stable base—rests flat on floor.	• Elevated on legs.
• Operates in 4'-4" of floor space. Folds flat to 5".	• Requires over 7' of floor space. Folds to 17" high.
• All chrome-plated steel construction.	• Wood and painted metal construction.
• Costs $399.	• Costs $470–559.

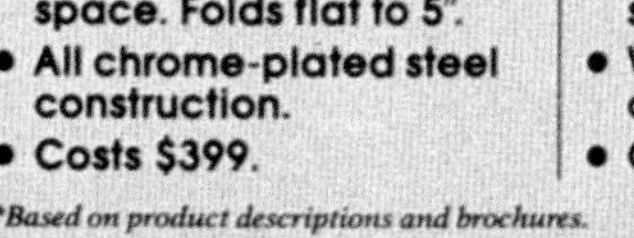

*Based on product descriptions and brochures.

BANANA REPUBLIC
·TRAVEL & SAFARI CLOTHING Co.·
CATALOGUE NO. 32 • SUMMER 1987 • ONE DOLLAR

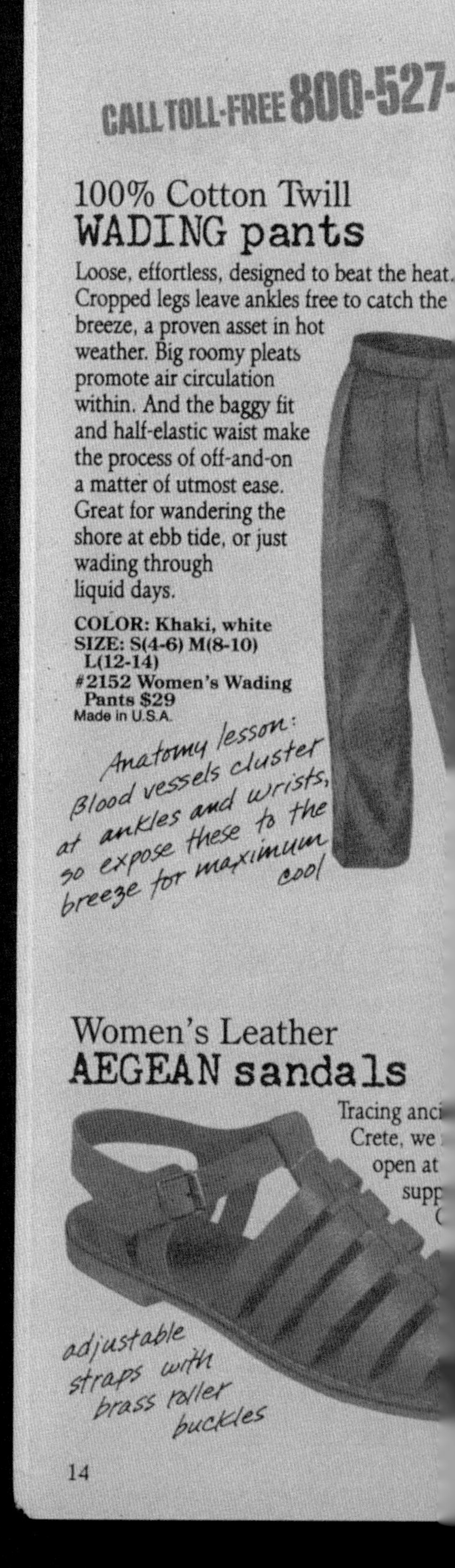

Title: "Banana Republic Catalogue #32"
Copywriters: Mel Ziegler, Nancy Friedman, David Darlington, Christie Allair
Art Directors: Terry Stelling, Mike Madrid, Craig Hannah, Robert Stein, An-Ching Chang, Peg Magovern
Agency: In-House
Client: The Banana Republic Travel & Safari Clothing Company

A perennial favorite, this Summer '87 edition of the Banana Republic Catalogue is entitled "Expatriates" and also features signed "Customer Letters" that appear throughout the booklet.

STRIPED JERSEY ON PAGE 28
side-seam pockets
white
soft pre-washed twill
…rkens …h age
…rom the roads of Rome to the cliffs of … timeless shoe design. Our Aegean Sandals, …r ventilation, are constructed like shoes to …n the feet, wherever your odyssey leads. …e-old Italian care from natural vegetable-…ther. Rippled rubber soles with slightly …l heels lend traction on tricky terrain. Suit-…ble for defying lions, evading Minotaurs, consulting oracles, or just tramping through the Cyclades in classical style.
COLOR: Natural
SIZE: 5½-10, medium width
#8047 Women's Aegean Sandals $49
Made in Italy
white
salmon
manila
WOVEN JUTE BELT ON PAGE 57
SANTA FE BELT ON PAGE 24
bleached chambray
100% Cotton PAINTER'S shirt
A no-fuss pullover of soft, lightweight cotton, our Painter's Shirt is cool and roomy enough to let your imagination and your brushstroke range freely. Cut like something your grandfather might have worn in the 20's, with a box pleat and long tail in the back, it's equally inspiring worn belted or hanging loose. A genuine study in summer comfort, be your subject sylvan landscape or side of barn.
By Bobbie Ann Mason
I'm not an artist but I refuse to let that stop me from wearing this swell shirt. Here are eleven extracurricular things to do in a Painter's Shirt: make a blackberry pie; play Parcheesi; read War and Peace; dance to "Woolly Bully;" go to the mall to buy nail polish; watch "M★A★S★H" reruns; jump rope; go bicycling; go on safari to Nebraska or Atlantic City or Asbury Park; go trekking along the Milford Sound in New Zealand; write a novel called Cotton, the Tale of a Shirt. I've done most of these, or thought about doing them. (Also, great news—the Painter's Shirt doesn't show cat hair!)
Bobbie Ann Mason
Literary artist Bobbie Ann Mason is the author of Shiloh and Other Stories and In Country.
COLOR: Bleached chambray, white, manila, salmon
SIZE: S M L
#1382 Painter's Shirt $36
Made in U.S.A.
S M L
MEN – 34-36 38-40
WOMEN 4-6 8-10 12-14
15

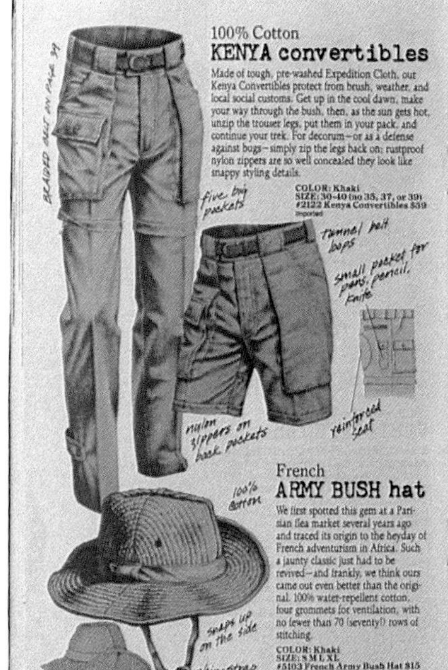

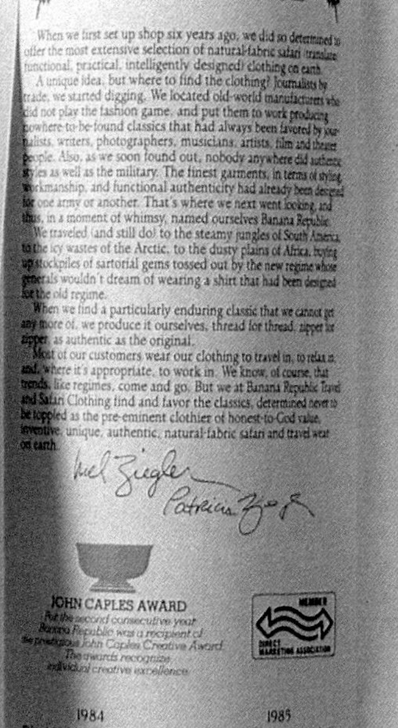

CALL TOLL-FREE 800-527-5200

TO SHOP BY PHONE

Our salespeople are on duty to take your orders 6 am to 7 pm weekdays (Pacific time), 8:30 am to 5 pm weekends (Pacific time). American Express, VISA, MasterCard and Diner's Club accepted. Just fill out the order form, give us a call and have your credit card number handy.

SUBSCRIBE! SUBSCRIBE!

Because we're ex-journalists, we naturally think of our catalogue as the official magazine of our imaginary republic. We set out to entertain our readers while giving them as much information as possible about our authentic, classic, functional, natural-fabric clothing and accoutrements. Our staff writers are reporters whose assignment is to tell the story of each item fully and conscientiously. No magazine is complete without reviews, and ours are written by some of the most distinguished writers on the planet. We also write about and illustrate our wanderings to discover and test new products. We think it's a very good read and the *Seattle Times* agrees—calls it the "hottest new publication in the country." If you're placing an order now or have ordered in the last two years, you'll be on our subscription list. Otherwise, to continue receiving the Banana Republic catalogue, please fill in the space below.

Name ______
Address ______
City ______ State ______ Zip ______

If you'd like to introduce us to friends, please provide information on their whereabouts and we'll send them a copy of our catalogue.

Name ______
Address ______
City ______ State ______ Zip ______

MOVING?

If you are moving, please write your old and new addresses in the spaces provided below. Please circle your new address.

Name ______
Address ______
City ______ State ______ Zip ______

Name ______
Address ______
City ______ State ______ Zip ______

DUPLICATE MAILINGS?

If you've received duplicates of our catalogue, please clip and send us all the mailing labels from the back cover and indicate the correct one. We'll tell the computer.

Outback Cloth
CORRESPONDENT'S
jacket
An overseas tradition that has stood the test of *Time*, as well as *Life*, *Newsweek*, UPI, and Reuters. Our new version, made of our pre-washed 100% cotton Outback Cloth, exudes character and venerability. Classic bush-jacket styling with epaulets, and bellows pockets with room enough for notebooks, tape recorder, and a flask of brandy for the chance icy encounter. The gathered waist adds dash; button sleeves roll up when the deadline rolls around. A jacket built for getting down and dirty in the field. Perfect for reporters who need to look as if they've been around even if they spent the war in the corner pub. Not recommended for *Pravda* correspondents, however—the jacket permits too much freedom of movement.
pewter
pre-washed
side entry pockets
bellows pockets
ivory
COLOR: Ivory, pewter
SIZE: XS S M L XL
#3093 Outback Cloth Correspondent's Jacket $69
Imported
2 pleated back pockets
khaki
pewter
100% pre-washed cotton
Men's
OUTBACK shorts
Hiking the harsh, demanding Outback, you carry as little extra equipment as possible and look for practical ways to distribute essentials. How best to manage this problem? Witness our Outback Shorts with expandable cargo bellows pockets and wide belt loops for fastening canteen, army knife, and compass.
COLOR: Khaki, ivory, pewter
SIZE: 30-40 (no 35, 37 or 39)
#2566 Men's Outback Shorts $36
Imported
flap patch pocket
ivory
40

100% cotton
navy
stone
manila
mocha
100% Cotton
OUTBACK shirt
button fly
India is famous for its hand-loomed fabrics, but what's often overlooked are its equally superlative milled textiles. Made of longer (thus stronger) fibers, these cottons are soft and lustrous, yet amazingly resistant to fraying and other signs of wear. We had one of India's premier textile mills weave a silky cotton for us in stripes adapted from the patterns of turn-of-the-century men's dress shirts. Then we designed a shirt inspired by the collarless, loose-fitting shirts worn by Australia's early jackeroos—the cowboys of the Outback. We think you'll be as pleased as we are by its handsome looks, its creamy feel, and its staunch dependability.
COLOR: Manila, mocha, stone, navy
SIZE: S M L XL
#1112 Outback Stripe Shirt $36 Imported
To find the size that fits you best, please see our size chart on the order form.
pre-washed
adjustable waist
Men's OUTBACK pants
On our last trip to Sydney, we dug up a particularly well-made pair of Australian army pants of WWII vintage. We replicated the ingenious design in Outback cloth and added a Dutch-inspired ankle tab.
COLOR: Khaki
SIZE: 29-38 (no 35 or 37)
#2106 Men's Outback Pants $49 Imported
ankle tab
100% pre-washed cotton
41

Title: "The Banana Republic Catalogue"

Copywriters: Mel Ziegler, Julie Smith, Nancy Friedman, David Darlington

Art Directors: Terry Stelling, Bonnie Dahan, Patricia Ziegler, Anatoly Belkin

The editorial thrust of the Banana Republic continues its expansion in these editions which feature cover stories and central themes within the stylized environment established in earlier versions.

Title: "Customer Services Book"
Copywriter: Mike Paul
Art Director: Paul Davies
Agency: McCarthy Cosby Paul
Client: Unisys UK Ltd.

From London comes this highly personalized package that includes a handsome 40-page booklet in an attache-type portfolio, a signed personal letter and no fewer than seven postage-paid reply devices offering management, consultative and practical services to senior business executives.

SYSTEMS SOFTWARE MAINTENANCE & SUPPORT

30

Hardware, software, machines and systems – the consequence of a fault developing in any is, at best, inconvenience; at worst – no one can tell. And Systems Software is no more immune than anything else.

UNISYS is superbly experienced and equipped to diagnose and correct System Software faults. Our combination of skills and back-up resources are your assurance that, should your System Software fail, your business won't.

Inconvenience is the mildest of consequences of a software fault; considerable expense waiting for the fault to be corrected is more common, plus hefty costs incurred through missed deadlines.

UNISYS Software Maintenance and Support Services can provide timely and valuable assistance, with sophisticated computer-based techniques for speeding the correction process.

To put all this to work for you, the most sophisticated device you need is a telephone.

One call connects you to the UNISYS Support Centre. Just as with Hardware Maintenance, the computer there holds an on-line database on which is listed every fault known to UNISYS, plus the corrections which have to be made in each case. The terminal operator can advise and help in the correction process while your call is underway.

Your equipment can, in fact, be linked directly to ours at the UNISYS Support Centre via the telephone system. From then on, we can run a full diagnostic program to locate and analyse the fault; it can even be corrected automatically in many cases.

Should the fault resist all attempts at remote correction, our specialists have direct access to UNISYS hardware manufacturing facilities and software development centres. If necessary, they can trace the problem right back to source and put right anything on the way.

In short, software faults are no more daunting to us than hardware faults; all that changes is the people who have the know-how and the resources to correct the situation. Fast.

UNISYS SERVICES

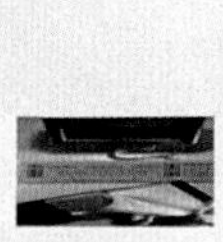

UNISYS SERVICES

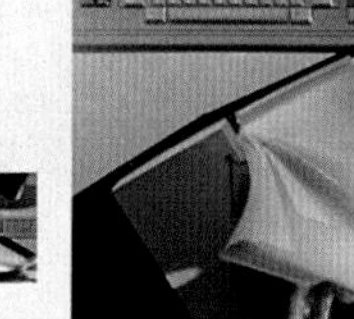

31

TECHNICAL WRITING

The range and scope of this service belies its name. It encompasses everything from origination – by writers with over a century of experience between them – through the complete artwork and proofing stages and right to printing and supply. Our advice and help at all stages, for both documentation and training purposes is totally unbiased; the objective is always the smooth, efficient operation of your system.

The constant – and constantly changing – need for printed materials is recognised by everyone.

It is also recognised throughout UNISYS management and catered for, with a range of skills and resources second to none, from document design to the production of books and manuals.

Between them, our writers have over a hundred years' experience, on which they have built a solid working knowledge of many specific customer environments. Our first priority is to define the actual needs in order to determine the library of manuals – and the amount and kind of training – best suited to your people.

It may be that the majority of your requirements can be met from our existing extensive documentation library. However, both documentation and training materials can be written exclusively for you, in which case there will be checks at every stage to ensure that the material meets your objectives.

Although it is normal to write your material to UNISYS style and content standards, we are perfectly happy to work to standards that you supply.

The service includes advice from a print Consultant regarding alternative print and production methods to suit your requirements and budget. We can, of course, sub-contract the artwork and printing on your behalf. UNISYS can negotiate extremely competitive rates for your benefit.

Your subject matter will normally be held for two years, or longer if you require. Updating the content is something that either we can do on your behalf or you can do for yourself directly from magnetic media that we can supply.

UNISYS

Unisys Limited
Stonebridge Park
London NW10 8LS

Telephone
01-965 0511
Telex
8951141
Fax
01-961 2252

Mr S Ayris
Senior Financial Consulta
Business Data Management Ltd
Christchurch House
Greyfriars Lane
Coventry
CV1

12th August 1987

Dear Mr Ayris

It is my great pleasure to present to you THE SERVICES BOOK from Unisys, a publication which, in its form and content - and particularly in what it offers - is unique, in the whole of our industry.

It outlines and introduces to you almost thirty management, consultative and above all practical services which comprise the Unisys Total Service Solution. Here you will find a range of widely differing yet closely allied and complementary offerings, from Supplies to Systems Design, Performance Monitoring to Project Management, Third Party Maintenance to Fourth Generation Development; somewhere in this book there is a service you need - now, sooner or later.

We are confident you will notice and appreciate this book's presentation which we believe reflects the quality of the service we are able to provide through the people whose knowledge, skill and commitment perform these services.

The key to your next step is your Account Manager. The experience and the resources behind them supports you. Additional information can be obtained through several sources. Your local Unisys Branch office; by calling our dedicated Linkline number - 0800 252 700 - or by completing the Reply Paid Card at the back of the book.

In any case your Account Manager will instantly be aware and in control of your enquiry and he will ensure the effective servicing of your business needs - he is the focal point of the Unisys Total Service Solution.

We are proud of our Customer Services, and of the relationship which exists between our people and yours. The skills and expertise which have gone into the development of the Unisys services described in this volume are yours to command.

I know you'll find that they live up to the high expectations that you will have after reading THE SERVICES BOOK.

Yours sincerely,

PETER ROBINSON
MARKETING DIRECTOR
CUSTOMER SERVICES

FREE PUBLICATIONS

UNISYS has developed for its customers a vast range of publications to assist in servicing their business needs both on Corporate, Service and Product specific needs.

We would welcome the opportunity to provide you or a business colleague with a free subscription to: (Please tick box)

THE SUPPLIES BOOK ...... a regular customer publication detailing over 3,000 computer supplies and accessories available from one central source ☐

THE SERVICES BOOK ...... providing information on an extensive range of UNISYS Value Added Services ☐

BUSINESS ...... the senior management magazine from UNISYS. Subjects include management issues technology features, news, city business, case studies and comment ☐

INNOVATION ...... a quarterly magazine informing you of new products and developments in technology. Providing a forum for ideas on system design and changing computer needs ☐

OTHER INFORMATION ...... Please indicate other UNISYS information you will find of interest to service your business needs.

IS YOUR NAME AND ADDRESS CORRECT?

1003835
MR S AYRIS
SENIOR FINANCIAL CONSULTA
BUSINESS DATA MANAGEMENT LTD
CHRISTCHURCH HOUSE
GREYFRIARS LANE
COVENTRY
CV1

PLEASE COMPLETE AND RETURN FREE OF CHARGE TO ADDRESS OVERLEAF

UNISYS SERVICES

CUSTOMER INFORMATION

I would like to receive further information on:

Applications Implementation ☐
Application Software Maintenance & Support ☐
Artificial Intelligence Consultancy ☐
Business Consultancy ☐
Capacity Management ☐
Computer Operations Auditing ☐
Customer Education ☐
Disaster Contingency Planning & Recovery ☐
Environmental Services ☐
Facilities Management ☐
Fourth Generation Development ☐
Hardware Maintenance ☐
Information Systems Strategies ☐
Migration Services ☐
Networks & Communication Services ☐
Organisational Reviews ☐
Performance Monitoring ☐
Professional Project Practices ☐
Project Auditing ☐
Project Management ☐
Software & Documentation Service ☐
Supplies Service ☐
System Design Services ☐
Systems Software Maintenance & Support ☐
Technical Writing ☐
Third Party Maintenance ☐
Turnkey Solutions ☐

IS YOUR NAME AND ADDRESS CORRECT?

If not, please fill in your correct information so that we may update our records to ensure you receive your UNISYS communications quickly. Please send my UNISYS information to:

Name ______
Job Title ______
Company ______
Address ______
______ Town ______
Postcode ______ Tel ______

PLEASE COMPLETE AND RETURN FREE OF CHARGE TO ADDRESS OVERLEAF

UNISYS INFORMATION

Title: "Levi Strauss & Company"
Copywriters: Kathleen Groh, David Moore
Art Directors: Elizabeth Addison, Marc Ziner
Agency: Stone & Adler, Inc.
Client: Levi Strauss & Company

"Family" is the focus in this full-color catalog illustrating that there is so much more than denim blue jeans is available from one of the most famous names in American apparel manufacturing.

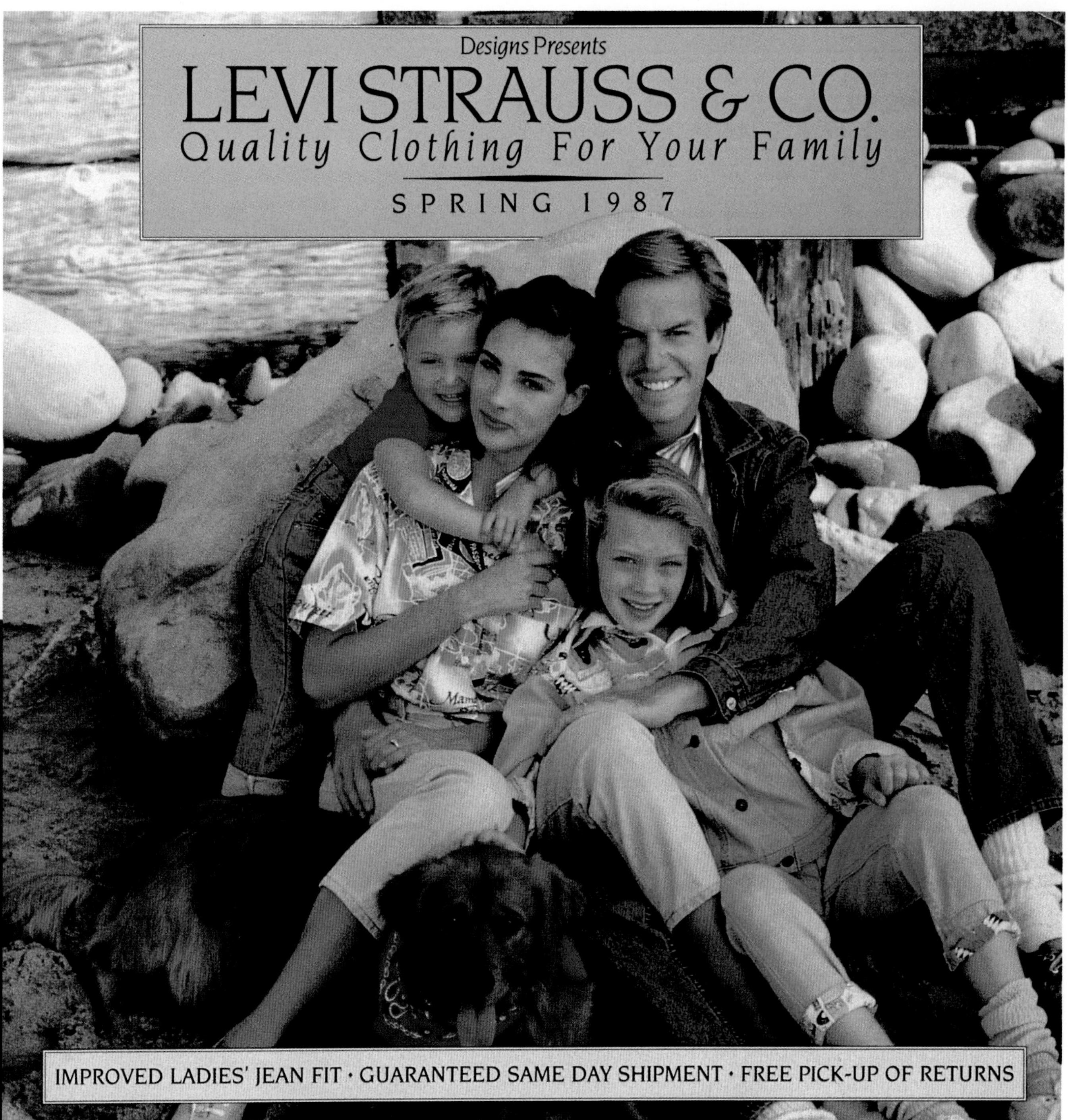
Designs Presents
LEVI STRAUSS & CO.
Quality Clothing For Your Family
SPRING 1987
IMPROVED LADIES' JEAN FIT · GUARANTEED SAME DAY SHIPMENT · FREE PICK-UP OF RETURNS

The Rosebook

Spring 1987

Title: "The Rosebook"
Copywriter: Jane Finder
Art Director: David Kasper
Agency: Cramer- Krasselt/Direct
Client: Armstrong Roses

A thousand words, perhaps, are said in the beautifully photographed still-life opening spread of this first-prize Caples Award winner. Throughout the

Armstrong Roses
P.O. Box 1020
Somis, California 93066

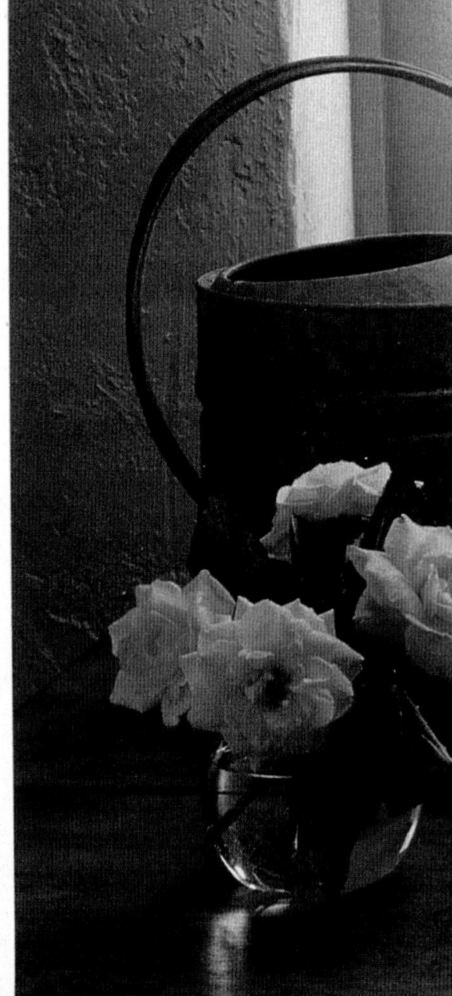

"And lovely is the Rose."

William Wordsworth, 1807

And lovely is the rose. A simple observation, as thought-provoking as a poem of several lines and stanzas. All by itself, the word "rose" can conjure sweet memories of beautiful colors, velvety petals, and that exhilarating, musky fragrance.

Since 1889 when young John Armstrong began his plant breeding business, we have been devoted to making roses lovelier and lovelier. Today, Armstrong employs hybridizers whose sole task is to develop garden roses with outstanding characteristics. Their hard work has resulted in over 200 new rose varieties, 34 All-American Rose Selections, and some of the most beloved roses of all time: Double Delight (see page 3), recently voted the world's favorite rose. Olympiad, the Official Rose of the 1984 Olympics (page 15). And Touch of Class (page 9), just claimed by France as its most beautiful rose.

Enjoy *The Rosebook.* As you view pages of indescribable shapes and colors, you'll understand why even a poet as prolific as William Wordsworth simply observed, "And lovely is the Rose." The beauty of a rose speaks for itself.

A Buyer's Guide To Roses.

Did you know the most critical factor in successful rose gardening is plant selection? Because although watering, fertilizing, sunlight and pruning are absolutely essential for healthy blooms, they can't change inferior roses. Here are a few questions to ask before purchasing any rose plant:

What grade is the rose plant?

Roses are graded 1, 1½, and 2 by the American Association of Nurserymen. The lower the number, the more canes and blooms to expect. All Armstrong roses *exceed* Grade 1 standards.

Where was the rose plant grown?

Roses are grown in many states, including North Carolina, Texas, Arizona, and California. By and large, today's finest rose growers are found in California, where excellent soil and climate provide the ideal environment. Armstrong roses are grown in Kern County, California, and are guaranteed to thrive anywhere in the United States.

How was the plant grown?

The farther apart roses are planted, the fuller, better-shaped they become. Most commercial roses are grown 12" apart. Armstrong roses are grown 18" apart.

How long has the
company been aroun
We'd advise you to buy
that is well establishe
track record. Armstro
opened their doors in
created over 200 new
well as 34 All-America
winners.

What kind of guara
comes with my roses
Because roses are livi
products, you should
thing less than a comp
guarantee. Every rose
was bred to bloom an
ously, and your satisf
guaranteed.

What are the advan
ordering from The
First and foremost, *T*
makes finding prime-
easy as making a pho
an order form. Our r
more healthy and flo
best-looking plant yo
all over town to find.
roses come with a mo
tee. You can even co
October 1, 1987 for a
refund if you're not
fied. The same guara
our fruits, trees, and
We hope this infor
this year's garden pr
before you buy, rem
go wrong with Arms

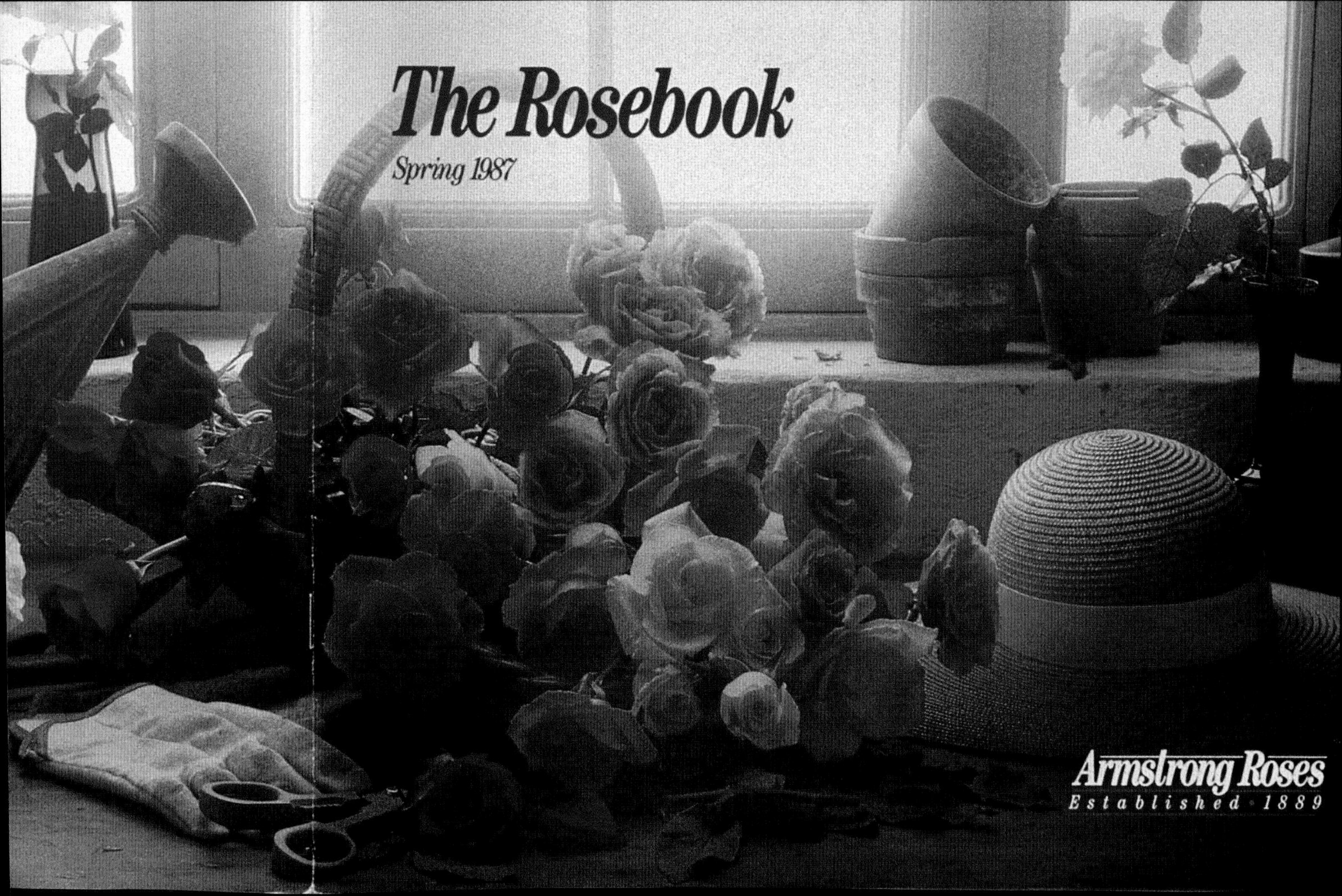

The Rosebook

Spring 1987

Armstrong Roses

Established 1889

Double Delight

"If there's room for only one rose, this is it." Hundreds of people must agree with Robert Smaus, award-winning garden editor of the Los Angeles Times Magazine. Because ever since this unique Hybrid Tea was introduced by Armstrong in 1977, we've been hard-pressed to keep up with demand. Why the obsession with Double Delight? Probably because its handsome red buds unfurl into huge, fluffy flowers, each containing a double delight: carmine red on the edges, true white at the center. The colors even change with the weather!

You'll also love the concentrated, spicy fragrance. Cut flowers have a long vase life and can literally scent an entire room. In the garden, its bush of glossy, deep-green foliage provides an elegant background for the colorful blooms. All-American Rose Selection (AARS) for 1977. Swim & Ellis, 1977. Plant Patent 3847.

Order C0271, $8.95 • 3 for $21.25

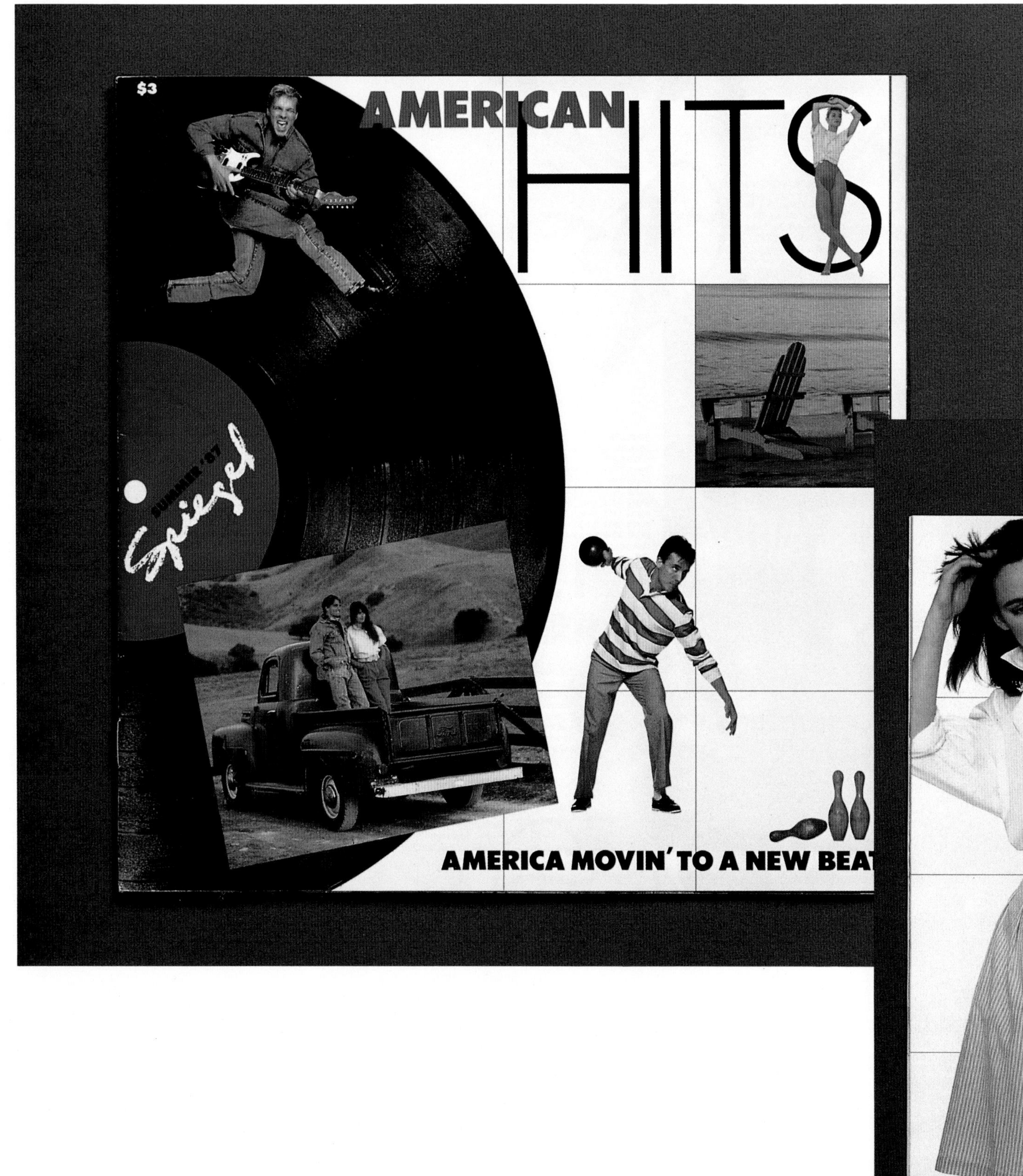
$3
AMERICAN HITS
SUMMER '87
Spiegel
AMERICA MOVIN' TO A NEW BEAT
28

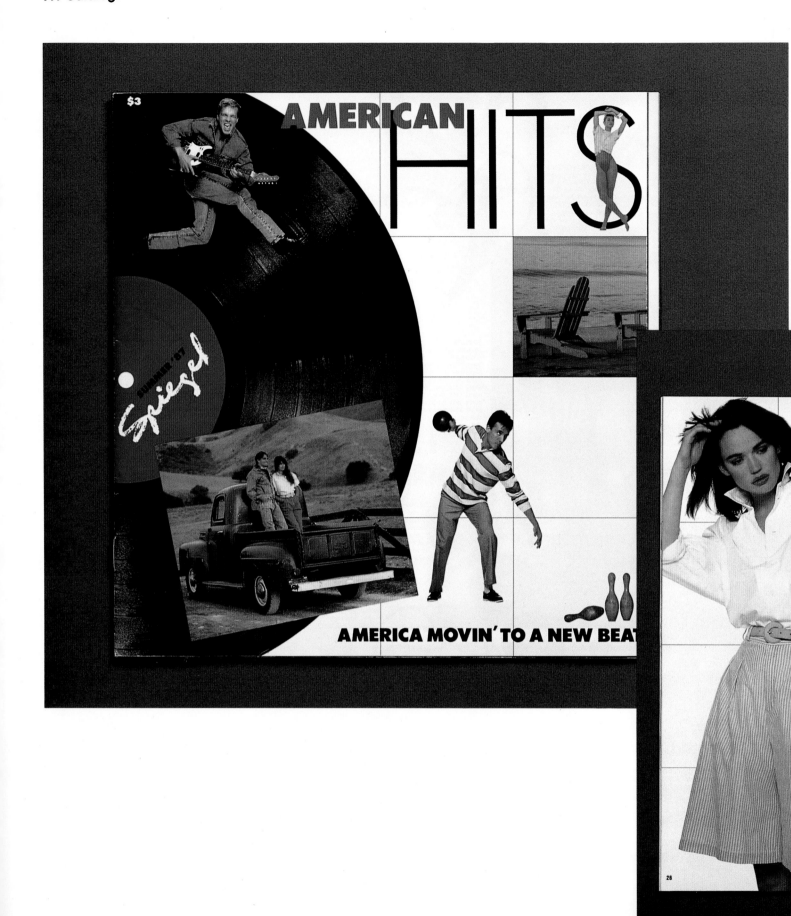

Title: "American Hits"
Copywriters: Michelle Hujar, J. Bezinque, K. Grestautas, J. Fumanski, G. Bilan
Art Director: David Brown
Agency: In-House
Client: Spiegel, Inc.

It's summer of '87 and America's young adults are the audience for this uptempo, contemporary collection from the acknowledged grand master of catalog retailing.

Title: "Connections"
Copywriter: Carl Goldberg
Art Director: Jeff Guido
Agency: Wunderman Worldwide
Client: IBM

An entirely different IBM catalog approach employs illustrations and magazine-type articles to create an editorial environment for its typewriter, word processing and data processing supplies.

Insurance Protection for Computer-Related Losses

by
David C. Tunick, Jeffrey A. Clark, Ronald S. Berman

Insurers now are writing policies for computer hardware and software companies to protect against losses caused by computer products. Computer system problems may result in liability, but vendors and their insurers can take some measures to prevent the liability-causing occurrences.

All three parties involved—the user, vendor and the vendor's insurance company—have the same goal: a system that meets the user's needs in a trouble-free manner.

Computer systems may become inoperable for a variety of reasons, including electrical or air-conditioning failure, water damage and improper programming. This can result in a computer disaster.

If data is lost on some storage media, such as the computer's memory or a disk, the user may need to spend hundreds of hours re-entering this information or may never be able to recreate the data if no handwritten records are available. The vendor may be blamed for failing to inform the user that the computer system was vulnerable to such a disaster, or for failing to take appropriate steps to avoid the problem.

One way of avoiding much of the problem is for the insurance company to require that the contract specify that the user must regularly save data on some backup medium, such as a disk or tape. This medium should be stored off-site, since the condition that wiped out the computer's memory (such as air-conditioning failure) also may cause damage to the backup storage medium. By doing this, the user can recover most of the data from the backup source if the computer fails and will have to re-enter only a small amount manually.

Another potential disaster can occur if the hardware becomes unusable for a long time. Therefore, the insurance company should require that the user have prompt access to backup hardware.

To summarize, the insurance company needs to implement a plan by which the computer acquisition process results in a properly working system. Of course, the plan may vary for different types of transactions, such as scanned or custom software acquisitions and hardware acquisitions.

The insurance company should have guidelines that must be followed by the vendor in each sale or licensing transaction, including the steps to be taken in the negotiation, contracting and post-delivery stages. While a properly conducted computer acquisition requires continuous effort, it minimizes the risk of litigation which can cost the insurance company thousands, or even millions, of dollars in indemnity and loss adjustment expense.

David C. Tunick is of counsel for Berman & Clark, a Santa Monica, Calif., law firm that specializes in computer-related legal matters. He is also professor of law at Loyola Law School, Los Angeles. Jeffrey A. Clark and Ronald S. Berman are partners in Berman & Clark.

Digested with permission from *Best's Review—Property/Casualty Insurance Edition.* © Copyright 1986 A.M. Best Company, Inc. All rights reserved.

4

IBM Diskettes for Optimum Performance

At IBM, we apply 30 years of computer experience to ensure that IBM Diskettes are the finest possible. This is your assurance of accurate data storage and retrieval for years to come.

The most advanced diskette technology

Invented by IBM, the diskette was designed for use as a diagnostic tool in the IBM System/360 Model 195. IBM then expanded its capability for data storage, and pioneered its use in this area.

The finest materials and workmanship

To ensure that your data are protected from physical stress and environmental changes, each IBM Diskette is manufactured with a specially formulated polyester film. This film is tested for uniformity, flatness and resistance to heat, cold and humidity.

To prevent read/write errors that may damage your work, the residual magnetism that may cause these errors must first be eliminated. IBM Diskettes have a microscopically fine oxide coating which eliminates harmful magnetism by evenly dispersing oxide grains in a random pattern.

Each diskette is then burnished and coated with a special lubricant to reduce friction and head wear and lengthen the life of both the diskette and your equipment.

Finally, every bit position on every track of every IBM Diskette is rigorously tested to make sure you get the performance and dependability you need.

After all, your work deserves a diskette with 100% first-pass reliability. Your work deserves an IBM Diskette.

Choose your diskettes packaged in a Library Case or Slipcase to protect your vital data and make it easier to file.

IBM 5-Year Diskette Limited Warranty

You're assured that IBM Diskettes will provide you with peak performance for a long, long time. Each one is warranted a full five years against defects in materials and workmanship. A defective diskette purchased from IBM will be replaced during the warranty period absolutely free. It's that simple.

Note: A copy of IBM's Limited Warranty on 5.25-inch diskettes is available free upon request from IBM Corporation, Attn: IBM DIRECT, One Culver Road, Dayton, NJ 08810.

Legend:
LC-Library Case
SC-Slipcase
DW-Displaywriter Format
FF-Fiftifile
OS/6-Office System/6 Format
w/p-Write Protect Notch
1D-Single-sided, double-density diskette
2D-Double-sided, double-density diskette
2HC-High-capacity, double-sided diskette
1-Single-sided, single-density diskette
2-Double-sided, single-density diskette

5.25-inch Diskettes	Diskettes Type	Usable Byte Capacity	Quantity per Package	Part Number	Price per Diskette at Quantity of 10-20	30-40	50-90	100+
1,200,000-byte Capacity Diskette	2HCw/p	1,200 KB	10/SC	6109660	$8.00	$7.75	$7.50	$7.25
	2HCw/p	1,200 KB	10/LC	6109661	8.20	7.95	7.70	7.45
	Specifically designed for use in the high-capacity drive of the IBM Personal Computer AT.							
Standard Diskettes	1Dw/p	160/180 KB*	10/SC	6023451	4.25	4.00	3.75	3.50
	2Dw/p	320/360 KB*	10/SC	6023450	4.75	4.50	4.25	4.00
	2Dw/p	320/360 KB*	10/LC	6060769	4.95	4.70	4.45	4.20

Order in lots of 10.
*Increased capacity from second release of DOS 2.X vs. DOS 1.X

8-inch Diskettes	Diskette Type	Sectors	Bytes per Sector	Usable Byte Capacity	Quantity per Package	Part Number	Price per Diskette at Quantity of 10-20	30-40	50-90	100+
Data Processing Diskettes in Slipcases	1	26	128	246,272	10/SC	2305830	$4.00	$3.75	$3.25	$3.00
	2	15	256	368,320	10/SC	2736700	5.25	5.00	4.50	4.25
	2D	26	256	985,008	10/SC	1766872	6.25	6.00	5.50	5.25
	2D	15	512	1,136,640	10/SC	1669044	6.25	6.00	5.50	5.25
	2D	8	1,024	1,212,416	10/SC	1669045	6.25	6.00	5.50	5.25
Word Processing Diskettes in Slipcases	1 DW	284,000 characters per diskette			10/SC	4498965	4.00	3.75	3.25	3.00
	2D DW	985,000 characters per diskette			10/SC	4496959	6.25	6.00	3.50	5.25
	1-OS/6	260,000 characters per diskette			10/SC	1669959	4.00	3.75	3.25	3.00

Order in lots of 10.

	Diskette Type	Sectors	Bytes per Sector	Usable Byte Capacity	Quantity per Package	Part Number	Price per Fiftifile at Quantity of 1	2+
Data Processing Diskettes in free Fiftifile*	1	26	128	246,272	50/FF	7035738	$162.50	$150.00
	2D	26	256	985,088	50/FF	7035749	275.00	262.50
	2D	15	512	1,136,640	50/FF	7035750	275.00	262.50
	2D	8	1,024	1,212,416	50/FF	7035751	275.00	262.50
Word Processing Diskettes in free Fiftifile*	1 DW	284,000 characters per diskette			50/FF	7034422	162.50	150.00
	2D DW	985,000 characters per diskette			50/FF	7034423	275.00	262.50

*Fiftifile sells separately for $28, see reverse side.

IBM DIRECT
1 800 IBM-2468

Connections
IBM
Supplies Catalog for Typewriters, Data Processing and Word Processing
Fall/Winter 1986
IBM DIRECT
1 800 IBM-2468
IBM
New! IBM Ribbons for non-IBM printers. See insert.

1

1. The decision to shoot jewelry on a model or not is always a dilemma. Diamonds are a girl's best friend, but it's hard to imagine them in a more perfect—or unlikely—setting than these pea pods. Courtesy of **Ted Pobiner Studios.**

and silver are highly reflective, and present problems like having the camera lens (and sometimes the photographer) show in the product. If it is a tiny reflection, it can either be retouched out on the transparency or etched out of the color separations. If, however, the surface showing the reflection is a large area, the photographer should try to disguise the camera by setting up a white paper tent around the equipment. Only the lens of the camera will show through a hole cut in the paper. The resulting reflection of the camera lens will be quite small, and easily corrected with photo retouching.

The shape of a ring is obviously round, meaning that the sides of the ring will reflect any images found there, much like peripheral vision in the eye. The use of reflector cards to block out these distracting images is helpful. The cards of white, gold, silver or grey are placed to the sides of the set at angles that are caught by the shiny surface of the ring.

Chains of necklaces must be laid out much like an engineer's drawing. Every link should be properly aligned and laying flat. This is usually done with a long pin or with a very fine pick, either by a patient and accomplished stylist or by a highly unusual photographer. A knotted or twisted link in a chain shows up glaringly. It may give a customer the impression that someone just didn't care enough to take the time to fix it, or even worse, convey a message that the chain will knot easily when worn.

Jewelry is normally photographed actual size in a catalog, but occasionally it should be shown larger than life. This decision might be called for if there is a lot of intricate, detailed design work that would only show up if the item is enlarged. In this event, a copy line that states that the merchandise is enlarged to show detail should always be added.

A dilemma always comes up in shooting jewelry as to whether to photograph it on a model or not. The decision should

depend on the m
dise; some items
better shown on
others will not n
model as a back
and will be fine sh
on a fabric or ot
tured backdrop.
earrings, for ex
would not be clear
stood unless th
shown on an ear
of the way that th
But be cautione
close, tightly cropp
of a portion of ear
of face may revea
fections and blem
even on the be
Retouching will b
sary (and that a
extra cost) to rem
imperfections and
cial hairs that will
tured on film.
A ring might be

THE S. D. WARREN
CATALOG OF CATALOG
PHOTOGRAPHY

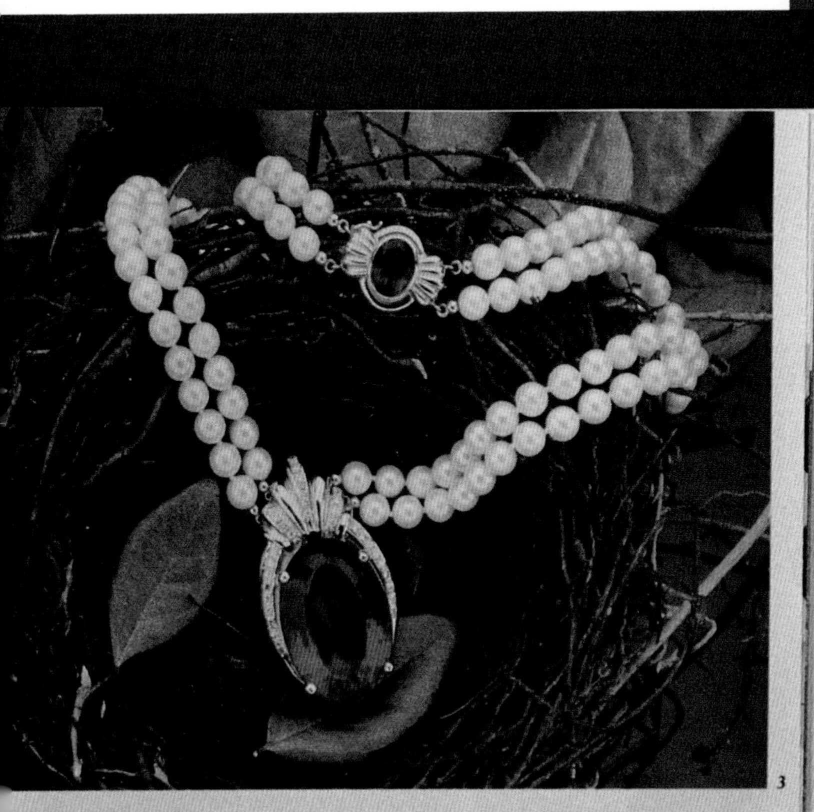

3

ı a more attractive
e when photographed
between manicured
ertips. The traditional
shot on a finger can
flat and unappealing,
cially if knuckles are
ving. (Even a *hand*
el has wrinkles in this
)
me necklaces will dis-
better when shown
nd the neck of a
el, rather than flat. The
lvantage here is that
re unable to show the
in the back. Since
customers will want
ow what kind of clo-
a necklace has, be
to cover that detail in
escriptive copy block.
ored gels (or strips of
on transparent film)
be used to help catch
ns of color in gems

like diamonds. They can be placed to the side and even hung up above the product (out of live camera area) to reflect color into the cut facets of the stones. Strategically placed reflector cards will accomplish the same thing, adding color in the facet areas which will lend definition and shape to the jewelry. The placement of the cards or gels will determine where the reflections will appear in the products. The photographer will set them up and make finite adjustment moves to capture the desired effect.

Black is a popular background color for photographing jewelry, particularly gold and silver items. It lends a rich frame without contamination of

2. Black is a popular background color for photographing jewelry. Here it adds to the mysterious allure of a twisted pearl necklace. Photographed by **Ted Pobiner Studios.**

3. Necklaces usually display better when they're around the neck, rather than lying flat. **Ted Pobiner Studios** *provides a wonderful alternative, entwining a priceless pearl necklace with a robin's nest.*

Chapter Seven 33

Title:	"The Catalog of Catalog Photography"
Copywriter:	Jo-Von Tucker
Art Director:	Jo-Von Tucker
Agency:	JVT Direct Marketing
Client:	The S.D. Warren Company

Clear evidence of the continuing growth of the catalog as a vital marketing tool is the appearance of the S.D. Warren catalog, a comprehensive guide to successful catalog photography. Itself a second-prize Caples Award winner for creative excellence, this piece features expert advice and stunning examples of superior work.

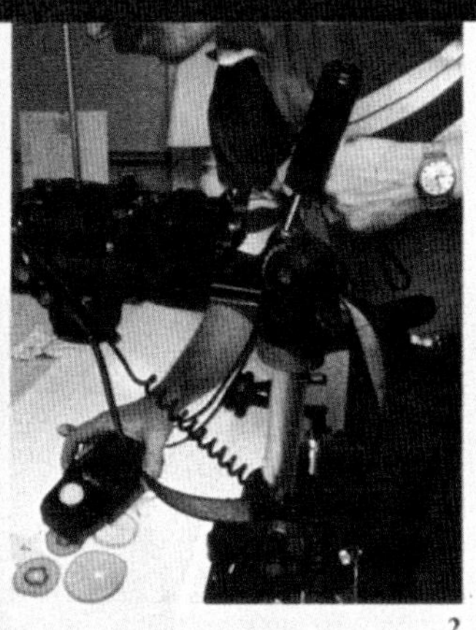

1. *A perception of dimension makes jewelry photography much more interesting. This ingenious approach was taken by* **Hing/Norton.**

2. *Food photography is often a complex art. The subjects need intense light to be shot properly, but have to be replaced or refreshed to withstand the high temperature.*

its color in the merchandise. Since metal jewelry is light in coloration, a black background provides maximum contrast. Black lucite or plexiglass is especially effective, because of the added perception of depth that can be attained with the resulting shadows. Lucite is highly reflective material for a table top shot. A perception of dimension makes a photograph of jewelry much more interesting.

A "high key" effect can be obtained with the use of white or frosted white backgrounds for jewelry shots. It provides a backdrop for the items that are lighter than the merchandise in color density. The same kind of shadows can be accomplished on white lucite as previously pointed out for black.

The use of highly textured backgrounds is also effective for jewelry photography. This choice will add contrast between the backdrop and the shiny items. Roughly textured wood bark, deep pile carpeting, woven fabrics like tapestries, heavily embossed papers...these are just a few of the available backgrounds that are appropriate for jewelry shots.

The lighting of jewelry photography is difficult and time-consuming. Many times a photographer will elect to use pin spots (very small individual lights that throw a concentrated and narrow beam of illumination) on a jewelry set. These p spots can be tightly co trolled in placement, a can add important defi tion where needed rings, bracelets, watch necklaces and pi Jewelry depictions ne shape and modeling to the most effective. T means that a full range deep shadows, mid-to and highlights is nec sary, and must be acc plished in the chos lighting technique.

FOOD PRODUCTS. Ph tographing food ite for a catalog require real specialist. Ph tographers who beco known as food special understand the imp tance of the visual app and have developed

4

style and flair needed to photograph food most effectively. These people usually do a lot of food shootings, working for magazines as well as for catalogs. Their studio facilities will include a well-equipped kitchen in which to prepare the food dishes.

A poorly photographed and reproduced food shot will not be appetizing, and therefore will not sell. Color is important in making the shots appealing and credible, and food styling helps to make a savory-looking presentation.

Food must be carefully prepared for photography and must look fresh. The presentation of the dishes and courses in a fine restaurant have a psychological impact on how the food tastes. In catalog photography, presentation is equally psychological, and contributes heavily toward motivating a customer to buy.

A food stylist (or home economist) is a necessary member of the food photography team. This person shops for the required fresh ingredients, prepares the food and arranges it in the serving dishes. They also provide the subtle decorations to "dress up" the food, touches like bows made of orange rind, mint leaves or sugar-frosted grapes, real or candied violets, and stemmed maraschino cherries. The food stylist sets the table (if a setting is needed), and even folds the napkins. Their knowledge of food preparation and food service is reflected in the photography, and helps to establish the catalog's credibility. Your shooting budget should include the money to retain a top-notch food stylist for the shots that will require this special attention.

Fresh fruit and produce should be spritzed (or sprinkled) with water and glycerine for a dewy, fresh-from-the-garden look. Brown edges on leafy foods can be clipped off, and spotty leaves should be replaced. Meats, if shown raw or uncooked, need to be the right color, never allowing the edges to change color or darken because they've been under the lights too long. It is important for cooked

3. *Food photography must look appetizing to be successful. The tempting arrangement shown here was photographed by* **Dennis Gottlieb.**

4. *A food stylist shops for fresh produce and herbs, simmers the soup and even breaks the croissants. A stylist's efforts helped* **Dennis Gottlieb** *to catch the activity in this French kitchen.*

Summer 1987

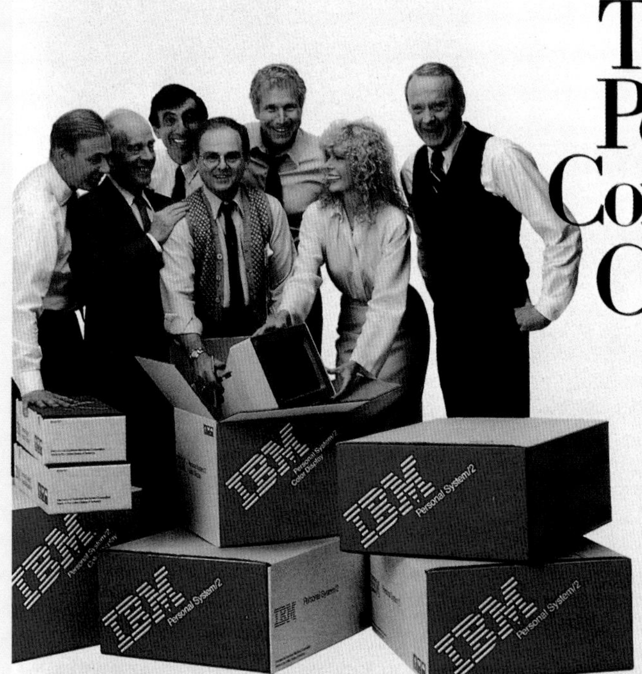

The IBM Personal Computing Catalog

- *The lid's off, and the next generation in personal computing is inside!*
- *The new IBM Personal System/2.*
- *Dazzling new displays. New printers and software.*
- *Over 100 products new to this catalog.*
- *See for yourself. It's the easy way to browse and shop IBM.*

IBM

IBM Personal System/2

Computers this capable used to take up whole rooms. Now, they sit neatly at your desk.

The next generation in personal computing has arrived. With faster, more reliable hardware that can handle increasingly complex applications. And the potential for more people to do more things simultaneously.

Leading the way into the next generation are machines so advanced we've chosen to call them systems—the IBM Personal System/2™ family of computers. With their introduction comes a revolutionary new architecture that brings you systems performance at a PC price; connectivity that opens a new world of multi-task and multi-user possibilities; graphics capabilities unimaginable five years ago; diskettes that hold significantly more data; and a host of standard features that make personal computing easier than ever before.

A **IBM Personal System/2 Model 80**
Our most advanced personal system, our first to harness the power of the 80386 microprocessor with the new IBM Micro Channel™ Architecture.

Model 80's 32-bit data path gives information twice as many "lanes" to travel in. So more programs *and* users can run on the system at once. That, plus an operating speed of up to 20 MHz, lets it run up to 3½ times faster than an IBM Personal Computer AT®.

Model 80 remembers more too. With a high-capacity 1.44MB 3.5" diskette drive. For fixed disks, choose from 44, 70, or 115MB. Double the capacity of each for up to 230MB of storage *or* mix and match the 70MB and 115MB drives. User memory starts at 1MB, and grows to an impressive 16MB. And, since system board memory on the Models -041 and -111 can expand to 2MB and 4MB respectively *without using any expansion slots*, you have all four 16-bit and three 32-bit slots available for other important options.

With such managerial potential, Model 80 excels as a file server, or as a gateway in a network. To complete the picture, it comes with Video Graphics Array (VGA) graphics, serial, parallel, keyboard and pointing-device ports.

Shown with the new IBM Personal System/2 Color Display 8514. Find out all about it on page 11.

8580-041 (1 MB, 44MB fixed disk) **$6,995.00**
8580-071 (2MB, 70MB fixed disk) **$8,495.00**
8580-111† (2MB, 115MB fixed disk) **$10,995.00**

†Available fourth quarter 1987.

A

The IBM Personal System/2 Model 80 available from:

IBM Authorized Dealer Advanced Products

Title: "IBM Personal Computing Catalog"
Copywriter: Bernie Libster
Art Directors: Wes Neal, Dana Martin
Agency: Grey Direct
Client: IBM

Most of the stars of the top-ranked M*A*S*H* television series are reunited in this tie-in with a broadcast network advertising campaign to promote a "dazzling" array of new computer hardware, software and ancillary products under the trusted IBM banner.

What's Inside, and Why.

This may be the most important introduction in the short history of personal computers," said Steven A. Ballmer, vice president of systems software for the Microsoft Corporation...[†] But, as significant as they are, IBM's new Personal System/2 computers are only part of our effort to develop total solutions that balance hardware, software and support.

For the whole story, see how IBM SolutionPac™ software achieves new levels of power and integration. Get up to speed on displays and printers that can enhance presentations beyond your greatest expectations. See how far we've come in networking, memory expansion, host attachment and more. And discover how IBM advances are taking personal computing into a future that reflects much of what you've hoped for in the past.

[†] ©New York Times Company/April 3, 1987

How to Buy.

IBM PERSONAL COMPUTING PRODUCTS:

IBM Authorized Advanced Products Dealer A new generation of IBM Dealers who have received advanced training with a special focus on *complete systems and total solutions.* See them for all your IBM Personal Computer and IBM Personal System/2 needs, and for support with the next generation of hardware and software.

Authorized IBM Personal Computer Dealer They handle IBM Personal Computers and the IBM Personal System/2 Model 30, and offer special assistance for those just getting started in computing. See the products you want to buy, and get knowledgeable advice and product demonstrations.

IBM Marketing Representative Ask our representatives how the products in this catalog fit into your business operation. They can fill your orders and arrange for quantity discounts.

Call IBM DIRECT toll free at 1 800 IBM-2468 for your closest IBM Dealer or check the telephone directory for the IBM branch office nearest you.

SUPPLIES:

Telephone Call IBM DIRECT *toll free* at 1 800 IBM-2468 Monday-Friday between 8 AM and 8 PM Eastern Time for fast service and delivery of supplies.

Mail Use the handy order form after page 20 of this catalog to order the supply items you need to keep your systems running smoothly.

How to Find It.

Hardware
2-4, 6-15, 20, 28-30

Discover the next generation in personal computing, plus the printers, displays, plotters and expansion options that work with them to make your work easier.

Service
16

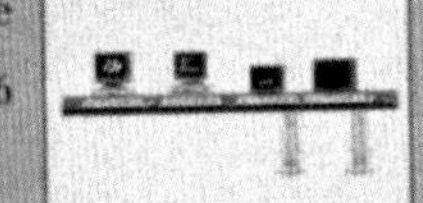

Find out all about IBM service plans. They're designed to suit your personal computing setup and needs. And there's a nationwide network that can help keep your systems in top form.

Software
17-19, 34

Introducing operating systems and IBM SolutionPacs for IBM Personal System/2, designed to help professionals do the whole job faster and more efficiently.

Supplies
21-25

You'll find just about everything you need to make your text and graphics look their very best, from high-quality ribbons to printwheels. Plus other essentials such as diskettes.

Communications and Networking
26-27, 31-33

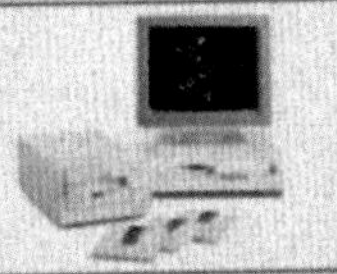

Local area networking, host-attach capabilities, terminal emulation, modems and more. Just about everything you need to communicate important information across the room or across the country.

For products bearing this symbol ✚ IBM provides no warranty, express or implied. These products are not manufactured by IBM. The manufacturer's warranty, if any, is the only warranty that applies.
Prices in this catalog are subject to change without notice.
Dealer prices and terms and conditions may vary from those listed in this catalog.
Photographs show engineering and design models.
Changes may be incorporated on production models.
© International Business Machines Corporation 1987

5

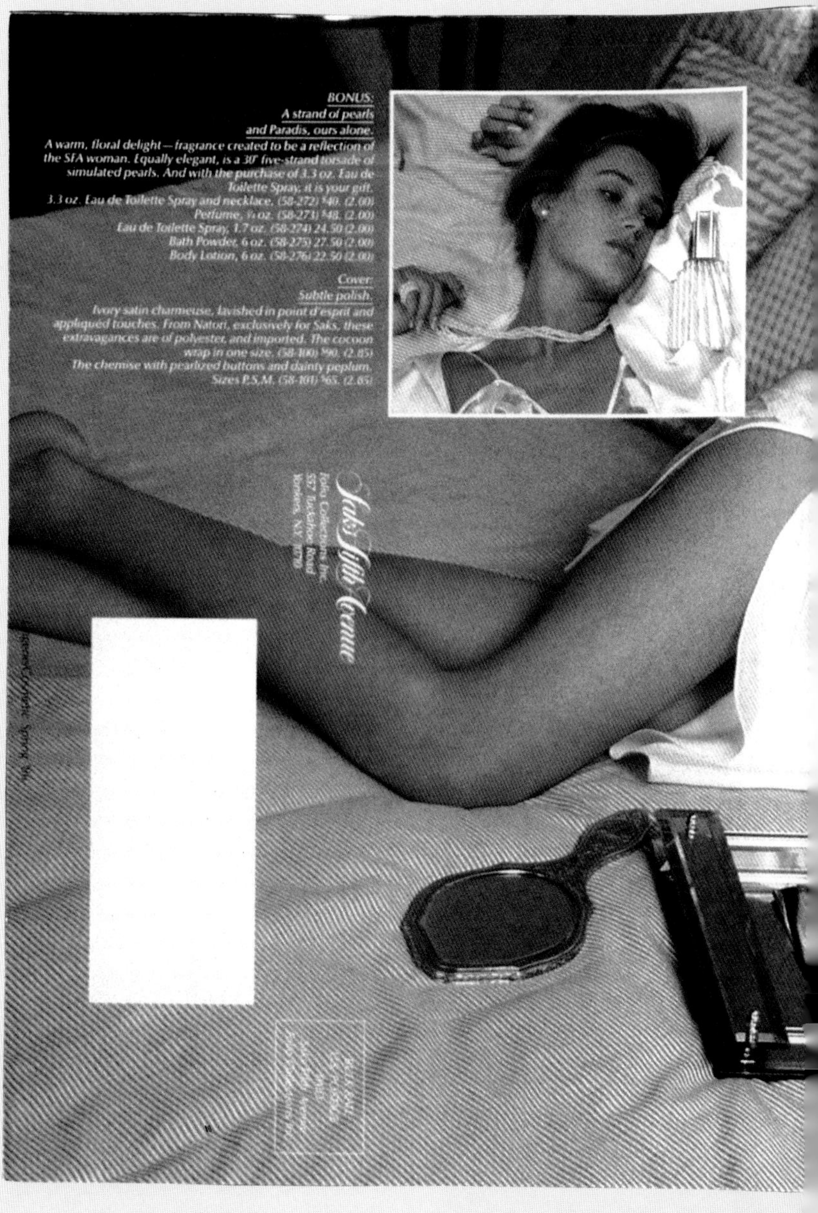

BONUS:
A strand of pearls
and Paradis, ours alone.
A warm, floral delight — fragrance created to be a reflection of
the SFA woman. Equally elegant, is a 30" five-strand torsade of
simulated pearls. And with the purchase of 3.3 oz. Eau de
Toilette Spray, it is your gift.
3.3 oz. Eau de Toilette Spray and necklace. (58-272) $40. (2.00)
Eau de Toilette Spray, 1.7 oz. (58-274) 24.50 (2.00)
Bath Powder, 6 oz. (58-275) 27.50 (2.00)
Body Lotion, 6 oz. (58-276) 22.50 (2.00)
Cover:
Subtle polish.
Ivory satin charmeuse, lavished in point d'esprit and
appliquéd touches. From Natori, exclusively for Saks, these
extravagances are of polyester, and imported. The cocoon
wrap in one size. (58-100) $90. (2.85)
The chemise with pearlized buttons and dainty peplum.
Sizes P.S.M. (58-101) $65. (2.85)
Saks Fifth Avenue

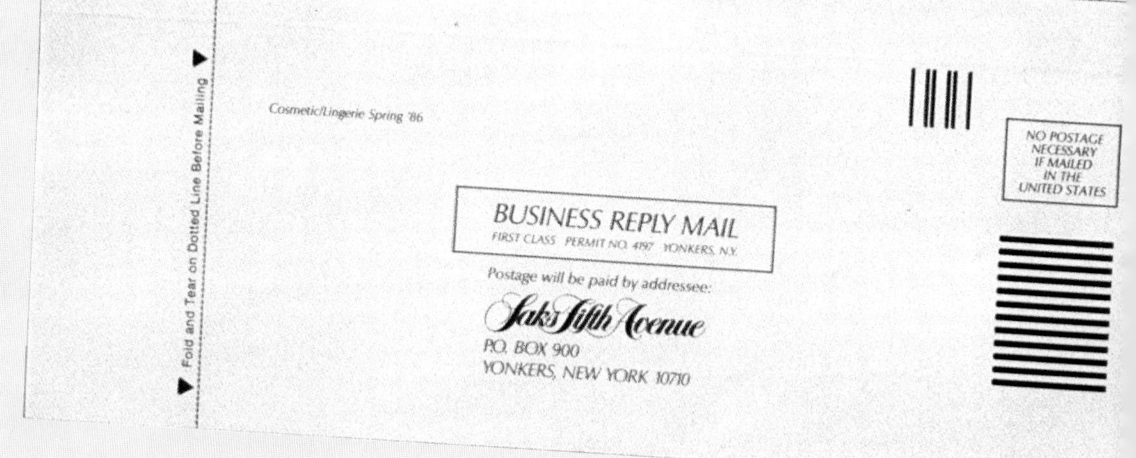

Fold and Tear on Dotted Line Before Mailing
Cosmetic/Lingerie Spring '86
NO POSTAGE NECESSARY IF MAILED IN THE UNITED STATES
BUSINESS REPLY MAIL
FIRST CLASS PERMIT NO. 4797 YONKERS, N.Y.
Postage will be paid by addressee:
Saks Fifth Avenue
P.O. BOX 900
YONKERS, NEW YORK 10710

Title: "Private Moments"
Copywriter: Felice Nasshorn
Art Directors: Linda Bruning, Leonard Restivo
Agency: In-House
Client: Saks Fifth Avenue

Cosmetics, fragrances and lingerie are presented here in sensual, feminine settings, supported by brief, breezy copy and simple ordering instructions from the famed New York department store.

BONUS:
Azzaro 9 by Loris Azzaro, Paris.
An original, classic French fragrance.
Celebrating those qualities of timeless beauty and excellence, is the rich composition of Azzaro 9. Here, a symphony of nine precious flowers is underscored by the refinement of woody notes and spiced touches. Experience this elegant, feminine fragrance today, only at SFA. As a special gift, receive a 5 ml. deluxe miniature Eau de Toilette with any purchase from the collection.

Parfum Flacon, 1 oz. (58-500) $130. (2.00)
Parfum Flacon, ½ oz. (58-501) $80. (2.00)
Parfum Flacon, ¼ oz. (58-502) $45. (2.00)
Eau de Toilette Natural Spray, 3.4 oz. (58-503) 42.50 (2.00)
Eau de Toilette Natural Spray, 1.7 oz. (58-504) 27.50 (2.00)
Eau de Toilette, 3.4 oz. (58-506) $40. (2.00)
Eau de Toilette, 1.7 oz. (58-507) $25. (2.00)
Pulse Points.

EXPERIENCE
ZARO 9
EN THE FLAP

AZZARO 9

in completing your order

S.C.

☐ Charge To My Saks Fifth Avenue Account
☐☐-☐☐☐-☐☐☐
CHECK OR MONEY ORDER ENCLOSED
FOR $
A/C CODE (SFA USE ONLY) SORRY, NO C.O.D.'S
☐ Please send me a Saks Fifth Avenue charge account application.
☐ Special Instruction

You may use your American Express or Diners Club card when ordering by mail or phone.
Please charge to my: ☐ American Express ☐ Diners Club
☐☐☐☐☐☐☐☐☐☐☐☐☐☐☐☐
PHONE NO. ( ) Home ( ) Business
Valid Date
Signature Expiration Date
A/C CODE (SFA USE ONLY)

ITEM NO.	QUANT.	SFA USE ONLY	ITEM DESCRIPTION	COLOR	SIZE	PRICE OF EA. ITEM	DELIVERY CHARGE	TOTAL PRICE

Please give name and address for each item to be shipped to an address other than your own.
NAME
ADDRESS
CITY/STATE ZIP
NAME
ADDRESS
CITY/STATE ZIP
NAME
ADDRESS
CITY/STATE ZIP
NAME
ADDRESS
CITY/STATE ZIP

*Warranty information can be obtained without charge upon written request to Saks Fifth Avenue at 557 Tuckahoe Road, Yonkers, N.Y. 10710

SUBTOTAL
TAX
TOTAL

Chapter
4
PBC INTERNATIONAL
ONE SCHOOL STREET
GLEN COVE, NY 11542

Direct response collateral advertising knows no boundaries. It can be a simple buckslip enclosed with a bill or tucked inside a package. It can be a matchbook cover, a cash register receipt, a booklet, a brochure, a huge poster, a small postcard, or even a die-cut placecard in the shape of a lobster. (See pages 158-159.)

Some direct marketing efforts rely heavily on collateral to add needed balance to a campaign. Think, for example, of how many "take one" displays filled with credit card applications there must be in all of the restaurants and retail shops throughout the world. Or, consider the wide variety of collateral pieces produced by banks and savings institutions to promote their financial products and services. There are literally dozens of ways that direct response collateral can be distributed.

Nevertheless, it has been observed that collateral is frequently underutilized or even overlooked during the development of a marketing plan. Such cases are unfortunate, because the cost of creating, producing and circulating collateral, often quite low, can yield significantly higher profit margins than those of more conventional advertising.

And while the multi-faceted nature of collateral allows it to escape precise definition, its similarities to the practice known as sales promotion sometimes cause it to be misunderstood. The difference between the two is that direct response collateral asks for action *now.*

More money is allocated to sales promotion, however, than to any other single budget item in the typical American marketing mix. It is quite possible that this lofty popularity may boost the use of direct response collateral, particularly when the enormous opportunities to build lasting customer relationships become apparent to more and more marketing people.

Creative people, meanwhile, have been busy producing some of the more imaginative collateral marketing communications to be found anywhere. Because the category is such a wide-open proposition, fresh approaches are frequent and welcome. It is noteworthy, too, that the scope of collateral can range from a tiny postage stamp sleeve to a complex, nine-part portfolio, complete with four accessory pieces and a three-dimensional display.

As the work in this chapter reveals, there is as much creative excellence to be found in collateral material as in any other area of direct response advertising. The inevitability of growth in the use of collateral promises abundant opportunity ahead for copywriters, designers and art directors to expand their horizons in this most diversified field of endeavor.

Title: "Enjoy the Freshest Catch"
Copywriters: Merry Bateman, Vipaporn Pramoj Na Ayudhya
Art Director: Lalit Lertmaithai
Agency: Ogilvy & Mather Direct (TH) Ltd.
Client: American Express (Thai) Ltd.

Lobster in Bangkok comes with a complementary bottle of wine when the customer presents these pieces at The Seafood Restaurants and uses the American Express Card.

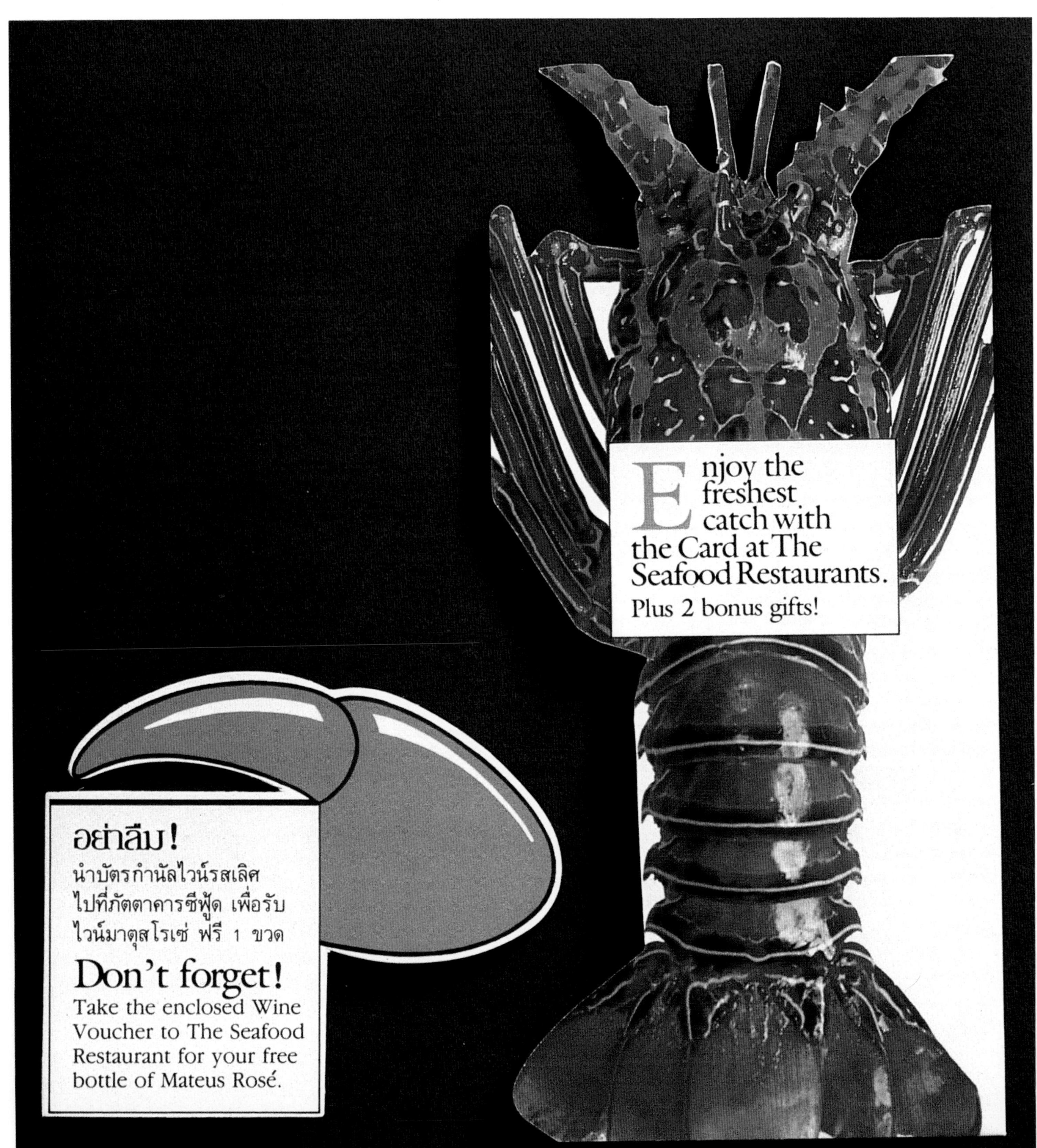

สดใหม่จากท้องทะเล มาเป็นอาหารรสเลิศ

เมื่อต้องการรับประทานอาหารทะเลชั้นเยี่ยม แน่นอน ภัตตาคารซีฟู้ดคือชื่อที่นักชิมทุกท่านวางใจ ด้วยรายการอาหารน่ารับประทานมากมาย หลายหลาก ปรุงแต่งอย่างสวยงามเอร็ดอร่อย ด้วยฝีมือพ่อครัวผู้ชำนาญ ไม่ว่าจะเป็นอาหารประเภทย่าง ทอด อบ นึ่ง ตลอดจนอาหารจีน ไทย หรือฝรั่ง

และเพื่อเพิ่มรสชาติความเอร็ดอร่อยให้สมบูรณ์แบบ อเมริกัน เอ็กซ์เพรส ร่วมกับภัตตาคารซีฟู้ด ขอมอบมาตุสโรเซ่ ไวน์สีชมพูเกรดเยี่ยม เป็นอภินันทนาการเมื่อท่านรับประทานอาหาร และชำระค่าอาหารและเครื่องดื่มด้วยบัตรอเมริกัน เอ็กซ์เพรส ตั้งแต่วันที่ 1 กรกฎาคม ถึงวันที่ 31 สิงหาคม 2530 โปรดอย่าลืมนำบัตรกำนัลที่แนบมาด้วยนี้มอบให้ทางภัตตาคารด้วย

สำหรับท่านที่ชำระค่าอาหารและเครื่องดื่มด้วยบัตรตั้งแต่ 1,500 บาทขึ้นไป ท่านยังจะได้รับบัตรกำนัลมูลค่า 250 บาทจากอเมริกัน เอ็กซ์เพรส ซึ่งท่านสามารถนำไปใช้เมื่อท่านรับประทานอาหารมื้อต่อไปที่ภัตตาคารซีฟู้ด ถนนเพชรบุรีตัดใหม่ และซีฟู้ดมาร์เก็ต ถนนสุขุมวิท

อเมริกัน เอ็กซ์เพรส มีความยินดีที่ได้จัดรายการพิเศษ "อร่อยที่ภัตตาคารซีฟู้ด" เพื่อมอบให้ท่านสมาชิกบัตรโดยเฉพาะ เราหวังว่าโบนัสพิเศษทั้งสองนี้จะช่วยเพิ่มความสำราญให้กับอาหารมื้อพิเศษของท่านได้เป็นอย่างดี

Delicious seafood prepared at its very best!

When you want a superb seafood dinner, The Seafood Restaurants are undoubtedly the best place to go. They offer the finest menu — an array of mouthwatering seafood prepared to perfection by master chefs just as you like it...barbecued, fried, steamed, Chinese, Thai or Western style.

Complement any Seafood dish you order with a complimentary bottle of semi-sweet Mateus Rosé Wine. When you dine with the Card between July 1 and August 31, 1987, be sure to use the enclosed Wine Voucher to receive your bottle of wine.

Remember, when you charge 1,500฿ or more, you will also receive an American Express Dining Voucher. Use it for your next visit to either of two convenient locations in Bangkok: The Seafood Market on Sukhumvit Road or The Seafood Restaurant on New Petchburi Road.

American Express is pleased to provide special privileges for Cardmembers at The Seafood Restaurants. We hope these bonus gifts will enhance your dining experience.

THE Seafood RESTAURANT
"IF IT SWIMS WE HAVE IT"

ซีฟู้ดมาร์เก็ต 388 ถนนสุขุมวิท โทร. 258-0218-9
ภัตตาคารซีฟู้ด 1980 ถนนเพชรบุรีตัดใหม่ โทร. 314-4312, 314-4173
เปิดบริการทุกวัน 11.00 - 24.00 น.

The Seafood Market 388 Sukhumvit Road Tel. 258-0218-9
The Seafood Restaurant 1980 Petchburi Road Tel. 314-4312, 314-4173
Open from 11:00 AM to Midnight, 7 days a week.

AMERICAN EXPRESS

THE STATISTICS MONSTER IS HERE!

Actually, it should come as no surprise. It happens at the same time every year. Classes begin, and the Statistics Monster rears its ugly head.

It's the unnatural, unreasonable fear many of your undergraduate students have about statistics. And along with making the class very unpleasant for them, it also makes it very difficult for you to teach.

Fortunately, now there's help. A book written specifically as a supplementary text for your students with "fear of statistics."

Statistics in Plain English, by Dr. Harvey J. Brightman, is just what it says—a statistics book that covers the most difficult topics in the language undergraduate students are the most familiar with—English.

PLAIN SPEAKING

It's obvious that it's a lot harder to teach a subject if you and your students don't have a language in common. But that's exactly what can happen in an undergraduate Statistics course, because, chances are, the text you're using is "written" in mathematics, a very foreign language to most business students.

Statistics in Plain English was written to address exactly that problem.

It uses clear, concise English, along with helpful illustrations, to cover some of the hardest topics in beginning Statistics. In a light, conversational tone, it helps to make the subject a lot more friendly, and the Statistics Monster a lot less menacing.

It also has special features to get the reader more involved, like carefully selected problems and puzzles that lead the student, step by step, to understand the ideas behind the formulas, and spaces that are left in the text for students to work out the answers as they're reading along.

Statistics in Plain English also lists, at the beginning of each chapter, a specific set of skills that will be mastered in that chapter. So the reader knows going in just what he or she will be able to do with the concepts and ideas covered.

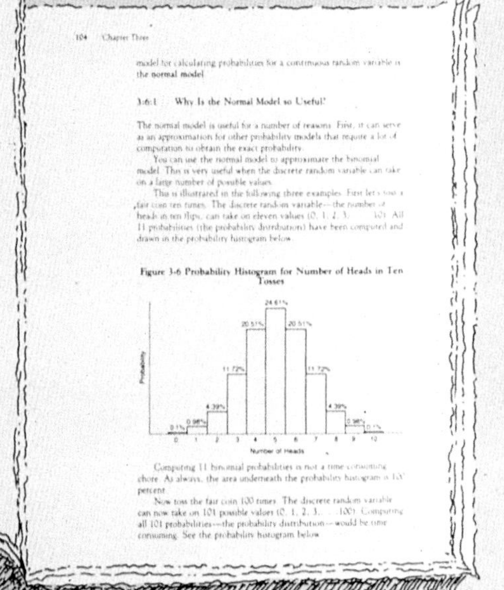

104 Chapter Three

model for calculating probabilities for a continuous random variable is **the normal model**

3:6:1 Why Is the Normal Model so Useful?

The normal model is useful for a number of reasons. First, it can serve as an approximation for other probability models that require a lot of computation to obtain the exact probability.

You can use the normal model to approximate the binomial model. This is very useful when the discrete random variable can take on a large number of possible values.

This is illustrated in the following three examples. First let's toss a fair coin ten times. The discrete random variable—the number of heads in ten flips, can take on eleven values (0, 1, 2, 3, . . . 10). All 11 probabilities (the probability distribution) have been computed and drawn in the probability histogram below.

Figure 3-6 Probability Histogram for Number of Heads in Ten Tosses

Computing 11 binomial probabilities is not a time consuming chore. As always, the area underneath the probability histogram is 100 percent.

Now toss the fair coin 100 times. The discrete random variable can now take on 101 possible values (0, 1, 2, 3, . . . 100). Computing all 101 probabilities—the probability distribution—would be time consuming. See the probability histogram below.

Here's a sample page from **Statistics in Plain English**. You can see how it'll help slay the Statistics Monster with a clear, readable, understandable and friendly text.

THE FIVE HARDEST TO

Statistics in Plain English, althoug designed to work as a supplemen covers all the basics. In fact, Professor Bri has, in his 14 years of teaching undergrad Statistics, compiled a list of what his stud have told him are the five hardest topics: tical dependence and independence, p bility distributions, sampling distributions estimation, analysis of variance, and reg analysis. The book is built around these to

It also provides a very up-to-date app since the verbal and visual presentations well with students' increasing use of pers computers. Mastering this material visua be an important first step toward succes data analysis on a microcomputer.

STATISTICS IN PLAIN ENGLISH

CHAPTER ONE:	Introduction and Descri Statistics
CHAPTER TWO:	Basic Probability
CHAPTER THREE:	Probability Distributions
CHAPTER FOUR:	Sampling, Confidence I and Hypothesis Testing
CHAPTER FIVE:	Experimentation and A of Variance
CHAPTER SIX:	Regression Analysis
AUTHOR:	Harvey J. Brightman Research Professor of Decision Sciences Georgia State Universit

THE ULTIMATE WEAP

Statistics in Plain English is not me replace any current texts. It was w work along with the books you're using n an aid to those students who are fighting

BUSINESS REPLY MAIL
FIRST CLASS PERMIT NO. 346 CINCINNATI, OHIO

POSTAGE WILL BE PAID BY ADDRESSEE

South-Western Publishing Co.
5101 Madison Road
Cincinnati, Ohio 45227

IT'S HERE.

Title: "It's Here"
Copywriter: Bruce Carlson
Art Director: Bruce Shaffer
Agency: Sive Associates, Inc.
Client: South-Western Publishing

Statistics and statistical language are as fearsome as the most horrible monster to many people. Here, in plain English and good humor, is a way to defend oneself against the dreaded onslaught.

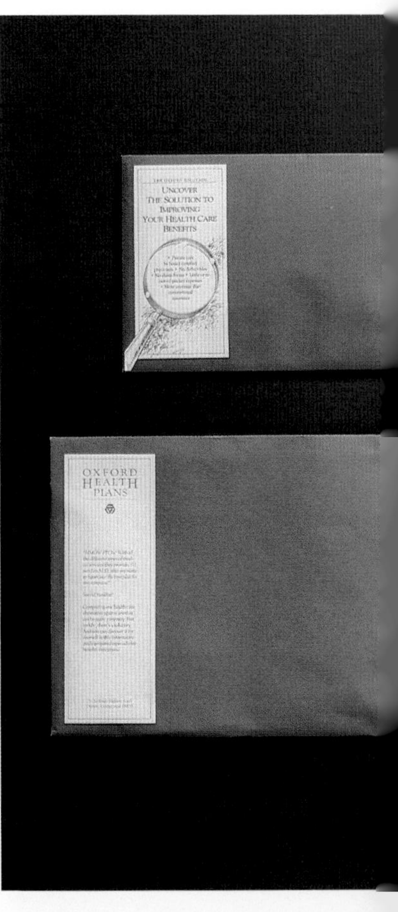

Title:	"The Oxford Solution"
Copywriter:	Karen Gedney
Art Director:	Patrick Fultz
Agency:	Millennium
Client:	Oxford Health Plans

Seventeen different elements combine into one very coherent presentation of the various group health plans offered to employees of major firms in the New York-New Jersey-Connecticut area. Obviously a formidable creative challenge, this collateral entry is extremely consistent and well-organized.

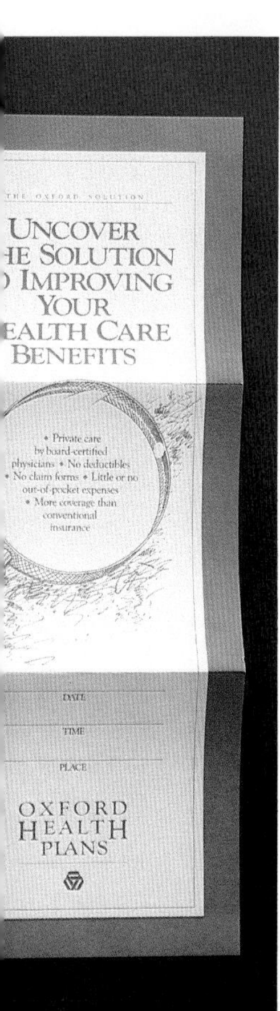
UNCOVER
HE SOLUTION
O IMPROVING
YOUR
EALTH CARE
BENEFITS
• Private care by board-certified physicians • No deductibles • No claims forms • Little or no out-of-pocket expenses • More coverage than conventional insurance
DATE
TIME
PLACE
OXFORD HEALTH PLANS

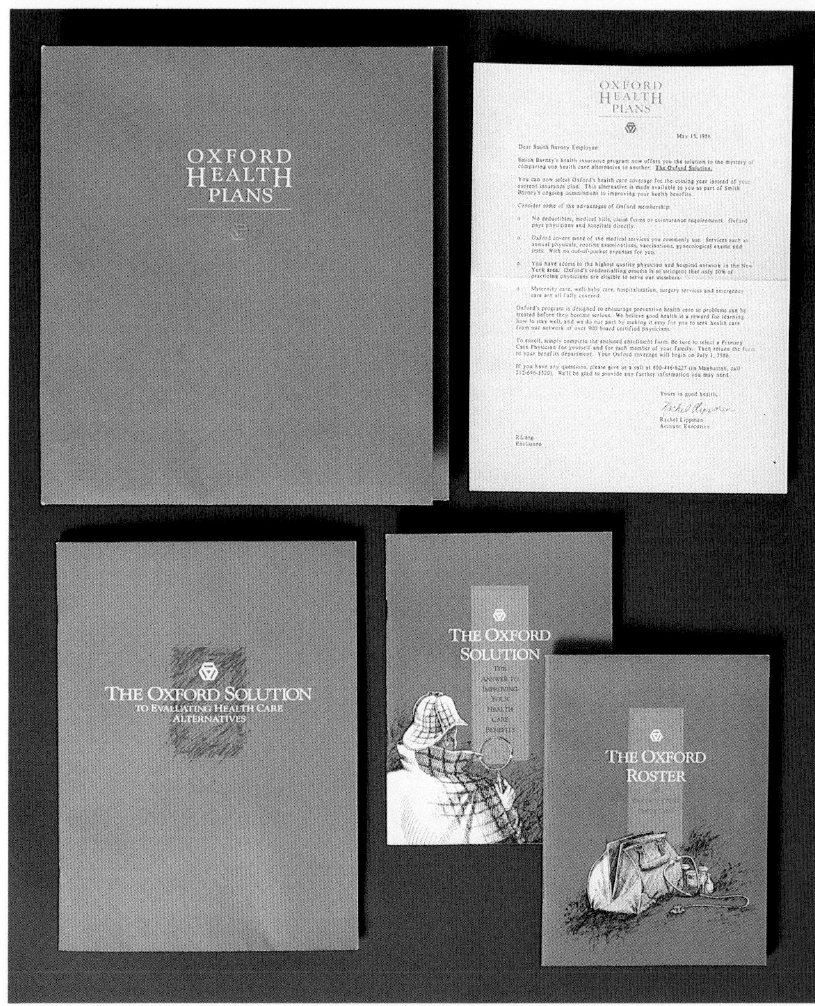
OXFORD HEALTH PLANS
OXFORD HEALTH PLANS
THE OXFORD SOLUTION
TO EVALUATING HEALTH CARE ALTERNATIVES
THE OXFORD SOLUTION
THE ANSWER TO IMPROVING YOUR HEALTH CARE BENEFITS
THE OXFORD ROSTER

The Financial Security Handbook

A guide for people who want to make the most from their money.

Budget

	Month	Year	Total
Total Income:	$_____	$_____	$_____
Minus Basic Expenses:			
Mortgage/Rent	$_____	$_____	
Food	_____	_____	
Insurance	_____	_____	
Auto	_____	_____	
Clothing	_____	_____	
Utility	_____	_____	
Medical	_____	_____	
Other	_____	_____	
			-$_____
Minus Discretionary Expenses:			
Entertainment	$_____	$_____	
Vacation	_____	_____	
Gifts	_____	_____	
Contributions	_____	_____	
Personal	_____	_____	
			-$_____
Minus Possible Expenses:			
Home Repairs	$_____	$_____	
Home Furnishings	_____	_____	
Auto Replacement	_____	_____	
Education	_____	_____	
Other	_____	_____	
			-$_____
Plus Savings: (IRAs, bank accounts, mutual funds, etc.)	$_____	$_____	+$_____
Minus Taxes: (Include Federal and State income tax, property tax, etc.)	$_____	$_____	-$_____
Equals Discretionary Income			=$_____

4

Do you know what your single biggest expense is?

Income tax. It can take more away from your income than any other expense. So it pays—literally!—to know about taxes, their effect on your income, and how to decrease your tax burden.

The IRS publishes dozens of easy-to-read, free booklets that will tell you everything you need to know. From Child Care Credit to Tax Information for Homeowners to Educational Expenses. And there are special booklets for self-employed individuals and business owners.

To get your free booklets, call the Internal Revenue Service office nearest you—the number is in your White Pages. It could be one of the most profitable phone calls you make this year.

(To find out how to save on taxes today while planning for retirement, turn to page 9.)

5

Title: "The Financial Security Handbook"
Copywriter: Paula Zargaj
Art Director: Jory S. Mason
Agency: Ingalls, Quinn & Johnson
Client: Sun Life of Canada

Pleasant pastel-color cartoon characters and simple line drawings illustrate this 20-page booklet which, with its smoothly written text sections, nicely manages to take an often intimidating subject and make it seem human and, after all, quite friendly.

Title: "R.S.V.P."
Copywriters: Laura DeFlora, Roz Cundell
Art Directors: Dan Levine, Bob Adameo
Agency: Ogilvy & Mather Direct
Client: American Express

Title: "Mead Top Sixty Awards"
Copywriter: Jo-Von Tucker
Art Director: Jo-Von Tucker
Agency: JVT Direct Marketing
Client: Mead Paper Company

For 38 years Mead Paper has presented Awards of Excellence in the Graphic Arts for creativity in design and printing quality on Mead coated papers. This 32-page 8 1/2" x 9 1/4" booklet includes the 56 winners and four Grand National Winners from the 1985 competition.

A SPECIAL INVITATION FROM AMERICAN EXPRESS.

THE FAVOR OF YOUR REPLY IS REQUESTED.

MEMBERSHIP HAS ITS PRIVILEGES.℠

The Card. 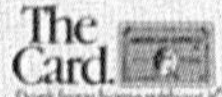
Don't leave home without it.℠

Morris Perlis
Executive
Vice President

Dear Prospective Member,

We're pleased to offer you this special invitation to become an American Express Cardmember.

It's the kind of invitation we think you'll be happy to accept.

Because once you become a member, you can be confident of receiving respect and recognition seldom found today. You will be treated as a member, not a number, enjoying a relationship with us that goes beyond the routine. American Express is a company totally dedicated to delivering you personal service worldwide.

And, when you use the enclosed invitation to apply and are approved for Cardmembership, you'll receive a special way to celebrate...

...we'll send you a **$25** Be My Guest® restaurant certificate good toward a meal at any restaurant that accepts the American Express® Card.

The Be My Guest certificate is a fitting way to begin enjoying privileges that are simply unavailable with ordinary credit cards.

What are some of these privileges?

One is no pre-set spending limit. Your purchases are approved based on your ability to pay as demonstrated by your past spending, payment patterns and personal resources. Naturally, we do not extend this privilege lightly.

Of course, such financial freedom would be meaningless without ample opportunity to exercise it. The Card is welcomed all over the world—at fine restaurants, retail establishments, hotels, airlines and car rental agencies.

And, if the Card is ever misplaced, lost, or stolen, you can have a new one—usually by the end of the next business day.

(continued)

AMERICAN EXPRESS TRAVEL RELATED SERVICES COMPANY, INC.
AMERICAN EXPRESS TOWER, WORLD FINANCIAL CENTER, NEW YORK, NY 10285-3000

A SPECIAL INVITATION TO DINNER.

We invite you to share a memorable meal *with our compliments* after you accept our special invitation to membership and become an American Express Cardmember.

We will send you a $25 Be My Guest® restaurant certificate once we issue the Card in your name. It's our way of welcoming you as a new American Express Cardmember.

All you have to do is present your certificate to the restaurant's maître d'—then have a wonderful time.

Your $25 Be My Guest restaurant certificate will be good toward a meal at any restaurant that welcomes the American Express® Card.

Membership has its privileges.℠

R. S. V. P.

BUSINESS REPLY MAIL
FIRST CLASS MAIL PERMIT NO. 110 NEW YORK, NY
POSTAGE WILL BE PAID BY ADDRESSEE

AMERICAN EXPRESS
TRAVEL RELATED SERVICES COMPANY, INC.
P.O. BOX 31557
SALT LAKE CITY UTAH 84131-9980

Chapter
5
PBC INTERNATIONAL
ONE SCHOOL STREET
GLEN COVE, NY 11542

SINGLE MEDIUM CAMPAIGNS

Perhaps nowhere in the direct marketing universe can the development of close relationships with customers be pursued more vigorously than in a campaign. Throughout this chapter and the next, which feature both single-medium and multi-media campaigns, you will see a number of different creative approaches in these two very challenging categories—altogether an extraordinary display of inventiveness and originality.

A single-medium campaign can be structured in many ways. It can consist of a short series of straightforward print ads or modest, two-color self-mailers. Or it can take the form of a major three-dimensional initiative, employing free samples mailed in cartons as well as all sorts of other attention-getting devices—software, hardware, even ready-to-wear items that can help drive home its point.

One advantage of campaigns is their ability to engage the customer's or prospect's curiosity and, step by step, raise his level of anticipation. The Chevrolet Dealer Solicitation on pages 182-183 is a good-natured, upbeat example of how a business campaign can establish and maintain solid rapport with its audience. Research had shown that dealers around the country were hesitant to use direct mail as a showroom traffic builder for three reasons. Chevrolet answered their objections one mailing at a time, using a language—namely, food–that is truly universal. And then, to end the campaign on a positive note, Chevrolet mailed one last candy bar as an incentive to join the program: Payday!

With the same ultimate goal but a completely different approach in tone and manner, the campaign launched by Mercedes-Benz and depicted on pages 184-185 reaches luxury car buyers directly with a test-drive offer that's hard to refuse—the key to the car. Also, note the great care taken in these efforts to mirror the general advertising image of Mercedes-Benz as an exclusive automobile obtainable by only an elite few. Before the reader even arrives at the dealer showroom, key in hand, he has already been affirmed as a member of a privileged group, and is likely to be favorably disposed toward the car he is about to drive.

While the direct mail campaign category boasts a wide variety of inventive creative solutions to marketing challenges, print advertising can make its own strong claim to a rich assortment of imaginative campaign efforts. And, although full pages and two-page spreads are often utilized to run long, persuasive copy convincing the reader to respond, effective campaigns can be mounted in much smaller amounts of space. On page 197, for example, the print ad series for Citizens Bank in Park Ridge resourcefully takes advantage of its own space limitations—and succeeds in bringing home its message with great clarity and visual impact.

Other print campaigns in this chapter, as you will see, use large, moderate and small amounts of space to establish relationships with their audience. You will also find direct mail campaigns and collateral efforts that range from expensive, custom-designed formats to pieces that are relatively modest in scope. Whatever its production budget, every one of the campaigns featured here is a distinctive example of originality of concept, well-balanced development and outstanding execution.

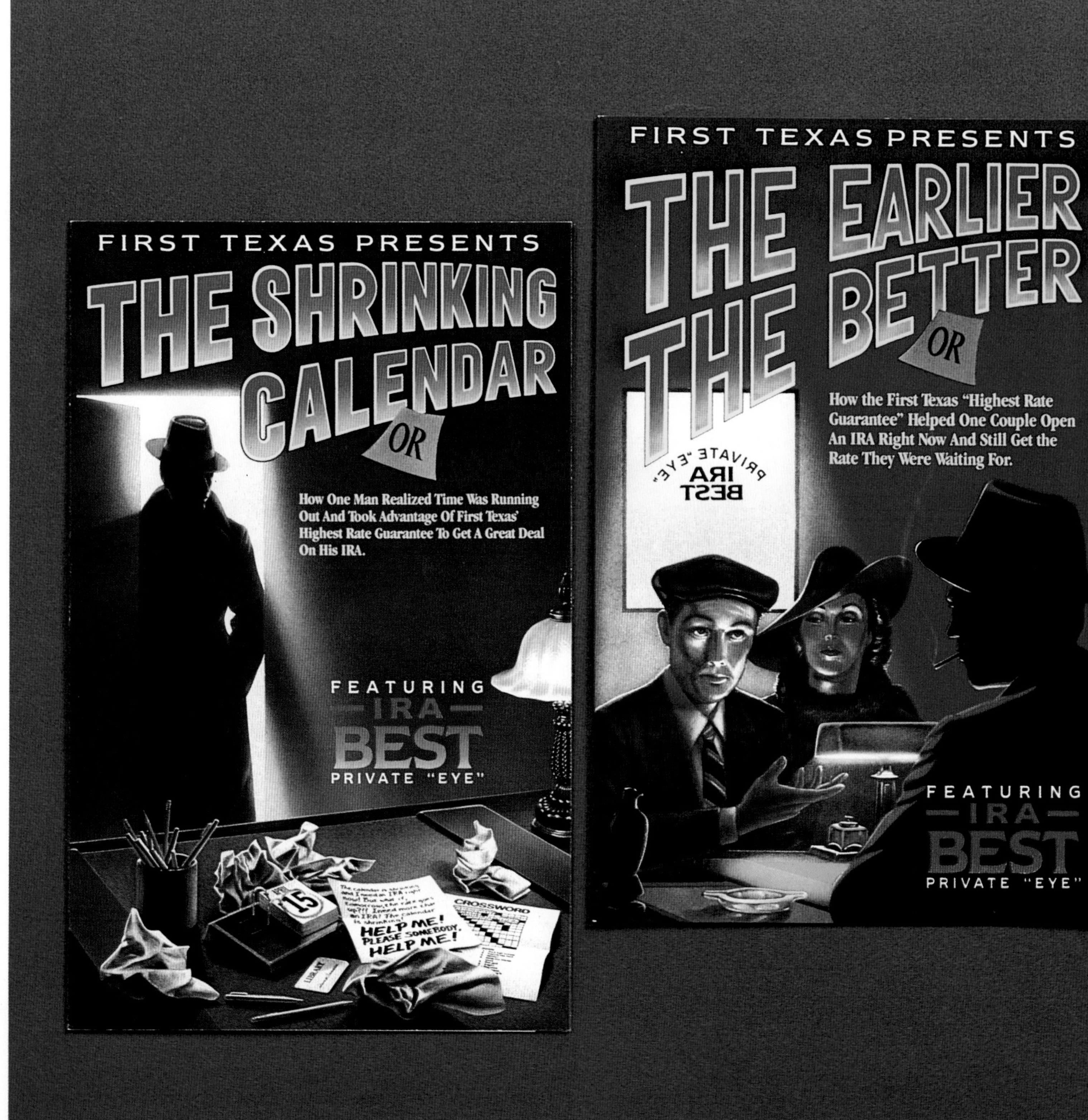

Title:	"The Adventures of IRA Best"
Copywriters:	Bob Dodd, George Campbell
Art Director:	Tonya Byers
Agency:	Bozell, Jacobs, Kenyon & Eckhardt Direct/Dallas
Client:	First Texas Savings Association

Nouveau fifties might be an appropriate genre from which to launch a discussion of this consumer campaign, which never lets the reader venture far from the trail of the evidence leading, of course, to the one best IRA solution of all.

FIRST TEXAS PRESENTS
THE LAST MINUTE
OR
How Ira Best Suddenly Remembered To Open His IRA And Hurried To First Texas Just In Time To Get A Break On His 1986 Taxes.
JOE'S
POLICE
FEATURING
IRA
BEST
PRIVATE "EYE"

FIRST TEXAS PRESENTS
THE LAST MINUTE
OR
FEATURING
IRA
BEST
PRIVATE "EYE"
PRIVATE "EYE" IRA BEST
"My office door clicked closed and there they stood. They wanted an IRA. They wanted it right now. And they wanted to be guaranteed a high rate. They wanted to know, could I help them find it?"
THIRD CLASS BULK RATE U.S. POSTAGE PAID First Texas Savings Association
John A. Sample
123 Sample Street
Sampletown, Texas
The solution was easy.
It can be even easier for you.
PRIVATE "EYE" IRA BEST
"My phone rang. A man was missing. He'd been acting strangely — worried about opening an IRA, worried about getting stuck at a low rate. Then, he disappeared. Where did he go? What happened?"
THIRD CLASS BULK RATE U.S. POSTAGE PAID First Texas Savings Association
James Ross Everett
1615 Woodcrest Lane
Carrollton, TX 75006
The solution was easy.
It can be even easier for you.

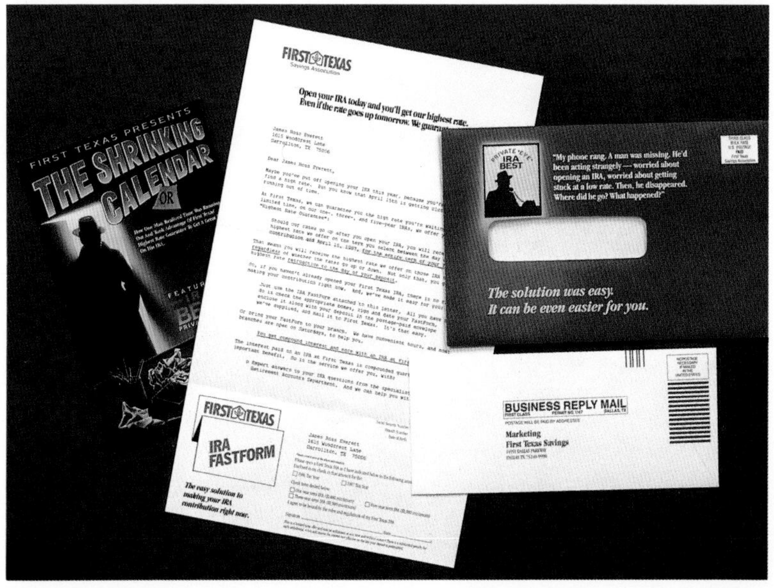
FIRST TEXAS PRESENTS
THE SHRINKING CALENDAR
OR
FIRST TEXAS
Savings Association
Open your IRA today and you'll get our highest rate.
Even if the rate goes up tomorrow.
PRIVATE "EYE" IRA BEST
"My phone rang. A man was missing. He'd been acting strangely — worried about opening an IRA, worried about getting stuck at a low rate. Then, he disappeared. Where did he go? What happened?"
The solution was easy.
It can be even easier for you.
FIRST TEXAS
IRA FASTFORM
The easy solution to making your IRA contribution right now.
BUSINESS REPLY MAIL
Marketing
First Texas Savings

"Thanks for sending the cake, Mom. It was probably delicious."

GET THE AT&T CALL ME CARD. THE EASY WAY TO CALL AND GET A TASTE OF HOME.

If you've got an appetite to speak to the folks back home, we've got a way you can do it that's quick and economical.

**THE CALL ME CARD.
IT'S ABSOLUTELY FREE FROM AT&T.**

The CALL ME Card is the easy, convenient way to talk to your family. It lets you call one place and one place only—home. Without having to fumble around for change. So it saves you time.

AND IT SAVES YOU MONEY.

Out-of-state calls made with the CALL ME Card cost less than collect or coin calls. So picking up the tab will be easier to swallow, whoever picks it up. All your calls will show up on the bill at home, right along with other telephone charges.

So come on. Do yourself—and your folks—a favor. Get the AT&T CALL ME Card. We think you'll find it makes calling… a piece of cake.

To get your AT&T CALL ME Card, mail the coupon at right. And we'll send an application home to your parents.

Or phone:

1 800 852-5432, Ext. 20

KEEP THE LINES OF COMMUNICATION OPEN.
GET THE AT&T CALL ME CARD. FREE.

Call 1 800 852-5432, Ext. 20, to get an application sent to your home. Or complete this coupon and mail back to: AT&T, Military CALL ME Card, P.O. Box 598, Teaneck, N.J. 07666.

Your Parents' Name ____ Parents' Phone No. ( )

Parents' Address ____

City/State/Zip ____

Your Name ____ Rank ____

Base ____ No. of Years in Service ____

Allow 6 to 8 weeks for delivery. Card not available in all areas, and only valid for domestic use. N20

Use of military situations does not imply endorsement by the armed services.

Title: "Call Me Card, Military Campaign"
Copywriters: Shelley E. Lanman, Michael Borden
Art Director: Bob Cesiro
Agency: Ogilvy & Mather Direct
Client: AT&T Public Communications

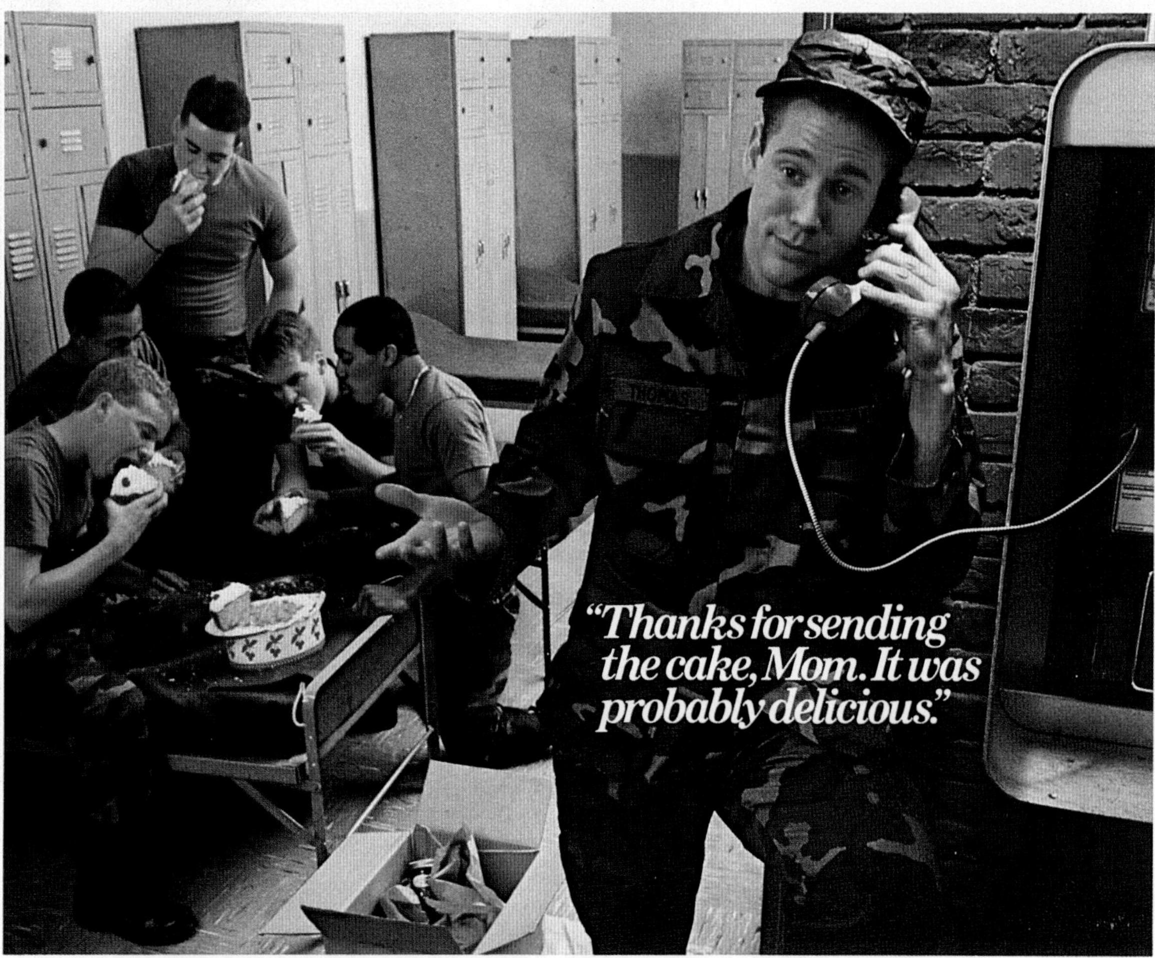
"Thanks for sending the cake, Mom. It was probably delicious."

GET THE AT&T CALL ME CARD. THE EASY WAY TO CALL AND GET A TASTE OF HOME.

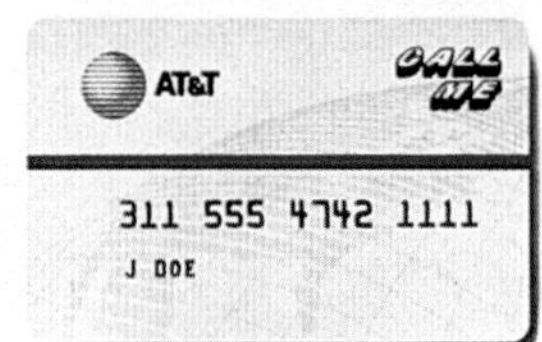
AT&T
CALL ME
311 555 4742 1111
J DOE

If you've got an appetite to speak to the folks back home, we've got a way you can do it that's quick and economical.

THE CALL ME CARD. IT'S ABSOLUTELY FREE FROM AT&T.

The CALL ME Card is the easy, convenient way to talk to your family. It lets you call one place and one place only—home. Without having to fumble around for change. So it saves you time.

AND IT SAVES YOU MONEY.

Out-of-state calls made with the CALL ME Card cost less than collect or coin calls. So picking up the tab will be easier to swallow, whoever picks it up. All your calls will show up on the bill at home, right along with other telephone charges.

So come on. Do yourself—and your folks—a favor. Get the AT&T CALL ME Card. We think you'll find it makes calling... a piece of cake.

To get your AT&T CALL ME Card, mail the coupon at right. And we'll send an application home to your parents.

Or phone:

1 800 852-5432, Ext. 20

KEEP THE LINES OF COMMUNICATION OPEN. GET THE AT&T CALL ME CARD. FREE.

Call 1 800 852-5432, Ext. 20, to get an application sent to your home. Or complete this coupon and mail back to: AT&T, Military CALL ME Card, P.O. Box 598, Teaneck, N.J. 07666.

Your Parents' Name ____ Parents' Phone No. ( )____

Parents' Address ____

City/State/Zip ____

Your Name ____ Rank ____

Base ____ No. of Years in Service ____

Allow 6 to 8 weeks for delivery. Card not available in all areas, and only valid for domestic use. A20

Use of military situations does not imply endorsement by the armed services.

AT&T

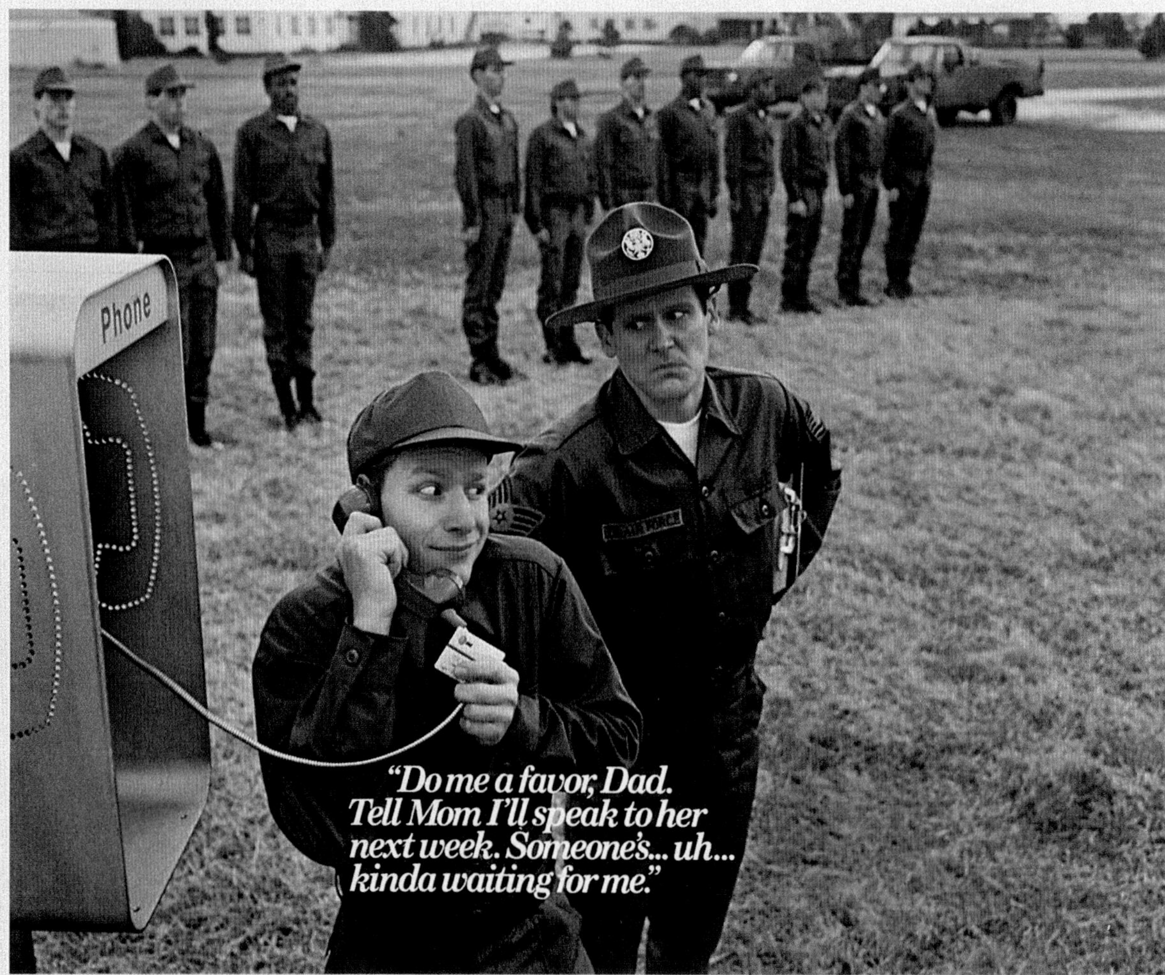

Phone
"Do me a favor, Dad. Tell Mom I'll speak to her next week. Someone's... uh... kinda waiting for me."

GET THE AT&T CALL ME CARD. THE EASY WAY TO TOUCH BASE WHEN YOU'RE ON BASE.

Now that you've become something of an expert at lining up, why not line up a quick and economical way to call the folks back home?

THE CALL ME CARD. IT'S ABSOLUTELY FREE FROM AT&T.

The CALL ME Card is the easy, convenient way to talk to your family. It lets you call one place and one place only—home. Without having to fumble for change. So it saves you time.

AND IT SAVES YOU MONEY.

Out-of-state calls made with the CALL ME Card cost less than collect or coin calls. So whoever pays for your calls home, pays less. Your calls will show up on the bill at home, along with other telephone charges.

So, come on—fall in . . . and make your calling easier. Get the AT&T CALL ME Card. For keeping in touch with home it makes a phone call almost as simple as—roll call.

To get your AT&T CALL ME Card, mail the coupon at right. And we'll send an application home to your parents.

Or phone:

1 800 852-5432, Ext. 20

KEEP THE LINES OF COMMUNICATION OPEN.
GET THE AT&T CALL ME CARD. FREE.

Call 1 800 852-5432, Ext. 20, to get an application sent to your home. Or complete this coupon and mail back to: AT&T, Military CALL ME Card, P.O. Box 598, Teaneck, N.J. 07666.

Your Parents' Name ______ Parents' Phone No. ( )

Parents' Address ______

City/State/Zip ______

Your Name ______ Rank ______

Base ______ No. of Years in Service ______

Allow 6 to 8 weeks for delivery. Card not available in all areas, and only valid for domestic use. F20

Use of military situations does not imply endorsement by the armed services.

Phone
HARRIS
"Do me a favor, Dad.
Tell Mom I'll speak to her
next week. Someone's...uh...
kinda waiting for me."

GET THE AT&T CALL ME CARD. THE EASY WAY TO KEEP THEM POSTED WHEN YOU'RE ON POST.

AT&T
CALL ME
311 555 4742 1111
J DOE

Now that you've become something of an expert at lining up, why not line up a quick and economical way to call the folks back home?

THE CALL ME CARD. IT'S ABSOLUTELY FREE FROM AT&T.

The CALL ME Card is the easy, convenient way to talk to your family. It lets you call one place and one place only—home. Without having to fumble for change. So it saves you time.

AND IT SAVES YOU MONEY.

Out-of-state calls made with the CALL ME Card cost less than collect or coin calls. So whoever pays for your calls home, pays less. Your calls will show up on the bill at home, along with other telephone charges.

So, come on—fall in... and make your calling easier. Get the AT&T CALL ME Card. For keeping in touch with home it makes a phone call almost as simple as—roll call.

To get your AT&T CALL ME Card, mail the coupon at right. And we'll send an application home to your parents.

Or phone:

1 800 852-5432, Ext. 20

KEEP THE LINES OF COMMUNICATION OPEN.
GET THE AT&T CALL ME CARD. FREE.

Call 1 800 852-5432, Ext. 20, to get an application sent to your home. Or complete this coupon and mail back to: AT&T, Military CALL ME Card, P.O. Box 598, Teaneck, N.J. 07666.

Your Parents' Name ( ) Parents' Phone No.
Parents' Address
City/State/Zip
Your Name Rank
Base No. of Years in Service

Allow 6 to 8 weeks for delivery. Card not available in all areas, and only valid for domestic use. A20

Use of military situations does not imply endorsement by the armed services.

AT&T

Two creative approaches are adapted for four different print advertisements as AT&T offers to help Army, Navy and Marine Corps recruits stay in touch with home.

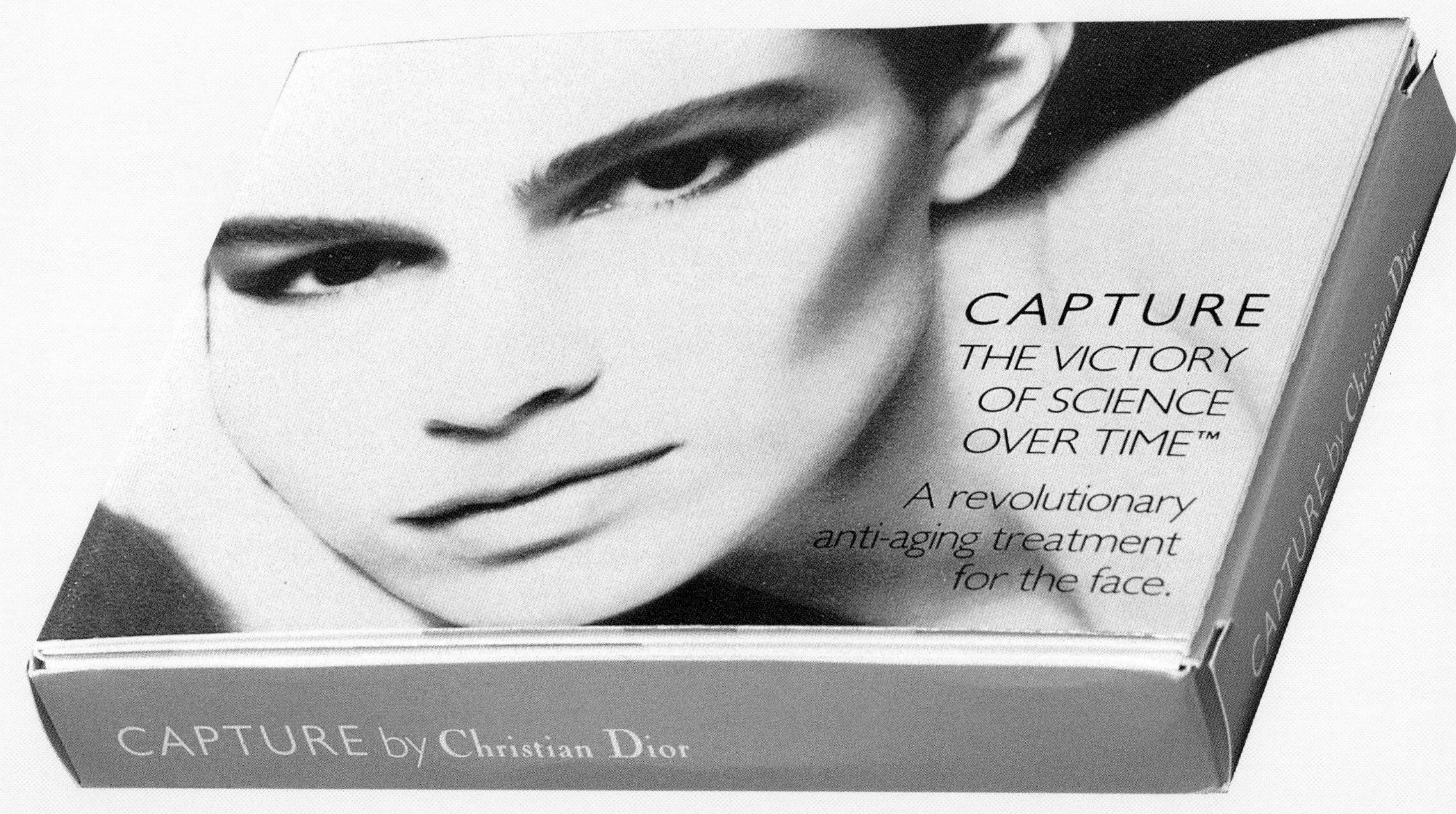

Title: "Capture"
Copywriter: Karen Herman
Art Director: Dale Friedman
Agency: Innotech Corporation
Client: Christian Dior Perfumes

So many claims made by so many apparently trustworthy brand names in the skin care area inspires Christian Dior to simply let the prospective customer—pinpoint-targeted through database management, of course—try the product for herself in this self-contained personal demonstration piece.

PULL TAB
TO ORDER
CAPTURE, by Christian Dior
Please send my gift of Résultante Moisturizing Day Cream, ½ ounce with my purchase of CAPTURE, 1 fluid ounce.
Delivery within
2-3 weeks of
receipt of order
pieces at $65.00
N.Y., N.J., OH, CT
add sales tax
Postage and Handling
3.50

CAPTURE

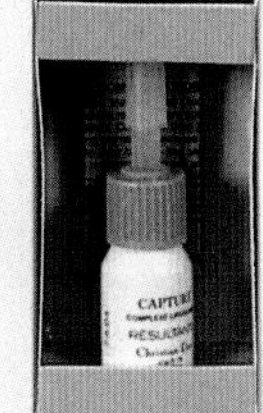

A TREATMENT DISCOVERY
Biologists at the Christian Dior Research Centre in association with the Pasteur Institute, Paris, have made an important new discovery based on an avant garde theory: with age, the cell membrane stiffens as hardening substances, such as cholesterol accumulate in its structure.

A CHRISTIAN DIOR ACHIEVEMENT
For the first time in cosmetology it has been possible to integrate Liposomes into a skin care product.

CHRISTIAN DIOR PATENTED* LIPOSOMES
Made of natural phospholipids (soy lecithin) Christian Dior Liposomes are spherical micro-capsules which have a molecular structure identical to cell membranes. In this form, they blend with the membrane to fluidify and promote its natural functions. Christian Dior Liposomes carry three international patents.

*U.S. Patent Nº 4,508,703 U.S. Patent Nº 4,621,023 French Patent Nº 2,540,381

THE SOLUTION: CAPTURE
An original creation in gel form which attacks the signs of skin aging. Based on tests on over 500 women, improvement can be seen from the first days. The wonderful result for women: less sluggish cells, more active cells give to skin a softer, smoother, firmer and more radiant tone.

HOW TO USE: 3 drops morning and night are all you need. Apply on a perfectly cleansed skin. **TO USE TRIAL SIZE FLACON ENCLOSED**: cut tip with scissors. Squeeze 2 to 3 drops on finger tips and apply to face and throat.

INSTRUCTIONS TO ORDER

- To order, pull pink tab to release Order Form.
- Tear off POSTAGE PAID ENVELOPE.
- Fill out Order Form.
- Use Check, Money Order or Credit Card to order CAPTURE.
- Place Order Form with payment back in the POSTAGE PAID ENVELOPE.

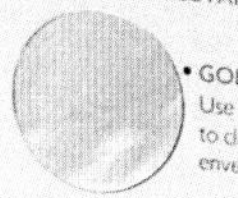

- GOLD SEAL. Use this gold seal to close envelope.
- **TO ORDER BY PHONE**
  Call toll-free —
  1-800-225-DIOR (1-800-225-3467)

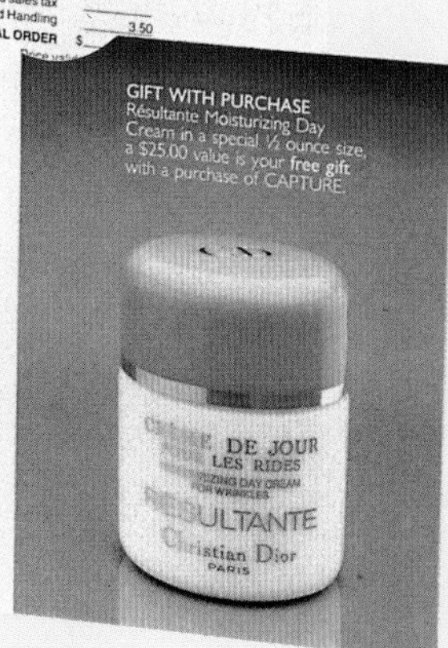

GIFT WITH PURCHASE
Résultante Moisturizing Day Cream in a special ½ ounce size, a $25.00 value is your free gift with a purchase of CAPTURE.
CRÈME DE JOUR
LES RIDES
RÉSULTANTE
Christian Dior
PARIS

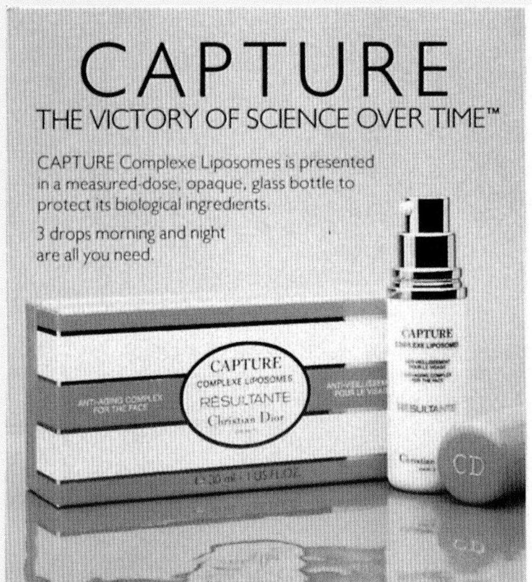

CAPTURE
THE VICTORY OF SCIENCE OVER TIME™
CAPTURE Complexe Liposomes is presented in a measured-dose, opaque, glass bottle to protect its biological ingredients.
3 drops morning and night
are all you need.
CAPTURE
COMPLEXE LIPOSOMES
RÉSULTANTE
Christian Dior
ANTI-AGING COMPLEX FOR THE FACE
CD

Christian Dior announces an achievement in skin care. This achievement is the result of research undertaken over 7 years in Christian Dior's Research Centre in association with the prestigious Pasteur Institute, Paris. The solution is CAPTURE containing Christian Dior's patented Liposomes, a biotechnological innovation that acts on 3 phases of skin aging:

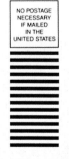

MEMBRANE AGING
—by restoring fluidity to cell membrane

CELLULAR AGING
—thymus extracts encourage cell renewal

TISSUE AGING
—collagen and elastine peptides help renew tissue to give the skin new firmness and tone.

CAPTURE by Christian Dior
A remarkable achievement

NO POSTAGE NECESSARY IF MAILED IN THE UNITED STATES

BUSINESS REPLY MAIL
FIRST CLASS PERMIT NO 17057 CINCINNATI, OHIO

POSTAGE WILL BE PAID BY ADDRESSEE

CAPTURE
CHRISTIAN DIOR PERFUMES, INC.
P.O. BOX 317634
CINCINNATI, OHIO 45231

Title:	"The Clue To The Best Copiers..."
Copywriters:	Dave Ullman, Josh Mandel
Art Director:	Beth Kosuk
Agency:	Cramer- Krasselt/ Chicago
Client:	A.B. Dick Copier Machines

America's topmost crimefighter plays a starring role in this clever business-to-business campaign that employs the "borrowed interest" advertising technique to enhance product name identification while having a bit of fun and delivering an important sales message at the same time.

YES, ED! THIS IS THE BEST COPY I'VE **EVER** SEEN! BUT YOUR ASCOT DOESN'T CUT IT.

WE WERE ALL SET FOR INTER-PLANETARY COPIER DOMINANCE UNTIL **DICK** CAME ALONG.

THAT'S THE THIRD OFFICE MANAGER THIS WEEK! THESE COPIER BREAKDOWNS HAVE **GOT** TO STOP!!

THERE'S **GOT** TO BE A MORE RELIABLE COPIER SOMEWHERE. BUT **WHOSE? WHOSE??**

"*Tracy??*" I spluttered. "Hey, he's a cop—not a copier expert."

"No, Sam," she said sweetly. "Not *that* Dick. A.B.Dick."

I tell ya, it was like a light went on in my head. Even I know A.B.Dick's new copiers are so reliable, they hardly ever break down.

They're also a cinch to use. Fact is, A.B.Dick copiers actually *help* you make copies right the first time. They guide you through, step by step, in good old American words—none of your sinister foreign symbols.

And talk about your copy quality! What with the advanced microelectronics and fiber optics, you get copies so beautiful, it could break your heart.

The A.B.Dick copier line-up includes everything from small tabletop models to heavy-duty consoles.

So if you're an office manager who's tired of taking the heat when the copier breaks down, you owe it to yourself to call your A.B.Dick sales office or mail the coupon today.

Or else, do us both a favor. And buy a bulletproof vest.

Call 1-800-447-4700 or mail this card today for a FREE A.B.Dick copier demonstration.

Dear Dick:

Yes! Show me the new line of trouble-free copiers from A.B.Dick —before it's too late!

Name_____

Title_____

Company_____

Address_____

City_____ State_____ Zip_____

Phone_____

ABDICK.

FORM# 92-9099

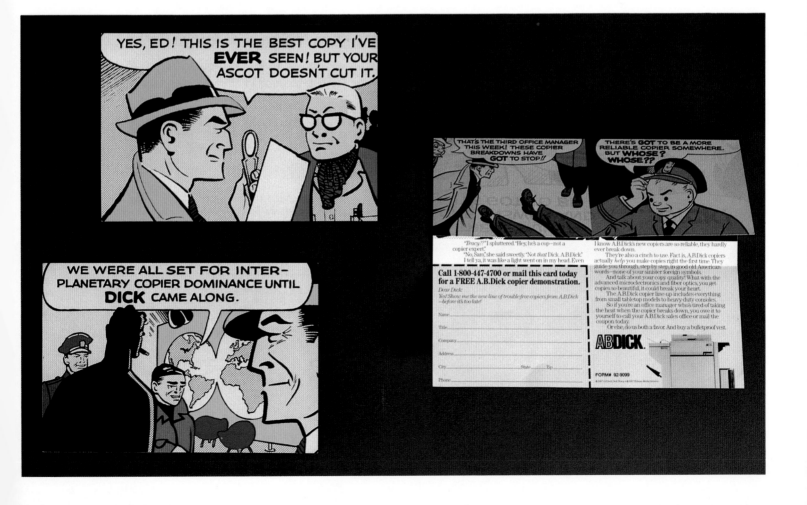

Cut taxes here.

Mail to: Merrill Lynch, Pierce,
Fenner & Smith Inc. Service Center
P.O. Box 2021, Jersey City, NJ 07303

☐ Please send me your free brochure, *How to Save Taxes on up to $2,000 in Income with the Merrill Lynch IRA.*

Name________
Address________
City________
State________ Zip________
Business Phone________
Home Phone________
Merrill Lynch customers, please give name and office address of your Financial Consultant:________

2772

The IRA brochure. Free from Merrill Lynch.

An IRA is more than just a retirement nest-egg. It's also a very easy way to cut taxes.

The Merrill Lynch IRA brochure, *How to Save Taxes on up to $2,000 in Income*, explains the two tax breaks you get when you open an IRA and answers the most frequently asked questions about IRAs. You'll learn who is eligible for an IRA, the range of investment alternatives, and the best time to open an IRA.

If you have any additional questions, a Merrill Lynch Financial Consultant will be happy to help you select an IRA that suits your personal needs and goals.

To receive a free copy of the IRA brochure, call toll free, Monday through Friday, 8:30 am to 12 midnight eastern time. In Alaska or Hawaii, call the Merrill Lynch office nearest you. Or just cut the coupon.

1 800-637-7455 Ext. 2772

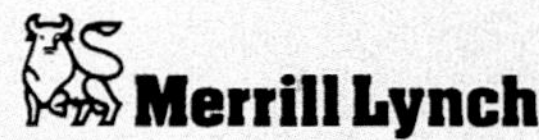

Improving your IRA is just a matter of making the right connection.

1 800-MERRILL
Ext. 6000

Connect with a Financial Consultant and transfer to Merrill Lynch.

When you connect with a Merrill Lynch Financial Consultant to transfer or open an IRA, you'll discover how to make your IRA an integral part of a comprehensive retirement program.

Your Financial Consultant can provide you with information on a variety of investment alternatives suitable for your retirement assets, including certificates of deposit, mutual funds, equities, and government-backed funds. Should economic conditions change, you will be able to make changes in your investment strategy based on the latest opinions of our top-ranked research team.

Our brochure, *Guide to Investment Selections for Retirement Plans*, outlines how you can tailor your retirement plan to your personal needs and financial objectives.

Call toll free Monday through Friday, 8:30 am to 12 midnight eastern time, for a free copy and ask for the phone number of the Merrill Lynch office in your area. In Alaska or Hawaii, consult your telephone directory.

We'd like to hear from you. And we think you'll like hearing what Merrill Lynch has to say.

Mail to: Merrill Lynch, Pierce, Fenner & Smith Inc.
Service Center, P.O. Box 2021
Jersey City, NJ 07303

☐ Please send me your free brochure, *Guide to Investment Selections for Retirement Plans.*

Name________
Address________
City________ State________ Zip________
Business Phone________
Home Phone________
Merrill Lynch customers, please give name and office address of your Financial Consultant:________

6000

Title: "Taxes"
Copywriter: Mark Levitt
Art Director: Roseanne Motti
Agency: Wunderman Worldwide
Client: Merrill Lynch

The ease of coupon and toll- free telephone direct response is given prominence in this tax- time print campaign that also features multiple-benefit promises in moderately short, to-the-point copy.

Fill out the short form that can save you money on taxes.

Mail to: Merrill Lynch, Pierce,
Fenner & Smith Inc. Service Center
P.O. Box 2021, Jersey City, NJ 07303

☐ Please send me your free report on *50 Tax Saving Ideas for Investors.*

Name ______

Address ______

City ______

State ______ Zip ______

Business Phone ______

Home Phone ______

Merrill Lynch customers, please give name and office address of your Financial Consultant:

______

______

2186

50 Tax Saving Ideas for Investors. Free from Merrill Lynch.

The long and the short of it is that no matter how much money you earn, what counts is what you get to keep—your after-tax return.

50 Tax Saving Ideas for Investors provides you with a guide to tax reducing strategies. Topics covered range from ways to accelerate deductions and postpone income to how to evaluate the impact of preference income. In addition, you'll find tips on how to reduce your tax bill with gifts and trusts as well as a discussion of tax investments.

To receive a free copy of this timely report, call toll free, Monday through Friday, 8:30 am to 12 midnight eastern time. In Alaska or Hawaii, call the Merrill Lynch office nearest you. Or just fill out the short form above and mail it in.

1 800-637-7455 Ext. 2186

Title: "Chevrolet Dealer Solicitation"
Copywriters: David Atnip, Joe Paonessa
Art Director: Terry Sharbach
Agency: CECO Communications
Client: Chevrolet Motor Division

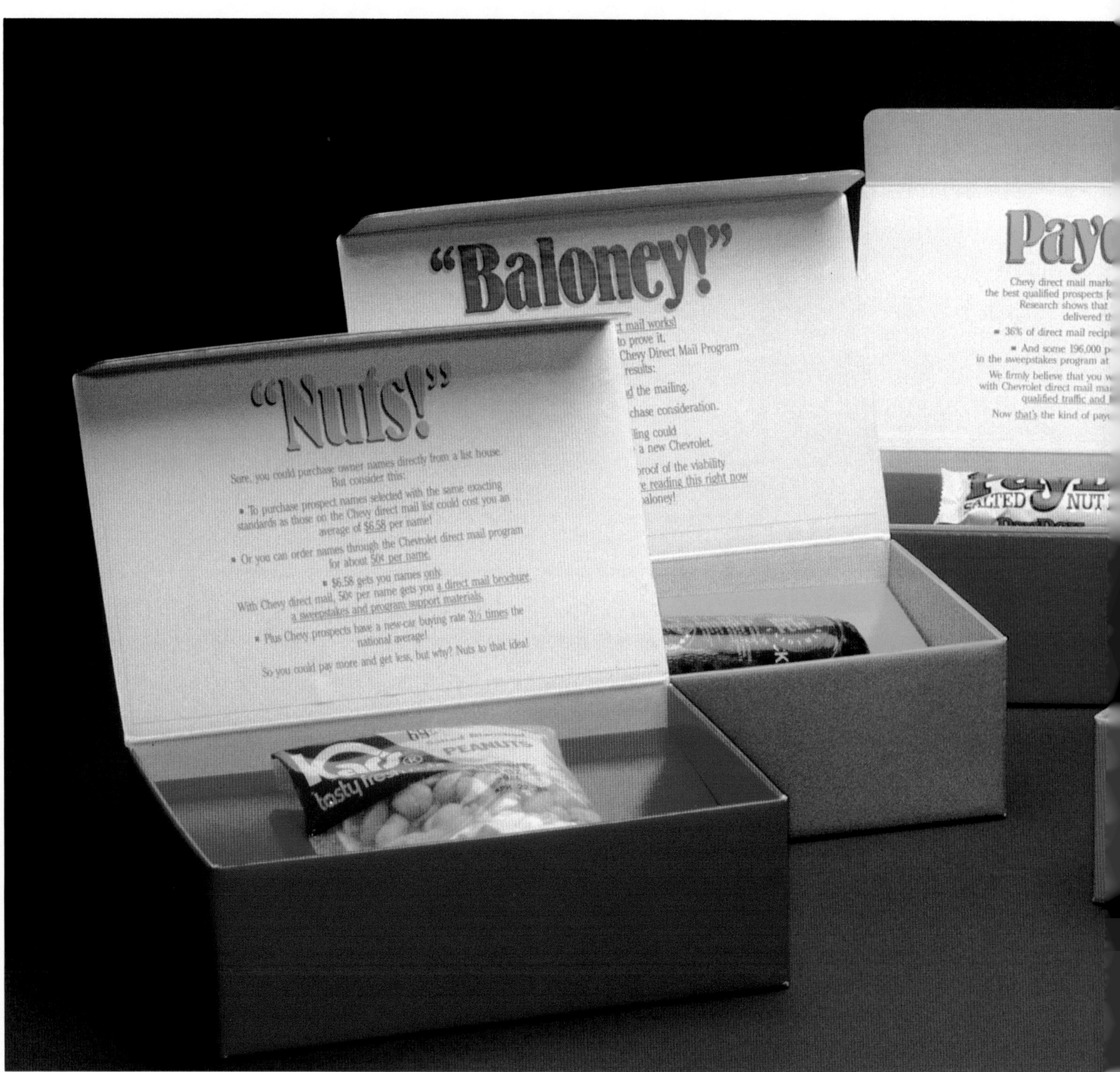

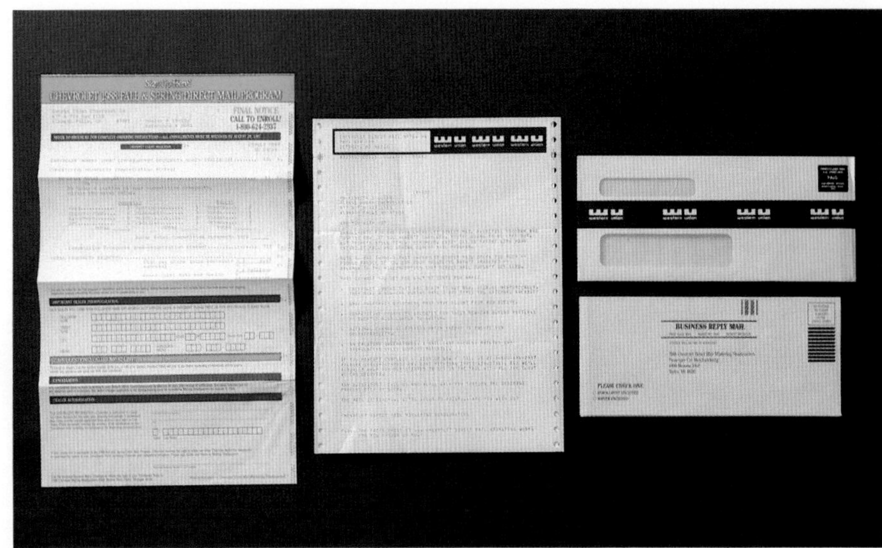

In an imaginative direct mail business campaign designed to overcome car dealers' apprehensions about the effectiveness of direct mail, the "teaser" headline on the front of each box sets up a high-impact, tasty message that drives each point home simply, quickly and with memorable effect. Follow-up telegrams solicit dealer participation in Chevrolet's national consumer direct mail efforts. "To anyone who has ever said, 'Direct mail costs too much,' we say: Nuts!" "To every person who has ever thought, 'Direct mail doesn't get read,' we say: Baloney!" "For every dealer who joins the direct mail program, every day will be like...Payday!" "To everyone who has ever claimed, 'National direct mail lists are not on target,' we say: Fiddle-Faddle!"

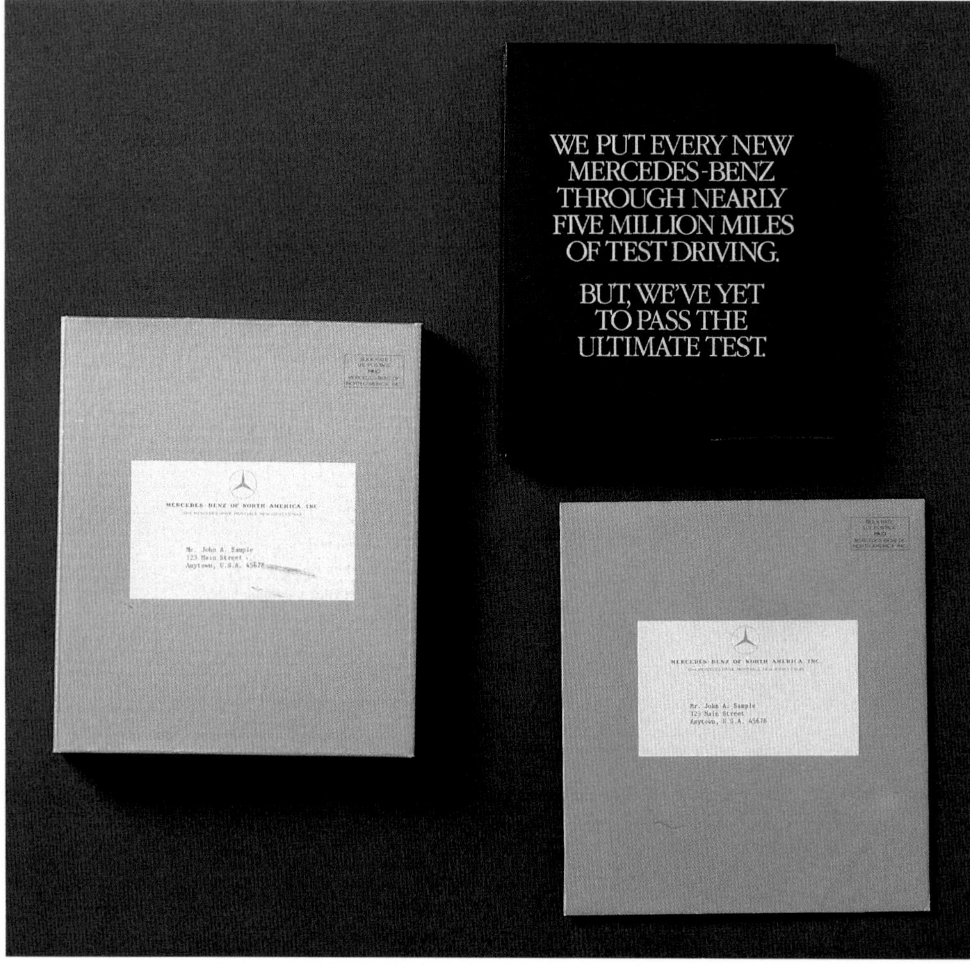

WE PUT EVERY NEW MERCEDES-BENZ THROUGH NEARLY FIVE MILLION MILES OF TEST DRIVING.
BUT, WE'VE YET TO PASS THE ULTIMATE TEST.
MERCEDES-BENZ OF NORTH AMERICA, INC.
Mr. John A. Sample
123 Main Street
Anytown, U.S.A. 45678

MERCEDES-BENZ OF NORTH AMERICA, INC.

BURGHARD VON CRAMM
VICE PRESIDENT SALES

ONE MERCEDES DRIVE
MONTVALE, NEW JERSEY 07645

September 21, 1987

Mr. John A. Sample
123 Main Street
Providence, Rhode Island 00000

Dear Mr. Sample,

"The best or nothing."

A hundred years ago, it was Gottlieb Daimler's personal motto
Today, all of us at Mercedes-Benz are committed to it.

This commitment is what makes Mercedes-Benz automobiles excel
in every area--from aerodynamic and interior design to performance
and engineering. It is what makes a Mercedes-Benz a Mercedes-Benz

Importantly, the commitment extends long past the day you purchase a new model.

Where a Mercedes-Benz proves its mettle is not on the test track or during a test drive. Year after year of hard use and year after year of outstanding service and owner satisfaction truly establish the basis of Mercedes-Benz worth.

It all starts with a forty-eight month or 50,000-mile new-ca
warranty, arguably the most comprehensive new-car warranty in for
today. Then, if you ever have a problem on the road--evenings, weekends or holidays, 365 days a year,--Mercedes-Benz Roadside Assistance is but a toll-free call away.

Yet the rewards of Mercedes-Benz ownership involve still mor
than the initial quality of the product and the benefits of an
attentive service network. Over the years, Mercedes-Benz automob

Title: "Test Drive Campaign"
Copywriters: Carolyn Crimmins, Judy Hultquist
Art Directors: Lynda Decker, Marvin Fried
Agency: McCaffrey & McCall Direct Marketing
Client: Mercedes-Benz of North America

Consumer personalization practically becomes an art form in this campaign to persuade luxury car owners to use a Mercedes-Benz for a day, as the name and address of the local dealership is linked with letters, information packages, a test-drive appointment card and even an actual Mercedes-Benz ignition key.

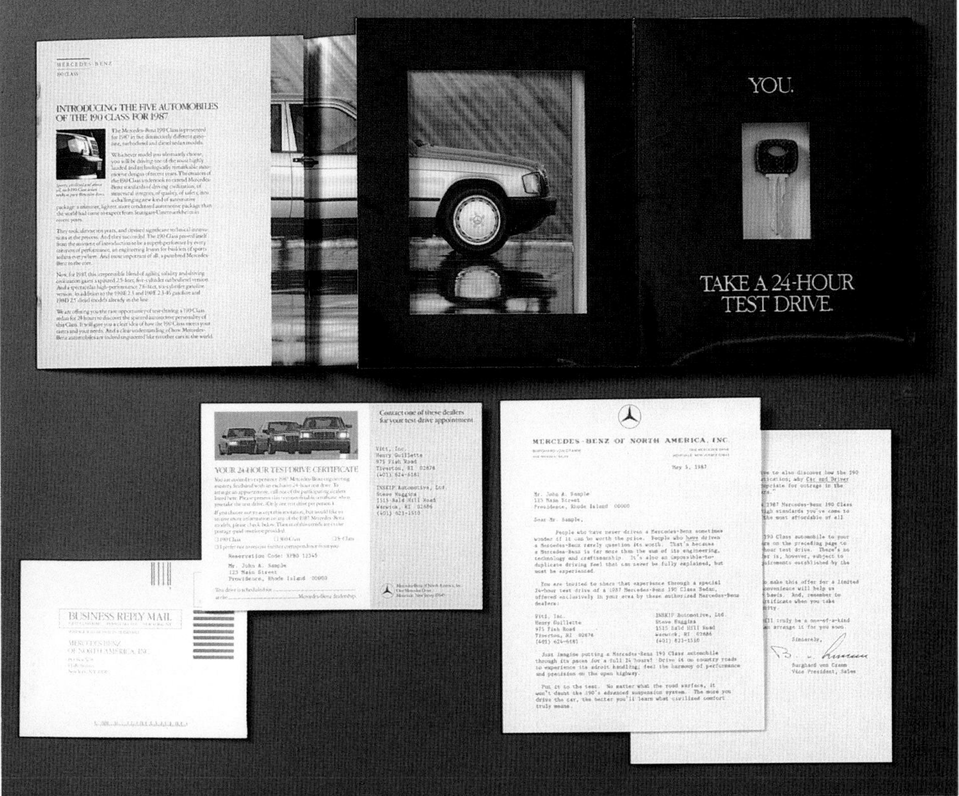

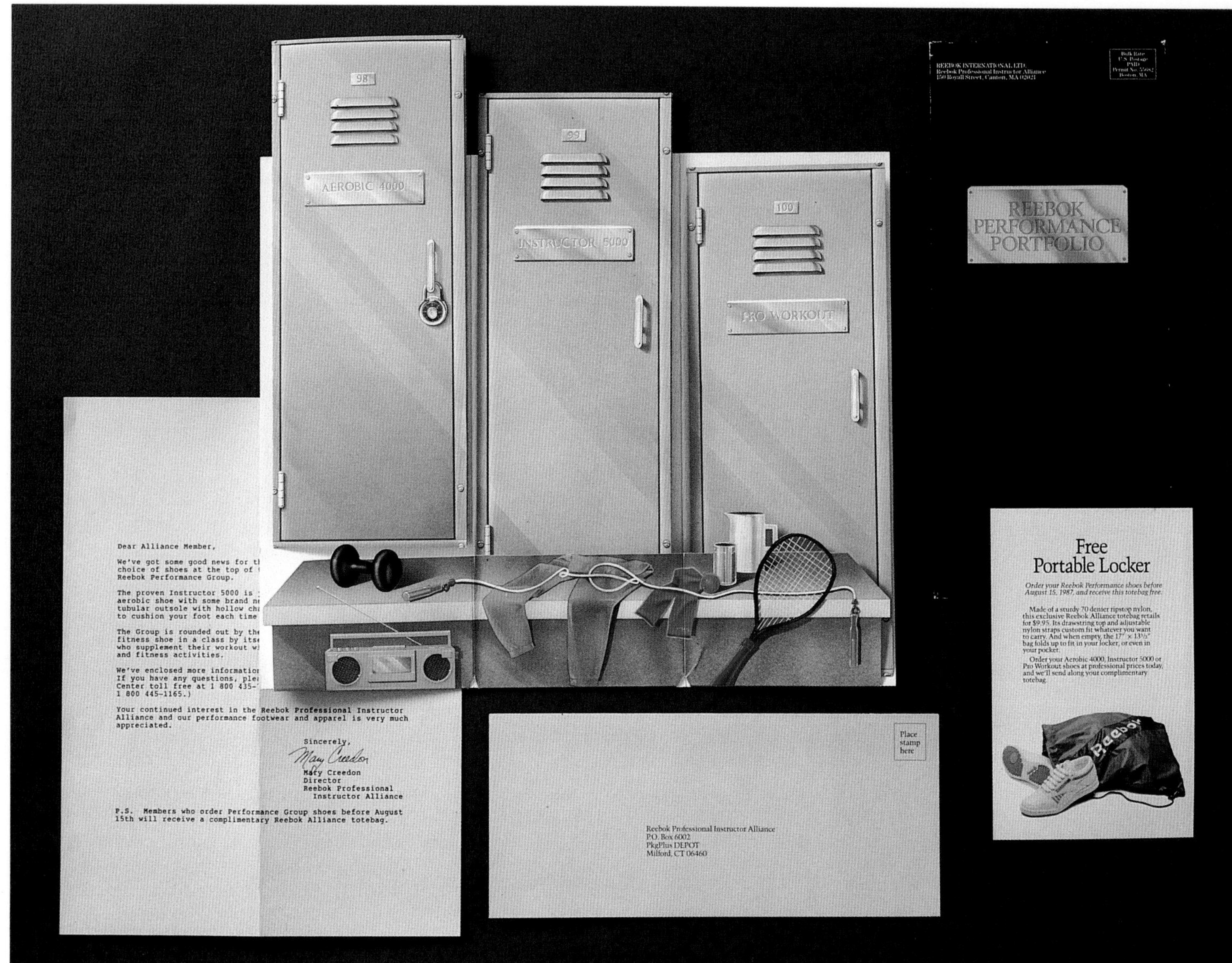

Title: "Reebok Performance Portfolio"
Copywriter: Suzie Becker
Art Director: Jory Mason
Agency: HBM/Creamer Direct
Client: Reebok International

What better way to spread the word about workout shoes than to tell aerobics instructors, who can then tell their students? As privileged members of the target audience for this handsome mailing piece extolling the advantages of Reebok's exercise footwear, instructors are also given an opportunity to obtain a free tote, creatively touted as a "portable locker."

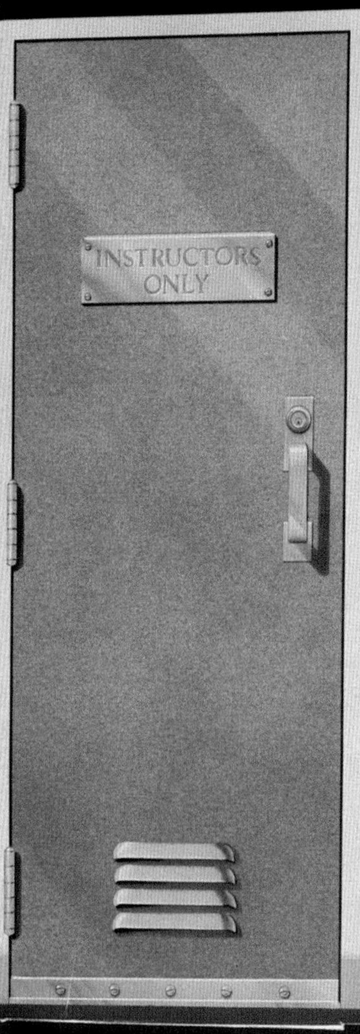

A proven performer.

The Instructor 5000® series was designed with aerobic professionals in mind. During its development in the Reebok Human Performance and Shoe Design Lab, we submitted the 5000 to an extensive wear test. Over 2,400 professional aerobic instructors did their most rigorous workouts in the Reebok Instructor 5000. We listened to what they had to say, refining the 5000.

It comes as no surprise then, that since its introduction, the Instructor 5000 has been widely regarded as the shoe for athletes who take their aerobics seriously.

Stability first and foremost.

Research into the biomechanics of aerobic exercise shows that all of the side-to-side motion of your intensive workouts puts an extraordinary amount of stress on your feet, class after class.

The Instructor 5000 was the first shoe designed to control excessive lateral motion in the forefoot. Reebok's unique Lateral/Medial Support Straps (patent pending) hold the forefoot securely in place, preventing it from rolling over during all types of aerobic workouts.

Maximum cushioning and shock absorption in the forefoot.

Not only does the 5000 offer forefoot stability, but it offers outstanding cushioning in this critical area of impact. A soft compression-resistant polyurethane bed is encapsulated in the forefoot of the EVA midsole for extra shock absorbency.

And the outsole features Reebok's Interactive Pillar System. More than 250 pillars work like independent shock absorbers to cushion your foot each time it lands.

How could a shoe that looks so good be so good for you?

This is the way we design shoes at Reebok. Superior performance, matched by superior looks. The Instructor 5000. A proven shoe that responds to the demands of professional instructors.

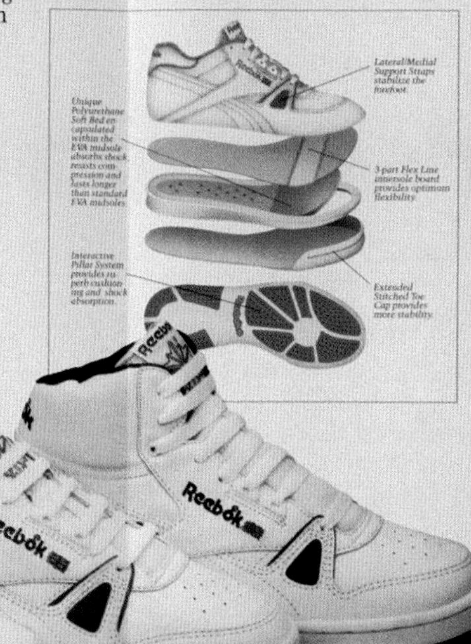

The right combination for a complete workout.

As you strive for total fitness, your workouts have become more and more diverse, and now may include weight training, court sports or running. At times, you need a shoe that can take you from the weight room to the court to the track. The Pro Workout combines key features of several sport-specific shoes to bring you a new class...a total fitness shoe.

At the Reebok Human Performance and Shoe Design Lab, we analyzed the demands placed on footwear during a variety of athletic activities, and with help from some of the most respected strength and conditioning coaches in the country, we developed the Pro Workout.

Next we put the shoe through one of the most extensive wear-testing programs ever, on a variety of surfaces, indoor and outdoor, for a variety of activities, continuously refining it right there in the lab.

And now, we have a shoe which will stand up to your toughest workout. The Pro Workout – for aerobics, weight training, court sports and running.

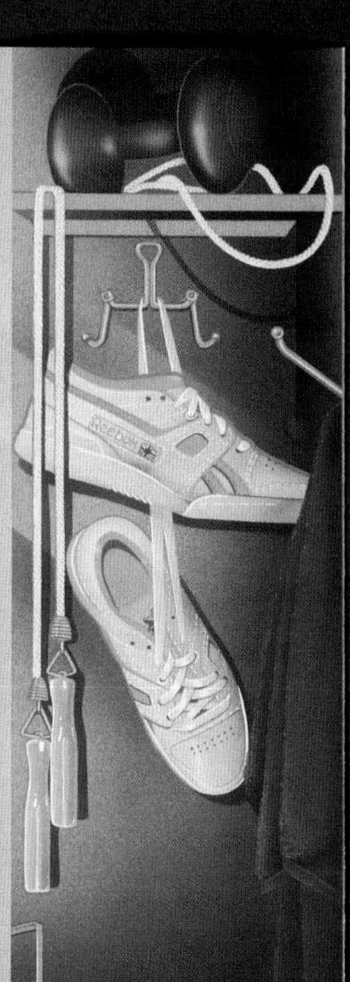

Introducing the Aerobic 4000

The newest performance model from the leader in aerobic shoes.

The Aerobic 4000 joins the Instructor 5000® at the top of the Reebok aerobic shoe line.

When we decided to develop this new performance aerobic shoe, we didn't settle for a few surface improvements. We went back to the Reebok Human Performance and Shoe Design Lab to construct an all new aerobic shoe.

The 4000 introduces two new features in aerobic shoes: a tubular outsole system and a Dynamic Cradle™ midsole system. In combination with our polyurethane forefoot support straps – they make for a technologically superior lightweight aerobic shoe.

New tubular outsole system

With the amount of time you spend on your forefoot during an aerobic workout, an unusual amount of stress falls on this part of your foot. The Aerobic 4000's new tubular outsole is designed specifically to soften this impact. Hollow channels between the midsole and outsole collapse independently on contact, then rebound, to provide a springy cushion exactly where you need it, when you need it.

Title: "Panorama"
Copywriter: Sid Meltzer
Art Director: Mary Ann Ahroon
Agency: Grey Direct
Client: Shell Oil Company

Nothing is as reassuring to a traveler as knowing he is welcome anywhere. The tone of Shell's comforting Signature direct mail campaign is typified in this four-element piece that makes any road seem quite lovely indeed.

Title: "Art Director's Sweepstakes"
Copywriter: James Wells
Art Director: Michael Smacchia
Agency: The Direct Marketing Agency
Client: Freelance Solutions

Self-mailers work independently and together in this efficient two-color series that not only promises to ease the art director's burden, but offers a nifty chance to win a hard-to-get, fun-to-watch giant television, too.

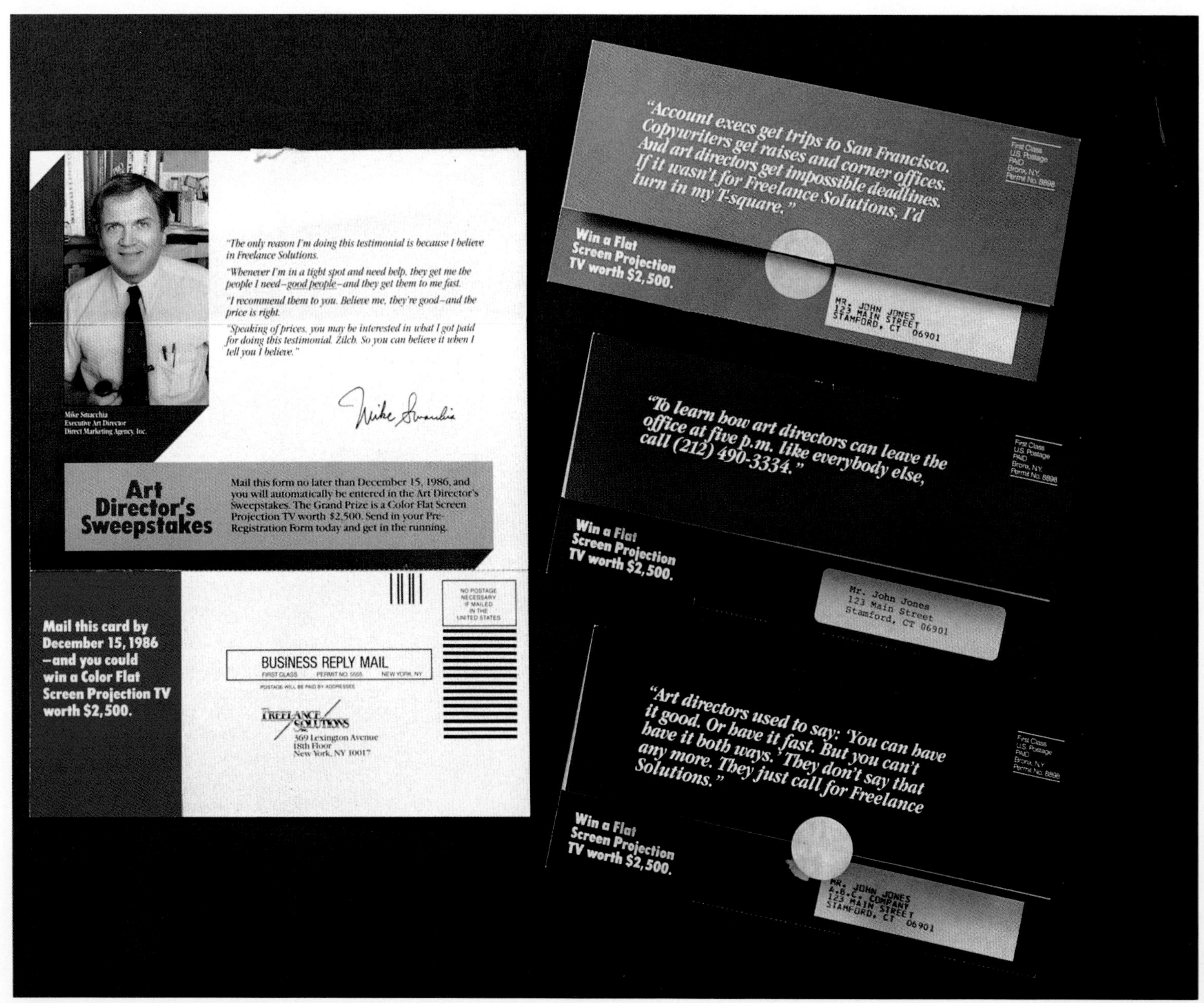

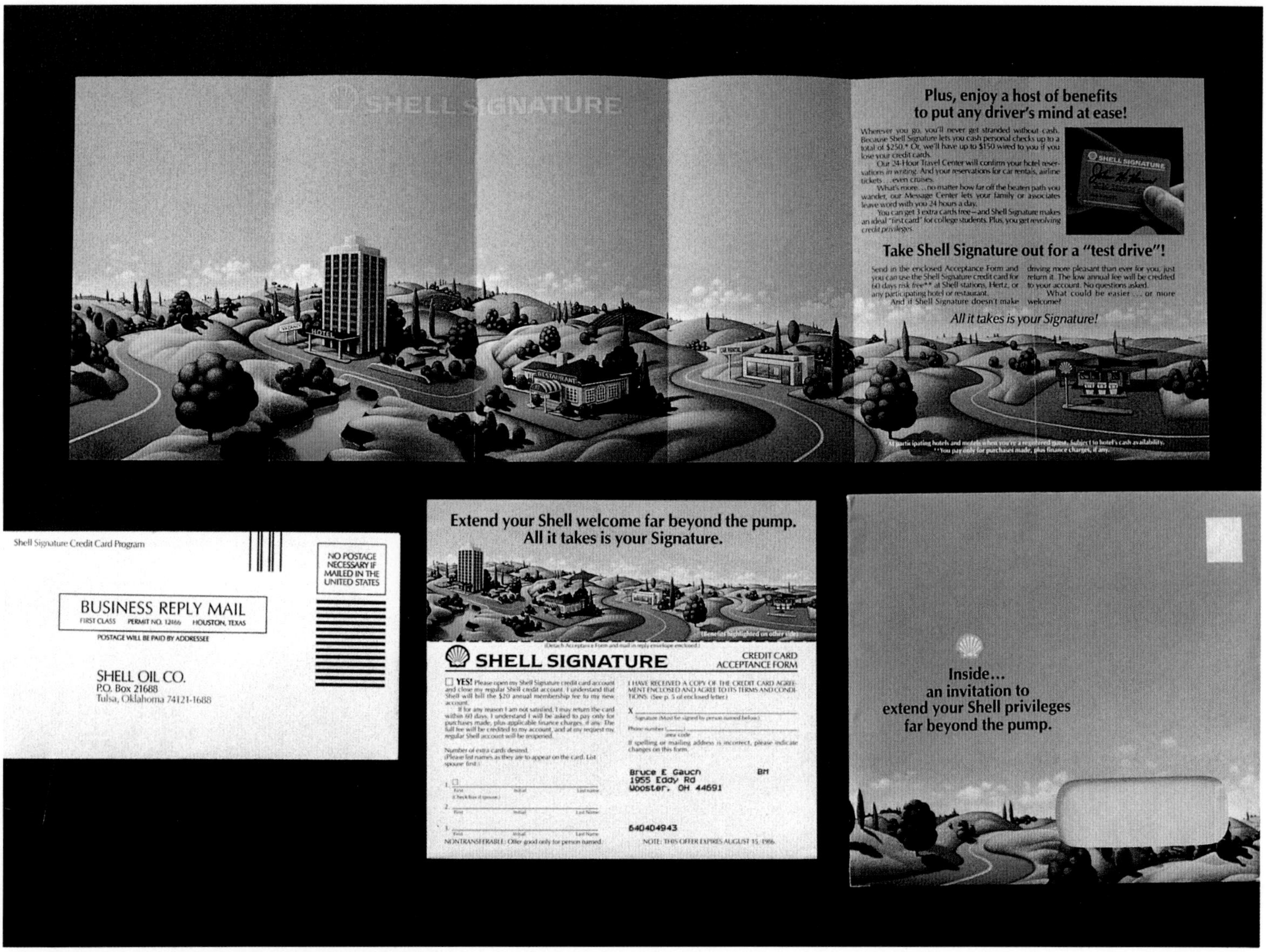

SHELL SIGNATURE

Plus, enjoy a host of benefits to put any driver's mind at ease!

Take Shell Signature out for a "test drive"!

All it takes is your Signature!

Shell Signature Credit Card Program

NO POSTAGE NECESSARY IF MAILED IN THE UNITED STATES

BUSINESS REPLY MAIL

FIRST CLASS PERMIT NO. 12466 HOUSTON, TEXAS

POSTAGE WILL BE PAID BY ADDRESSEE

SHELL OIL CO.
P.O. Box 21688
Tulsa, Oklahoma 74121-1688

Extend your Shell welcome far beyond the pump. All it takes is your Signature.

SHELL SIGNATURE

CREDIT CARD ACCEPTANCE FORM

Inside... an invitation to extend your Shell privileges far beyond the pump.

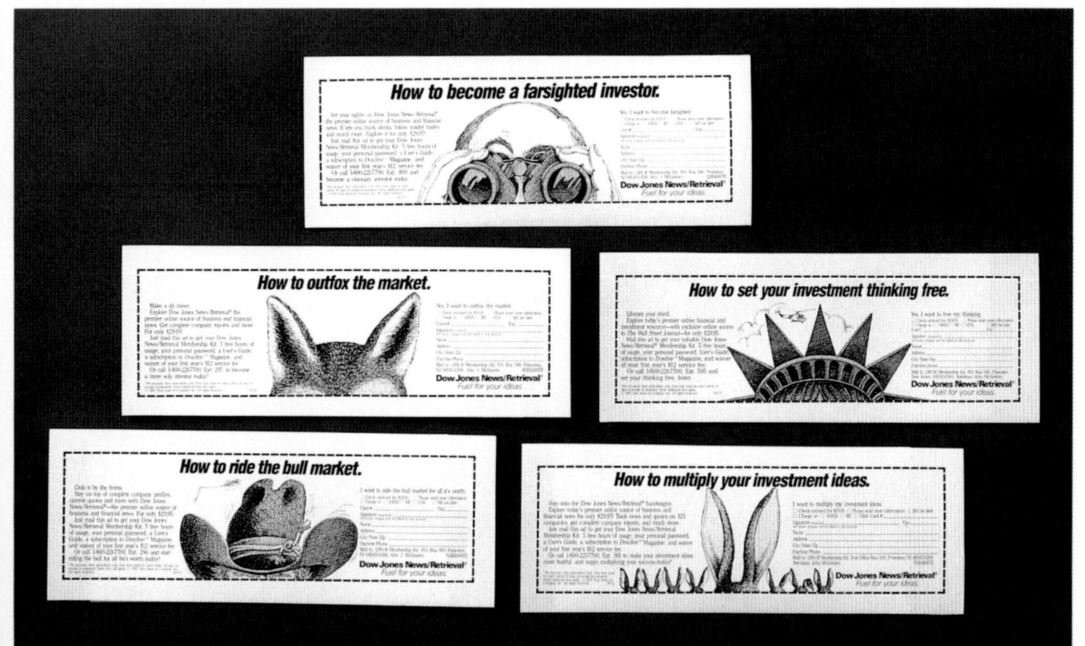

Title: "Barron's Campaign"
Copywriter: Bill Spink
Art Director: Joan Van der Veen
Agency: Gillespie Advertising
Client: Dow Jones News/ Retrieval

Moderate amounts of print advertising space are used here in sequence to build image continuity while conveying numerous service benefits and an attractive offer to business readers of a prestigious financial weekly.

AMERICAN EXPRESS "SERVICES PLUS" SALES KIT
SIMPLE HOW-TO INSTRUCTIONS
Apply Today.
APPLICATIONS FOR SMALL CLIENTS
THE AMERICAN EXPRESS CORPORATE CARD SYSTEM
LEAD SHEET
PROSPECT INFORMATION
LEAD SHEET FOR LARGER CLIENTS
SAMPLE COVER LETTER
1-800-221-4102
American Express
In Arizona 602-222-3572
ROLODEX CARD
AMERICAN EXPRESS
Services Plus
CORPORATE CARD

WE JUST ADDED A NEW DIMENSION TO THE TRAVEL BUSINESS THAT OPENS UP A WHOLE NEW WORLD FOR TRAVEL AGENTS.

Mr. Sample A. Sample
President
123 Main Street
Anytown, USA 00000
AMERICAN EXPRESS
Services Plus
CORPORATE CARD

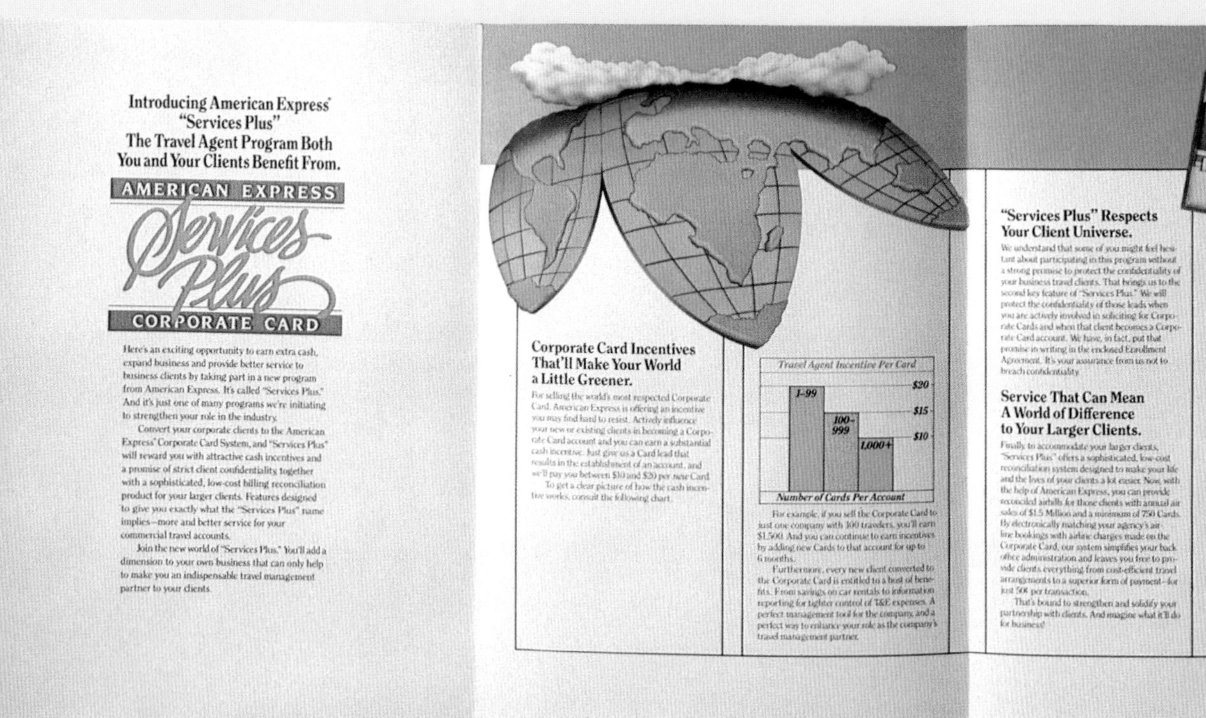

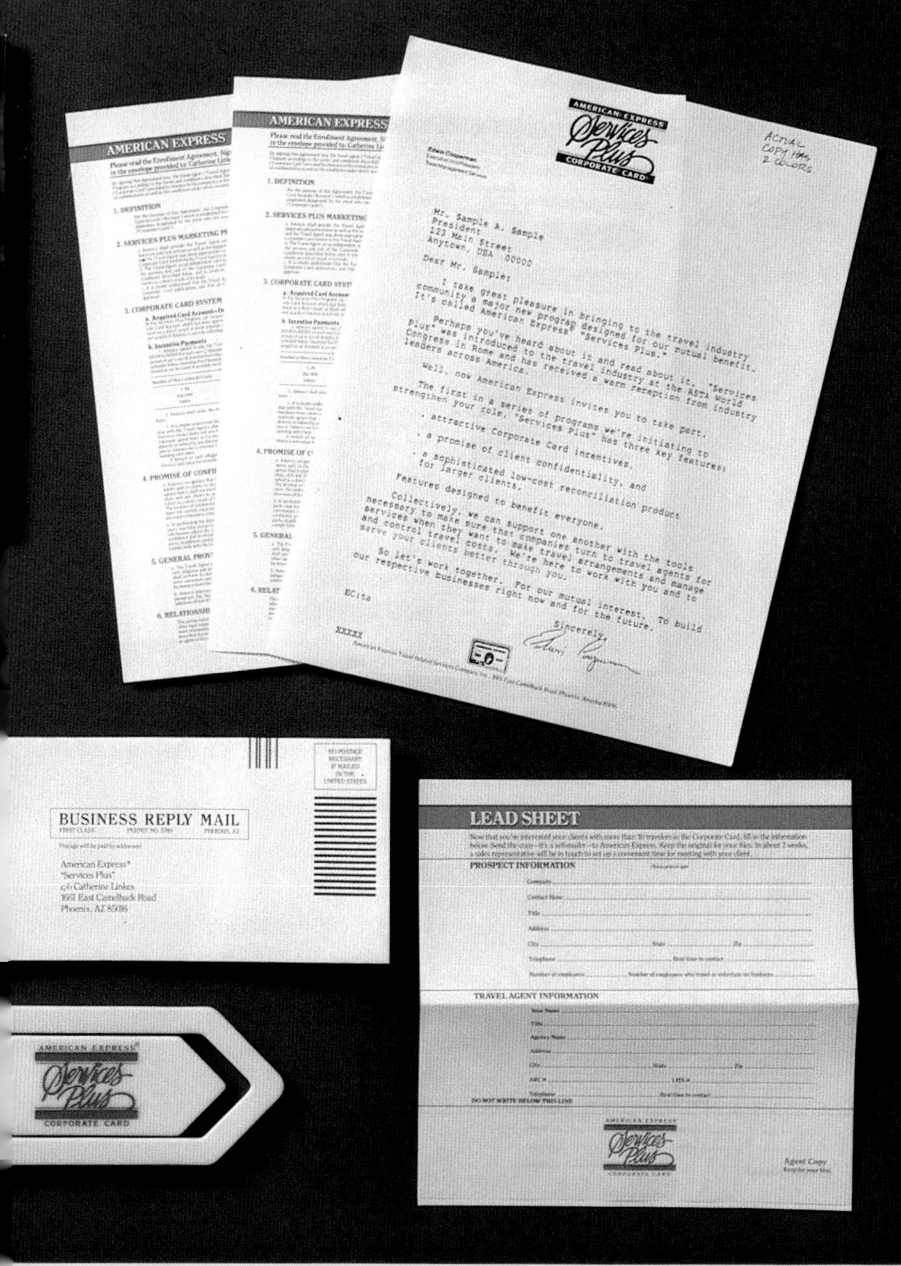

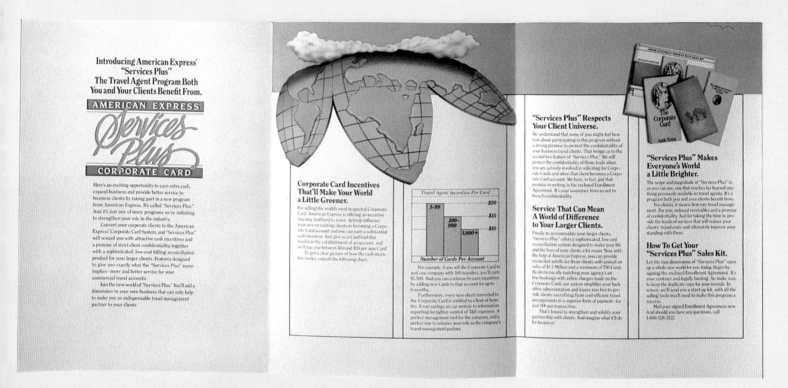

Title: "Services Plus"
Copywriters: Peg Pulcini, Leila Vuorenmaa
Art Directors: Bill Clarke, Michael Cancellieri
Agency: Ogilvy & Mather Direct
Client: American Express

This business campaign uses direct mail to proffer a comprehensive Travel Agency Incentive Program, first introduced in Rome at the ASTA World Congress, to qualified members of the American Society of Travel Agents.

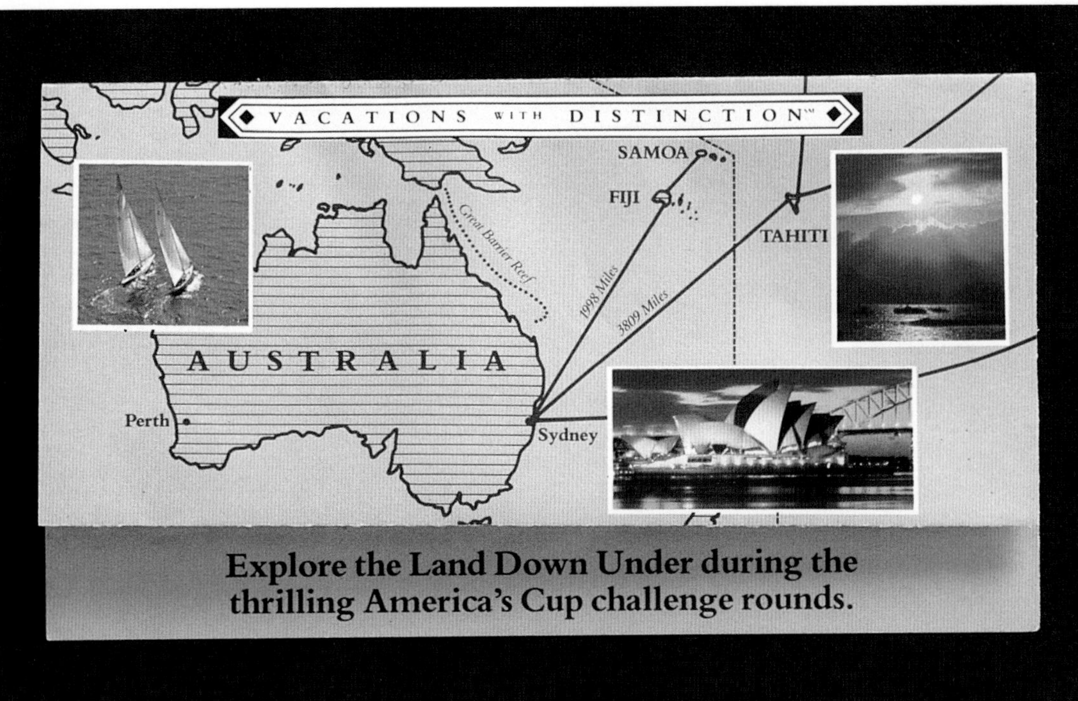
VACATIONS WITH DISTINCTION℠
SAMOA
FIJI
TAHITI
Great Barrier Reef
1998 Miles
3809 Miles
AUSTRALIA
Perth
Sydney
Explore the Land Down Under during the thrilling America's Cup challenge rounds.

VACATIONS WITH DISTINCTION℠
Lincolns Inn
Royal Courts of Justice
Aldwych
Kingsway
Shaftesbury
Temple
Victoria
Waterloo Br
RIVER THAMES
National Theatre
Cheapside
Guild
Celebrate this holiday season with a very special theatre tour of London.

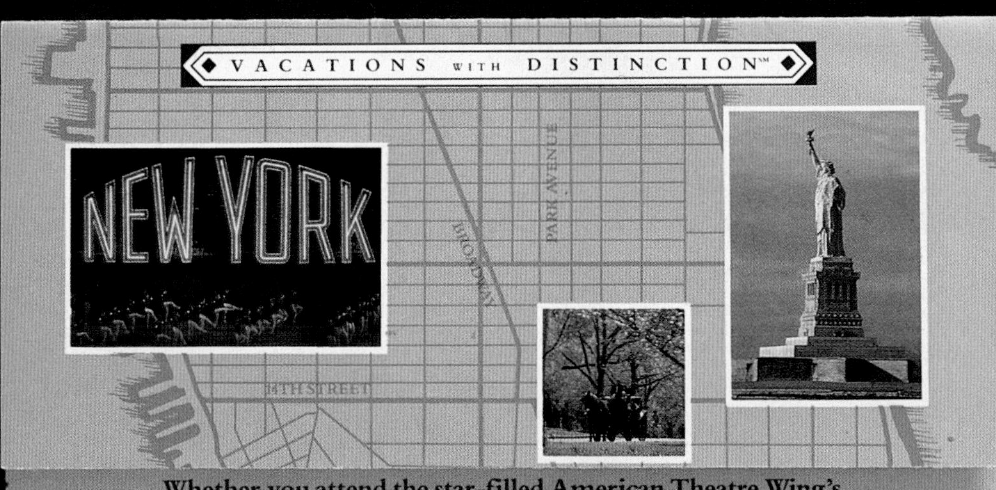
VACATIONS WITH DISTINCTION℠
NEW YORK
BROADWAY
PARK AVENUE
14TH STREET
Whether you attend the star-filled American Theatre Wing's Tony Awards Show in June or join in the Statue of Liberty Celebration in July, it's certain to be an unforgettable weekend in New York.

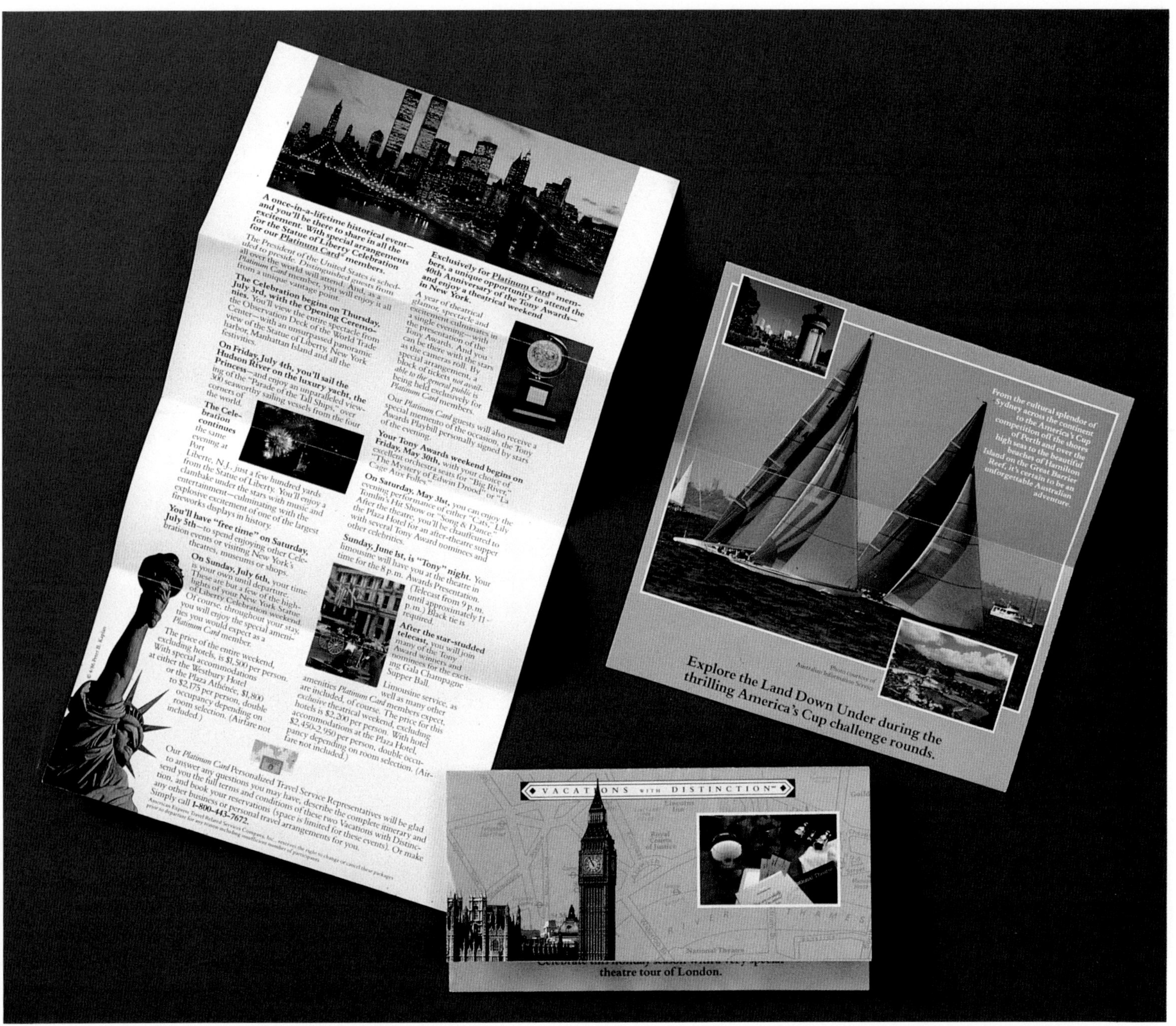

Title: "Vacations with Distinction"
Copywriters: Betsy Oshlo, Jim Schmidt
Art Directors: Richard Shuback, Deborah Lyons
Agency: McCann Direct
Client: American Express

Very special events are brought within easy reach through these three mailing pieces that invite Cardmembers to the Indian Ocean, Olivier's London, the lights of Broadway or the Statue of Liberty's now-famous anniversary celebration.

Title: "Centuries ago..."
Copywriters: James M. Casey, Julie Maloyan
Art Directors: Grant Kollar, George Szabo
Agency: Lowe-Marschalk Direct Marketing
Client: Xerox Direct Marketing

The often-overlooked, uncommonly rich history of copying becomes a tangible foundation for Xerox's informative, unpretentious discussion of its development and importance in this accessible three-part business campaign.

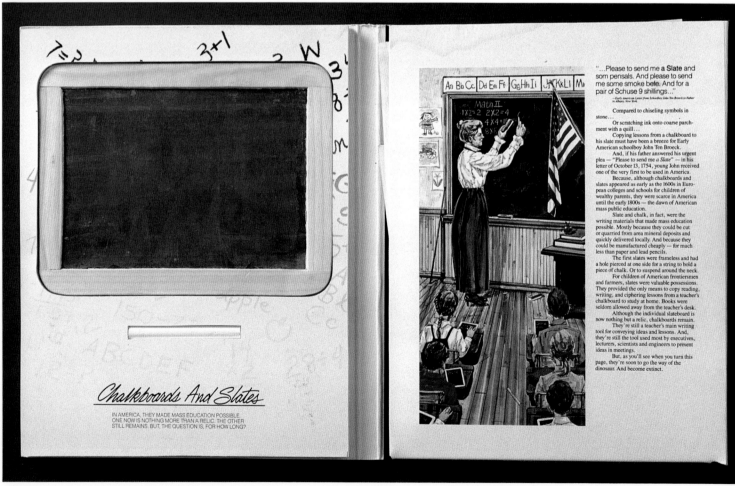

Chalkboards And Slates

IN AMERICA, THEY MADE MASS EDUCATION POSSIBLE. ONE NOW IS NOTHING MORE THAN A RELIC. THE OTHER STILL REMAINS. BUT, THE QUESTION IS, FOR HOW LONG?

"...Please to send me a Slate and som pensals. And please to send me some smoke befe. And for a pair of Schuse 9 shillings..."

Compared to chiseling symbols in stone...

Or scratching ink onto coarse parchment with a quill...

Copying lessons from a chalkboard to his slate must have been a breeze for Early American schoolboy John Ten Broeck.

And, if his father answered his urgent plea — "Please to send me *a Slate*" — in his letter of October 13, 1754, young John received one of the very first to be used in America.

Because, although chalkboards and slates appeared as early as the 1600s in European colleges and schools for children of wealthy parents, they were scarce in America until the early 1800s — the dawn of American mass public education.

Slate and chalk, in fact, were the writing materials that made mass education possible. Mostly because they could be cut or quarried from area mineral deposits and quickly delivered locally. And because they could be manufactured cheaply — for much less than paper and lead pencils.

The first slates were frameless and had a hole pierced at one side for a string to hold a piece of chalk. Or to suspend around the neck.

For children of American frontiersmen and farmers, slates were valuable possessions. They provided the only means to copy reading, writing, and ciphering lessons from a teacher's chalkboard to study at home. Books were seldom allowed away from the teacher's desk.

Although the individual slateboard is now nothing but a relic, chalkboards remain.

They're still a teacher's main writing tool for conveying ideas and lessons. And, they're still the tool used most by executives, lecturers, scientists and engineers to present ideas in meetings.

But, as you'll see when you turn this page, they're soon to go the way of the dinosaur. And become extinct.

In 1776, Thomas Jefferson spent three sleepless weeks drafting and making copies of the Declaration of Independence. To the point, he once quit.

Thomas Jefferson felt honored when, on June 10, 1776, members of the Second Continental Congress selected him to "send a message to the King" and draft a declaration of independence.

And, rightly so. For in its search for an author, Congress stipulated a "Man with gift for words. Clear in concept. Brilliant in execution. And an abundance of that God-like virtue: Patience!"

If historians are correct, "patience" could well have been at the top of the list. Because, besides naming Jefferson author, Congress appointed four other wordsmiths of the day — John Adams, Robert R. Livingston, Roger Sherman, and Benjamin Franklin — to "review and inspire a great work."

To write his drafts, Jefferson housed himself in a boarding room across from what is now Philadelphia's Independence Hall. Spending most days meeting, he wrote mostly at night and burned candles to the quick scratching out draft after draft with quill, ink and parchment.

Even if satisfied with a night's draft, Jefferson's agony was often prolonged until dawn. Copies were needed for committee review the following morning. And Congress, through an oversight, neglected to appoint a "copyist." So Jefferson handwrote them.

As usual with committees, changes in words and phrases were numerous. Sending Jefferson, night after night, back to his room to write new drafts. And more copies.

Two weeks of constant changes and Congressional bickering later, in a rare display of anger, Jefferson quit the committee and threatened even to leave Congress "for the quiet of my beloved home and wife."

John Adams and Ben Franklin soon appeased him, however. Through the promise of a "helping hand" — a secretary — to help write the needed copies.

Two days later, on June 28th, Jefferson and his committee submitted "a rough draft" to Congress, which finally approved "The Declaration" on July 4, 1776.

The rest is history. Along with one little known fact:

Though he hated making copies, Jefferson so loved the principles stated in his 876-word document, he penned at least five full copies early in July 1776.

To give to his friends.

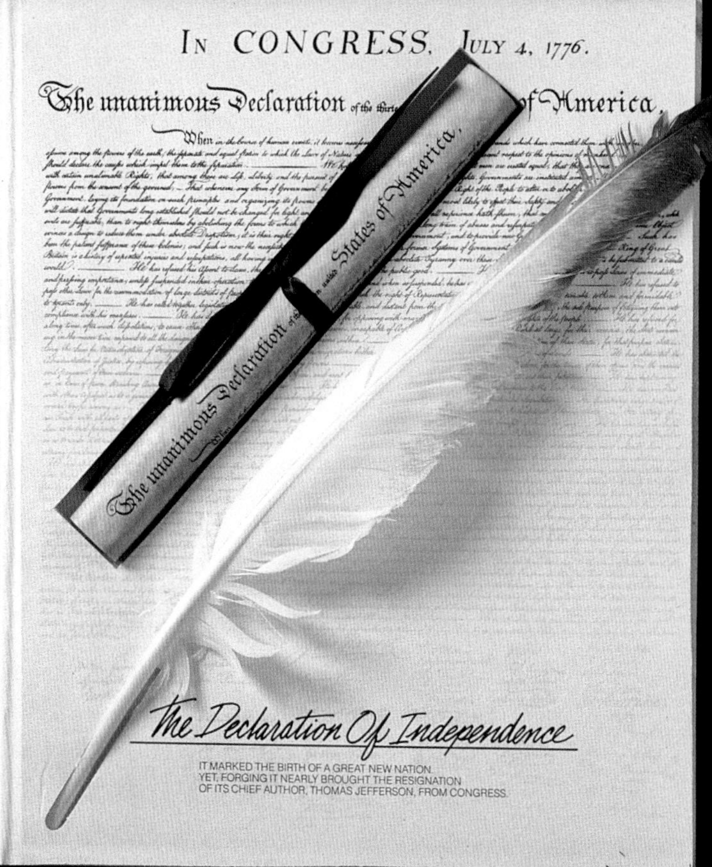

IT MARKED THE BIRTH OF A GREAT NEW NATION.
YET, FORGING IT NEARLY BROUGHT THE RESIGNATION

Unearthed in 1799 near Rosetta, Egypt, a huge stone bearing ancient inscriptions unlocked centuries of two lost languages.

You can imagine the excitement of its discoverers that late August of 1799.

Three French Legionnaires, digging a trench as a latrine to serve their outpost's new encampment near Rosetta, Egypt, uncovered what scholars later proved to be the foundation of an ancient inn.

Sensing the possible discovery of a few "take home" artifacts, they dug further. And found, buried deep within, one of the most important and valuable artifacts of all:

The Rosetta Stone — a huge stone tablet that unlocked the meanings of two lost languages (Hieroglyphics, the symbolic writings of Egyptian kings and priests who lived centuries before Christ; and Demotic, the language and writings of common villagers and tribesmen who roamed Egypt) because it was inscribed with an equally ancient, but "known" language: Greek.

The stone itself was immense — measuring 3' 9" long by 2' 4" wide by 11" thick. And scholars who have studied and translated its inscriptions have discovered why.

It was a "public notice" in stone. A decree written by Egyptian priests to commemorate the coronation of King Ptolemy V and his piety and generosity toward the Egyptian people during his first nine years of reign. (The commemoration took place in 196 B.C.)

In three languages for all Egyptians and foreign visitors to see, its inscriptions told of Ptolemy's gifts of corn and money to priests, his forgiveness of debts owed by commoners to his government, his reduction of taxes, his conquests against enemies of Egypt, and his rebuilding of ruined shrines and sacred buildings.

The original stone and, scholars believe, as many as six laborious copies were cut into slabs of basalt and, for mass communication, ordered displayed "in temples of the first, second, and third orders…throughout the land."

Many or all of those copies may still exist, buried beneath tons of hard-packed sand.

They all await rediscovery. Of an early-day "national message" chiseled and copied in stone.

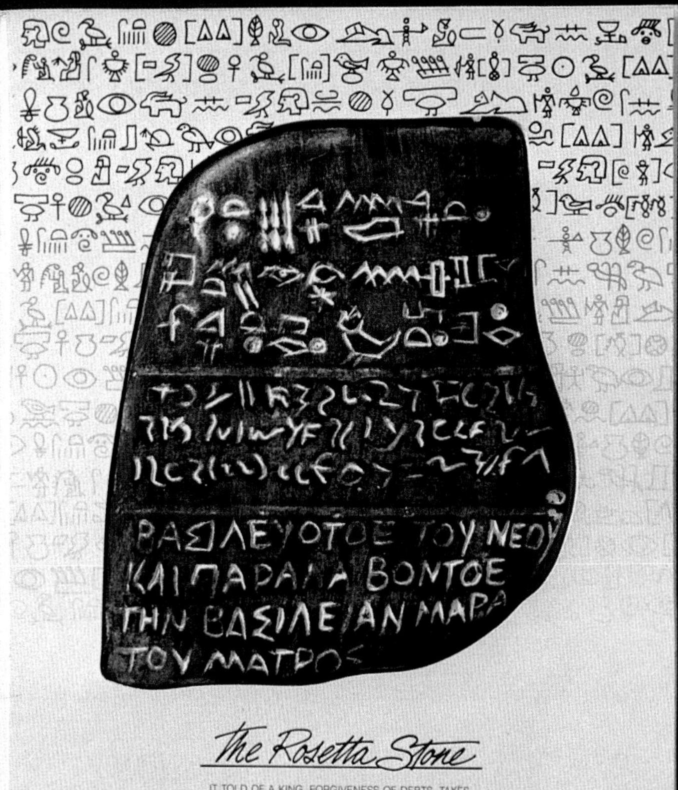

The Rosetta Stone
IT TOLD OF A KING, FORGIVENESS OF DEBTS, TAXES
AND REBELLIOUSNESS. BUT, MOST OF ALL, IT OPENED
THE DOOR TO CENTURIES OF HIDDEN MEANINGS.

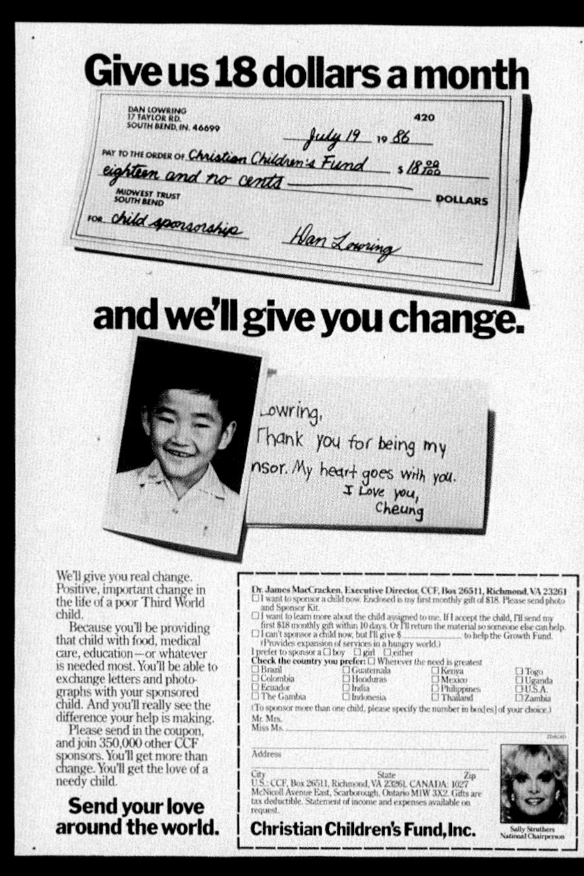

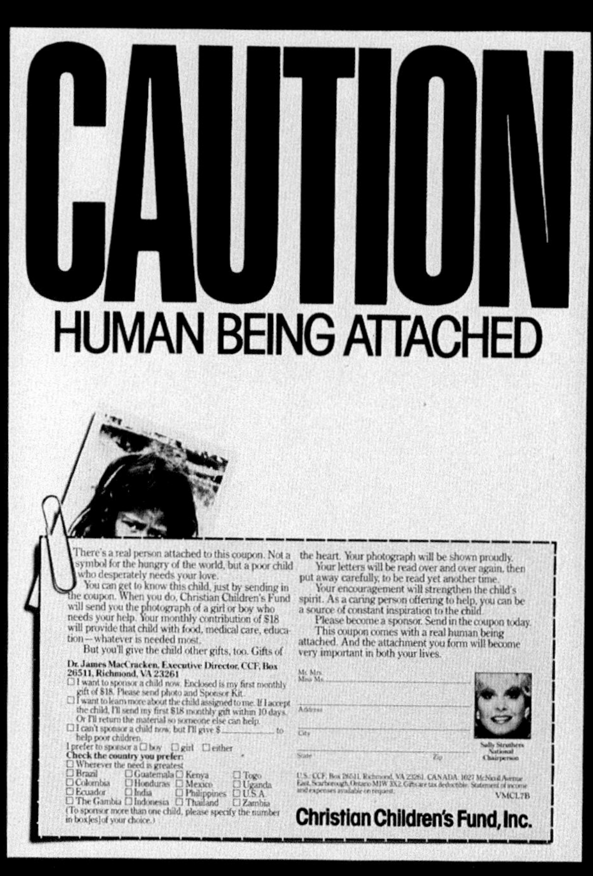

Title: "Christian Children's Fund"
Copywriter: Bill Hawkey
Art Director: Dick Bennett
Agency: Kaiser Kuhn Bennett
Client: Christian Children's Fund

Although variety is a key aspect of this black- and-white consumer print series, in design as well as copy approach, the recognition factor of celebrity spokesperson Sally Struthers is maintained in the response device throughout the campaign.

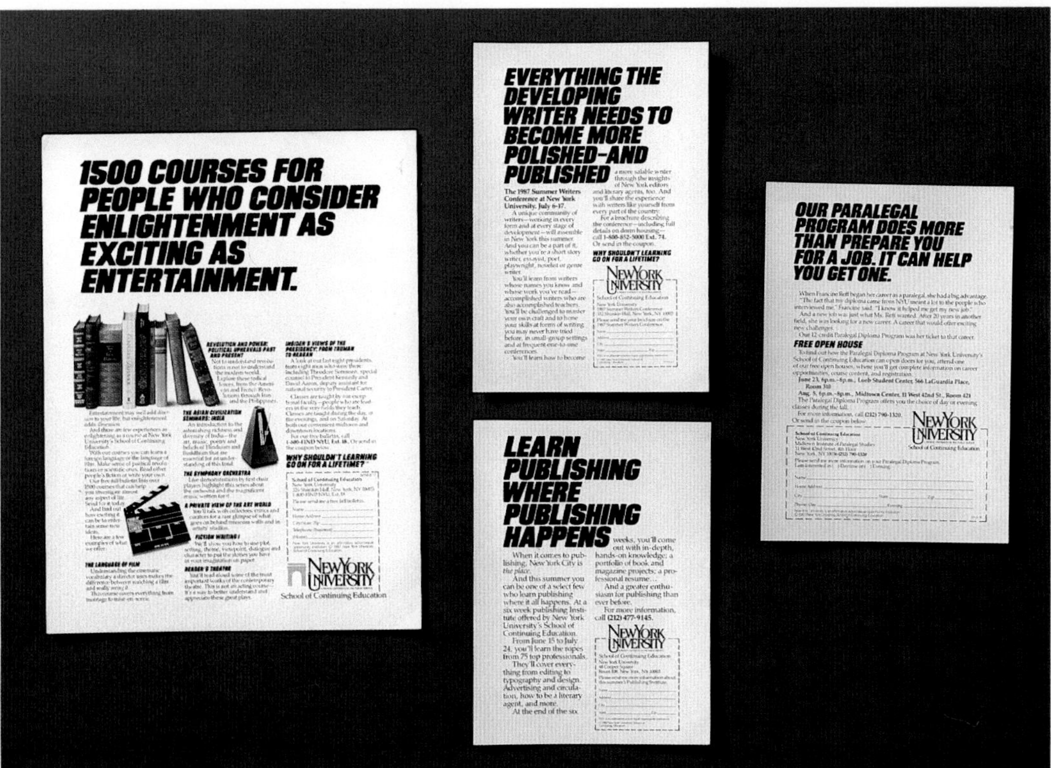

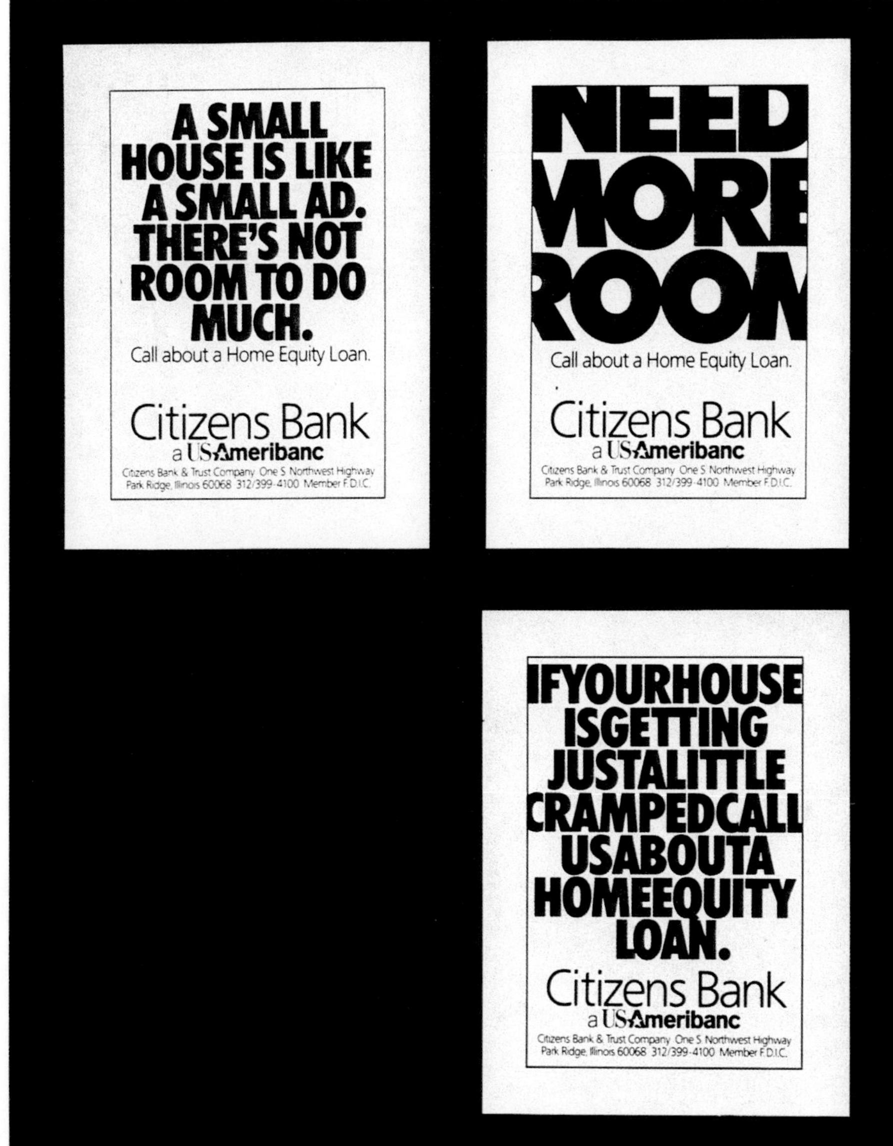

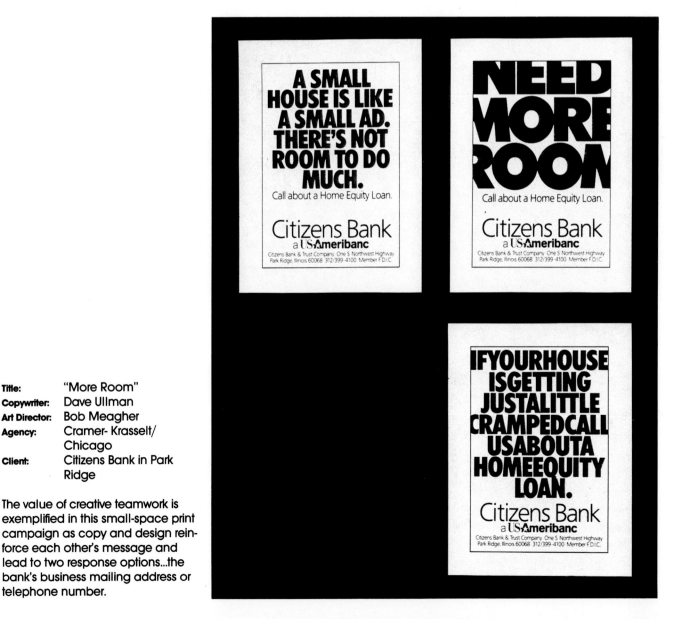

Title: "More Room"
Copywriter: Dave Ullman
Art Director: Bob Meagher
Agency: Cramer- Krasselt/ Chicago
Client: Citizens Bank in Park Ridge

The value of creative teamwork is exemplified in this small-space print campaign as copy and design reinforce each other's message and lead to two response options...the bank's business mailing address or telephone number.

Chapter
6
PBC INTERNATIONAL
ONE SCHOOL STREET
GLEN COVE, NY 11542

MULTIMEDIA CAMPAIGNS

Media opportunities for direct marketers are, in a word, expanding. Thanks to innovations and new economies in direct mail printing formats, technological advances on the electronic media front, ever-improving database manipulation, and the ongoing segmentation within the publishing field that allows an advertiser to reach highly-targeted readerships—never has there been a more favorable set of circumstances for the increased importance of the multimedia direct marketing campaign.

The fact is, for many years there was no such thing as a multimedia campaign in direct marketing. Not all that long ago, each medium was treated as a separate entity. If a direct mail piece or a print ad was successful, it was mailed or published again and again. There was not much experimentation with transferring a successful creative approach from one media into another. Indeed, there was generally little or no reason to even try such adaptations—given the fact that a genuine breakthrough direct mail package might remain profitable for three, five, or even up to ten years. Similarly, a print ad that pulled well can enjoy a lifespan of dozens or often hundreds of insertions in different newspapers and magazines.

Within the world of mainstream advertising, of course, the multimedia campaign is, and for many generations has been, an indispensable and powerful way to saturate a market, keep prospects interested, reinforce the image and the promise of a product, and increase the probability of recall when a purchase opportunity is at hand.

Since in direct marketing the purchase opportunity or means of obtaining more information is presented right there, on the spot, it's easy to understand how a single channel of communication was considered sufficient.

In the mid-1970s, as the large general advertising agencies began acquiring direct marketing shops or launching their own direct response divisions, the extensive presence of multimedia campaigns in mainstream marketing plans undoubtedly influenced a number of direct marketing practitioners to explore such possibilities for their own specialty area.

But of equal or greater significance is the broad potential among the different media outlets themselves. Television time, first with remnant broadcast buys and more recently on cable networks and through regional or local cable operators, has become more affordable for direct response advertisers. Print advertising space, most of which is discontinued for direct marketers, can reach specific groups of readers with remarkable efficiency. Mailing lists are rapidly evolving to become rich databases of information, managed with sophisticated computers that identify not merely individuals, but also their repeat purchasing patterns, average amount of money spent per transaction, seasonal preferences, and even such details as changes in colors, styles and sizes ordered.

Each medium, furthermore, is carefully measured for the performance and cost-effectiveness of each marketing effort, and these track records are routinely logged and analyzed in search of larger lessons. That information, in turn, is shared with colleagues during industry conventions and seminars, in books and articles published by the trade press, and at the hundreds of meetings and conferences held each year by the many different direct marketing clubs and organizations around the world.

With so much ongoing refinement having occurred over the years, it is no wonder that the multimedia campaign has emerged as a formidable, vigorous direct marketing tool whose usefulness continues to gain strength. For copywriters and art directors, the dynamics involved in creating a winning campaign are as challenging as those of any other conceivable direct response assignment. Not surprisingly, creative people are rising to the occasion and producing top-notch work, as evidenced by the examples on the following pages.

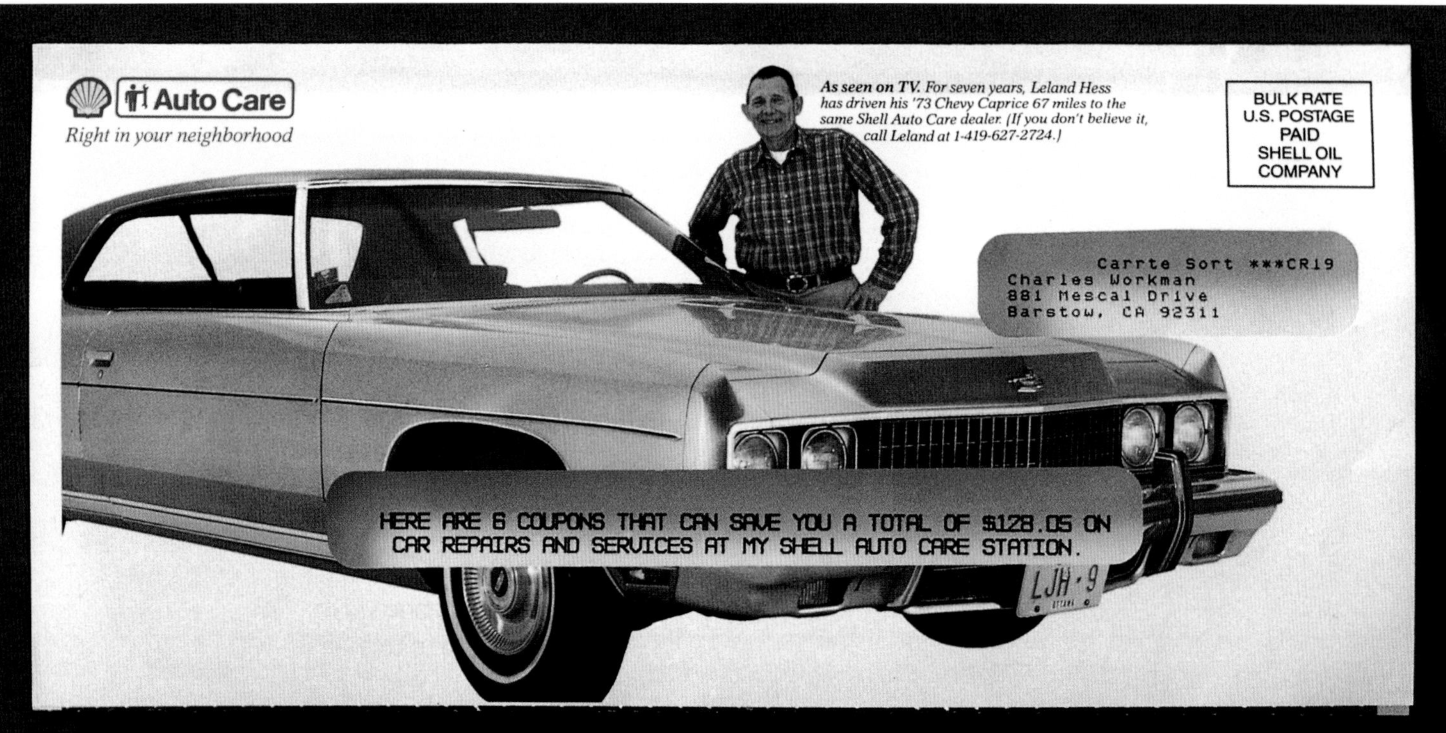

Leland Hess, Auto Care customer

This man drives 67 miles
to *his* Shell Auto Care station.

You, however, are luckier than he is.
Your Shell Auto Care station is *right in the neighborhood.*

You *also* get:

- **A 4,000-mile, 90-day written warranty on repairs.** If you have a problem with a warranted repair, it will be fixed at no charge to you or your money will be refunded.
- **A nationwide warranty.** Repairs are backed by over 1,600 Shell Auto Care dealers nationwide—to protect you when you travel.
- **A written estimate.** Your approval prevents unwanted repairs.
- **Original parts returned as proof of replacement.**
- **Certified mechanics.** Certified by the National Institute for Automotive Service Excellence. Look for the ASE emblem.

A 000 956 3

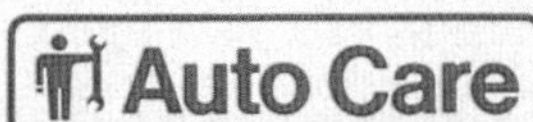

Carrte Sort ***CR19
Charles Workman
881 Mescal Drive
Barstow, CA 92311

Dear Mr. Workman,

I can repair most makes and models of passenger cars and trucks, gasoline and diesel engines, foreign and domestic. I am a trained mechanic. I have over 25 years' experience. I employ 4 certified mechanics. Last year my station handled over 6,000 repairs. About 95% of my business comes from satisfied repeat customers. Bring these coupons to my station, or call 256-2037 for an appointment. I would like to be the person who takes care of your car.

Jack Theroff
Jack Theroff
Owner
Dry Gulch Shell Service
1601 E Main St
Barstow, CA 92311

HERE ARE 6 COUPONS THAT CAN SAVE YOU A TOTAL OF $128.05 ON
CAR REPAIRS AND SERVICES AT MY SHELL AUTO CARE STATION.

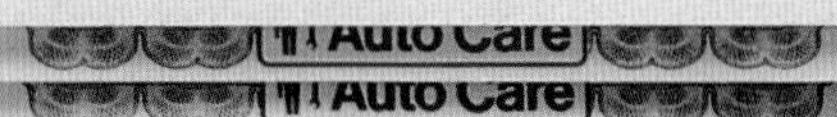

Title:	"Going the Distance"
Copywriter:	Barry Callen
Art Directors:	Bob Marberry, Susan Chinchar, Harold Hutcheson
Agency:	Ogilvy & Mather Direct
Client:	Shell Oil Company

Putting an innovative twist on the trusted "satisfied-customer testimonial" device, the self-mailer portion of this campaign invites the reader to call the satisfied customer directly, at home, to verify the quality of Shell Auto Care. Other campaign elements include a comprehensive auto maintenance diary, a four-element 6″ x 9″ direct mail package and money-saving discount coupons for various automotive services.

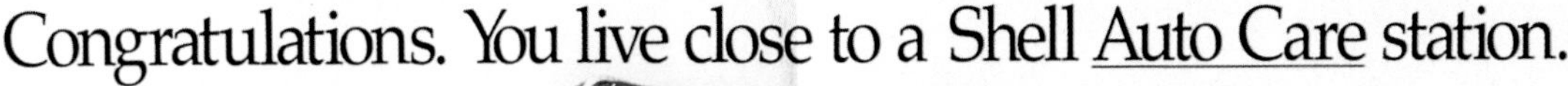

You are receiving this letter because you live close to a Shell Auto Care station. Your Auto Care Dealer provides certified mechanics, written warranties, a nationwide warranty, return of original parts, and written estimates.

Your Shell Auto Care Dealer is a *professional* who invests in the latest equipment and training. As a result, you can get a wide variety of repair services right in your neighborhood, including: tune-ups, brake repair, wheel alignments, and air conditioning repair. And he has a complete line of products for your car, including: gasoline, oil, tires, batteries, antifreeze, and wiper blades.

A good mechanic is harder to find. But every Auto Care station has certified mechanics.

Your neighborhood Shell Auto Care Dealer is special. Only one out of three Shell stations carries the Auto Care sign.

Certified mechanics with years of experience

It's not your imagination. A good mechanic is harder to find. In 1950 there was one mechanic for every 54 cars. Today there is only one mechanic for every 108 cars.

The days of the backyard mechanic are gone forever. Your mechanic needs *training* to cope with the 15,000 parts and computer controls in the average car of today. Yet the National Institute for Automotive Service Excellence has estimated that *only half* of all U.S. automobile mechanics *are competent* to perform a full range of diagnostic and repair functions in one or more vehicle systems.

Every Shell Auto Care station has certified mechanics—certified first by Shell and then by the National Institute for Automotive Service Excellence (ASE), an independent nonprofit testing organization.

Only mechanics with years of experience who can diagnose and treat current car problems get ASE certification.

Written estimates to prevent unwanted repairs

Your Auto Care Dealer provides written estimates of the cost of the repair before work begins. To protect against overcharge or unwanted repairs, no work is done until you approve the estimate.

A written estimate puts you in control of the bill. No work is done until you approve the estimate.

Parts returned as proof of replacement

Upon request, your Shell Auto Care Dealer will return your original parts in a plastic bag, as proof of replacement. The only exception is when old parts have to be traded in.

A 4,000-mile, 90-day written warranty backs all repairs

All repairs are backed in writing for 4,000 miles or 90 days, whichever comes first. Only the best dealers are willing to back their repairs in writing.

Did your parts really need to be replaced? An Auto Care Dealer will return your original parts for your inspection.

A new Nationwide Warranty to protect you when you travel

Surprise! Most car repair shops have a warranty that is good only at their station. Their warranty is no good if you travel to another city or state.

This year Shell Auto Care proudly introduces the Nationwide Warranty. Your repair is now backed by 1,678 Shell Auto Care Dealers *nationwide*. Your 4,000-mile, 90-day warranty travels with you.

If you experience a problem with a repair that is under warranty, an Auto Care Dealer will fix the repair at no charge.

Before you leave on a trip, ask your Auto Care Dealer for a Nationwide Warranty Glovebox Holder for your repair receipts. The Glovebox Holder has a 24-hour toll-free number (1-800-942-9898) that you can call from anywhere in the United States to find the nearest Auto Care Dealer, or the nearest authorized dealer.

Any repair that is under warranty is backed by 1,678 Auto Care Dealers nationwide, to protect you when you travel.

If you experience a problem on the road, just present the nearest Auto Care dealer with your repair receipt. He will check to make sure your problem is covered by the warranty. If the repair is covered, he will fix your car at no charge.

Now you have warranty protection when you go on the road.

Next time, see your neighborhood Shell Auto Care Dealer.

Title: "XR4Ti Challenge"
Copywriters: Steve Petz, Jim Plegue
Art Directors: Diane Kangas, Karl Shaffer
Agency: Wunderman Worldwide/ Y&R Detroit
Client: Lincoln-Mercury/Ford North American Automotive Operations

Jumbo-sized and #9 direct mail, as well as print advertising entices sports car lovers to accept a "Challenge Kit," which in turn provides them with booklets, checklists, a video and rosters of dealerships and test-drive locations nationwide, all toward the goal of encouraging showroom traffic and hands-on interest in this hot little roadster.

ACCEPT THE XR4Ti ROAD TEST CHALLENGE!

And get your FREE CHALLENGE KIT—A road test guide for this performance coupe from Merkur.

Our challenge was to create a German-bred sports coupe unsurpassed by the competition. Your Challenge is to road test it, uncover its remarkable capabilities and then tell us how we did.

Your **FREE CHALLENGE KIT** tells you where you can take a special road test of XR4Ti, and it gives you two full-color books to guide you through it. The Kit is a unique look at the way you test and evaluate the performance features of a car such as the XR4Ti.

You Get:

THE XR4Ti CHALLENGE—An 8-page book which shows you the professional way to give XR4Ti a complete road test from the viewpoint of three-time world champion race car driver Jackie Stewart.

THE AUTOBAHN FACTOR—An 8-page book discussing how the design and engineering of Merkur automobiles are influenced by the demanding roads of Germany. It tells you the kind of performance to expect when you road test an automobile with the German breeding of XR4Ti.

AN EVALUATION—A point-by-point outline for your road test. Use it to tell us how XR4Ti performed in the Challenge.

Details about your special road test and the **XR4Ti CHALLENGE KIT** are **only** available from XR4Ti Challenge Headquarters, and our special road test is on for just a short time. So...

Call 1-800-882-9010

or complete the coupon below and mail it **today.**

I accept the XR4Ti Road Test Challenge. Send me details on my special road test and my **CHALLENGE KIT** right away.

Name

Address

City State ZIP

MERKUR XR4Ti

Advancing the art of driving.

Send completed coupon to: **XR4Ti Challenge Headquarters P.O. Box 7022 Lincoln Park, MI 48146-9990**

MXRC01

Ad No: WRK-919-87-146
Ad Size: 8⅜ x 11⅛
Client: XR4Ti Challenge
Art Dir.: D. Kangas Production: Tingstad

Lettergraphics - AdGravers
WRK
KB08556 7/16/86

Lincoln-Mercury-Merkur Division
Ford Motor Company
P.O. Box 7022
Lincoln Park, MI 48146

MERKUR XR4Ti

Lebanon Lincoln-Mercury-Merkur
Riverside Lincoln-Mercury-Merkur
Foxgate Lincoln-Mercury-Merkur
Schilling Motors, Inc.
Heritage Lincoln-Mercury-Merkur
Beaman Lincoln-Mercury-Merkur, Inc.
Oak Ridge Lincoln-Mercury-Merkur

THE XR4Ti ROAD TEST CHALLENGE

Immediate Reply Requested

MXWE1A

Lincoln-Mercury-Merkur Division
Ford Motor Company
P.O. Box 7022
Lincoln Park, Michigan 48146

MERKUR XR4Ti

Mr. Neil Donovan
304 Pleasant St #3
Winthrop, MA 02152

Immediate Reply Requested

THE XR4Ti CHALLENGE

DRIVE IT!

THE AUTOBAHN FACTOR

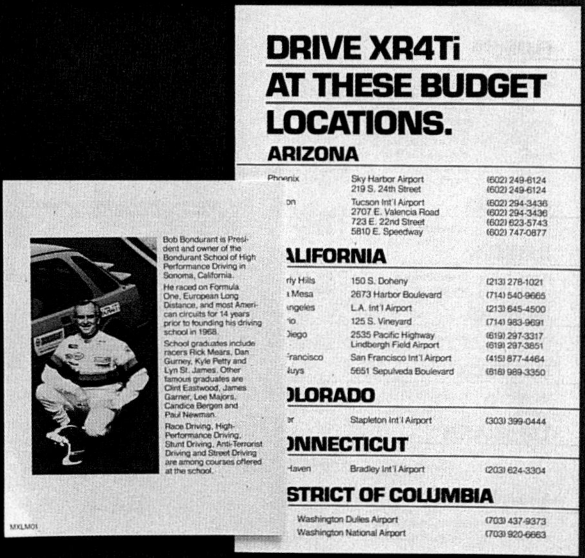

DRIVE XR4Ti AT THESE BUDGET LOCATIONS.

ARIZONA

Phoenix	Sky Harbor Airport 219 S. 24th Street	(602) 249-6124 (602) 249-6124
on	Tucson Int'l Airport 2707 E. Valencia Road 723 E. 22nd Street 5810 E. Speedway	(602) 294-3436 (602) 294-3436 (602) 623-5743 (602) 747-0877

ALIFORNIA

rly Hills	150 S. Doheny	(213) 278-1021
Mesa	2673 Harbor Boulevard	(714) 540-9665
ngeles	L.A. Int'l Airport	(213) 645-4500
io	125 S. Vineyard	(714) 983-9691
Diego	2535 Pacific Highway Lindbergh Field Airport	(619) 297-3317 (619) 297-3851
rancisco	San Francisco Int'l Airport	(415) 877-4464
uys	5651 Sepulveda Boulevard	(818) 989-3350

OLORADO

r	Stapleton Int'l Airport	(303) 399-0444

ONNECTICUT

Haven	Bradley Int'l Airport	(203) 624-3304

STRICT OF COLUMBIA

Washington Dulles Airport	(703) 437-9373
Washington National Airport	(703) 920-6663

Bob Bondurant is President and owner of the Bondurant School of High Performance Driving in Sonoma, California.

He raced on Formula One, European Long Distance, and most American circuits for 14 years prior to founding his driving school in 1968.

School graduates include racers Rick Mears, Dan Gurney, Kyle Petty and Lyn St. James. Other famous graduates are Clint Eastwood, James Garner, Lee Majors, Candice Bergen and Paul Newman.

Race Driving, High-Performance Driving, Stunt Driving, Anti-Terrorist Driving and Street Driving are among courses offered at the school.

MXLM01

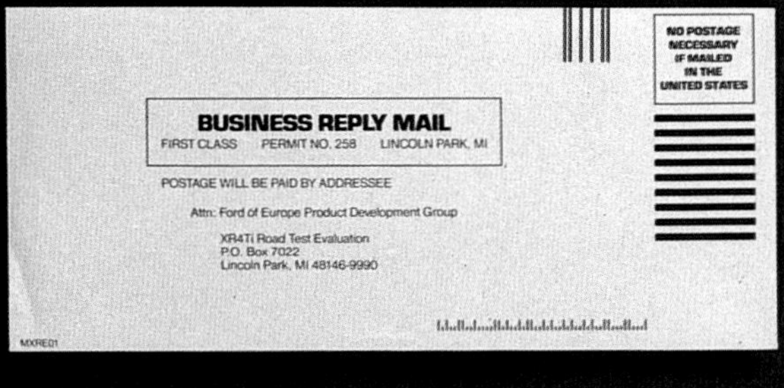

NO POSTAGE NECESSARY IF MAILED IN THE UNITED STATES

BUSINESS REPLY MAIL
FIRST CLASS PERMIT NO. 258 LINCOLN PARK, MI

POSTAGE WILL BE PAID BY ADDRESSEE

Attn: Ford of Europe Product Development Group

XR4Ti Road Test Evaluation
P.O. Box 7022
Lincoln Park, MI 48146-9990

MXRE01

ROAD TEST XR4Ti AT THESE MERKUR DEALERS

Alabama

Albertville	Billy Thrash Lincoln-Mercury-Merkur, Inc.
Anniston	Anniston Lincoln-Mercury-Merkur
Birmingham	Bart Starr Motor Company, Inc. Champion Lincoln-Mercury-Merkur, Inc.
Decatur	Cloverleaf Lincoln-Mercury-Merkur, Inc.
Dothan	Williams Lincoln-Mercury-Merkur, Inc.
Enterprise	Bernie Hughes Lincoln-Mercury-Merkur
Gadsden	Lowe Lincoln-Mercury-Merkur
Huntsville	Ray Pearman Lincoln-Mercury-Merkur
Jasper	Gene Reeves Lincoln-Mercury-Merkur
Mobile	Robinson Brothers Lincoln-Mercury-Merkur
Montgomery	Youngblood-Perry Lincoln-Mercury-Merkur
Selma	Driggers Motor Company
Sheffield	Schilling Motors, Inc.
Tuscaloosa	Bill De Loach Lincoln-Mercury-Merkur

Alaska

Anchorage	Stepp Brothers Lincoln-Mercury-Merkur

Arizona

Glendale	Sunland Lincoln-Mercury-Merkur
Mesa	Fiesta Lincoln-Mercury-Merkur
Phoenix	Covey Lincoln-Mercury-Merkur Sales, Inc.
Tempe	Jack Ross Lincoln-Mercury-Merkur
Tucson	Selby Motors

Arkansas

Fayetteville	Goff McNair Motor Co.
Fort Smith	Putnam Lincoln-Mercury-Merkur
Hot Springs Natl Pk.	Meredith Motors, Inc.
Jonesboro	McCarty Motor Company
Little Rock	Schilling Motors, Inc.
Pine Bluff	Summers Lincoln-Mercury-Merkur
Searcy	Capps Motor Company, Inc.

California

Bakersfield	Westwind Lincoln-Mercury-Merkur
Bellflower	Ray Fladeboe Lincoln-Mercury-Merkur
Berkeley	Berkeley Lincoln-Mercury-Merkur Sales
Beverly Hills	Gregg Motors Lincoln-Mercury-Merkur
Burlingame	Shen Lincoln-Mercury-Merkur
Carlsbad	North County Lincoln-Mercury-Merkur
Concord	Diablo Lincoln-Mercury-Merkur, Inc.
Costa Mesa	Johnson & Son Lincoln-Mercury-Merkur
Downey	Joe Cram Lincoln-Mercury-Merkur
Escondido	Escondido Lincoln-Mercury-Merkur
Fremont	Fremont Lincoln-Mercury-Merkur
Fresno	Frank J. Sanders Company
Fullerton	Fairway Lincoln-Mercury-Merkur
Glendale	Star Lincoln-Mercury-Merkur
Hayward	Mission Blvd. Lincoln-Mercury-Merkur, Inc.
Hollywood	Hollywood Lincoln-Mercury-Merkur
Huntington Beach	Beach Lincoln-Mercury-Merkur
Irvine	Ray Fladeboe Lincoln-Mercury-Merkur
Long Beach	Boulevard Lincoln-Mercury-Merkur
Los Angeles	O'Connor Lincoln-Mercury-Merkur
Los Gatos	McHugh Lincoln-Mercury-Merkur
Menlo Park	Stanford Lincoln-Mercury-Merkur
Merced	McAuley Motors, Inc.
Modesto	Rule-Dale Lincoln-Mercury-Merkur
Monrovia	Sierra Lincoln-Mercury-Merkur
Montclair	University Lincoln-Mercury-Merkur
Montebello	Montebello Lincoln-Mercury-Merkur
National City	Frank Motors
North Hollywood	Mayberry Lincoln-Mercury-Merkur
Oakland	Negherbon Lincoln-Mercury-Merkur
Oroville	Pahl Goodhue Lincoln-Mercury-Merkur
Pasadena	Pasadena Lincoln-Mercury-Merkur
Placerville	Lutz Lincoln-Mercury-Merkur
Redding	Redding Lincoln-Mercury-Merkur
Redlands	Jim Glaze, Inc.
Richmond	Mira Vista Lincoln-Mercury-Merkur
Riverside	Riverside Lincoln-Mercury-Merkur
Roseville	Frank Andrews
Sacramento	Niello Lincoln-Mercury-Merkur Winter Lincoln-Mercury-Merkur
Salinas	Salinas Lincoln-Mercury-Merkur
San Bernardino	Camino Lincoln-Mercury-Merkur
San Carlos	Village Lincoln-Mercury-Merkur
San Diego	Miramar Lincoln-Mercury-Merkur Townsend Lincoln-Mercury-Merkur
San Francisco	Auto Plaza Lincoln-Mercury-Merkur
San Gabriel	San Gabriel Valley Lincoln-Mercury-Merkur
San Jose	Almaden Lincoln-Mercury-Merkur J. Kerley Lincoln-Mercury-Merkur
Santa Ana	Santa Ana Lincoln-Mercury-Merkur
Santa Barbara	Gregg Motors, Ltd.
Santa Maria	Rentrow Auto Center, Inc.
Santa Monica	Lynch Lincoln-Mercury-Merkur
Santa Rosa	Prestige Lincoln-Mercury-Merkur
Stockton	Gene Gabbard, Inc.
Sunnyvale	Sunnyvale Lincoln-Mercury-Merkur
Thousand Oaks	Ladin Lincoln-Mercury-Merkur
Torrance	Torrance Lincoln-Mercury-Merkur
Vallejo	Larry Albedi Motors
Van Nuys	Westway Lincoln-Mercury-Merkur
Ventura	Weber Motor Company
Visalia	Kitchen Motors
Watsonville	Marty Franich Lincoln-Mercury-Merkur
West Covina	West Covina Lincoln-Mercury-Merkur
Whittier	Urich Motor Company
Woodland Hills	Woodland Hills Lincoln-Mercury-Merkur
Yuba City	Bill Hamon Lincoln-Mercury-Merkur

Colorado

Aurora	Osborn Lincoln-Mercury-Merkur
Boulder	Valley Lincoln-Mercury-Merkur, Inc.
Colorado Springs	Gene Osborn Lincoln-Mercury-Merkur
Denver	Johnny Haas Motors, Inc.
Englewood	The Kumpf Motor Car Company
Greeley	Stanley Lincoln-Mercury-Merkur
Pueblo	Dale Spradley Motors, Inc.

Connecticut

Bridgeport	Key Lincoln-Mercury-Merkur, Inc.
Bristol	Crowley Lincoln-Mercury-Merkur
Brookfield	Greentree Lincoln-Mercury-Merkur
East Hartford	Newman Lincoln-Mercury-Merkur
Georgetown	Georgetown Lincoln-Mercury-Merkur
Manchester	Moriarty Brothers, Inc.
Middletown	Town & Country Auto Sales, Inc.
Milford	Stevens Lincoln-Mercury-Merkur
New Haven	Crest Lincoln-Mercury-Merkur, Inc.
Norwich	Norwich Lincoln-Mercury-Merkur
Shelton	Curtiss-Ryan Lincoln-Mercury-Merkur
Stamford	Lincoln-Mercury-Merkur of Stamford, Inc.
Torrington	Countryside Lincoln-Mercury-Merkur
Wallingford	Merriam Motors, Inc.
Waterbury	Shaker's, Inc.
West Simsbury	Hoffman Lincoln-Mercury-Merkur

1

MERKUR SCORPIO
Advancing the art of driving.
IMPORTED FROM GERMANY
Exclusively at a Lincoln-Mercury-Merkur dealer.

SCORPIO

Edsel B. Ford II
General Marketing Manager
Lincoln-Mercury Division
Ford Motor Company
P.O. Box 7041
Lincoln Park, Michigan 48146-7041

BULK RATE
U.S. POSTAGE PAID
FORD MOTOR COMPANY

Here's The Scorpio Preview Collection You Asked For

SCORPIO

Edsel B. Ford II
General Marketing Manager
Lincoln-Mercury Division
Ford Motor Company

Mr. John Sample
123 Koln St.
Anytown, USA 12345

Scorpio Preview Collection. As an Audi
formance and handling offered by German
ion mailing should help you appreciate
ing and comfort Scorpio offers.

ed look at Scorpio from standard anti-lock
senger seatbacks. Open the large fold-out
llent look at the room and comfort offered
ring Notes point out some of the design
the viewpoint of the Chief of Design, Hans
you about the Merkur brand -- its Ford of
s that make it a name you'll be hearing

l literature that will tell you about the
Scorpio ownership. The Scorpio Quality
pio's Guaranteed Resale Value (pegged to
program (with benefits that protect you
er Program, and more.

iving Review, to help you familiarize
test, and a complete driving evaluation
you think of Scorpio.

ction isn't the same as seeing the car in
s some of the excitement that Scorpio has
next new car, call your nearest Merkur
driving performance, price and return on
eal competitor.

Sincerely,

the United States in limited numbers.
aler and make an appointment before you go
f a road test opportunity.

ln Park, Michigan 48146 9990

SCORPIO

H.G. Gaffke
Chief of Design
Ford Werke A.G.
Köln
West Germany

The Scorpio project was one of the most demanding and exciting assignments in my own and my colleagues' careers. We started with a clean sheet of paper because our charter was to create a new vehicle that had virtually nothing in common with its predecessor. This is a rare opportunity, to design and develop an all-new automobile, and it resulted in a very special product.

The development focus for Scorpio came from customer input. Functionality, modern technology and high-quality appointments were the design parameters.

We realized that the interior dimensions and comfort were the key requirements, and we designed the vehicle from inside out to meet these requirements. The exterior needed to be fresh, modern, exciting and aerodynamically efficient.

When Scorpio won the European "Car of the Year" award, the Scorpio team knew we had the job done well. I think that, when you drive Scorpio, you will agree.

THE MERKUR STORY

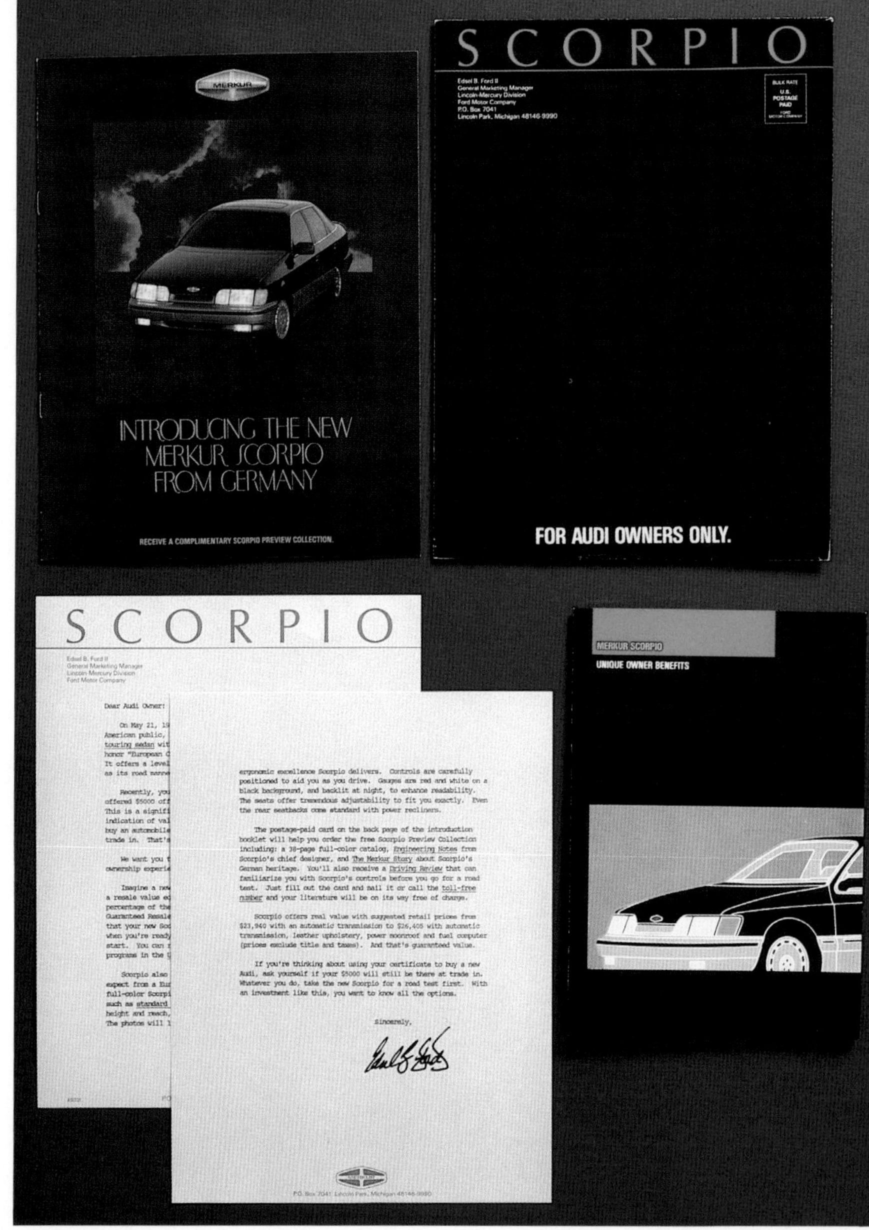

Title: "Scorpio Announcement"
Copywriters: Dennis Staszak, Steve Petz, Fred Stafford
Art Directors: Diane Kangas, Karl Shaffer
Agency: Wunderman Detroit/ Young & Rubicam Detroit
Client: Lincoln-Mercury/Ford

This major launch of a new car imported from Germany by Ford's Lincoln-Mercury division began with an eight-page insert in magazines to generate qualified potential customers, who were then sent this impressive direct mail display and invited to test-drive the Scorpio of their choice.

M E R K U R

SCORPIO

NOW YOU CAN HAVE YOUR BLACK FOREST CAKE...

It's a streak in the night set to capture your imagination. Its name is Scorpio. And it projects a boldness seldom exhibited by the European establishment.

STRIKINGLY DIFFERENT.
Scorpio designers were given the freedom to create a new, dramatic shape that is both aerodynamic and space efficient. It is powered by a smooth 2.9 liter, fuel injected V-6 developed for the unlimited speed autobahns of Germany. The suspension is fully independent to provide excellent handling and a smooth ride while its brakes employ the world's most advanced system: ABS with discs at all four wheels.

THE MOST HONORED.
Scorpio won more awards than any other new car when introduced in Europe. Eighteen in all, among them the German Road Safety Award and Europe's coveted Car of the Year title for 1986. In a vote by 56 journalists representing 17 countries throughout Europe, Scorpio finished first ahead of the Saab 9000 and the Mercedes-Benz 200 and 300E models.

LINCOLN-MERCURY DIVISION Ford

ENTION.
erience
l level of
on that
er you've
se. Like a
articipating
you bring
r service.

Scorpio RoadCare is also provided. It's all part of Lincoln-Mercury-Merkur's dedication to customer satisfaction.

MERKUR

Advancing the art of driving.

Buckle up—together we can save lives.

MERKUR SCORPIO

UNIQUE OWNER BENEFITS

IF THE
LITTLE
THINGS
BUG
YOU

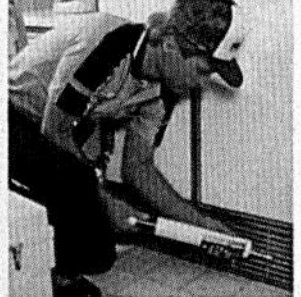

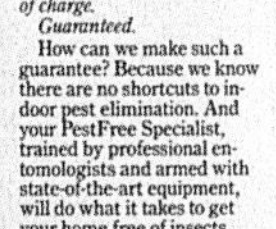

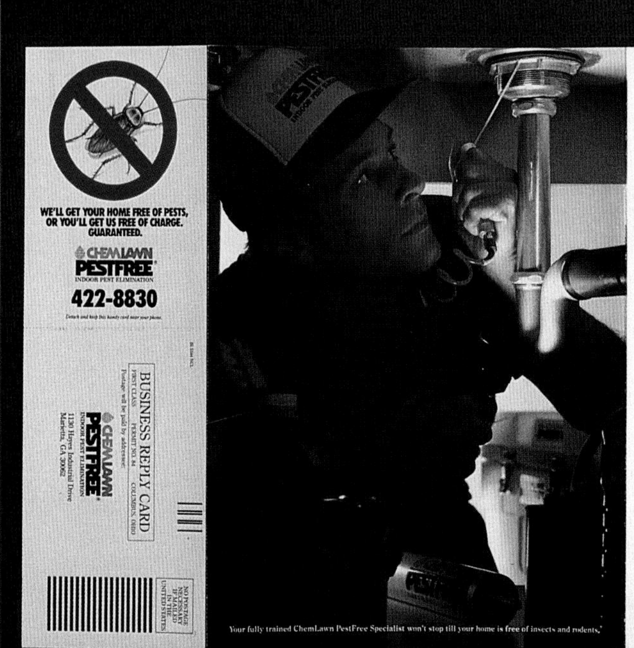

Title: "Guaranteed"
Copywriter: Leila Vourenmaa
Art Director: Michael Cancellieri
Agency: Ogilvy & Mather Direct
Client: Chemlawn Pestfree

The largest headline type that can possibly fit onto the front of a not-so-large self- mailer and a simple, straightforward guarantee repeated in each brochure and collateral piece emphasize Chemlawn's understanding of, and solution for, the consumer's frustration at the presence of different ugly little insects and rodents.

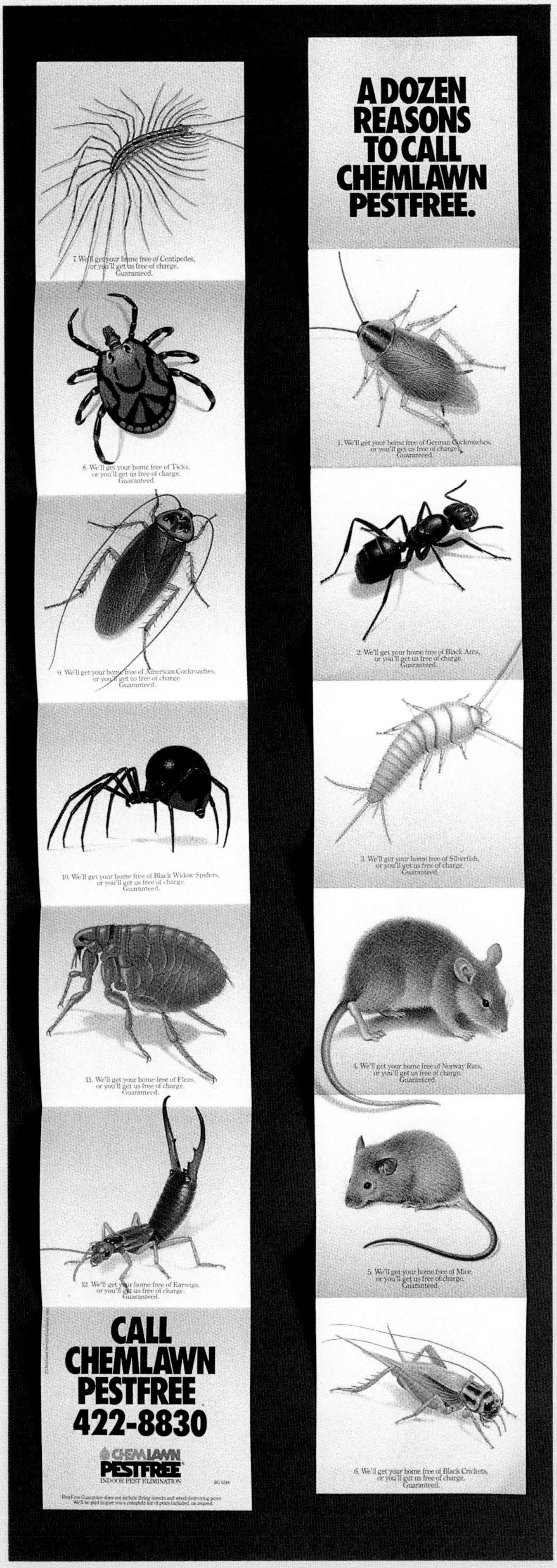

7. We'll get your home free of Centipedes, or you'll get us free of charge. Guaranteed.

8. We'll get your home free of Ticks, or you'll get us free of charge. Guaranteed.

9. We'll get your home free of American Cockroaches, or you'll get us free of charge. Guaranteed.

10. We'll get your home free of Black Widow Spiders, or you'll get us free of charge. Guaranteed.

11. We'll get your home free of Fleas, or you'll get us free of charge. Guaranteed.

12. We'll get your home free of Earwigs, or you'll get us free of charge. Guaranteed.

CALL CHEMLAWN PESTFREE 422-8830

CHEMLAWN PESTFREE INDOOR PEST ELIMINATION

A DOZEN REASONS TO CALL CHEMLAWN PESTFREE.

1. We'll get your home free of German Cockroaches, or you'll get us free of charge. Guaranteed.

2. We'll get your home free of Black Ants, or you'll get us free of charge. Guaranteed.

3. We'll get your home free of Silverfish, or you'll get us free of charge. Guaranteed.

4. We'll get your home free of Norway Rats, or you'll get us free of charge. Guaranteed.

5. We'll get your home free of Mice, or you'll get us free of charge. Guaranteed.

6. We'll get your home free of Black Crickets, or you'll get us free of charge. Guaranteed.

n termites are.
h year throughout the U.S., they
total of $500 million in damage.
mites can enter your home through
as small as 1/64 of an inch. They can
rough any piece of wood that has
ontact with the soil. And they bur-
ough the center of the wood with-
earing on the outside. If no wood is
e, they gain access by building mud
in crawl spaces.
nce inside your house, termites
will attack any wood or wood by-
product they can find. Wood,
books, wallpaper and
sheet rocking are all
rich in the cellulose

they live on. So these harmful pests can cause extensive damage to your property before you even notice it.

FULLY TRAINED TERMITE SPECIALISTS

At ChemLawn PestFree® we have fully trained Termite Specialists who are advised by top pest control and chemical experts in the country. They'll know exactly how to protect your home from termites.

Our Termite Specialists are licensed and certified by the state they operate in. So you're assured that your home is being treated by a fully qualified professional.

ChemLawn PestFree inspects your house thoroughly—from eaves to basement.

UARANTEED PEACE OF MIND

s can attack your home at any
. You could worry about the possi-
damage. Or you could get peace of
th ChemLawn PestFree's Inspec-
rranty.
Termite Specialist will do a thor-
pection of your house without
If no wood-destroying organisms
d, he'll issue a one-year warranty
ninal fee.
nLawn's warranty guarantees you
50,000 in protection in ridding
me of termites and repairing any

at wood by working along the grain—so they
ge a piece of wood extensively without being
the outside.

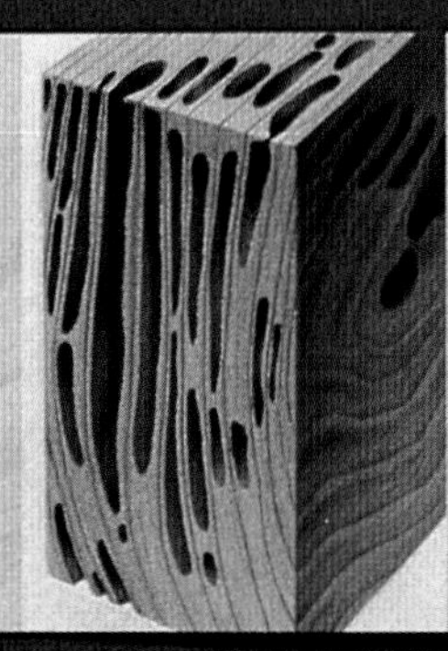

damage they've caused—during the life of the warranty.

A SAFE, EFFECTIVE TERMITE TREATMENT TO PROTECT YOUR HOME

If termites are discovered, our Termite Specialist will use Dursban® TC to create a barrier between your house and the termites in the soil underneath. Dursban TC has been proved a safe, effective termiticide. It doesn't just repel termites, it kills them. And it achieves this at relatively low dosage rates. Dursban TC has been proved safe enough for indoor usage so you won't have to worry about chemical contamination.

Your ChemLawn Termite Specialist will inject Dursban TC all around your house to form a shield underneath. He'll inject the chemical into all voids and cracks where termites might gain entry.

Once your specialist has done his job, he'll refill the holes in the plaster and masonry. He'll schedule your treatment to suit you and since the entire treatment takes only a day, you won't be inconvenienced.

When your ChemLawn Termite Specialist has finished you'll have an impenetrable shield between your home and the millions of termites in the soil underneath it.

And after he's treated your home he'll issue you a $250,000 warranty to protect you if termites attack again.

MOTHER NATURE NEEDS ALL THE HELP CHEMLAWN CAN GIVE HER.

You know the ugliness and injury insects and disease can cause your defenseless trees and shrubs.

What you're probably not aware of is how easily the damage can be avoided.

Often, many homeowners do nothing until they actually see the problem. Leaves eaten through. Trees and shrubs so weakened that they're prime targets for disease.

But Mother Nature doesn't have to suffer like this. You can spare her the agony with an Insect & Disease Treatment from ChemLawn Tree & Shrub Care.

ONLY $00.00 PROTECTS YOUR TREES AND SHRUBS FROM INSECTS AND DISEASES. GUARANTEED.

With just a single treatment from ChemLawn Tree & Shrub Care now, you can protect your trees and shrubs from life-threatening insects and disease all season long.

We guarantee it.

Just give us a call, and within days a trained specialist will come out to your home and spray all the trees and shrubs on your property up to 0,000 sq. ft. (average landscape size) for only $00.00.

Our environmentally safe spray* will protect bark and foliage from hundreds of debilitating diseases and voracious insects including aphids, caterpillars, beetles, leaf miners, spider mites, and scale insects. Leaving your trees and shrubs to grow greener, fuller, and healthier.

CHEMLAWN TREE & SHRUB CARE WILL CUSTOM-DESIGN A PROGRAM OF SCIENTIFIC CARE AT NO EXTRA CHARGE.

While your tree and shrub specialist is at your home spraying your trees and shrubs he'll also give you a complete analysis of their condition —absolutely free, and without any obligation on your part.

Based on his findings he'll custom-design a year-round program specifically for your landscape's needs. One that's guaranteed to make your trees and shrubs the absolute best they can be.

By coming back all season long to feed and care for your trees and shrubs, he'll be able to spot, and stop problems *before* they cause any real damage.

And he's always available for free consultations and service calls.

Best of all, this *guaranteed* service is only $00.00. Less than it would cost you to replace even one young tree that might fall victim if left unprotected.

So don't wait till you see the damage. Call ChemLawn Tree & Shrub Care for your guaranteed Insect & Disease Treatment today.

Mother Nature will appreciate the help.

*ChemLawn is committed to the safety of our customers and the environment. All tree and shrub insect and disease control materials selected for use by ChemLawn have been registered for use on landscapes by the United States Environmental Protection Agency and the appropriate state agency, and have passed our own rigorous selection standards. With ChemLawn you have the confidence that our applications equal or exceed the safety of the tree and shrub care products sold in retail stores and you have the advantage of professional handling and application of these materials.

CALL 000-0000

CHEMLAWN TREE & SHRUB CARE GUARANTEES GREENER, FULLER, HEALTHIER TREES AND SHRUBS.

WHO SAYS MONEY DOESN'T GROW ON TREES?

According to real estate experts, a well-cared-for landscape can add up to 15% to the resale value of your home.

And an attractive landscape certainly makes your home easier to sell when the time comes.

But you know, right now you probably have a sizeable investment to protect. Just one medium sized tree with a 10" diameter costs up to $2,500 to replace.

Yet insects, disease or malnutrition can threaten several trees and shrubs at once.

A SPRING FEEDING FROM CHEMLAWN WILL HELP YOU PROTECT YOUR INVESTMENTS.

Your trees and shrubs are most vulnerable to insects and disease now, while they're trying to recover from a winter without food.

They're starving for attention that you can easily provide.

Because ChemLawn Tree & Shrub Care will feed all your hungry trees and shrubs for only $00.00 on up to 0,000 square feet of property.

Spring Feeding makes those little and not-so-little investments stronger, healthier and more disease resistant.

What's more, ChemLawn guarantees it.

WE'LL CUSTOM-DESIGN A COMPLETE PROGRAM OF SCIENTIFIC CARE AT NO EXTRA CHARGE.

When your ChemLawn Tree & Shrub Care specialist feeds your trees and shrubs, he'll also analyze their health in the most critical areas absolutely free.

Based on the results of his analysis your specialist will custom-design a year-round program of care for your plants, without any obligation on your part.

If you should choose to let ChemLawn care for your trees and shrubs, your personal specialist will make sure they're as green and healthy as they can be. And he'll always be available for free consultations and free service calls.

So let us start you on your way to a greener, healthier landscape for just $00.00. Call for our Spring Feeding. We guarantee you'll begin to see a noticeable difference in the quality of your trees and shrubs.

There really is no surer way to give those investments a chance to mature.

CALL 000-0000

CHEMLAWN TREE & SHRUB CARE GUARANTEES GREENER, FULLER, HEALTHIER TREES AND SHRUBS.

ONLY $35.00 FEEDS THE ENTIRE FAMILY ALL SPRING.

While you spent the winter inside, all snug and protected, your trees and shrubs suffered through the harsh, cold winter without anything to eat.

YOUR TREES AND SHRUBS ARE STARVING FOR ATTENTION THAT YOU CAN EASILY PROVIDE.

Right now they're at their most vulnerable stage of the year. In their weakened condition, they're extremely susceptible to the onset of insects and disease.

If you care how they look in the coming months, let us care for them now. With a deep rooted feeding at our low introductory price.

For a limited time only, ChemLawn Tree & Shrub Care will come to your home and feed all of your trees and shrubs—up to 0,000 square feet of property. That's the average landscape size.

We'll give each and every one of them a total root-zone feeding to overcome the soil depletion that took place last winter. So every tree and shrub on your property will get the nutrients they need to grow healthy and strong. *Guaranteed.*

When your ChemLawn Tree & Shrub Care Specialist feeds your trees and shrubs, he'll also analyze their health in the most critical areas—absolutely free.

WE'LL CUSTOM-DESIGN A COMPLETE PROGRAM OF SCIENTIFIC CARE AT NO EXTRA CHARGE.

Based on the results of his analysis your specialist will custom-design a program of care for your trees and shrubs, without obligation. Since his analysis pinpoints specific problem areas, you can be sure that *your* program best suits *your* needs.

Your specialist will keep coming back all year long to care for your trees and shrubs. He's always available for free consultation and free service calls.

So why not start on your way to greener, healthier trees and shrubs today? Call for their Spring Feeding. We guarantee you'll begin to see a noticeable difference in their quality.

And after all, $00.00 isn't much to make sure such valuable members of your household get the nourishment they need.

CALL 000-0000

CHEMLAWN TREE & SHRUB CARE GUARANTEES GREENER, FULLER, HEALTHIER TREES AND SHRUBS.

Title: "Kimberly Farms"
Copywriters: Shelley E. Lanman, Susan Enterline, Jenny Raybould
Art Directors: Phyllis Cayton, Neil Wagner
Agency: Ogilvy & Mather Direct
Client: Kimberly- Clark

Through a die-cut square window on the cover of a heavy card-stock three-panel portfolio, the tobacco grower's attention is captured by a pleasant and familiar sight—a healthy leaf held in the hand. Inside, and in other mailing pieces and in-store collateral, the benefits of Kimberly Farms' new high-grade see bed covers are explained in detail.

THEY'LL BE USING KIM
THE REMARKABLE NEW SEE
LASTS AT LEAST TWO FULL P

In the risky business of tobacco farming, it often seems that all you can count on are the hazards. Drought. Insects. Disease. Price fluctuation.

There are so many things you *can't* control when it comes to growing tobacco.

Now, there's something you can really be sure of. KIMBERLY FARMS Seedbed Covers. They're new, from Kimberly-Clark.

GOOD FOR 2 SEASONS OR MORE

TWO SEASONS—OR MORE—FOR THE PRICE OF ONE.

KIMBERLY FARMS Seedbed Covers are different from anything you've used before. They can actually last through two full seasons—and sometimes longer—with proper care.

How is that possible? One reason is the special fabric they're made of. Strength analysis tests show it's more durable than other synthetics. Yet it's lightweight.

What's more, a unique part of the fabric's makeup helps prevent deterioration due to the sun's rays. (Other synthetic covers don't have this feature.) How does this affect strength retention? After 22 weeks of intensive exposure to sunlight, the KIMBERLY FARMS Cover maintained nearly 5 times the strength of the leading competitor. It's a difference you can feel. So KIMBERLY FARMS Covers will last at least twice as long as the leading synthetic cover under normal use.

And that's a difference you can take to the bank.

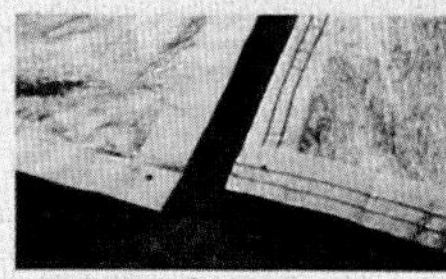

KIMBERLY FARMS Cover's tan-colored hem—and the competition's hem—just take a look at the difference.

KIMBERLY FARMS GIVES YOU THE COMPETITIVE EDGE.

As you know, seedbed covers are especially prone to wear and tear at the hems and corners, where wind, over-handling, and other factors can really take their toll. Here, too, KIM FARMS Covers offer a clear advantage. The tan-c is made from an even stronger fabric than the r cover. We doubled it over, then stitched it dow heavy-duty thread, for the most secure hold down holes are made by a special heat process that reduces tearing. So grommets aren't needed.

But the real beauty of this unique edge shows at the end of the transplanting season. Then you'll see and feel how much stronger the KIMBERLY FARMS Cover still is than other synthetic covers.

CONTROLLED, HEALTHY SEEDLING GROWTH... TESTS PROVED IT.

Of course, the bottom line is this: How will KIMBERL Seedbed Covers perform on your seedbeds?

Tobacco beds co (above) consist at Blue Mea

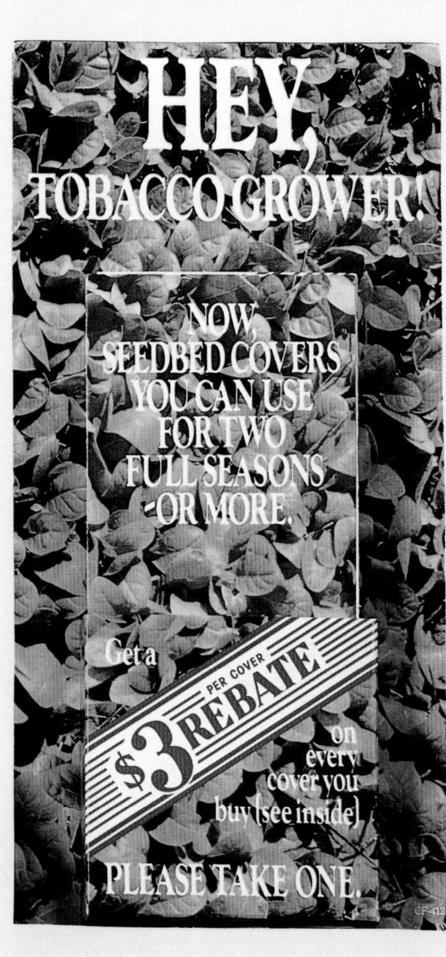

HEY,
TOBACCO GROWER!
NOW SEEDBED COVERS YOU CAN USE FOR TWO FULL SEASONS -OR MORE.
Get a
$3 PER COVER REBATE
on every cover you buy [see inside]
PLEASE TAKE ONE.

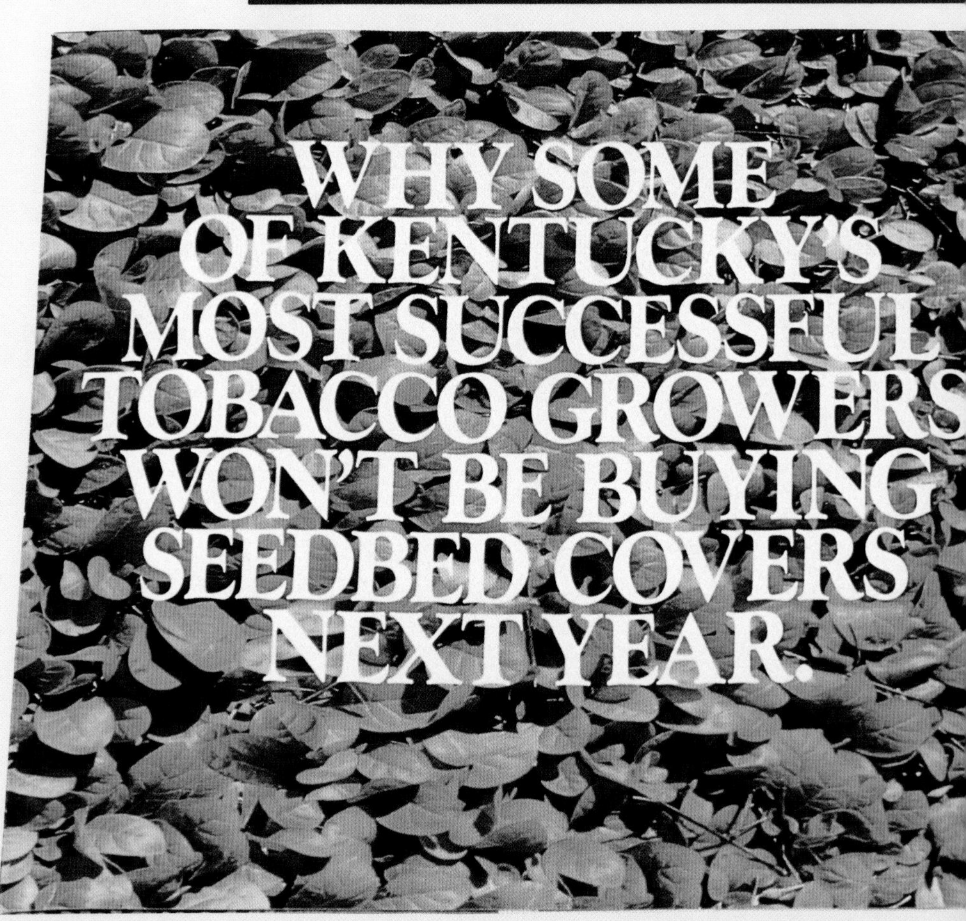

WHY SOME OF KENTUCKY'S MOST SUCCESSFUL TOBACCO GROWERS WON'T BE BUYING SEEDBED COVERS NEXT YEAR.

LY FARMS™- COVER THAT NG SEASONS.

vell, according to the evidence. In ducted on 100 Kentucky tobacco ring the 1984 seedbed season, LY FARMS Covers provided effective n against frost and heavy rainfall.

Most importantly, the KIMBERLY FARMS Covers demonstrated an outstanding "greenhouse" effect. Sunlight and moisture pass freely through the fabric, keeping plants warm and moist. Of course, control over your plants' growing environment helps you control their growth . . . a big advantage.

This greenhouse effect could enable you to plant later in the year—and still be sure you won't miss the prime transplanting season.

With this control over plant growth, you could find more plants ready at the first transplanting. And plants picked first generally produce the best adult u're likely to have a better crop down the line.

y won't rot or mildew.

EASY STORAGE WITHOUT ROT OR MILDEW.

At the end of the season, you can roll and fold or braid KIMBERLY FARMS™ as you would cotton covers. Their compactness and light weight make storage fast and easy. And while you'll want to shake off excess dirt before storing them, don't worry about left-on dirt damaging the covers. The fabric won't be affected.

Unlike cotton covers, KIMBERLY FARMS Covers will look as good coming out of storage as they did going in. In fact, the special fiber is not adversely affected by organic matter, so there's absolutely no risk of fabric rot or mildew in storage.

UNIVERSITY OF KENTUCKY PUT IT TO THE TEST—AND IT WORKED.

COMPARE THE THREE MAJOR SEEDBED COVERS

	Cotton Cover	The Leading Synthetic Cover	KIMBERLY FARMS Cover
Good for at least 2 seasons	Yes, if not rotted	No	Yes
Rebate offered	No	No	Yes $3/cover
Resistant to rot and mildew	No	Yes	Yes
Protects against frost	Yes	Yes	Yes
Protects against heavy rainfall	Yes	Yes	Yes
Average cost per year for a 12'x100' Cover	Varies	$23.97*	$14.47**

*recommended retail price **with rebate

KIMBERLY FARMS vs. the rest. The facts speak for themselves.

There's no need to take our word for KIMBERLY FARMS Covers' qualities. U.K. tests have proven them.

During the growing seasons of 1983 and 1984, the University ran extensive tests of the performance of KIMBERLY FARMS Covers compared to other synthetics. They found:

- After a full planting season, the KIMBERLY FARMS Covers were still intact and ready to be used again the next season.
- After two seasons—one 8-week and one 10-week—the KIMBERLY FARMS Covers retained virtually 100% of their strength. The leading competitor retained only 54% of its strength after just one season.
- There was a discernible difference in under-cover temperatures. The KIMBERLY FARMS Cover averaged 4° higher at night than the leading competitor.
- Most important, when plants were ready for the field, researchers found the KIMBERLY FARMS bed produced significantly more transplantable plants than the competition.

KIMBERLY FARMS GIVES YOU THE BEST OF BOTH WORLDS.

In University of Kentucky tests KIMBERLY FARMS maintained a warmer nighttime temperature—an average of 4° higher than the leading synthetic tested.

Only KIMBERLY FARMS Covers give you at least two seasons' use for little more than the cost of other synthetics, which usually last only one season.

But they can do more for you than just save money.

As U.K. tests show, KIMBERLY FARMS Covers can help you grow healthy, strong tobacco plants. And when the tobacco fields are greener, there's another type of green that grows faster: the kind that grows in the bank—not in the ground.

$3 PER COVER REBATE

For a limited time, you can save even more on KIMBERLY FARMS™ Covers. Just send us the coupon below. Include your sales slip and the proof of purchase card from inside each package. We'll send you $3 for every KIMBERLY FARMS Seedbed Cover you purchase.

You'll find KIMBERLY FARMS Covers at your regular farm supply store or Co-op Store.

I JUST GOT MY 2 SEASONS' WORTH OF KIMBERLY FARMS™ COVERS. PLEASE SEND MY REBATE OF $3 PER COVER.

Enclosed with this coupon are my sales slip (with price for covers circled) and proof of purchase card from inside each package.

For ____ covers purchased, please send me $____

Name ____

Address ____

Telephone ( ) ____

Name of store where purchased ____

City ____

Mail to: Kimberly Farms Rebate Offer, c/o Kimberly-Clark Corporation, P.O. Box 93040, Atlanta, GA 30377-9990

Offer expires July 31, 1985 A15

WHOEVER HEARD OF A SEEDBED COVER WITH A HIGH PROFIT MARGIN?

Bet you didn't—until now.

It's been this way for years. There are some things you have to stock simply because your customers *need* them. And forget about making any money selling them.

Tobacco seedbed covers, for instance. Your growers pick up a few each year—just in time for the growing season—and you make a small profit on each one. Maybe. Because by the end of the season, you're likely to have excess inventory that you wind up marking down—sometimes cutting out your whole profit in order to clear the floor space. Just one of those things you have to live with. A simple fact of life.

Well, not any more.

KIMBERLY FARMS™ gives the dealer a good deal more.

Now, we can understand if you're skeptical. After all, how many grand, empty promises of greater profits have you been sent in the last few years?

KIMBERLY FARMS' tan-colored hem—and the competition's plain one—the difference is obvious.

This isn't one of them. We're not making any promises we can't back up. The fact is, at the suggested retail price of $31.95 for the 12' x 100' cover and $28.95 for the 12' x 75' and 9' x 100' sizes, you'll make a significantly higher average profit per KIMBERLY FARMS Cover than you will on the leading synthetic cover. Your KIMBERLY FARMS distributor will be glad to give you the cold, hard numbers.

There is, however, one catch. We've made the KIMBERLY FARMS Cover so well, growers can use it for *two* full seasons. Your customers may only have to buy them once in two years.

So where does that leave you? Still with a welcome gain over the profit you were making on those other covers! (And you'll have it all up front, instead of waiting another year for the second installment.)

A better deal for growers, too.

Of course, no one in his right mind expects to make a profit on a product that won't sell. So you should know that your customers will be asking for KIMBERLY FARMS, for several excellent reasons.

Attractive packaging designed to be noticed.

First off, KIMBERLY FARMS is the *only* cover designed to last through two full seasons. So while they cost a bit more initially, KIMBERLY FARMS Covers really *save* your customers money in the long run. The actual yearly cost

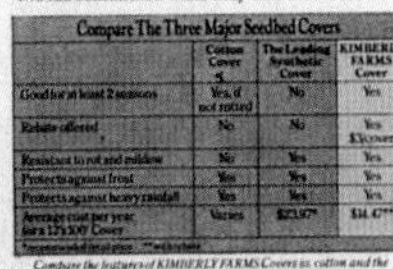

Compare The Three Major Seedbed Covers

	Cotton Cover	The Leading Synthetic Cover	KIMBERLY FARMS Cover
Good for at least 2 seasons	Yes, if not rotted	No	Yes
Rebate offered	No	No	Yes $3/cover
Resistant to rot and mildew	No	Yes	Yes
Protects against frost	Yes	Yes	Yes
Protects against heavy rainfall	Yes	Yes	Yes
Average cost per year for a 12'x100' Cover	Varies	$23.97*	$14.47**

*recommended retail price **with rebate

Compare the features of KIMBERLY FARMS Covers vs. cotton and the leading synthetic. The facts speak for themselves.

Kimberly-Clark, Nonwoven Fabrics Division
1400 Holcomb Bridge Road, Roswell, GA 30076

Announcing the new KIMBERLY FARMS™ Tobacco Seedbed Cover. Put through its paces by University of Kentucky agriculturists. Tested and acclaimed by leading growers in the state. And priced to bring you more profit than you usually earn on other covers.

Register now as a participating dealer, and you'll receive a handy pocket calculator--free, with our compliments.

Dear Dealer:

It's a hard fact of life.

You're in business to make a profit. Yet there are products it simply doesn't pay you to sell--products you stock purely to provide a service to your customers and to avoid losing ground to the competition.

Like tobacco seedbed covers. They take up space in your store, bring in--at best--lower profits than other products you sell, and at worst get off--loaded at a loss as the end of the season approaches.

That may be how it was last season.

But now that's all in the past. Because this season you can place your order for KIMBERLY FARMS.

HEALTHY CROPS FOR THE GROWER--HEALTHY PROFITS FOR YOU

KIMBERLY FARMS Seedbed Covers are made of a tough, nonwoven synthetic fabric refined and improved over more than five years of intensive research and development. They're designed to help produce healthy crops for the tobacco grower--and at the same time, a better crop of profits for you.

In fact, KIMBERLY FARMS is quickly gaining recognition as the tobacco cover of the future.

... season of strictly controlled University of Kentucky tests, ... current top-selling synthetic. The fabric is so

(over, please)

Why growers will be asking for KIMBERLY FARMS by name.

Kimberly-Clark, Nonwoven Fabrics Division
1400 Holcomb Bridge Road, Roswell, GA 30076

for the 12' x 100' cover is only $14.47 (with $3 rebate), compared to $23.97 recommended retail price for the leading synthetic cover.

And we're giving growers a $3 rebate on every cover they buy, making KIMBERLY FARMS even more attractive.

. . . On a cover that offers proven performance.

But where KIMBERLY FARMS Covers will prove *most* attractive to your customers will be on their tobacco seedbeds. Just look at the test results. KIMBERLY FARMS Covers provided:

- **An improved "greenhouse" effect.** Tests conducted by the University of Kentucky showed that temperatures under the KIMBERLY FARMS Covers averaged 4° warmer at night than the leading synthetic cover.
- **A full crop for two full seasons.** In those tests, the KIMBERLY FARMS seedbed produced significantly more transplantable plants than the leading competitor.
- **A unique double reinforced hem** that resists tearing and fraying through *two* full seasons.
- **Effective protection** against heavy rainfall and frost.

Full-color, 2-page advertisements in KENTUCKY FARMER will get your customers mighty interested.

What do growers think? Here's an opinion from one of the best—Bill Balden, Progressive Farmer's 1983 Kentucky Farmer of the Year. He said: "I would definitely be willing to pay extra to get the KIMBERLY FARMS Cover . . . even as much as 25% more. And I would tell my neighbors the same thing."

We're here to help you sell.

Attention-getting point-of-sale materials inform and persuade your customers at the most crucial time—when they're ready to buy.

When a product has such instant appeal and obvious benefits, you'd think it would just sell itself. Well, not quite. It takes some doing to spread the word. And Kimberly-Clark is ready to back you in a big way. We've instituted an extensive program of advertising and promotion to introduce growers to KIMBERLY FARMS.

We're running two-page color ads in Kentucky Farmer magazine. An informative brochure will be sent to every tobacco farmer in this area. And we're ready to supply *you* with powerful in-store material—poster, counter card, take-one, and product display—to bring home the message where the final buying decision is made—right in your store.

Display designed for maximum results using minimal floor space.

But most important, we've done our homework, with tests at the University of Kentucky and on farms throughout Kentucky. Test results have proven our claims, and gotten people talking. Which gives you the advantage of the best sales tool of all—word of mouth.

Yet another way you can count on us . . .

Are you ready to add up those extra profits? We'd like to help by sending you this handsome, credit card size pocket calculator. It's ultra-thin and solar-powered—so it never needs batteries. With 4 functions and easy-to-read LED quartz display, it will come in handy in managing your business.

It's yours as our gift, when you register as a participating dealer. Plus you'll be sent, absolutely *free*, in-store point-of-purchase materials to help you display and sell KIMBERLY FARMS Covers.

Handsome, trim 4-function calculator—a useful tool—yours, free, from KIMBERLY FARMS.

Be sure you're covered now.

Whatever you do, don't delay. You'll want to be fully informed *before* the growing season rolls around.

Enclosed is a sample copy of the announcement we'll be sending to growers. It's packed with even more information about KIMBERLY FARMS Covers. We've also enclosed a small sample of the cover material for you to examine.

Make sure you're stocked and ready for your customers. And, come planting season, you can watch your profits grow right along with their crops.

PRESENTING KIMBERLY FARMS™ SEEDBED COVERS.

At last, a seedbed cover designed to promote healthy growth–of profit.

WHOEVER HEA
A SEEDBED COVE
A HIGH PROFIT M
Bet you didn't–unt

It's been this way for years. There are some things you have to stock simply because your customers *need* them. And forget about making any money selling them.

Tobacco seedbed covers, for instance. Your growers pick up a few each year—just in time for the growing season—and you make a small profit on each one. Maybe. Because by the end of the season, you're likely to have excess inventory that you wind up marking down—sometimes cutting out your whole profit in order to clear the floor space. Just one of those things you have to live with. A simple fact of life.

Well, not any more.

KIMBERLY FARMS™ gives the dealer a good deal more.

Now, we can understand if you're skeptical. After all, how many grand, empty promises of greater profits have you been sent in the last few years?

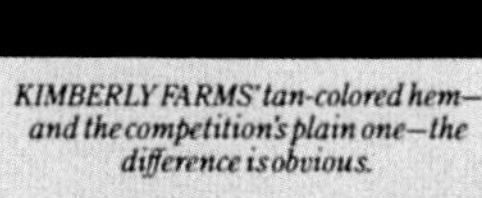

KIMBERLY FARMS' tan-colored hem—and the competition's plain one—the difference is obvious.

This isn't one of them. We're not making any promises we can't back up. The fact is, at the suggested retail price of $31.95 for the 12′ x 100′ cover and $28.95 for the 12′ x 75′ and 9′ x 100′ sizes, you'll make a significantly higher average profit per KIMBERLY FARMS Cover than you will on the leading synthetic cover. Your KIMBERLY FARMS distributor will be glad to give you the cold, hard numbers.

There is, however, one catch. We've made the KIMBERLY FARMS Cover so well, growers can use it for *two* full seasor
to buy them once

wit
you
cov
inst
the

Al

Of
in h
exp
a p
product that won
you should know
customers will be
for KIMBERLY FA
several excellent

First off, KIM
FARMS is the *only*
designed to last t
two full seasons.

Compare T
Good for at least 2 seas
Rebate offered
Resistant to rot and mil
Protects against frost
Protects against heavy
Average cost per year for a 12′x100′ Cover
*recommended retail price

Compare the features leading syn

tially, KIMBERLY
tomers money in

OF
ITH
GIN?

v.

ers may only have

that leave you? Still
n over the profit
n those other
have it all up front,
nother year for
ent.)

growers, too.

tive packaging designed to
be noticed.

st a bit more ini-

bed Covers	
ne Leading Synthetic Cover	KIMBERLY FARMS Cover
No	Yes
No	Yes $3/cover
Yes	Yes
Yes	Yes
Yes	Yes
$23.97*	$14.47**

vers vs. cotton and the
themselves.

lly *save* your cus-
e actual yearly cost

A few more privileges for the privileged few.
MANUFACTURERS HANOVER
GrandElite
MasterCard

Ah, the benefits of success. If you already know them well, read on.

Because now Manufacturers Hanover would like to add one more.

A most remarkable credit card. Our GrandElite® MasterCard® card.

While other credit cards come with very pedestrian credit lines, ours offers you as much as $25,000. (Of course, actual credit lines are subject to approval).

And you can use it not only for credit, but for cash. At over 10,000 conveniently located Automated Teller Machines. All across the country and in Canada.

Or you can access your credit line instantly with personalized GrandElite Master Checking checks. Which can make the GrandElite MasterCard card an essential financial tool for sudden investment opportunities.

Yet, no matter what your station in life, you didn't get there by being financially unaware.

So our GrandElite MasterCard card offers you something else that's very special: a lower finance charge than most major banks.* Manufacturers Hanover was the first major bank in the U.S. to reduce its credit card rates.

If the idea of carrying a credit card with all these advantages–and many others–fits well with your lifestyle, we invite you to find out more by calling our toll-free number now.

You'll get some very privileged information.

GrandElite®
MasterCard®
1 800 431-6100

We realize your potential.
MANUFACTURERS HANOVER
The Financial Source.® Worldwide.

*The annual fee is $40 and the ANNUAL PERCENTAGE RATE is 17.8 percent.

Member F.D.I.C.

Is your credit card designed for the way you lived five years ago?

Then welcome to your next credit card. The Premier VISA card from Manufacturers Hanover.

You'll enjoy some benefits that are very special, indeed.

Like a credit line that truly reflects how far you've come. Up to $25,000, in fact. (Of course, actual credit lines are subject to approval.)

And you'll find over 10,000 Automated Teller Machines that will recognize your card and your success. All across the country and in Canada.

You'll even pay a lower finance charge* than with most major banks. Because Manufacturers Hanover was the first major bank in the U.S. to bring credit card rates down.

So if the card in your wallet now doesn't do all this for you—and much more—maybe it's time it went the way of your first stereo or even your first apartment.

To learn more about the Premier VISA card from Manufacturers Hanover, call our toll-free number now.

We may just have a great future together.

Premier VISA
1 800 431-6100

*The annual fee is $40 and the ANNUAL PERCENTAGE RATE is 17.8 percent.

Member F.D.I.C.

MANUFACTURERS HANOVER
VISA
We realize your potential.
MANUFACTURERS HANOVER
The Financial Source.® Worldwide.

Title: "Premier VISA, Grande Elite MasterCard"
Copywriters: Ed Subitzky, Joyce Lapin
Art Director: John Olds
Agency: Wunderman Worldwide
Client: Manufacturers Hanover Trust

These print ads, working in conjunction with two television spots, speak only to very successful achievers from the upper echelons of the demographic spectrum about two rather potent credit cards from the two leaders in the field.

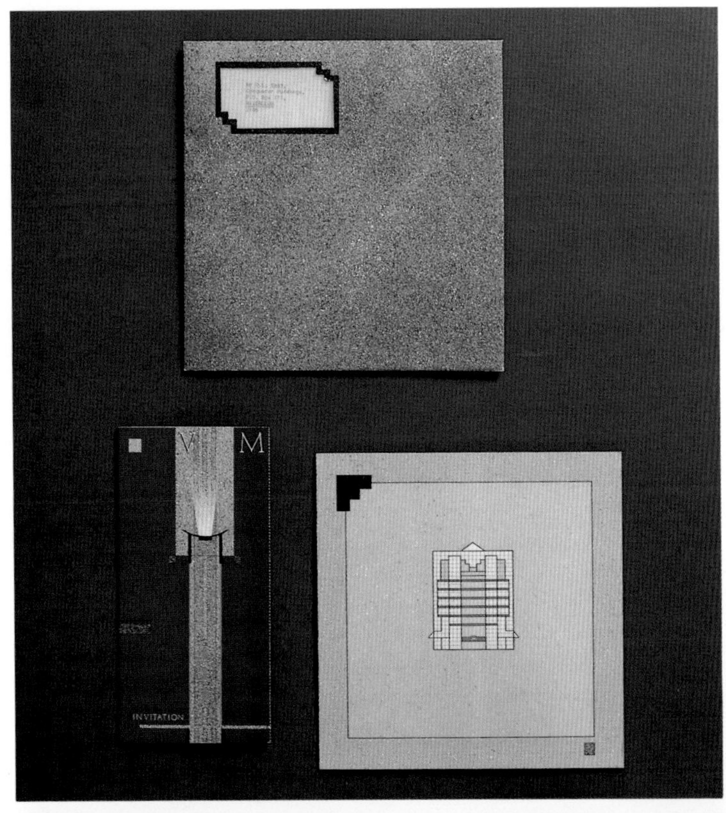

Charles Rennie Macintosh

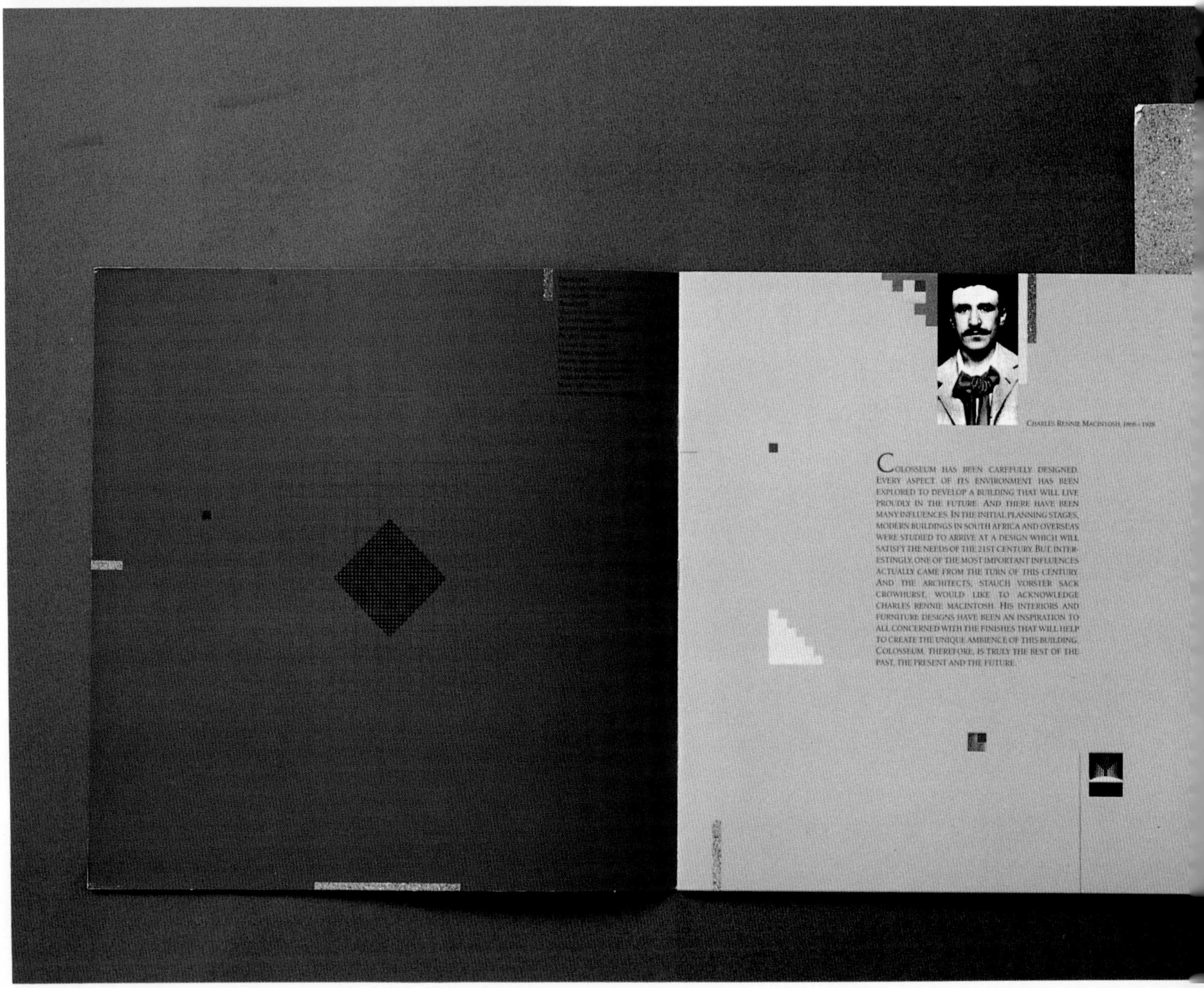

Colosseum has been carefully designed. Every aspect of its environment has been explored to develop a building that will live proudly in the future. And there have been many influences. In the initial planning stages, modern buildings in South Africa and overseas were studied to arrive at a design which will satisfy the needs of the 21st century. But, interestingly, one of the most important influences actually came from the turn of this century. And the architects, Stauch Vorster Sack Crowhurst, would like to acknowledge Charles Rennie Macintosh. His interiors and furniture designs have been an inspiration to all concerned with the finishes that will help to create the unique ambience of this building. Colosseum, therefore, is truly the best of the past, the present and the future.

Title:	"Colosseum"
Copywriter:	Dave East
Art Director:	Ross Chowles
Agency:	Wunderman Worldwide
Client:	Prudential Properties

As ground was being broken at the construction site in Johannesburg, this mailing piece and a series of print ads with the same theme were positioning an important new office building as an exclusive business location.

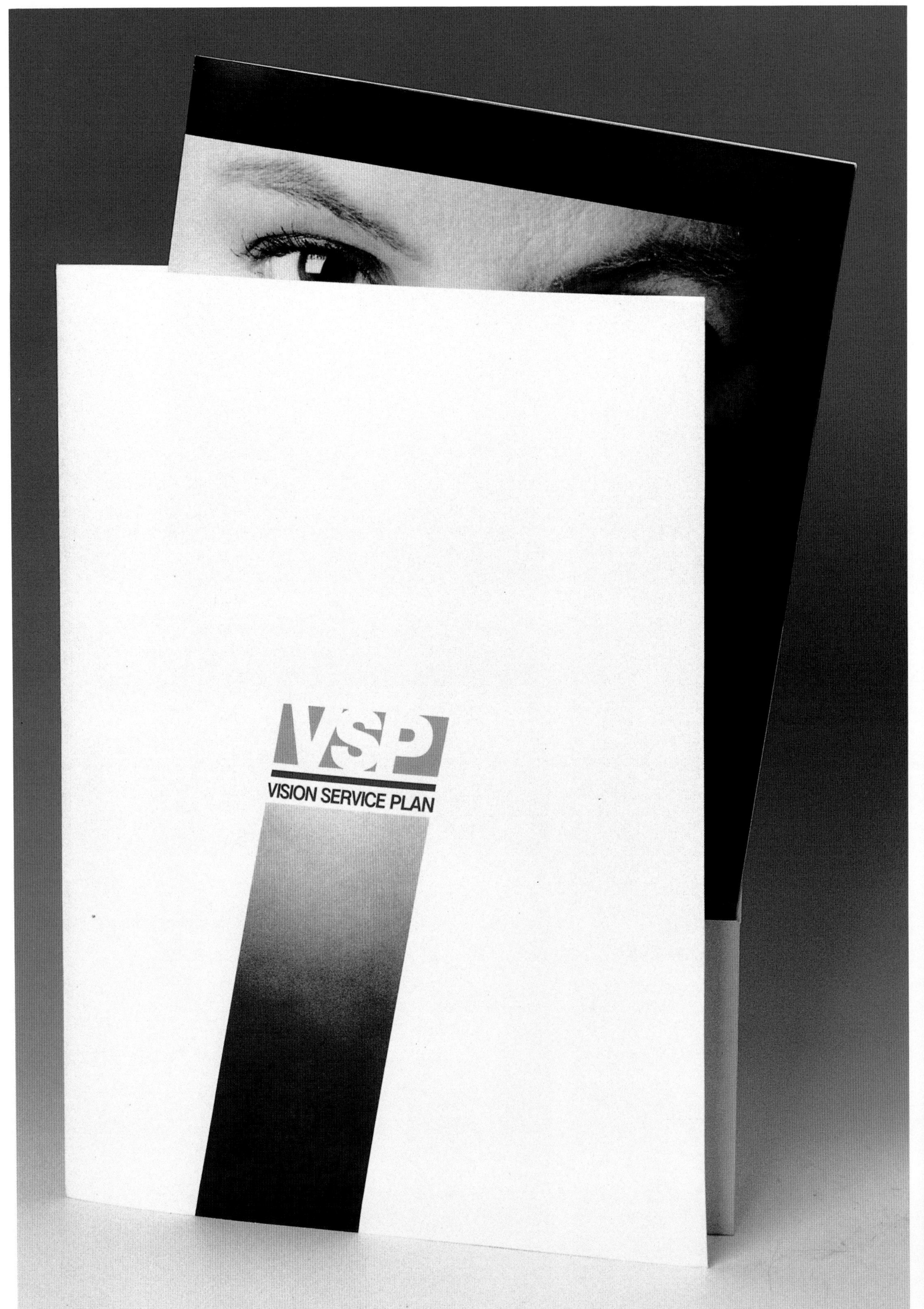
VSP
VISION SERVICE PLAN

Title: "Vision Service Plan"
Copywriter: Pam Isham
Art Director: Steve Hammond
Agency: Henry-Gill, Inc.
Client: Vision Service Plan

Eyeglasses and eye care often are not included in business group health plans, so Vision Service's coverage capabilities are explained in this print, direct mail and collateral campaign with a careful focus on clarity and detail.

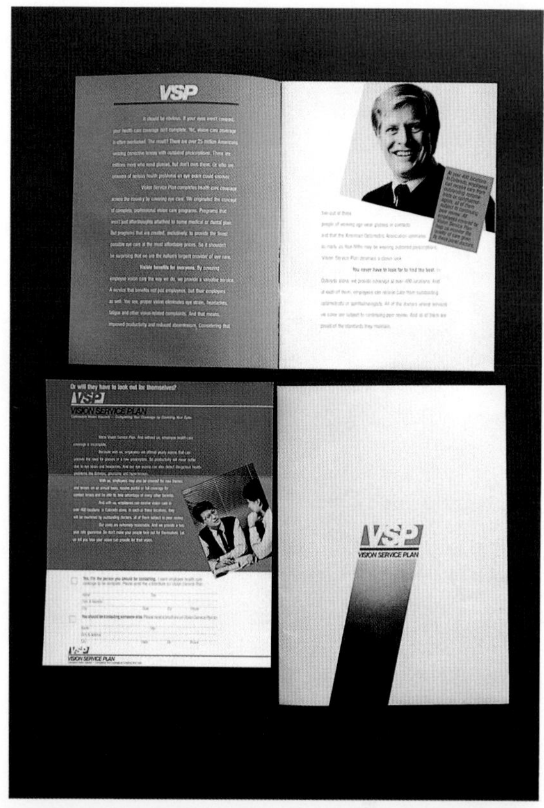

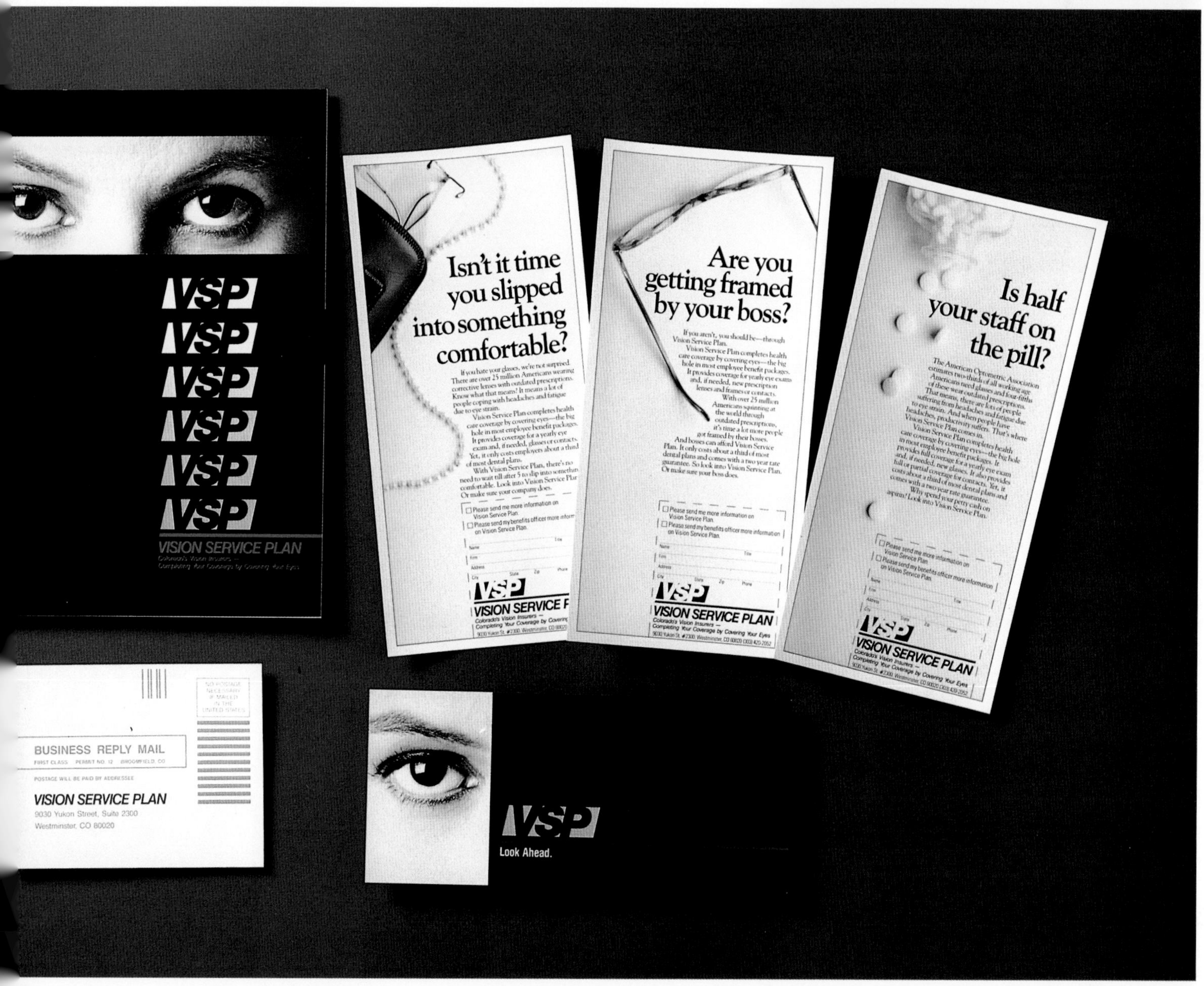

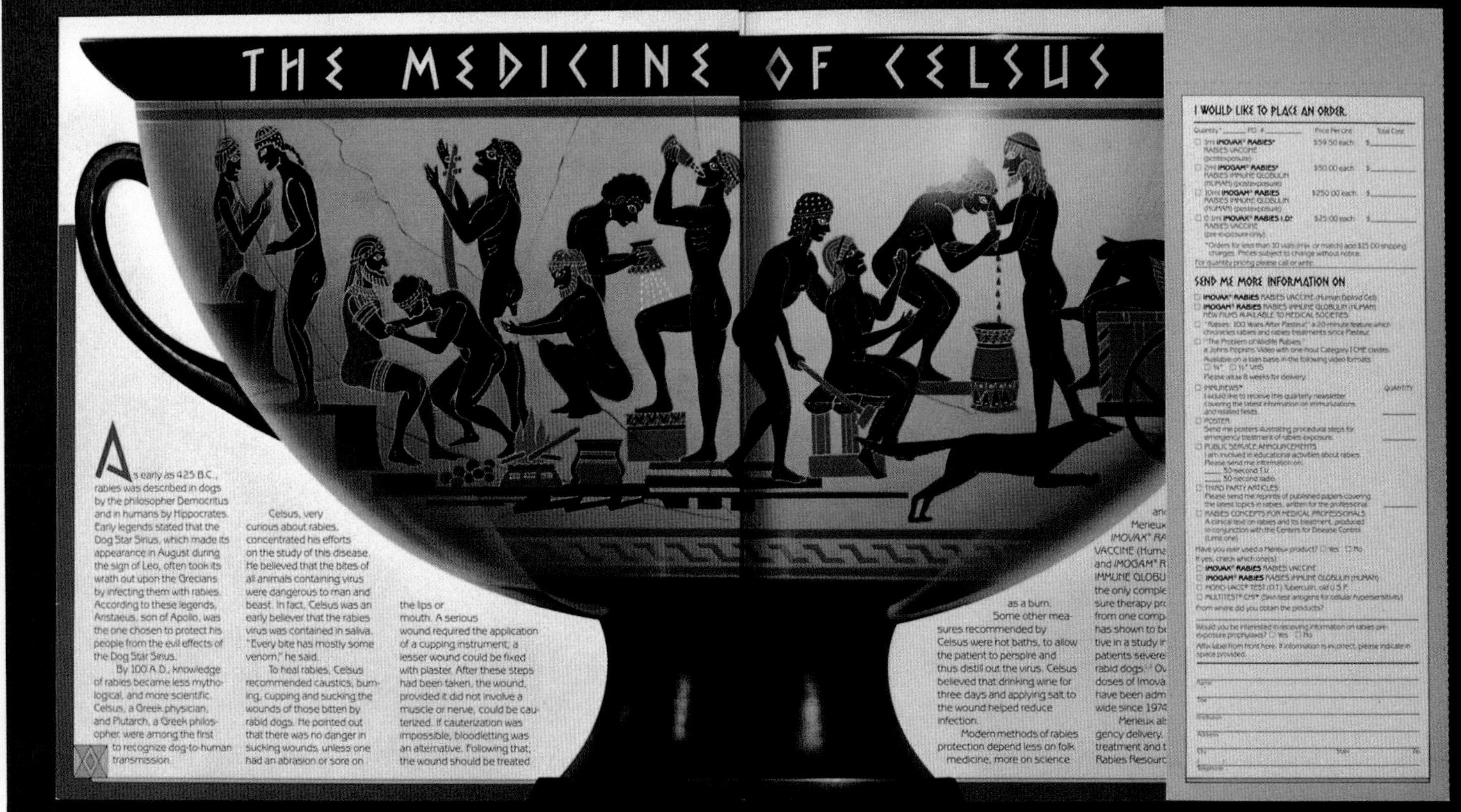

THE MEDICINE OF CELSUS

As early as 425 B.C., rabies was described in dogs by the philosopher Democritus and in humans by Hippocrates. Early legends stated that the Dog Star Sirius, which made its appearance in August during the sign of Leo, often took its wrath out upon the Grecians by infecting them with rabies. According to these legends, Aristaeus, son of Apollo, was the one chosen to protect his people from the evil effects of the Dog Star Sirius.

By 100 A.D., knowledge of rabies became less mythological, and more scientific. Celsus, a Greek physician, and Plutarch, a Greek philosopher, were among the first to recognize dog-to-human transmission.

Celsus, very curious about rabies, concentrated his efforts on the study of this disease. He believed that the bites of all animals containing virus were dangerous to man and beast. In fact, Celsus was an early believer that the rabies virus was contained in saliva. "Every bite has mostly some venom," he said.

To heal rabies, Celsus recommended caustics, burning, cupping and sucking the wounds of those bitten by rabid dogs. He pointed out that there was no danger in sucking wounds, unless one had an abrasion or sore on the lips or mouth. A serious wound required the application of a cupping instrument; a lesser wound could be fixed with plaster. After these steps had been taken, the wound, provided it did not involve a muscle or nerve, could be cauterized. If cauterization was impossible, bloodletting was an alternative. Following that, the wound should be treated as a burn.

Some other measures recommended by Celsus were hot baths, to allow the patient to perspire and thus distill out the virus. Celsus believed that drinking wine for three days and applying salt to the wound helped reduce infection.

Modern methods of rabies protection depend less on folk medicine, more on science

I WOULD LIKE TO PLACE AN ORDER.

SEND ME MORE INFORMATION ON

Title: "A Modern Solution to an Ancient Problem"
Copywriters: Lisa Hersch, Lucia Huczek
Art Director: Don Kapp
Agency: Baxter, Gurian & Mazzei
Client: Merieux Institute, Inc.

The dreaded disease rabies has, over the millennia, maintained its forceful presence among physicians, pharmacists, veterinarians and public health officials, not to mention ranchers, outdoor game enthusiasts and animal safety groups. Merieux's comprehensive mail and collateral series embodies both folklore and the scientific and medical progress that has been made against this merciless killer.

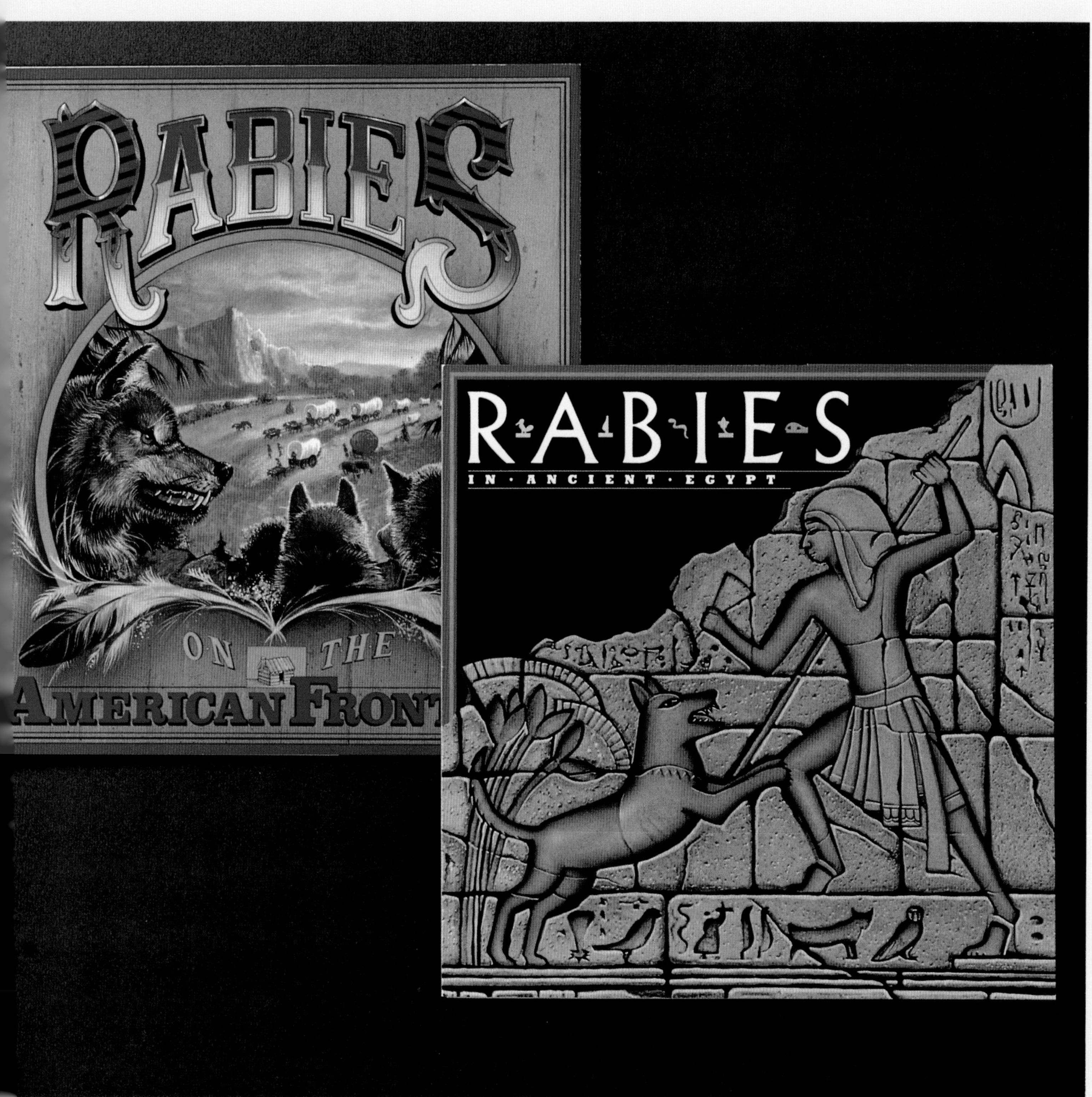
RABIES
ON THE
AMERICAN FRONT
R·A·B·I·E·S
IN · ANCIENT · EGYPT

THE CURE OF
PHARAOH'S WIZARDS
In Pharaoh's time, the treatment of rabies was left in the hands of wizards, whose powerful chants, threats and magical potions were used to ward off evil canine spirits.
Before a victim could be treated, the wizard had to exorcise the evil spirit. Using a potion made from poison and animal saliva, the wizard recited the following incantation:
"O thee dog who is one of ten dogs belonging to Anubis, by thy spell take away this poison; ward off from me thy saliva. If thee do not take away from me now thy saliva, I will take thee in the court of Osiris' temple."
After the incantation, the wizard then recommended treatment for the victim. Mashed garlic was to be applied to the wound, and the same incantation recited upon it until the victim was cured.
While the ancient Egyptians depended on wizardry, today's healthcare professional depends on Merieux.
Merieux is the only company that offers a complete and effective postexposure treatment program: IMOVAX® RABIES RABIES VACCINE (Human Diploid Cell) and IMOGAM® RABIES RABIES IMMUNE GLOBULIN (HUMAN).
In fact, 45 patients bitten by rabid wolves and dogs were treated with Merieux postexposure therapy. One-hundred percent were effectively protected—even when treated 14 days after being bitten!*
Merieux also offers a complete rabies resource service, including lectures, literature and a 24-hour, 7-day toll-free hotline to place orders and to assist you with emergency medical questions on the dosage and treatment of rabies.
For further information, please mail the attached postage-paid reply card. Or call 800-327-2842. In Alaska, Florida and Hawaii, call collect (305) 593-9577.
MERIEUX
A MODERN SOLUTION TO AN ANCIENT PROBLEM
*"Immune complex-like" reactions may occur in approximately 6% of persons receiving booster vaccines, much less frequently in persons receiving primary immunization. MMWR, July 20, 1984.

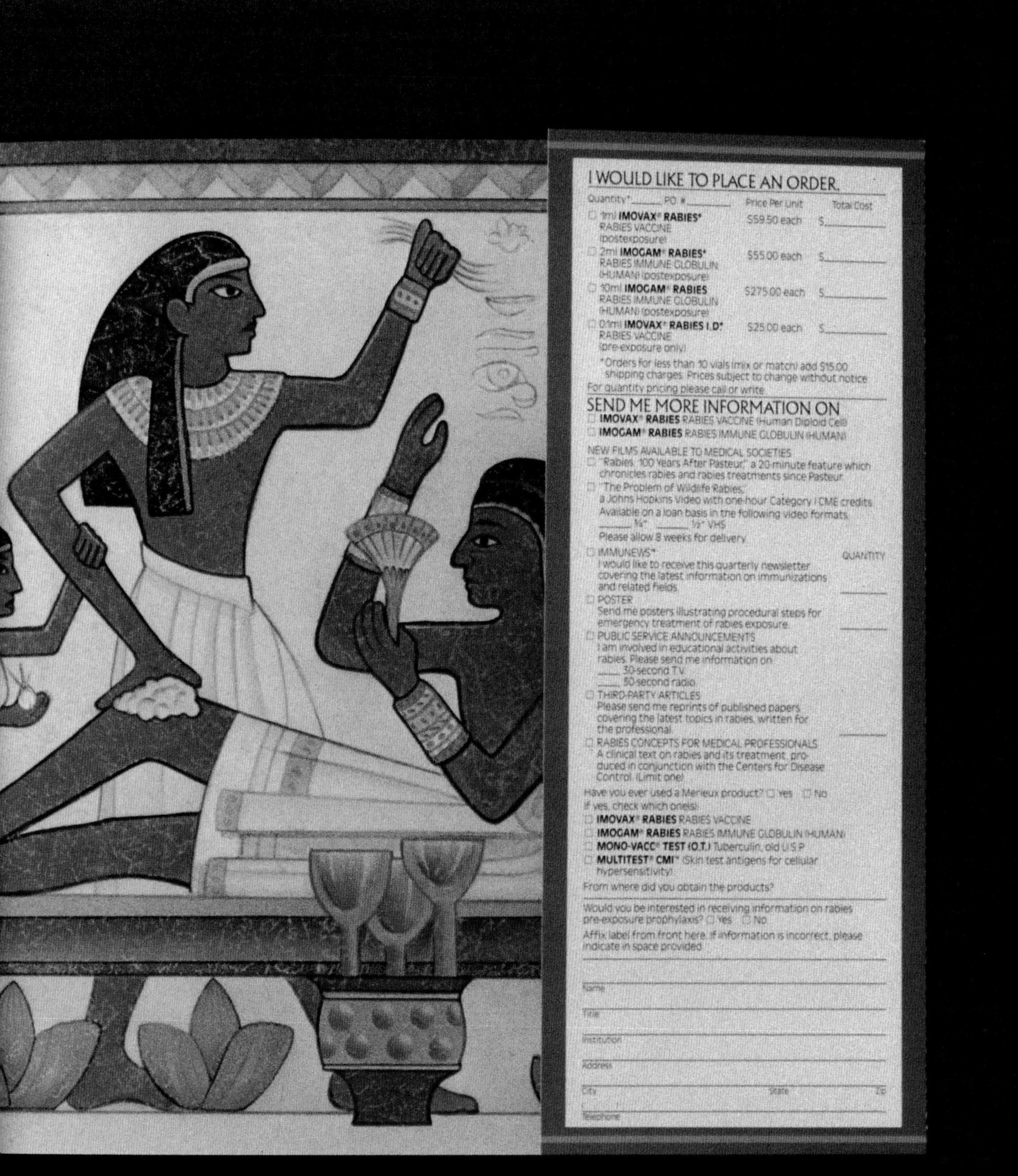
I WOULD LIKE TO PLACE AN ORDER.
Quantity* ______ P.O. # ________
Price Per Unit
Total Cost
1ml IMOVAX® RABIES* RABIES VACCINE (postexposure)
$59.50 each
$______
2ml IMOGAM® RABIES* RABIES IMMUNE GLOBULIN (HUMAN) (postexposure)
$55.00 each
$______
10ml IMOGAM® RABIES RABIES IMMUNE GLOBULIN (HUMAN) (postexposure)
$275.00 each
$______
0.1ml IMOVAX® RABIES I.D.* RABIES VACCINE (pre-exposure only)
$25.00 each
$______
*Orders for less than 10 vials (mix or match) add $15.00 shipping charges. Prices subject to change without notice
For quantity pricing please call or write
SEND ME MORE INFORMATION ON
IMOVAX® RABIES RABIES VACCINE (Human Diploid Cell)
IMOGAM® RABIES RABIES IMMUNE GLOBULIN (HUMAN)
NEW FILMS AVAILABLE TO MEDICAL SOCIETIES
"Rabies: 100 Years After Pasteur," a 20-minute feature which chronicles rabies and rabies treatments since Pasteur.
"The Problem of Wildlife Rabies," a Johns Hopkins Video with one-hour Category I CME credits. Available on a loan basis in the following video formats
______ ¾" ______ ½" VHS
Please allow 8 weeks for delivery.
QUANTITY
IMMUNEWS®
I would like to receive this quarterly newsletter covering the latest information on immunizations and related fields.
POSTER
Send me posters illustrating procedural steps for emergency treatment of rabies exposure.
PUBLIC SERVICE ANNOUNCEMENTS
I am involved in educational activities about rabies. Please send me information on
____ 30-second T.V.
____ 30-second radio
THIRD-PARTY ARTICLES
Please send me reprints of published papers covering the latest topics in rabies, written for the professional.
RABIES CONCEPTS FOR MEDICAL PROFESSIONALS
A clinical text on rabies and its treatment, produced in conjunction with the Centers for Disease Control. (Limit one)
Have you ever used a Merieux product? Yes No
If yes, check which one(s):
IMOVAX® RABIES RABIES VACCINE
IMOGAM® RABIES RABIES IMMUNE GLOBULIN (HUMAN)
MONO-VACC® TEST (O.T.) Tuberculin, old U.S.P.
MULTITEST® CMI™ (Skin test antigens for cellular hypersensitivity)
From where did you obtain the products?
Would you be interested in receiving information on rabies pre-exposure prophylaxis? Yes No
Affix label from front here. If information is incorrect, please indicate in space provided.
Name
Title
Institution
Address
City
State
Zip
Telephone

T·H·E MADS

In the early frontier days of the United States, rabies prevention and cure fell into the domain of magic—and the madstone.

Madstones, sometimes called moonstones, were actually hairballs or gallstones taken from the stomachs of white deer or cows. The rarity of such formations in these types of animals served to emphasize the stone's magical properties.

Before a madstone could be used, it had to be boiled in milk until it turned white in order to remove all impurities that would weaken its magical properties. The madstone was then either carried as an amulet to ward off rabies attacks, or placed on the wound itself. The longer the stone "stuck" on the wound, the better the chances for a cure would be.

Madstones were an imaginative means of treating rabies. But today's healthcare professional prefers science—and Merieux.

Merieux is the only company that offers a complete and effective postexposure treatment program: **IMOVAX® RABIES** RABIES VACCINE (Human Diploid Cell) and **IMOGAM® RABIES** RABIES IMMUNE GLOBULIN (HUMAN).

In fact, 45 patients bitten by rabid wolves and dogs were treated with Merieux postexposure therapy. 100% were effectively protected—even when treated 14 days after being bitten! *

Merieux also offers a complet rabies resource service, including lectures, literature and a 24-hour, 7-day toll-free hotline to place orders and to assist you with emergency medical questions on the dosage and treatment of rabies.

SEND ME MORE INFORMATION ON

- ☐ **IMOVAX® RABIES RABIES VACCINE** (Human Diploid Cell)
- ☐ **IMOGAM® RABIES RABIES IMMUNE GLOBULIN (HUMAN)**
- ☐ **NEW FILM AVAILABLE TO MEDICAL SOCIETIES**
  "Rabies: 100 Years After Pasteur," a 20-minute feature chronicling rabies since Pasteur. Available on a loan basis. Please allow 8 weeks for delivery.
  ☐ ¾" ☐ ½" VHS

QUANTITY

- ☐ IMMUNEWS™
  I would like to receive this quarterly newsletter covering the latest information on immunology. ______
- ☐ POSTER
  Send me posters illustrating procedural steps for emergency treatment of rabies exposure. ______
- ☐ LECTURES
  Please send me information on speaker availability, etc. ______
- ☐ PUBLIC SERVICE ANNOUNCEMENTS
  I am involved in educational activities about rabies. Please send me information on:
  ☐ 30-second T.V.
  ☐ 30-second radio.
- ☐ THIRD PARTY ARTICLES
  Please send me reprints of published papers covering the latest topics in rabies, written for the professional. ______
- ☐ RABIES CONCEPTS FOR MEDICAL PROFESSIONALS
  A clinical text on rabies and its treatment, produced in conjunction with the Centers for Disease Control. (Limit one) ______

Have you ever used a Merieux product?
☐ Yes ☐ No

If yes, check which one(s):

- ☐ IMOVAX® RABIES RABIES VACCINE
- ☐ IMOGAM® RABIES RABIES IMMUNE GLOBULIN (HUMAN)
- ☐ MONO-VACC® TEST (O.T.) (Tuberculin, old)
- ☐ MULTITEST® CMI™ (Skin test antigens for cellular hypersensitivity)

From where did you obtain the products?

______

Would you be interested in receiving information on rabies pre-exposure prophylaxis?
☐ Yes ☐ No

Affix label from front here. If information is incorrect, please indicate in space provided.

NAME ______

TITLE ______

INSTITUTION ______

ADDRESS ______

CITY ______ STATE ______ ZIP ______

( ) ______
TELEPHONE

HP

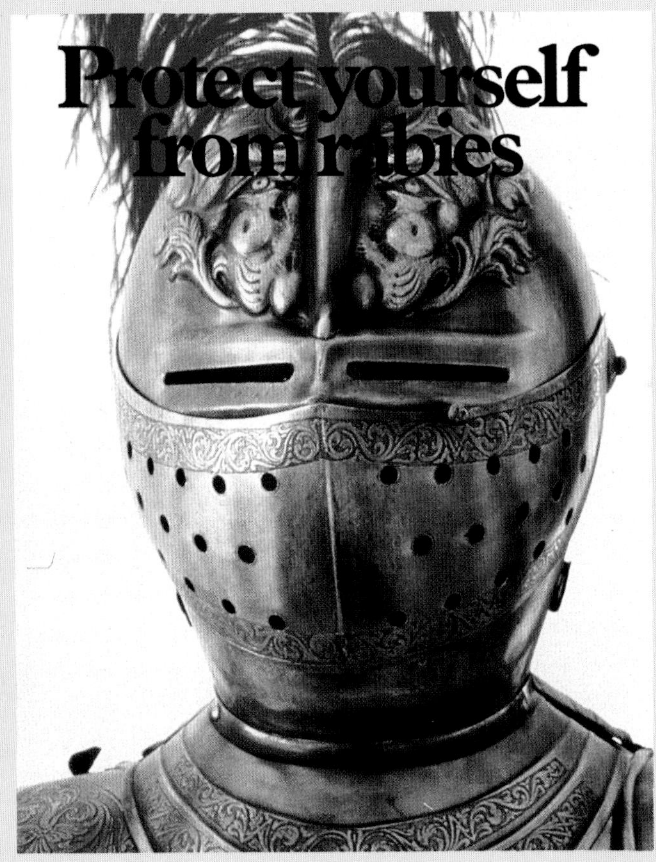
Protect yourself
from rabies

one way
JOHN R. KAY, D.V.M.

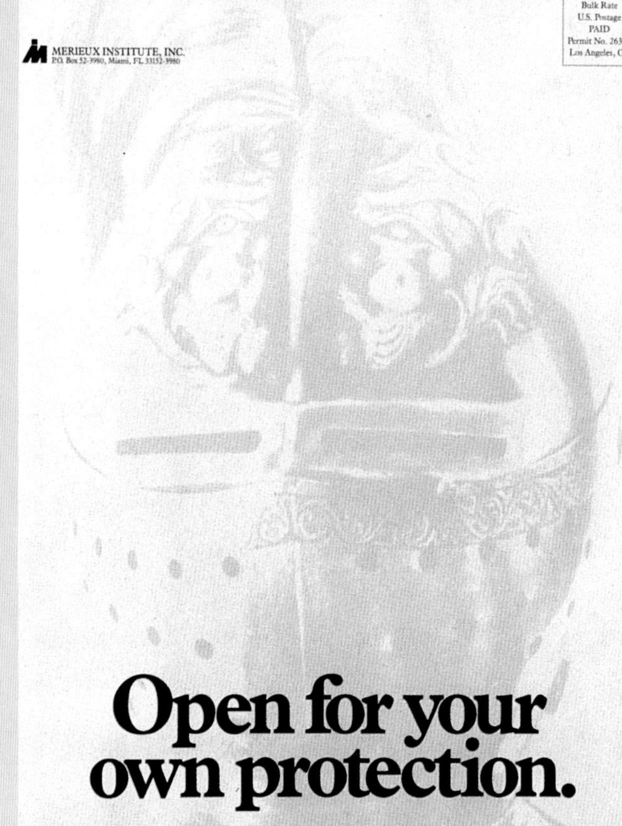

or another.

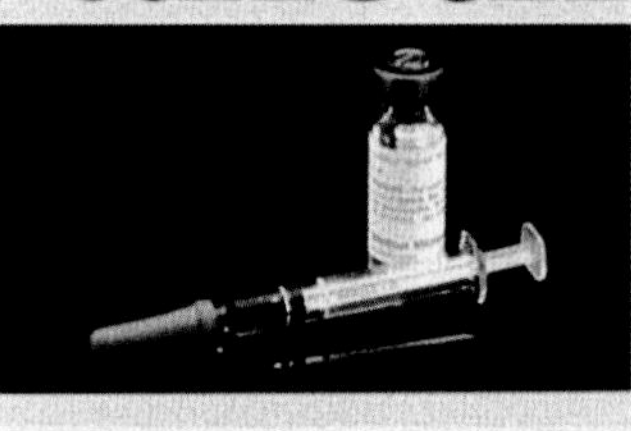

Now
rabies b
RABIE
Merieu
Thre
0, 7, an
need*–
phylaxi
reduces
by redu
to two c
Globul
later, h
is requi
a benef
as those
Note: "
observe
doses o
IMC
prefille
preserv
the syri
conveni
Prote

IM
F

*MMWR July
of rabies bun

P
In

BUSINESS REPLY MAIL

FIRST CLASS MAIL PERMIT NO. 459 MIAMI, FLORIDA

POSTAGE WILL BE PAID BY ADDRESSEE

MERIEUX INSTITUTE, INC.
Attn: Marketing Manager
P.O. BOX 523980
MIAMI, FL 33152-9958

NO POSTAGE
NECESSARY
IF MAILED
IN THE
UNITED STATES

Chapter
7
PBC INTERNATIONAL
ONE SCHOOL STREET
GLEN COVE, NY 11542

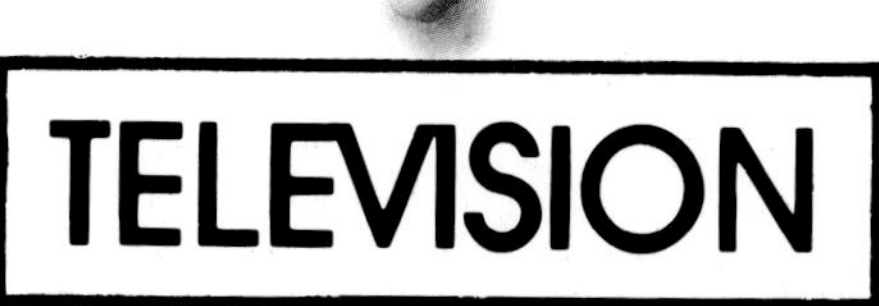

TELEVISION

A few years ago, the creative director of one of the world's leading direct response advertising agencies was about to deliver a speech to 20 or 30 creative directors from general, image-oriented advertising agencies. The subject of the speech was direct response television, and before she began to speak, this well-known, highly-respected direct marketing executive tossed out 20 or 30 bags of popcorn, one to each member of her audience, with the admonition that they'd better get comfortable in their seats, sit back, and enjoy the movies.

Her good-humored introduction, of course, acknowledged the fact that the standard two-minute length of direct response commercials seems like a long, long time to many people—especially to advertising professionals who create only :10s, :15s, :30s and :60s.

Although shorter formats can work in certain situations, the great majority of successful direct response TV spots are :120s. It has been determined that 120 seconds is usually the minimum amount of time it takes a viewer to understand he is being asked to respond, think about the offer, make his decision, and actually carry out his response or remind himself to do so later.

Viewers must also have ample access to the specific offer and ordering information necessary to complete the sale. When a telephone number is made available to accept orders, which is almost always the case, it should be superimposed on the screen for at least 20 seconds and be repeated by the announcer, if there is one and there usually is, a minimum of three times.

All of the commercials in this chapter are First Prize Caples Award winners, including "Celebration." This classic direct response subscription solicitation for *Bon Appetit* magazine *does* follow all of the rules, and sacrifices nothing in the process.

Part of the conventional wisdom, for example, is that too much entertainment in a commercial will weaken its power to motivate the viewer to act. But the 10th Annual Caples Awards First Prize winner for *Money* magazine, "Rollover," seems not to lose strength but to gain it, and the viewer's undivided attention as well, through delightfully special animation that makes dollar bills do magic tricks.

And in the *Sports Illustrated* spot, the toll-free telephone number is not spoken at all, but presented visually at the end of the commercial. The 60-second spot for Control Data Institute includes the phone number in the voiceover only once, but the number is so easy to remember that multiple repetitions are not considered crucial.

All of the commercials in this chapter are First Prize Caples Award winners, including "Celebration." This classic direct response subscription solicitation for *Bon Appétit* magazine *does* follow all of the rules and sacrifices nothing in the process.

Whatever the differences between these TV efforts, they all have in common the ability to immediately get the viewer's attention and then keep it. Basic guidelines and stylistic considerations notwithstanding, that is what all good television commercials must do—and this is why these fine examples succeed.

Money
Money
1-800-221-6100

HOW TO
HOW TO SAVE ON TAXES
FREE
1-800-221-6100

WHERE PROS PUT THEIR OWN IRAS
Money
SPECIAL REPORT
THE BEST WAYS TO CUT YOUR TAXES
These three people have made fortunes

1-800-221-6100

Title: "Rollover"
Copywriters: Andrew Cohen, Steve Petoniak
Art Director: Ron Hartley
Agency: Direct Resources, Inc.
Client: Money Magazine

Dazzlingly clever special effects in this 2-minute commercial work well with a pleasant fantasy concept and to-the-point copy to solicit subscriptions for one of Time, Inc.'s more popular publications. Two on-camera characters—Ron, a *Money* subscriber, and Andy, a non-reader—provide the action and have some dialogue, but most of the copy is read by an off-camera announcer.

ANNOUNCER: Wouldn't it be nice to have total control over your money?

RON (talking to dollar bill, which responds to each command): Sit. Rollover. Stand up. Lie down, please. Multiply.

ANNOUNCER: To be able to tell it to do exactly what you'd like it to do. Well, Money Magazine would like to help you achieve more control over your money. With an offer that doesn't have to cost you any money.

RON (holding open his wallet): OK, everybody, in here.

ANNOUNCER: Just call this number now. We'll send you your first issue of Money risk-free. Meaning if you don't like it, you keep it free. Otherwise, we'll send you more of Money showing you how to spread your investments more profitably. Increase the value of your home or real estate more wisely. Even how to help your vacation dollars go further.

ANDY (talking to dollar bill that does not respond): Sit. Grow. Speak.

ANNOUNCER: So call now and examine your first issue of Money without paying any money. We'll also send you Money's Financial Advisor, free. It's the best of Money, helping you to invest better, save on taxes, retire worry free. Look everything over. If you feel Money's for you, then we'll continue your subscription with a total of 13 issues payable in four monthly installments of just $7.99 each. Otherwise write "cancel" on your bill and keep the first issue free. The Financial Advisor is free, regardless. 1-800-221-6100.

ANDY (talking to dollar bill, which responds): Sit. Multiply.

ANNOUNCER: So examine how to take better control of your money without paying any money. Call for Money's risk-free offer. 1-800-221-6100.

ANDY: A little higher, please.

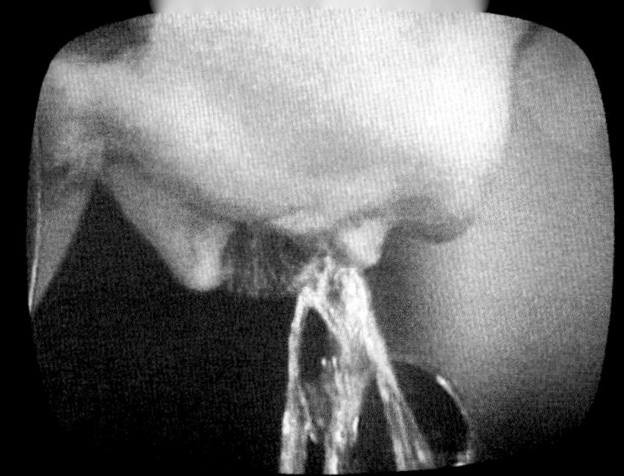

ts Illus

Sports Illustrated

Sports Illustrated
Get the feeling.

Title: "The Big Deal"
Copywriter: John Gruen
Art Director: Jim Good
Agency: Ogilvy & Mather
Client: Sports Illustrated

The emotion builds from the first frame in this cinema verite' spot, shot live at a night baseball game, as a relief pitcher prepares to take the mound and try to give his team a victory. A percussive, tension-filled music track, quick-cut editing and fragments overhead from players' conversations ("Yea, he's ready..." "Nervous? Aw, don't be concerned...") add to the excitement. It's almost like being there in the dugout, which is exactly the idea. Minimal voiceover copy from the announcer drives the point home: "Sports Illustrated...get the feeling."

1-800-TRAIN ME

1-800-TRAIN ME
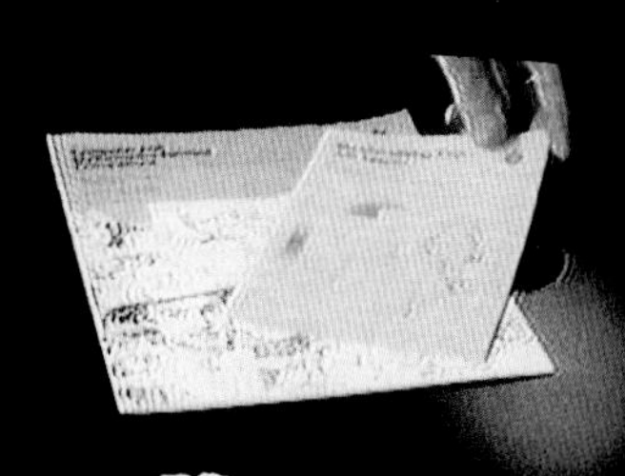

CONTROL DATA INSTITUTE
1-800-TRAIN ME

CONTROL DATA INSTITUTE
1-800-TRAIN ME

CONTROL DATA INSTITUTE
1-800-TRAIN ME

Title:	"Zombies"
Copywriter:	Bert Gardner
Art Director:	Ron Anderson
Agency:	Bozell & Jacobs Direct
Client:	Control Data Institute

Just when it begins to seem there will be no end to the eerie, awful monotony of the rank-and-file workers' fate in this 60-second spot, a hopeful ray of sunshine brings cautious optimism into the picture. As the color tones become deeper and more real, a friendly human hand adds piece after piece to the free "career planning kit" available to the viewer merely by placing one toll-free telephone call. A warm, reassuring voice, reading sparkling, carefully-crafted copy, explains the situation clearly and simply...

ANNOUNCER: A mindless job drains the life out of people. When you go to work, your brain goes dead. But one thing that could be particularly nice is a new career, in a field that's vital, alive and growing—the field of computer programming. In just six-and-a-half months, Control Data Institute could teach you the skills you need to find a rewarding future in computer programming. Call Control Data Institute at 1-800-TRAIN ME. It could bring you back to life. If you call now, we'll send you a free career planning kit filled with information on financial aid, job placement, interviewing and more. Call Control Data Institute. Bring your future to life.

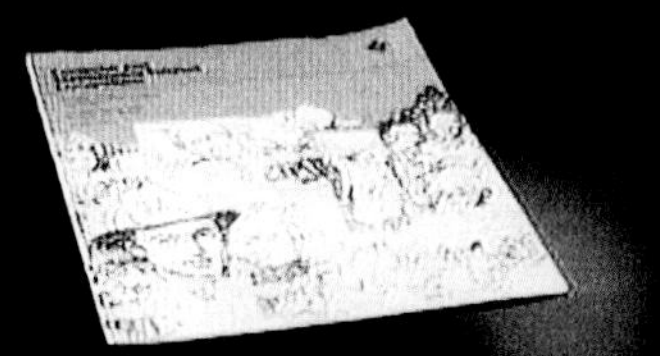

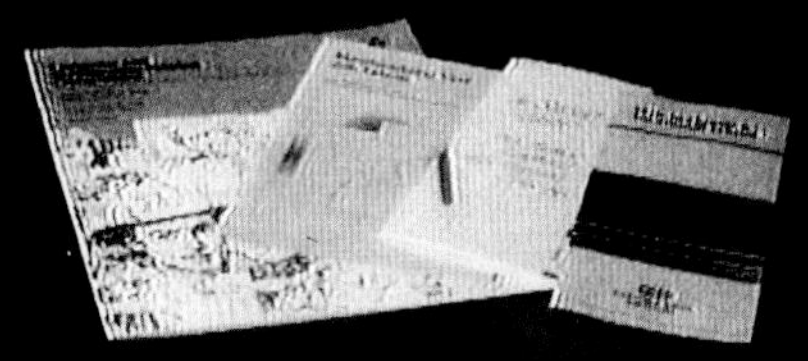

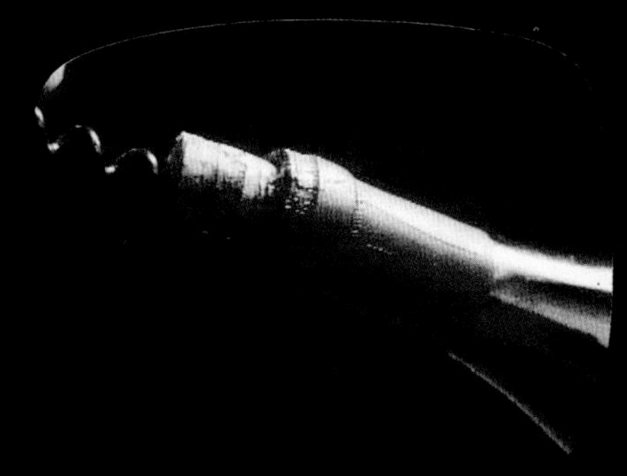

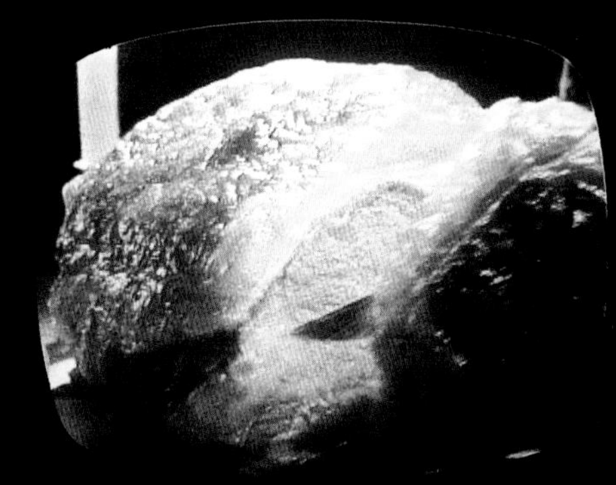

Bon Appétit
Spectacular show-off cakes
French cuisine made easy
Do-ahead buffet for 20

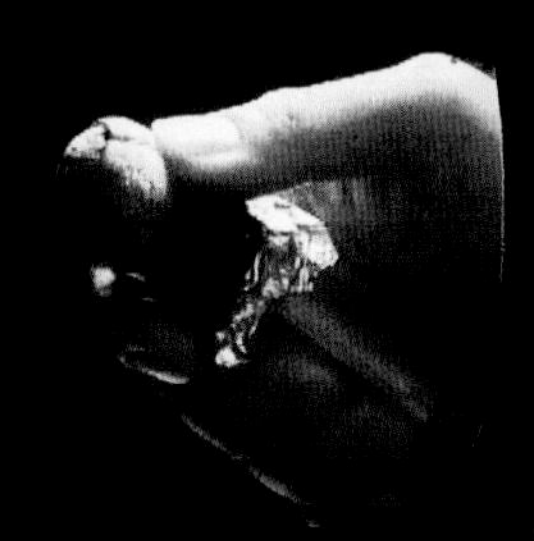

Bon Appétit

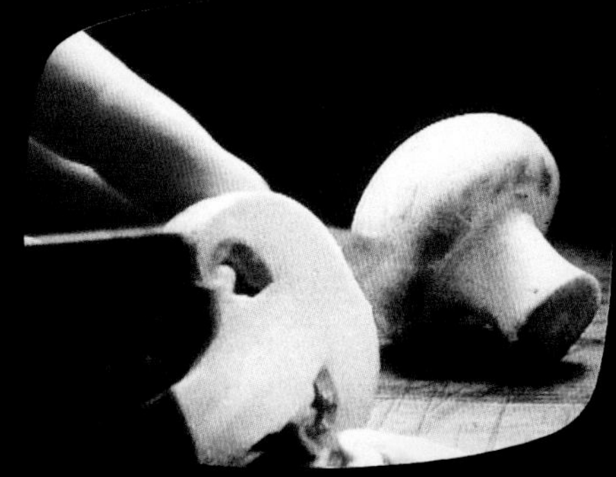

Country Inn Buffets
FREE
1-800-331-1000

Bon Appétit
ASK ABOUT OUR ADDED SAVINGS OFFER
1-800-331-1000

Title:	"Celebration"
Copywriter:	Art Brooks
Art Director:	Jerry Genova
Agency:	Rapp & Collins
Client:	Knapp Communications, Inc.

This First Prize winner from the 7th Annual John Caples Awards reflects classic television commercial production values on every level: design, direction, photography, editing, music, sound effects and voiceover script.

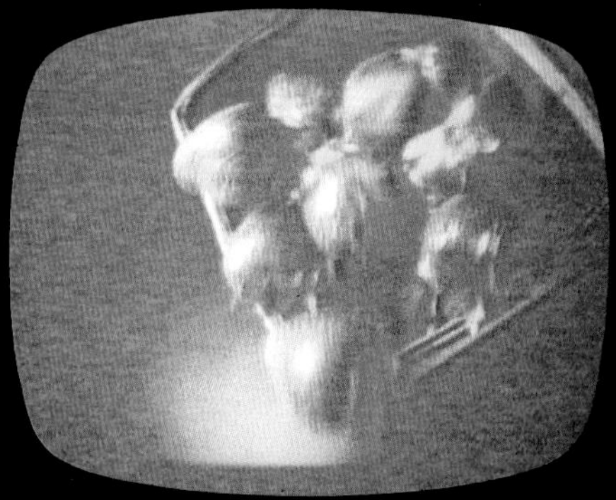

MUSIC: Up and under throughout.

SFX: Pop of wine bottle cork.

ANNOUNCER: Welcome...to a very special celebration...

SFX: Whoosh of flame.

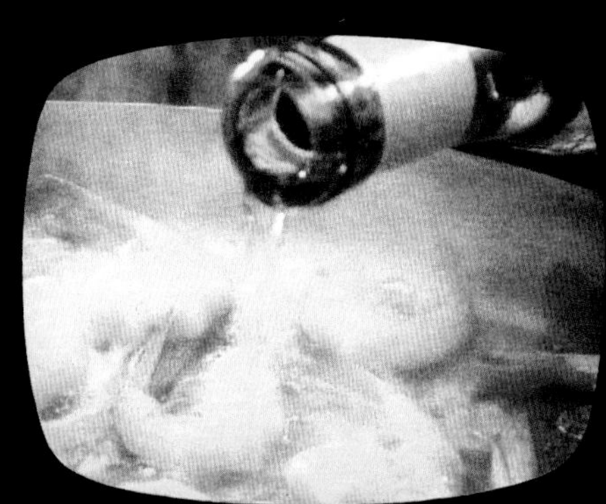

ANNOUNCER: ...a celebration that looks like this, tastes like this, sounds like this, and has an aroma like this. A celebration that magically transforms the everyday into something memorable. A celebration that begins with a magazine called...Bon Appe'tit.

SINGERS: Celebrate life with Bon Appe'tit.

ANNOUNCER: Come celebrate...

SFX: Champagne cork popping.

ANNOUNCER: Savor the good things of life. Experience the world's great foods...like Pasta Primavera... Mediterranean shrimp saute...Come share the Bon Appe'tit celebration...

SINGERS: Celebrate...

ANNOUNCER: ...with brilliant full-color photographs...with captivating, authoritative articles, month after month. Even when you're too busy to cook, celebrate with delectable, time-saving recipes...easy to prepare, using easy-to-find ingredients. One hundred recipes in each issue, all kitchen-tested by Bon Appe'tit. Celebrate with an intimate dinner for two.

SINGERS: Celebrate...

ANNOUNCER: Or an informal party for twenty-two. Celebrate at one of the world's acclaimed restaurants, then let Bon Appe'tit give you master chef's prized recipes...to prepare at home. Celebrate the holidays! Celebrate all year round. Phone now for our special offer, 12 big issues of Bon Appe'tit for only $9.95. You save 34% off the regular subscription rate of $15. And, free with your paid subscription, you get this colorful 20-page booklet of menus and recipes—the buffet secrets of America's finest country inns. Phone toll-free: 1-800-331-1000.

SINGERS: Celebrate life with Bon Appe'tit!

Index

CLIENTS

AGENCIES

ART DIRECTORS

COPYWRITERS

Print Advertising
8th ANNUAL JOHN CAPLES AWARDS

1st Prize **Copy:** Bob Higbee
Art Direction: Joe Schick
Agency: The Direct Marketing Agency In-House
Client: The Direct Marketing Agency

3rd Prize **Copy:** Claire O'Brien
Art Direction: Stefanie Palermo
Agency: Ogilvy & Mather
Client: NannyCare

Consumer Catalogs
10th ANNUAL JOHN CAPLES AWARDS

1st Prize **Copy:** Jane Finder
Art Direction: David Kasper
Agency: Cramer-Krasselt/Direct
Client: Armstrong Roses

2nd Prize **Copy:** Deborah Bishop, Doug Payne, Tim Murray
Art Direction: Pat Margis, Noren Schmitt, Trisha Stricklan, Carole Czapla
Agency: The Sharper Image In-House
Client: The Sharper Image Corp.

3rd Prize **Copy:** Mel Ziegler, Nancy Friedman, David Darlington, Christie Allair
Art Direction: Terry Stelling, Mike Madrid, Craig Hannah, Robert Stein, An-Ching Chang, Peg Magovern
Agency: Banana Republic In-House
Client: Banana Republic

Honorable Mention **Copy:** Deborah Bishop, Doug Payne, Tim Murray
Art Direction: Pat Margis, Noren Schmitt, Trisha Stricklan, Carole Czapla
Agency: The Sharper Image In-House
Client: The Sharper Image Corp.

Business Catalogs
10th ANNUAL JOHN CAPLES AWARDS

1st Prize **Copy:** David Lesser
Art Direction: Ann O'Daniel
Agency: Wunderman Worldwide
Client: IBM

2nd Prize **Copy:** Jo-Von Tucker
Art Direction: Jo-Von Tucker
Agency: JVT Direct Marketing Corp.
Client: The S.D. Warren Company

3rd Prize **Copy:** Mike Paul
Art Direction: Paul Davies
Agency: McCarthy Cosby Paul
Client: Unisys UK Ltd.

Honorable Mention **Copy:** Bernie Libster
Art Direction: Wes Neal, Dana Martin
Agency: Grey Direct
Client: IBM

Consumer Catalogs
9th ANNUAL JOHN CAPLES AWARDS

1st Prize **Copy:** Jennifer Ellsworth, Pleasant Rowland
Art Direction: Myland McRevey
Agency: Pleasant Company In-House
Client: Pleasant Company

2nd Prize **Copy:** Mel Ziegler, Julie Smith, Nancy Friedman, David Darlington
Art Direction: Terry Stelling, Patricia Ziegler, Anatoly Belkin
Agency: Banana Republic In-House
Client: Banana Republic

3rd Prize **Copy:** J. Shankman, C. Salack, M. Harless, L. Killian
Art Direction: Bradford Matson
Agency: Spiegel, Inc. In-House
Client: Spiegel, Inc.

Honorable Mention **Copy:** Eileen Haas
Art Direction: Bjorn Kartomten
Agency: The MoreNow Corp.
Client: Terry D'Auray, Sierra Club

Business Catalogs
9th ANNUAL JOHN CAPLES AWARDS

2nd Prize **Copy:** Robert R. Zemon, Rich Bayan
Art Direction: Stiner Pieri, Jim Wascoe
Agency: Day-Timers Advertising In-House
Client: Day-Timers Inc.

3rd Prize **Copy:** John Klawitter
Art Direction: Gene Bramson, Karen Ashby, Robert Bashore, Antje Goebelmann
Agency: Bramson & Assoc.
Client: Shomex Productions

Honorable Mention **Copy:** David Lesser, Mel Bruck
Art Direction: Gary Grayson, Tim McCord
Agency: Wunderman, Ricotta & Kline
Client: IBM

Business Catalogs
8th ANNUAL JOHN CAPLES AWARDS

1st Prize **Copy:** Wally Williams
Art Direction: Mark Crim
Agency: Keller-Crescent S/W
Client: Justin Boot Co.

2nd Prize **Copy:** Jim Ferguson
Art Direction: Mark Crim
Agency: Keller-Crescent S/W
Client: Chippewa Shoe Co.

3rd Prize **Copy:** Mel Ziegler, Julie Smith
Art Direction: Terry Stelling
Agency: Mel Ziegler
Client: Banana Republic Travel & Safari Clothing

Honorable Mention **Copy:** Mary Ann Donovan, Jacqueline Stern
Art Direction: Ann O'Daniel
Agency: Wunderman, Ricotta & Kline
Client: General Foods

Consumer Collateral
10th ANNUAL JOHN CAPLES AWARDS

1st Prize **Copy:** Laura DeFlora, Roz Cundell
Art Direction: Dan Levine, Bob Ademeo
Agency: Ogilvy & Mather Direct
Client: American Express

2nd Prize **Copy:** Merry Bateman, Thailand Copy—Vipaporn Pramoj, Na Ayudhya
Art Direction: Lalit Lertmaithai
Agency: Ogilvy & Mather Direct (TH) Ltd.
Client: American Express (TH) Co., Ltd.

3rd Prize **Copy:** Bob Matheo
Art Direction: Chuck Dickinson
Agency: Bob Matheo, AdMaker
Client: C.I.C. Industries

Honorable Mention **Copy:** Paula Zargaj, Edward Bernard
Art Direction: Candi Orsi, Stephen Wight
Agency: Hill, Holliday Direct
Client: J. Bildner & Sons

Honorable Mention **Copy:** Samuel Kirschenbaum
Art Direction: Timothy Claffey
Agency: Bozell, Jacobs, Kenyon & Eckhardt Direct/Chicago
Client: Mundelein College

Business Collateral
10th ANNUAL JOHN CAPLES AWARDS

1st Prize **Copy:** Leah Roth
Art Direction: Paul Howard
Agency: Granola Graphics
Client: ASI/Focus Plus

2nd Prize **Copy:** Alan Goldstein
Art Direction: Jeff Potter, Steve Wheeler
Agency: Ogilvy & Mather Direct/Chicago
Client: Sears Business Systems Center

Consumer Collateral
9th ANNUAL JOHN CAPLES AWARDS

2nd Prize **Copy:** Paul Zargaj
Art Direction: Jory S. Mason
Agency: Ingalls, Quinn & Johnson
Client: Sunlife of Canada

3rd Prize **Copy:** Steve Snapp, Melanie Price
Art Direction: Michael Chinnici
Agency: Foote Cone Belding Direct
Client: Bermuda Tourism

Business Collateral
9th ANNUAL JOHN CAPLES AWARDS

2nd Prize
Copy: Karen Gedney
Art Direction: Patrick Fultz
Agency: Millennium
Client: Oxford Health Plans

3rd Prize
Copy: Peter Lloyd
Art Direction: Cheryl Meninger
Agency: Sive Associates, Inc.
Client: Southwestern Publishing

Honorable Mention
Copy: Jo-Von Tucker
Art Direction: Jo-Von Tucker
Agency: Jo-Von Tucker & Associates
Client: S.D. Warren Paper Co.

Collateral
8th ANNUAL JOHN CAPLES AWARDS

2nd Prize
Copy: Diana Garza, Araceli Moreno
Art Direction: Mike Psaltis, Ted Amber, David Krieger
Agency: Adelante Advertising, Inc.
Client: Schenley Affiliated Brands

Single Medium Consumer Campaigns
10th ANNUAL JOHN CAPLES AWARDS

Honorable Mention
Copy: John Robertson, Steve Law
Art Direction: Barbara Thompson
Agency: Dizinno & Partners
Client: PSA

Honorable Mention
Copy: Carolyn Crimmins, Judy Hultquist
Art Direction: Linda Decker, Marvin Fried
Agency: McCaffrey & McCall Direct Marketing
Client: Mercedes-Benz of North America

Honorable Mention
Copy: Sid Meltzer
Art Direction: Mary Ann Ahroon
Agency: Grey Direct
Client: Shell Oil

Single Medium Business Campaigns
10th ANNUAL JOHN CAPLES AWARDS

1st Prize
Copy: David Atnip, Joe Paonessa
Art Direction: Terry Sharbach
Agency: CECO Communications
Client: Chevrolet Motor Division

2nd Prize
Copy: Bill Spink
Art Direction: Joan Van der Veen
Agency: Gillespie Advertising, Inc.
Client: Dow Jones News/Retrieval

3rd Prize
Copy: James Wells
Art Direction: Michael Smacchia
Agency: The Direct Marketing Agency
Client: Freelance Solutions

Honorable Mention
Copy: Dave Ullman, Josh Mandel
Art Direction: Beth Kosuk
Agency: Cramer-Krasselt/Chicago
Client: A.B. Dick

Single Medium Consumer Campaigns
9th ANNUAL JOHN CAPLES AWARDS

2nd Prize
Copy: Bill Hawkey
Art Direction: Dick Bennett
Agency: Kaiser Kuhn Bennett Inc.
Client: Christian Children's Fund

3rd Prize
Copy: Dianne Edlemann, Carey Smith
Art Direction: Judy McCabe Smith
Agency: Ogilvy & Mather Direct
Client: Atlanta Ballet

Honorable Mention
Copy: Scoti Bryant, Joyce Smith, Susan Jones
Art Direction: Diane Lausar, Bruce Stephen
Agency: Frankel & Co.
Client: United Healthcare Corp.

Single Medium Campaigns
8th ANNUAL JOHN CAPLES AWARDS

1st Prize
Copy: Bert Gardner
Art Direction: Ron Anderson
Agency: Bozell & Jacobs
Client: Control Data Institute

3rd Prize
Copy: Shelley E. Lanman, Michael Borden
Art Direction: Bob Cesiro
Agency: Ogilvy & Mather Direct
Client: AT&T Public Communications

3rd Prize
Copy: Richard Sprano, Vincent Chieco
Art Direction: Joseph Cupani, Judi Kolstad
Agency: Ogilvy & Mather Direct
Client: Chemlawn

Honorable Mention
Copy: Dennis Harrington
Art Direction: Nick Mirkay
Agency: Direct Mail Corp.
Client: RehabCare

Multimedia Consumer Campaigns
10th ANNUAL JOHN CAPLES AWARDS

1st Prize
Copy: Barry Biederman, Chuck Bromley
Art Direction: Mel Rustom, Angelo LaCalandra
Agency: Biederman & Co.
Client: New York University School of Continuing Education

2nd Prize
Copy: Barry Callen
Art Direction: Bob Marberry, Susan Chinchar, Harold Hutcheson
Agency: Ogilvy & Mather
Client: Shell Oil Company

2nd Prize
Copy: Steve Petz, Jim Plegue
Art Direction: Diane Kangas, Karl Shaffer
Agency: Wunderman Worldwide
Client: Lincoln Mercury

3rd Prize
Copy: Dennis Staszak, Steve Petz, Fred Stafford
Art Direction: Diane Kangas, Karl Shaffer
Agency: Wunderman Detroit, Y&R Detroit
Client: Lincoln Mercury

Honorable Mention
Copy: Mary Ann Donovan
Art Direction: Jane Walsh
Agency: Wunderman Worldwide
Client: Manufacturers Hanover Trust

Honorable Mention
Copy: Bob Drevney, Ted Barnett
Art Direction: Don Johnson, Bill Dolan
Agency: Leo Burnett U.S.A.
Client: Philip Morris

Multimedia Business Campaigns
10th ANNUAL JOHN CAPLES AWARDS

1st Prize
Copy: Dave East
Art Direction: Ross Chowles
Agency: Wunderman Worldwide
Client: Supervision Food Services

2nd Prize
Copy: Dave East
Art Direction: Ross Chowles
Agency: Wunderman Worldwide
Client: Prudential Properties

3rd Prize
Copy: Steve Joyce
Art Direction: Jon Padgett
Agency: Good-Koupal Advertising/Public Relations
Client: Ameritech Communications

Honorable Mention
Copy: Lisa Hersch, Lucia Huczek
Art Direction: Don Kapp
Agency: Baxter, Gurian & Mazzei, Inc.
Client: Merieux Institute

Multimedia Consumer Campaigns
9th ANNUAL JOHN CAPLES AWARDS

2nd Prize
Copy: Shelley E. Lanman, Jenny Raybould
Art Direction: Robert Cesiro, John Palisay
Agency: Ogilvy & Mather Direct
Client: Sylvan Learning Centers

3rd Prize
Copy: Dave Ullman/TV, Alan Fonorow/DM
Art Direction: Bob Meagher
Agency: Cramer-Krasselt/Chicago
Client: Lincoln Park Zoo

Honorable Mention
Copy: Kim Fritz, Michael Gould
Art Direction: Allen Hicks, Jesse Faber
Agency: Grey Direct
Client: Bank of America

Honorable Mention
Copy: Ed Subitzky, Joyce Lapin
Art Direction: John Olds
Agency: Wunderman, Ricotta & Kline
Client: Manufacturers Hanover Trust

Multimedia Business
9th ANNUAL JOHN CAPLES AWARDS

1st Prize
Copy: Kathi Stark, Steve Snapp, Jim Pieretti, Wendy Wishnie
Art Direction: Melanie Price, John Woldin, Mitch Lunsford, Tom Ozga
Agency: Foote Cone Belding Direct
Client: AT&T

2nd Prize
Copy: Pam Isham
Art Direction: Steve Hammond
Agency: Henry-Gill, Inc.
Client: Vision Service Plan

3rd Prize
Copy: Paul Levett
Art Direction: Mal Karlin
Agency: Lowe Marschalk, Inc.
Client: Xerox Corp.

Honorable Mention
Copy: Bill Fidel
Art Direction: F. Byron Tucker
Agency: Eisner & Associates, Inc.
Client: Minolta

Multimedia Campaigns
8th ANNUAL JOHN CAPLES AWARDS

1st Prize
Copy: Leila Vuorenmaa
Art Direction: Tina Cohoe
Agency: Cohoe & Vuorenmaa
Client: Allan & Gray Corp.

2nd Prize
Copy: Leila Vourenmaa
Art Direction: Michael Cancellieri
Agency: Ogilvy & Mather Direct
Client: Chemlawn Pestfree

Honorable Mention
Copy: Shelley E. Lanman, Susan Enterline, Jenny Raybould
Art Direction: Phyllis Cayton, Neil Wagner
Agency: Ogilvy & Mather Direct
Client: Kimberly-Clark

Television
10th ANNUAL JOHN CAPLES AWARDS

1st Prize
Copy: Andrew Cohen
Art Direction: Ron Hartley
Agency: Direct Resources Inc.
Client: Time Inc.

2nd Prize
Copy: David Hecht
Art Direction: Rodger Minyard
Agency: Wunderman Worldwide
Client: Time Life Books

3rd Prize
Copy: Jim Maltese
Art Direction: Jim Maltese
Agency: Ayer Direct
Client: AT&T Communications

Honorable Mention
Copy: Janice Ferri
Agency: A. Eicoff & Company
Client: Time Life Books

Television
9th ANNUAL JOHN CAPLES AWARDS

1st Prize
Copy: John Gruen
Art Direction: Jim Good
Agency: Ogilvy & Mather
Client: Jose Perez

2nd Prize
Copy: Mark Levitt
Art Direction: Ellen Fitzgerald
Agency: Wunderman, Ricotta & Kline
Client: Time Life Books

3rd Prize
Copy: Andrew Cohen
Art Direction: Robert McDuffy
Agency: Direct Resources, Inc.
Client: Fortune Magazine (Time Life, Inc.)

Honorable Mention
Copy: Edward Bernard
Art Direction: Stephen Wight
Agency: Hill, Holliday, Connors Cosmopulos Direct
Client: The Boston Globe

Television
8th ANNUAL JOHN CAPLES AWARDS

1st Prize
Copy: Bert Gardner
Art Direction: Ron Anderson
Agency: Bozell & Jacobs Direct
Client: Control Data Institute

2nd Prize
Copy: Robert Potter
Art Direction: Robin Bray, Peter Schwartz
Agency: Time Life Books In-House
Client: Time Life Books

3rd Prize
Copy: Dave Ullman, Jay Kaskel
Art Direction: Bob Meagher
Agency: Cramer-Krasselt/Direct
Client: Mayor's Gant TaskForce

Radio
10th ANNUAL JOHN CAPLES AWARDS

Honorable Mention
Copy: Don Garbe
Agency: J. Goldstein Marketing Communications
Client: Kaufman and Broad

Honorable Mention
Copy: Nevil Cross
Agency: Lawrence Butner Advertising
Client: Air & Space Smithsonian Magazine

Radio
9th ANNUAL JOHN CAPLES AWARDS

2nd Prize
Copy: Jeff Ostroth, Steve Pimsler
Agency: Kobs & Brady Advertising
Client: Home Box Office

Radio
8th ANNUAL JOHN CAPLES AWARDS

Honorable Mention
Copy: Bill Fidel, Barry Leibowitz
Agency: Eisner & Associates, Inc.
Client: Holiday Spa

Honorable Mention
Copy: Terry Seaford
Agency: Dana
Client: Dow Jones